SLAVE IN A PALANQUIN

Slave in a Palanquin

COLONIAL SERVITUDE AND
RESISTANCE IN SRI LANKA

Nira Wickramasinghe

Columbia University Press
New York

Columbia University Press
Publishers Since 1893
New York   Chichester, West Sussex
cup.columbia.edu
Copyright © 2020 Columbia University Press
All rights reserved

Library of Congress Cataloging-in-Publication Data
Names: Wickramasinghe, Nira, author.
Title: Slave in a palanquin : colonial servitude and resistance
in Sri Lanka / Nira Wickramasinghe.
Description: New York : Columbia University Press, [2020] |
Includes bibliographical references and index.
Identifiers: LCCN 2020006925 (print) | LCCN 2020006926 (ebook) |
ISBN 9780231197625 (cloth) | ISBN 9780231197632 (paperback) |
ISBN 9780231552264 (ebook)
Subjects: LCSH: Slavery—Sri Lanka—History. | Slaves—Sri Lanka—History. |
Sri Lanka—History—1505–1948.
Classification: LCC HT1315.S72 W53 2020 (print) | LCC HT1315.S72 (ebook) |
DDC 306.3/62095493—dc23
LC record available at https://lccn.loc.gov/2020006925
LC ebook record available at https://lccn.loc.gov/2020006926

Cover design: Julia Kushnirsky
Cover illustration: Charmaine Samarasinghe

Contents

List of Illustrations vii
Acknowledgments ix

Introduction 1

I A Dutch Fiscal's Murder: Interrogating the Identity of Slaves, Blacks, and "Kaffirs" 16

II From Colombo to Galle: Enslaved Bodies in an Archive of Violence 51

III Slave in a Palanquin: Jaffna in the Early Nineteenth Century 89

IV The Chilaw "Experiment": Labor for Freedom 126

V The Plaint of an Emancipated Slave: A Play in Two Acts 160

VI Eclipse of the Slave: Traces, Hauntings 189

Glossary 209
Notes 213
Bibliography 263
Index 291

Illustrations

0.1. The Indian Ocean in the early nineteenth century   3
1.1. Slave Island, Colombo   20
2.1. Sri Lanka in the early nineteenth century   54
2.2. Ethnic distribution of proprietors   55
2.3. Deed of transfer of slave, June 30, 1809   63
2.4. Gender distribution of slaves in Colombo   71
2.5. Age of slaves in Colombo   71
2.6. List of prisoners, Supreme Court circuit for Colombo, February 1822   73
3.1. Jaffna and Vanni   92
3.2. Palanquin ca. 1820   93
3.3. List of prisoners accused of selling free persons as slaves   104
3.4. Slave certificate, Jaffna kachcheri, 1830   111
3.5. List of emancipated slaves under regulation of government no. 8 of 1821   113
3.6. Slave register, parish of Nallore, 1818–1832   124
4.1. West coast of Sri Lanka   127
4.2. Number of slaves per caste   135
4.3. Register of slaves emancipated by government, September 24, 1824   148
6.1. Baptism record, Dutch Reformed Church, Colombo District, 1831   201

Acknowledgments

I am deeply grateful to individuals, friends, and strangers in various institutions who contributed to this project by sharing their time and experience. I benefited from the resources and the help of library staff of the Sri Lanka National Archives (Colombo and Kandy branches), the National Archives, the British Library, and the SOAS library in London, the Bodleian library at Oxford and the National Archives in the Hague. As a scholar whose career began in the precomputer age, I saw the way I do research change completely with the technological surge of the 1990s. I realize, in hindsight, that the digital age has made me less reflective in my data collection but at the same time allowed me to gather information quickly and efficiently. I am now a compulsive scan, file, and read-later scholar! If not for scans and digital photography, this book might have remained an idea and never been written. I composed it "in between," while teaching and grappling with heavy administrative duties, first as chair of the program in South and Southeast Asian Studies and then as academic director of research at the Leiden University Institute for Area Studies (LIAS). Leiden University provided me with a peaceful and comfortable work space, enriched by interactions with wonderful colleagues. I must also acknowledge a semester-long partial teaching release, a small grant from the Digital Humanities Centre at Leiden University, a small research grant from the Asian Modernities and Tradition (AMT) profile area for travel to archives in London and for copyediting. Most of the archival research in Europe and Sri Lanka, however, was conducted in my own free time, and writing happened during long and dark Leiden winter days, when I had returned home after a full day's work. Writing this book felt like a reward to myself after I had finished looking after the work and home fronts.

Except for chapter 3, which contains sections of an article I coauthored with Alicia Schrikker—"The Ambivalence of Freedom: Slaves in Jaffna, Sri Lanka, in the Eighteenth and Nineteenth Centuries," *Journal of Asian Studies* 78 (3): 497–519—none of the other chapters have appeared in print. I thank Alicia and the *Journal of Asian Studies* for allowing me to use parts of the article. A small portion of the introduction overlaps slightly with the introductory chapter of my coedited volume, *Being a Slave: Histories and Legacies of European Slavery in the Indian Ocean*, published by Leiden University Press in 2020. Early versions of the chapters have been presented and discussed in various gatherings: at the LIAS Global History network meeting (2016), the Amsterdam International Institute for Social History workshop on slavery (2017), the World History seminar (2017), the Center for South Asian Studies at Cambridge University (2019), the Center for South Asian Studies at Edinburgh University (2019), in Colombo as a keynote for the Ibn Battuta Foundation launch event (2018), and at conferences and workshops organized by the American Institute for Lankan Studies in 2017 and 2018. I drew from chapter 1 for a lecture I delivered at the Global History and Culture Centre at Warwick University in 2019.

I am deeply indebted to my colleagues and friends who offered comments and advice on various versions and helped me sharpen my project. Among them—and I am sorry not to be able to name everyone—I must single out Tsolin Nalbantian, Sanjukta Sunderason, Alicia Schrikker, John Rogers, Jonathan Spencer, and Mahmood Kooria. Marina Carter and Robert Ross read the entire manuscript. Patrick Peebles generously shared some archival material and notes. Michael Laffan, Ronit Ricci, Bhavani Raman, Tom Hoogervorst, Sujit Sivasundaram, Bindu Menon, and Eva Ambos offered comments at various stages, and Sanderien Verstappen edited the bibliography. Yvette Ferdinands and Sanayi Marcelline did brilliant work as researchers in the Kandy and Colombo archives. Thisara Perera drew the maps, and Koen Berghuis improved on them. Doreen Bogaart and Harkirat Singh painstakingly compiled the slave registers. Peter Verhaar created graphs and tables from the slave register data. Abhijit Wickramasinghe provided the photograph of the palanquin, and Pratik

Wickramasinghe helped me with the charts. Many others listened to my talks and made encouraging noises that helped so much in moments of self-doubt. I must also thank my editor Caelyn Cobb for fearlessly taking on a project centered on a small Indian Ocean island, Monique Briones for guiding me with humor and enthusiasm through the production phase and Anita O'Brien for her perceptive copyediting. My two reviewers made some sharp and productive comments, which I was able to take on board to revise and improve on the manuscript. All mistakes that remain are mine alone.

As always, my family enthusiastically supported what they saw as my latest whim. My mother did occasionally warn me "not to speak too much of my slaves" when I attended dinner parties in Colombo. I am so grateful for her lovely painting of a palanquin traveling on a Jaffna road bordered with fan-leafed palmyra trees. A final thought for my dear sons, Abhijit and Pratik, who have been unconditional allies in this adventure, although they tend to look at me and my work with a mix of indulgence and amusement.

Introduction

No life is as small as it might appear from a distance.
Vast worlds lie buried within the smallest details of ordinary life
—ANAND PANDIAN AND M. P. MARIAPPAN

What conditions must exist for men and women to cease to accept their lives as they are? This book relates the lives of enslaved men and women who carved a moral self for themselves by resisting what they perceived as injustice. It is the story of a place and a time when the ordinary lives of individuals burst into the archive somewhat inadvertently. This book, which analyzes a series of linked events that took place in early nineteenth century Sri Lanka, emanates from the somewhat presumptuous belief that reading traces and hauntings will help reawaken an awareness of what happened and set off changes in a present replete with unresolved pasts.[1] Rather than attempt to repair wrongs already done, this book aims to understand the practices of becoming and being of enslaved people in a local context that was braided with the global.[2]

I do not look on enslaved people as numbers in a maritime trade but as subjects that fashioned their own lives within the limits of the social relations that played out in Sri Lanka's maritime provinces. These were territories that had been conquered in the sixteenth century by the Portuguese, ruled in the seventeenth and eighteenth centuries by the Dutch Vereenigde Oostindishe Compagnie (VOC), and finally taken over in 1796 by the British. During three centuries an island known chiefly for its cinnamon and elephants also functioned as a "carrefour," in the way Denys Lombard describes Java in his celebrated work *Le Carrefour Javanais*, though in the case of Sri Lanka it was also a crossroad of slave routes.[3]

This is not a book about the abolition of slavery, "the embarrassing institution" that has spawned a rich and variegated global scholarship, but about the battles against adversity—*during* the period of British abolition, the early nineteenth century—of individual slaves who, like children, servants, the poor, and women, were not seen as capable of "moral autonomy."[4] In comparison to slave societies in the early nineteenth century in the Atlantic and Indian Ocean worlds, the crown colony of Ceylon seemed to be of little significance. Its slave population never exceeded thirty-six thousand.[5] The turn to the particular is therefore called for, as there was little of the grand drama that drives the narratives of standard histories of slavery and emancipation in many other regions.

In Sri Lanka today, slave pasts are unknown or partially known. The conventional wisdom is either that slavery did not exist or, if it did, that it was confined to African slaves commonly known as "Kaffirs," brought to the island by the Portuguese and the Dutch, or was limited to a few possessions by Dutch proprietors. In short, it was mild and not a subject worth investigating, as there were no slave revolts as in St. Domingue and abolition did not require, as in the United States, a bloody civil war. In Sri Lanka slavery ended rather inconspicuously in 1844, paving the way for another type of labor regime and bondage—the plantation system, which differed from early forms of labor organization such as the reaping of cinnamon by members of the Salagama caste. For these reasons it is not entirely surprising that very few comprehensive studies of slavery and emancipation even mention Sri Lanka.[6]

This book is as much about the present as the past, in the sense that it reaches out to create a relation between the traces of the past and the ghosts that loom in the present, the afterlives. The slave hovers around today, like an absent present murmuring what must not be said aloud: that all histories are complex and that claims of origin, purity, and innocence of communities belong to the realm of myth. I explore the traces effaced and left and the lack of remembrance of and about enslaved people.[7] The ending of enslavement in Sri Lanka calls for different ways of seeing.

The trajectory of Sri Lanka from the early nineteenth century has been sketched in many ways: as a journey toward modernity, as a move toward democracy and freedom, and as a descent into communal chaos, violence, and evil. The lives of the enslaved open to us a vast world hitherto unknown, where there was no single trajectory but many routes taken that bifurcated or came together. When I focus on individuals, I do not reduce history to the epiphenomenal but try to develop a vocabulary that evokes and registers those who lived in this historical time. This book attempts a way of writing that represents their pain and struggles and conjures, describes, narrates, and explains a forgotten world. Fugitive lives are often difficult to seize on, and for this reason some of the stories are sketchy and remain unfinished.

This book crisscrosses a number of fields and disciplines and runs the risk of satisfying no one. It falls neither into the field of Indian Ocean slavery studies nor of Sri Lankan history as it is conventionally conceived of, since it looks beyond the shores of the island toward sea journeys and lands across the Indian Ocean. It does not attempt a chronological reconstruction of the making of "modern" Sri Lanka—a paradigm that has been crucial to nationalist historiography—since it is built on the premise that the past never abandons the present and can be drowned or reactivated. It may, however, pass the test of relevance so crucial these days. It is about unveiling, finding the shadows and the contours left by the absence of enslaved people, as well as removing the disguises put there to take us down paths that lead away from the ghosts, toward statues erected by states and dominant groups. In this sense this book is an engaged history of the present.

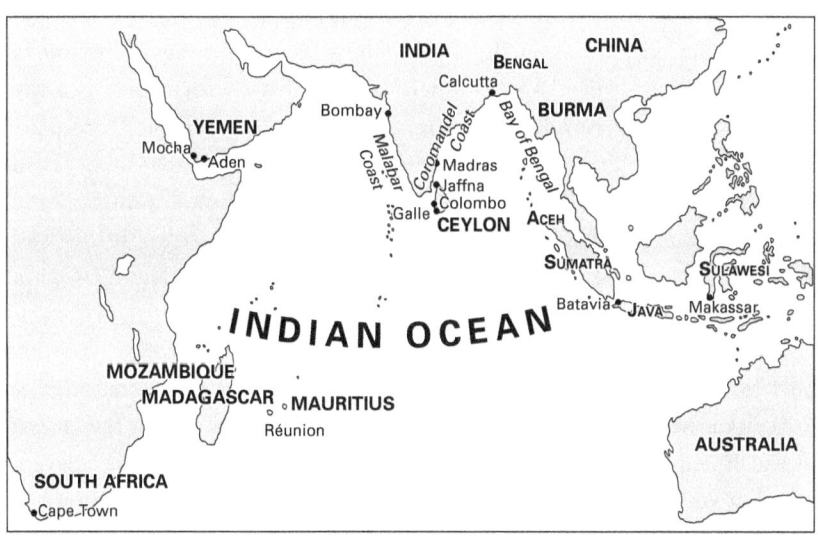

Figure 0.1 The Indian Ocean in the early nineteenth century

Setting the Stage

The stage needs to be set, and it is a large swathe of land and sea that we traverse. Enslaved people moved; they were forcibly transported across the Indian Ocean, as testified to by the lives of the men and women involved in the murder of the fiscal of Colombo in 1723, related in chapter 1, or by the life of a woman enslaved in Galle, described in chapter 2. Although the book centers on the maritime provinces of the island, the predominantly Sinhalese South and the predominantly Tamil North, other places across the sea surreptitiously enter the frame. The history of enslaved people cannot be divorced from the histories of other places, the places these people came from or where they went. In this sense the book is not confined to the boundaries of the island but is inserted in a wider territorial and oceanic loop.

From the seventeenth century, the port cities of Colombo and Galle, which served as transit points for enslaved people from South India and Southeast Asia and within the VOC shipping network, were second in importance only to Batavia. The bureaucracy of shipping has thus yielded a first type of data that comes to us from shipping lists and logbooks of ship captains. Colonial officials kept records of all the ships, passengers, and cargo that entered and left ports under their control.[8] It has been estimated, for instance, that four ships a year would depart from the Dutch Republic to Sri Lanka, and up to fifteen a year navigated from Sri Lanka to the republic, with a halt at the Cape. The port settlements of Sri Lanka were, moreover, crucial spaces where ships called en route between the Western and Eastern Indian Oceans.[9] The traffic between the Coromandel Coast and Colombo was far greater still: in 1705–1706, 103 boats sailed into Colombo. Colombo was in the path of the southwest monsoon and hence, unlike Batavia, was not a key port for company ships. It thus had to share much of the shipping traffic with Galle in the South and Jaffna in the North.[10]

During the wars that pitted France against other European powers between 1792 and 1815, Britain acquired the Indian Ocean territories of Sri Lanka, Mauritius, and the Cape Colony.[11] Britain was then the largest of the Europe-based empires and had been the dominant slave-trading country among them since the seventeenth century. During this transitional imperial period, debates in the British Parliament about abolishing the slave trade and related plans to ameliorate or reform the condition of the empire's slaves were chiefly concerned with British sugar colonies in the West Indies. India, still under East India Company rule, remained until the late 1830s conspicuously absent from the abolitionist debate. As Andrea Major convincingly argues, "Not all slaveries were considered equal."[12] Parliament made the slave trade illegal in 1807, and by the 1820s and 1830s an increasingly globalized antislavery movement was fiercely debating the legitimacy of "property in men" and the idea of payment of compensation to slaveholders in exchange for the freedom of their slaves. The culmination of these debates in Britain was a compromise: the Slavery Abolition Act of August 28, 1833, provided for the award of twenty million pounds sterling to the owners of "slave property" in the British colonies but exempted Sri Lanka, St. Helena, and the territories under East India Company rule, such as India.[13] The delegalization of slavery in India that occurred in 1843 thus had no provisions compelling local elites to enforce it, and enslaved people were not informed of their new status.[14]

By comparison, the early dismantling of slavery in the crown colony of Ceylon from 1816 and other forms of experimentation in land tenure, labor, taxation, and trade were quite unlike the Indian situation. At the time the Colebrooke-Cameron Commission was sent to the island in 1828, mainly to explore new forms of productivity and address the continuing deficit in the revenue of the colony, a number of changes, including the dismantling of coerced labor, had already been set in motion.[15] Legal scholars have recently identified, for instance, an earlier report, the "Ceylon Calendar of 1821," as a key testimony of "the new administrative focus" that signaled the emergence of novel social and political arrangements.[16] Furthering this endeavor, which charts a genealogy of modernity that predates the Colebrooke-Cameron reforms, in the present work I introduce a modified perspective on social change insofar as my concern is with "state effects," in particular the way mundane material practices of the state acted on subaltern people in the decades preceding the Colebrooke-Cameron Report.[17]

A Singular Story

In 1815—the year in which the British conquered the interior kingdom of Kandy—the entire island came under colonial rule for the first time. At this time there were three areas in Sri Lanka where slavery was still in practice: the maritime provinces formerly controlled by the Portuguese and the Dutch East India Company and under British East India Company rule between 1796 and 1802; the Jaffna peninsula; and the Kandyan areas in the central highlands, where categories of slaves were described in the Kandyan treatise of law, the *Niti-Nighanduwa*. Before the arrival of the Europeans, slavery had been practiced in the north-central and southern areas of the island during the Anuradhapura period (fourth century BCE to eleventh century CE) and the Polonnaruwa period (eleventh century CE to fourteenth century CE) in conjunction with public institutions such as Buddhist temples, royal households, and guilds. Families of slaves are clearly listed in records such as the Galapata-vihara inscription (twelfth to thirteenth centuries).[18]

This book focuses on the southern and northern maritime provinces, which came under colonial rule as early as the sixteenth century, and does not cover the special case of slavery in the Kandyan provinces. The Kandyan kingdom, the last independent kingdom, survived for another two centuries and finally succumbed to the British in 1818, after a widespread rebellion of the Kandyan aristocracy. Enslavement in the Kandyan provinces was often voluntary, as people sold themselves into slavery to settle a debt or obtain a loan and were then subject to the customary Kandyan law.[19]

In the southern areas, the enslaved people who worked in Dutch or local homes as servants or artisans more often hailed from South India or the East Indies. This was quite different to the situation in the north of the island, where the enslaved were Tamils from oppressed castes. There, by sanctioning and tapping into a perceived local practice of slavery and legally constituting them as slaves, Dutch colonial rulers had further strengthened the power of the dominant caste Vellalars over their subordinates.[20] This was done through bureaucratizing processes of registration, legal codification, and litigation. While the Dutch transformed an existing form of bondage in the Tamil areas, creating a slavery that looked much more like European slavery, British rule introduced a number of measures, acts, and incentives from 1816 to dismantle slavery as it was practiced in the entire island. The present volume follows the lives of a few enslaved people as they were touched by these changes and at moments when they challenged their condition. A slave who rode the palanquin of his master in Nallur, Jaffna, epitomizes this moment of upheaval.

Sri Lanka was an anomaly that resembled neither the Indian subcontinent nor other Indian Ocean islands. Its forms of enslavement were linked to the Dutch creation of a form of slavery resembling European slavery through a transformation of caste in the Hindu North, to debt in the Kandyan areas, and to Portuguese and Dutch needs for domestic and agricultural labor in the southern maritime territories. They were a mélange of Indian Malabar Coast praedial caste-based forms of slavery and Cape Colony's racialized forms of servitude. If slavers were not always "white," in the Cape the enslaved were never other than "black." The variety of slave systems and forms of bondage is such that it cannot be easily encapsulated in terms such as "South Asian slavery" or "Sri Lankan slavery."[21] It may not be useful to include, as has been done in some recent studies, quite disparate forms of servitude, from palace women in the Chola Empire, to Turks in the army of the Delhi sultans, to indebted peasants in western India, in the catchall category "South Asia." Thinking of the multiple genealogies and modes of exerting power over another's body could be a productive approach. Furthermore, there is a need to treat with caution an implicit idea among some scholars working on Indian forms of slavery that South Asian / Indian slavery works through intimacy and kinship ties.[22] This view is challenged inter alia by Matthias van Rossum's recent work on slavery in Cochin, which is based on a detailed analysis of VOC archives.[23] For insight into the intertwined history of freedom and unfreedom and the need to address them as entangled in the common history of capital, one may need to go back to Gyan Prakash's masterful demonstration of the reconstitution by British rule in nineteenth-century Bihar of a range of dependent labor ties in the inverse image of free labor. His work shows that after the abolition of slavery in 1843, the Kamias, enslaved agricultural laborers in Bihar, were transformed into bonded laborers. They became free but enslaved by debt.[24] Freedom is clearly a misleading antithesis to slavery. There is no easy or single definition of slavery in Sri Lanka, where the bundle of traits of Western slavery are rarely visible. Orlando Patterson's definition of slavery as "the permanent, violent domination of natally alienated and generally dishonoured persons" may apply to some but not all domestic slaves working in the port cities of the island.[25] But it does not fit, in any sense, the situation in the northern province where the enslaved Nalavars, Pallars, and Coviyars had a sense of belonging to the land where they lived and worked. Igor Kopytoff's identification of slavery as the "legitimate exercise of a bundle of different rights over another person" by slaveholders may be more fruitfully applied to the northern maritime province.[26]

Sri Lanka became in many ways a testing ground for the British government through its representative, the governor, that set in motion processes to gradually abolish slavery as soon as the island came under its control after the interlude of East India Company rule between 1796 and 1802. In the decades that followed, acts of gradual emancipation of slaves were passed and official pronouncements made regarding the need to free slaves. These decades have been referred to as a period of amelioration of slavery when the ideas of the antislavery lobby in Parliament and the Evangelical movement threw their weight behind the forces of emancipation. West Indian planters responded by introducing some policies to mitigate the blatant abuses inherent in slavery through distribution of food and clothing and conversion through the medium of education and religion. This amelioration policy met with much derision on the part of abolitionists who did not see it as a path to emancipation.[27] Sri Lanka's experience with abolition bears many common features of amelioration practices in other crown colonies and is for this reason singularly distinct from the subcontinent.

The Descent Into the Ordinary

The lives of dominated people, in the singular—lives of trouble, chance, nerve, and ruse—make the matter of this book, which takes the shape of a "descent into the ordinary."[28] It does not strive to create a vast tapestry but rather to look at the "epic of the ordinary" formed by oblique alignments and tangential engagements that took place in the shadow of the grand dramas recounted by historians.[29] It relates individual stories of enslaved people who were moved from the Malay world and the Indian subcontinent to Sri Lanka and whose lives were captured and recorded by colonial archiving because they stepped out of line at a particular moment. Meghan Vaughan's portraits of enslaved men and women in Mauritius, Marina Carter's exploration of life experiences of indentured workers, and, more recently, Clare Anderson's meticulous retracing of the lives of convicts have considerably enriched our understanding of the lives of subaltern people in the nineteenth century across the Indian Ocean.[30] Ably researched works by Kerry Ward, Ronit Ricci, and Michael Laffan have recently followed the journeys of Southeast Asian exiles and convicts between Java, Cape Colony, and Sri Lanka.[31] A rich and well-established historiography on slavery in the Cape of Good Hope has yielded fascinating stories of enslaved people, parts of whose lives appeared in the VOC archive. This happened at moments of crisis or conflict when it was necessary for them to be recorded.[32] Nigel Worden's sharp observation that "slaves survived in the paper archive by default rather than by design" is reflected in the Sri Lankan archive too.[33] More recently, Sue Peabody's master-slave narrative of Madeleine, a woman sold into slavery in the 1760s in Chandernagor, and her son Furcy explores the paradoxes of what it meant to be a slave and then free in the Mascarene Islands. The changes in fortune that were bequeathed to Furcy, a man who was born a slave and then became a bourgeois head of household and a slaveholder himself, would have happened to others too.[34]

Historians writing on Sri Lanka's colonial past have rarely focused their attention on the lives and practices of subaltern men and women who did not keep journals or diaries, and if they wrote letters they did it with the help of a petition writer. On the other hand, accounts of the trials and triumphs of exceptional figures, politicians, and rulers by professional and public historians are numerous. In Sri Lankan historiography, the realm of the popular is seen as made of a collective, rather than of individuals endowed with names and faces. Studies of popular collective revolts, movements, and political parties rarely turn to the singular except to linger briefly on leaders of these movements.[35] The margins have had a different meaning for feminist historians who have created a corpus that has unearthed the extraordinary lives of exceptional women in conditions of adversity: medical practitioners, suffragettes, trade union leaders. Yet all belonged to privileged literate backgrounds and left a trail of paper sources for feminist historians to document.[36] Historians of labor have turned to communities of work: plantation labor on coffee or tea plantations and, more recently, in garment factories or migrant workers as a collective rather than focusing on individual lives.[37] The individual is conspicuously absent from the historiography of the nineteenth century unless the subject is royal, heroic, or villainous.[38]

Works of historical and cultural anthropology ranging from later Annales historians' studies of revolt to the seminal Indian historiography on peasant resistance were inspiring and helped me think about modes of reading and representing violence.[39] Together with the Annales and Subaltern studies' decoding of counterinsurgency discourse, my debt is to the luminous work of Veena Das on victims of violence, with its reading of silences and recomposition of people's lives.[40] There has been little attention given to enslaved peoples in nineteenth-century Sri Lanka and especially to their connection to other places in the Indian Ocean world. So while I draw from familiar forms of history writing, I explore an uncharted archive that allows new subject matter and vantage points. This book aims to deepen an engagement with areas and people who have been overlooked by the dominant historiography.

It is a historian's lament that people from India, Indonesia, or Sri Lanka who were enslaved in the Indian Ocean world between the seventeenth and nineteenth centuries have produced, to my knowledge, only a few autobiographies, in contrast to the rich body of works on the Atlantic world. Among them is the little-known, unpublished memoir of Wange van Balie, which describes his life as an enslaved person in the Indonesian Archipelago.[41] The fifty-nine pages handwritten by van Balie, who was emancipated in the Netherlands after following his final master there, is unique in many ways. He describes his youth on a farm on the island of Magarij, his subsequent enslavement, and life under various masters until 1810. Paul Bijl interprets the manuscript as the performance of "acts of equality" by the author. He argues that van Balie wrote the text to engage with his Dutch readers and claim his equality as an autonomous human being who had the capacity to empathize. Slaves appear as actors in a few other texts. The life of Untung Surapati, the "national hero of Indonesia," born in the late seventeenth century as a slave in Bali, is recounted in Javanese historical poems or ballads. The Mughal Punjab eighteenth-century manuscript Kitab-i-Qissa-I Tahmas Miskin was written in Persian by an ex-slave. Its author, Tahmas Miskin, a young boy from a village called Barzat in Turkey, was forcefully taken during a raid by Persian soldiers.[42] Din Muhammad, who worked in the East India Company's Bengal army and followed his former master to Cork in the mid-eighteenth century, wrote an autobiography in which his past as a slave in a British household during a time of famine is occluded.[43]

Apart from these rare examples, the Indian Ocean world lacks the genre of literature now known as "slave narratives" or "freedom narratives" that accounts for the lives of African slaves in North America and the Caribbean from capture to emancipation. There are a few Arabic-language narratives of slave experience, such as that of Abu Bakr of Timbuktu, in bondage in Jamaica, and some narratives of liberated Africans, the most famous being that of Samuel Ajayi Crowther, who was rescued from a slave ship by the British Navy and resettled in Sierra Leone.[44] These are rare, however, compared to the corpus written by formerly enslaved people in North America and the Caribbean, which includes the canonical writings of Harriet Tubman, Harriet Jacobs, Frederick Douglass, and Olaudah Equiano. These texts are invaluable sources to understand capture, enslavement, transportation, and finally emancipation. Yet while they strive to speak from the perspective of the enslaved, many of them remain texts that were edited by prominent abolitionists for use in their antislavery campaigns.[45] Written in autobiographical and sociological modes for a primarily white and female readership, they were constrained by the demands placed on them by their main sponsor and consumer, the abolitionist movement, which wanted texts that were written in a specific style and sounded "truthful and believable."[46]

By contrast, the texts that pepper the colonial archive—petitions, testimonies of slaves, and letters about them—are not compelled to show a visible sign of reason or a shared humanity. They come to us mediated, partially recorded, and drawing on different types of conventions and tropes. These texts that document performances of enslaved people are not produced to prove the humanity and personhood of slaves but stage them at the center of events where their own claim for recognition comes to the fore.[47] Thus, in spite of a lack of personal accounts such as slave diaries, autobiographies, letters, and stories, there is an alternative in judicial records when they have been preserved. Legal cases have often become a mainstay of cultural history, despite being mediated and translated records where the historian performs the role of a sleuth who investigates events that are incomplete or subject to the vagaries of memory.[48]

An Archive of Practices, Names, and Numbers

My strategy is to capture the slave at the moment he or she acts and performs, thus relating a slice of his or her life. Rather than focusing only on utterances, I forge an archive of practices, of people doing things, these things being precisely what allowed them to enter the archive. The texts I read at the National Archives and British Library in London, the Sri Lanka National Archives in Colombo, and the National Archive in The Hague are a variety of documents: petitions by enslaved or formerly enslaved people claiming justice and dignity; court records where the enslaved appear as witnesses, victims, or accused culpable of transgressions, hence reported in the official legal apparatus; notarial records where enslaved people receive largesse from their proprietors. I read in these texts heroic gestures by ordinary men and women that could be qualified as a politics of resistance to a status quo or simply as evidence of the emergence of the "political" in men and women who were confronted with situations where they refused to accept the terms set for them by society.[49] There are, however, many things that we cannot know from a hostile archive. Stories take us down false trails and dead-ends. I have therefore tried to force the archive in search of discards, dissonances, and anomalies.

For each story of an enslaved person in the north and south of the island, another important source of information is the slave register, an enumerative procedure that took place in the nineteenth century as an outcome of the movement to abolish slavery in the British Empire. Slave registers on Sri Lanka, a series of large, hand-filled, bound books, have not until now been exploited as a historical source.[50] In Sri Lanka as in other colonies, measures were taken to ensure that proprietors duly registered their slaves. Although this operation was not designed to count slaves, it is an enumeration of a specific sort. The slave registers listing enslaved people in the island of Sri Lanka were created in 1818–1832 and are today at the National Archives in London. They provide information not exclusively about slaves, listed alphabetically in each parish or district, but also about proprietors. In 1819 the Office for the Registry of Colonial Slaves was established in London, and copies of the slave registers kept by the colonies were sent to this office. Registration generally occurred once every three years. The registers continued through to 1834, when slavery was officially abolished in most territories, but in the case of Sri Lanka registration continued until 1844—the year in which the crown colony abolished slavery. These later registers are visible only in pieces in the correspondence of collectors and have not survived as complete documents.[51] Registers tabulate names of enslaved individuals, number each of them, and list them in columns. They provide some interesting information for the maritime provinces: date of registration, name of slave, sex, age, name of children of female slaves, age and sex of children.[52] Thus, although they deal with the "collective," the registers of enslaved people prove themselves to be extremely useful to frame the individual stories this book relates.

This book is organized around six core questions. The first five chapters braid individual stories of enslaved people within a broader theme—race and blackness, bodily violence, caste and slavery, free and unfree labor, the performance of freedom. The final chapter reflects on the way slavery haunts the present, how it reverberates while adopting different disguises, and tries to understand for whose benefit slavery is invisible or invoked.

The first chapter begins with the story of the murder of a Dutch fiscal in 1723 and its afterlives to explore the gradual blackening of slaves in texts and in the collective memory of the people of Sri Lanka. It details the rewriting of history around the space called "Slave Island" in Colombo, where a murder by Indonesian slaves gets transformed into a Kaffir slave revolt in popular memory and guidebooks. I then turn my attention to the census and Blue Books of the first half of the nineteenth century, the main administrative documents where the "slave" was mentioned as a collective category and, ironically in a colony where the majority of people were under British colonial rule, contrasted with "free" black subjects. This chapter explores the social and political conditions that produced these recorded taxonomies and the political and moral projects that were served by the appearance and disappearance of certain categories of classification.

Chapter 2 follows four enslaved people in the southern part of the island, from Colombo to Galle, as they appear in the fissures of an archive of law and violence. Violence is present in its multiple and cruelest forms in the burdened life of an enslaved woman, Selestina, who kills her newborn child in 1820; in the murder of an enslaved man, Valentine, running away from servitude on a Maradana Road; in a woman from Cochin sold in Galle; and in a child in Galle kidnapped as merchandise for the Arabian slave market. In all four cases one gets a glimpse of people's refusal to accept the terms set: infanticide as protest, flight interrupted by murder, appeals to colonial justice all signal a clear desire for moving out of enslavement or the conditions that come with it.

Chapter 3 begins with an event: in 1819 in Jaffna, a Coviyar slave named Cander Wayreven was whipped under orders of the collector of Jaffna, the highest British official in the area, for traveling in the palanquin of his master and thus going against what was conceived as the prevailing law by allegedly overstepping his position and status. Wayreven's case and others too reveal that in spite of the ambivalence displayed by British officials in Sri Lanka to defend and uphold antislavery and proabolition policies initiated in the metropole since the beginning of the nineteenth century, small spaces of resistance were opening in Jaffna society in many different and unusual ways. This murmur of British liberalism's rejection of slavery gave enslaved peoples the psychological thrust to act.

The Chilaw experiment in slave emancipation related in chapter 4 began in 1820 as a prelude to better-known experiments in freeing labor in the British West Indian colonies. It seemingly applied a simple rule: freedom in exchange for labor. According to this scheme, hundreds of Coviyar, Nalavar, and Pallar slaves from Jaffna whose freedom was purchased by the colonial government were sent to Chilaw in the southwestern part of the island in the early decades of British rule to perform hard labor on canals and other public works. Through a reconstruction of the lives of these emancipated slaves in Chilaw, the chapter demonstrates that modernity and liberal thought were ever present in the procedures informing the gradual abolition of slavery, decades before the Colebrooke-Cameron reforms.

Chapter 5 is a detailed exposé of the revolt of an emancipated slave in Colombo in 1826. Packier Pulle Rawothan, a resident of Colombo, applied to the headmoorman (headman of the Muslims) of the district to obtain permission for his son to be circumcised.[53] Some members of the Moor (Muslim) community of Colombo reacted angrily to this request, spawning a war of reports, petitions, and complaints, culminating in a court case filed by Rawothan in the provincial court of Colombo against eight members of the Moor community.[54] The issue was simply that Rawothan was "of slave extraction," castigated as "a cooly and the son of a maid slave of Pakkeer Pulle" and thus not eligible to perform "such honorary ceremonies the respectable Moors are only entitled to perform." The thirty-two handwritten pages filed in the records of the Colombo kachcheri exist as a testimony of the legitimate strategies of claim making that were available to and used with some confidence by disgruntled subjects of the colony, exemplifying that the crown colony was not dissimilar to what has been aptly called the "Document Raj" across the Palk Straits.[55]

The final chapter explores the eclipse of enslaved people from the collective memory of people in Sri Lanka. After slavery was abolished in 1844, how and why did enslaved people become invisible in the North and the South? The main form of forgetfulness was the willingness to accept a layer of memories that conflated slavery with "Kaffirs" or Africans. But there were also various mechanisms in the Sinhalese-majority South—conversion, baptism, appropriation of "ethnic" (Portuguese Burgher) identity or of a labor identity (coolie)—that may have contributed to the complete disappearance of traces of slavery. In the North, among dominant Tamils, invisibility is a symptom of a refusal to remember a difficult past shared by enslaved people and slaveholders.

CHAPTER I

A Dutch Fiscal's Murder

Interrogating the Identity of Slaves, Blacks, and "Kaffirs"

> The documents we read were not written for us.
> —MARTIN A. KLEIN[1]

There is an enduring belief in Sri Lanka that at some undetermined point in history "Kaffir" slaves rebelled, creating such havoc in Colombo that it led to them being severely suppressed and then confined to a ward of the city that then became known for posterity as Slave Island. The less well-known murder of the Dutch fiscal, Barent van der Swaan, and his wife by their Asian domestic slaves in Colombo in 1723 is intimately connected to this apocryphal story.[2] The reverberations of this violent event across three centuries offer a key to tracking shifts in the manner in which "slaves," "blacks," and "Kaffirs" were represented and their lives and deaths recorded during successive colonial and postcolonial regimes.

The term "Kaffir," from the Portuguese word *caffre*, is borrowed, according to the *Encyclopaedia of Islam*, from the Arabic *kafir*, which originally meant obliterating or covering in verses in the Qur'an and later acquired the more general meaning of infidel or nonbeliever.[3] It remains today as Kapiri in Sinhala and Kapili in Tamil, to qualify present-day Afro–Sri Lankans whose ancestors were believed to have been forcefully brought to the island as slaves and mercenaries by the Portuguese from various parts of the African continent. Exact lineages are difficult to trace as one has to rely on facts and figures given in colonial sources and vernacular literary works, where the strength, ferocity, and numbers of the enemy forces are often exaggerated in descriptions of battles. One can only assume that early Africans would have merged, over centuries, into the local population. African soldiers were brought to fight in the British Army during the Kandyan campaign in the nineteenth century. Records show that they were slaves purchased by the British in Goa and Bombay and brought to the island to be trained as soldiers. They served as free men in the Caffre Corps, later called the Third and Fourth Ceylon Regiment.[4] Some Afro–Sri Lankans who today form a distinct community in Puttalam claim to be descendants of those soldiers from the Third Ceylon Regiment who were given land to settle on after retirement. Others believe their ancestors came from Kaffa in Ethiopia.[5] This book, however, is not about the Kaffirs, who are commonly seen as an ethnographically distinct community associated with slavery and empire, but about enslaved people whose ambiguous origins take us to an interconnected Indian Ocean world made of a crucible of peoples from India, Sri Lanka, the East Indies, and Africa, men and women who shared a similar fate.

I suggest in this chapter that a metamorphosis happened in popular culture in the form of a gradual "blackening" of the slave in texts and in the collective memory of the people of Sri Lanka from the mid-nineteenth century onward through a merging of two initially distinct colonial categories of "slave" and "black." This led to an erasure of the diversity of the origin of enslaved people and the equivalence of slave with African, a bias that academic history has until now failed to address.[6] The history of men and women who were forcefully brought to Sri Lanka from the East Indies and India disappeared, replaced by a new, simplified history of slavery in Sri Lanka conceived as black/African (Kaffir) slavery that resonated with the dominant model of Atlantic slavery.

Another semantic phenomenon that has occurred in many places where violent colonial encounters shattered societies and touched Sri Lanka equally is the shift over time in the meaning of "black" and "blackness." The meaning of the former term shriveled, shifting from an amorphous one of conquest in the sixteenth to eighteenth centuries to one endowed with a sharp racial undertone, alongside the growth of racialized ideas about indigenous "oriental" peoples. In Sri Lanka until 1838, "blacks" encompassed Sinhalese, Tamils, Muslims, and other nonwhites. Blackness, like race, had no scientific pretensions until the late nineteenth century, as it was most often used as a category of classification in the early censuses and as a term of inferiority cast on all dominated peoples who simply looked different from the norm, the white male. Achille Mbembe reminds us of Frantz Fanon's famous point that just as the figure of the black does not exist, neither does the white, both being fantasies of the imagination.[7] The white was indeed little more than a fantasy of the European imagination that the West tried to naturalize and universalize. Yet ironically, while a century earlier blackness was forcefully contained in a racialized African identity, in the twentieth century blackness would free itself to become a radical claim and rallying point for political solidarity among peoples of African and Asian descent.[8]

This chapter begins with a foray into a hitherto unexplored event, the murder of a Dutch fiscal in eighteenth-century Colombo, in order to understand the processes at stake in the recording and memorialization of enslaved people. What details are recorded and emphasized for posterity, and what is left out? I trace the fractured journey of the categories of slave, black, and Kaffir and inquire into the political and moral projects that were served by the resilience, disappearance, and metamorphosis of slaves and blacks in the nineteenth century. After piecing together existing data on the murder of 1723 and its afterlives, I explore the few sources that provide clues to the origin of slaves in the southern maritime region of the island and finally trace the journeys of the categories "slave" and "black" in the official colonial record.

A Murder in 1723

Let us begin with the events recorded in recent popular guidebooks and travel writings that are purported to have happened in Slave Island, today a ward of Colombo, the capital city of Sri Lanka. Slave Island (fig. 1.1) is located directly south of the fort area, between the Colombo harbor and Beira Lake, where once stood a fortress built by the Portuguese and the Dutch as the center of power. The account written in 1984 by the reputed surveyor R. L. Brohier of the growth of the Kaffir slave population in Colombo and their violent rebellion remains the most detailed. Yet one searches in vain for archival sources or precise dates that sustain his story. Most present explanations of the events are found in popular writings that draw generously from Brohier's account, often failing to cite its author.

Since he is considered reliable and has produced such a trail of followers, his rendering of the events needs to be cited at length:

> The Kaffirs were trafficked from the East coast of Africa in the neighbourhood of Mozambique . . . they were used as mercenary troops, camp fellows and carriers. The Portuguese introduced the Kaffir to Ceylon about the year 1630 from their settlement at Goa on the coast of Malabar. The Dutch drew largely on this pool of labour to work under the overseers when they set out to build the citadel at Colombo.[9]

In Brohier's account, slaves found in Sri Lanka's southern maritime province were clearly and unambiguously Africans, who had been forcibly brought from Mozambique through Goa, the capital of the Portuguese viceroyalty in India. Furthermore, the momentous events leading to the death of the fiscal, Barent van der Swaan, are depicted as something much larger than a murder, since the language Brohier used is one of a large-scale slave insurrection and a conspiracy:

> In the early years of the 18th century the Kaffir population of Colombo had grown to *such numbers* that it gave them a sense of their own strength. This enabled them to stage an *insurrection* in the citadel. Besides committing much violence in the streets to private property, they conspired and murdered the Fiscal, Barent van der Swaan, and his good wife, when they lay asleep. The details of the tragedy hold that the murderer, a *Kaffir servant*, had hidden under the bedstead, and when his master and mistress had turned into sleep crawled out behind them and using a dagger "with two unerring stabs sent them to eternity." Eventually the *Kaffir Insurrection* was suppressed. The authorities thereafter decided that all the slave-labour working in the citadel must be regimented.[10]

Reading through Brohier's account, it seemed to me curious that a slave insurrection of presumably large numbers of African slaves would go unnoticed or at least unreported by generations of professional historians who have written on Dutch rule in Sri Lanka.[11] Furthermore the peculiar mix of vagueness (the absence of dates) and precision in the form of exact details (the dagger, the bedstead) in Brohier's telling belongs more to the realm of

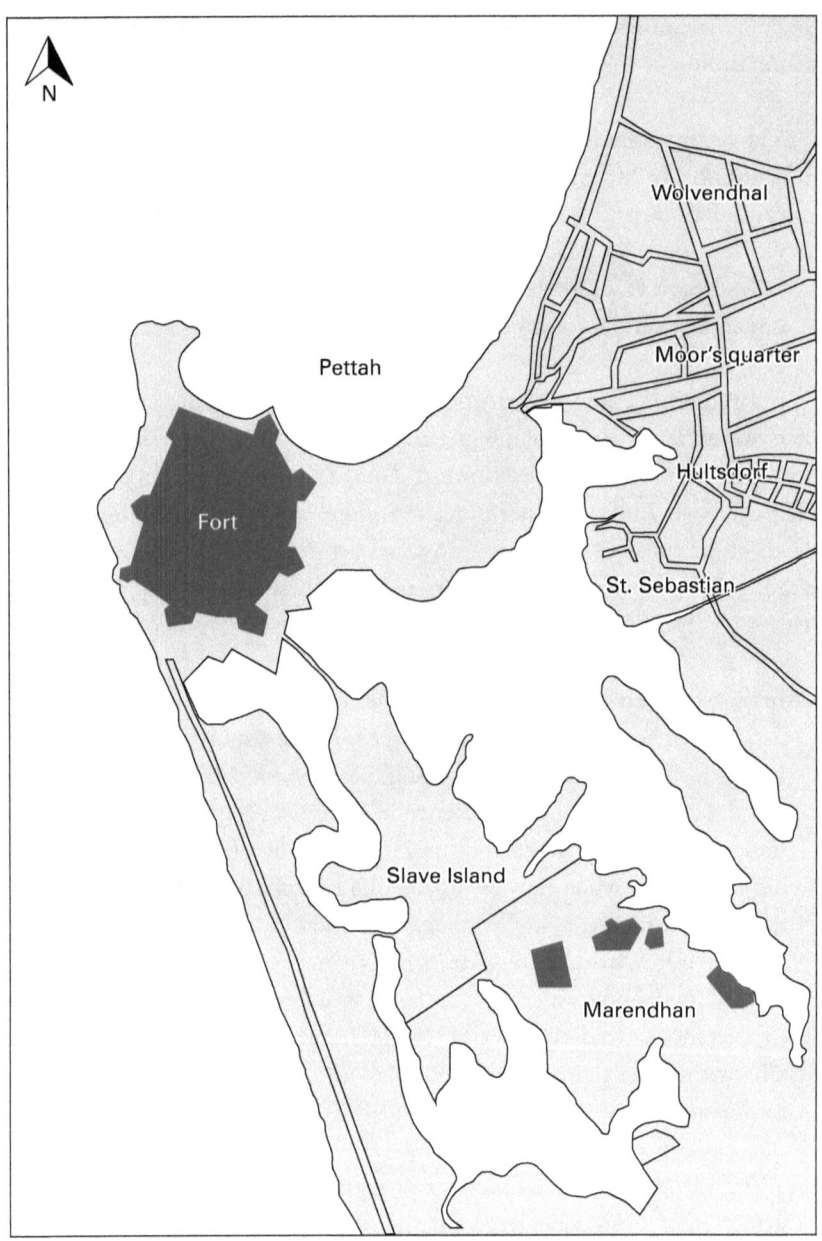

Figure 1.1 Slave Island, Colombo

myth than to that of professional history. Curiosity pushed me into hunting for answers through a foray into a Dutch VOC archive that I was quite unfamiliar with. Colleagues recommended looking at the criminal case records in the form of criminal rolls of the period. The dating of the events was made possible by the conjuncture of the death of Governor Isaac Augustin Rumpf, which secondary sources confirmed as happening in June 1723. Rumpf's funeral account by Francois Valentijn, published a few years later, did not make any reference to a large-scale "Kaffir" insurrection, although it did mention the unrest caused by cinnamon peelers that same year: "In this year the cinnamon peelers rose against us. . . . Also in this year (1723) a rare event occurred when the fiscal, Barent van der Swaan, with his wife, was murdered by his slaves, unfortunately, in Colombo. Upon hearing this, his hon. passed away three days later, on the 11 of June 1723 (so people say) he died out of shock."[12]

Interestingly, an account by R. G. Anthonisz, the government archivist, from 1906 tallies with Valentijn's record of the event. Anthonisz writes that Rumpf, governor from 1716 to 1723, died suddenly from "a shock received on hearing of the assassination of the Fiscal Barent van der Swaan and his wife by their slaves."[13] He does not mention any instance of a slave rebellion.

Distinct, braided, and parallel narratives appear to have emerged after the event. One that describes the event as a murder committed by domestic slaves, followed by the death of the governor evident after 1723, fades away as we move into the twentieth century, leaving some traces, as in a recent online resource that draws from uncited sources to explain the naming of Slave Island: "One night a slave of a Dutch household in the Fort had murdered an entire family. As a result all the slaves in the Fort were lodged in huts just outside the Kasteel or Fort. . . . The slaves, after carrying water, firewood, and attending to janitorial work in the households in the Fort, were at the end of the day rowed to Slave Island every evening through steps of the Sally Port."[14] The narrative that came into existence in the nineteenth century about a murder and a rebellion of Kaffir slaves has spawned multiple avatars in contemporary popular culture.

The criminal rolls of 1723, however, do not refer to widespread disturbances or any other violent context and only give us a picture of the object of the court case, namely, the deaths of Barent van der Swaan and his wife, which are noted as horrific (*gruvelijk*). For the crime committed, twelve enslaved people, described as "slaves of van der Swaan," were taken prisoner and charged in court for murder. Their names and ages are listed:

1. Kedoe   23 to 24 years
2. Scipio   22, 23
3. Lotty   19, 18
4. Wintura   26, 28
5. Titus   26
6. Tenna   24
7. Rake   22
8. Rande   20
9. Cong   17
10. Dana   12, 13
11. Clona   30, 31
12. Rosetta   12, 13

The most revealing information given is about the place of origin of these slaves (*lijfeigenen*), which was scribbled under their names. Contrary to the common perception of African/Kaffir slaves being involved in the violence, the fourth-named Wintura and seventh, Rake, were "Balinese" and "Christian," while others were "born on the island of Timor and heathen (together) slaves."[15] VOC sources suggest quite categorically that those involved in the violence were not Kaffirs. Thus by the late twentieth century, when Brohier wrote his seemingly authoritative book on Colombo, the origin of the slaves had undergone a metamorphosis, from East Indies, Balinese, and Timorese to a new identity as "Kaffirs."

The term "Kaffir" (nonbeliever in Arabic), used by Arab slavers to refer to indigenous people of East, Central, and West Africa, was adopted by European colonizers to qualify various people from Africa and was never applied in Sri Lanka to people of Asian origin. Asian slaves appear in Dutch textual records under the generic term *slaaven*, while Africans are included in both the "slaaven" and "Kaffir" categories. The discrepancy between the story as it is recorded in the official VOC archive and its appearance in a new garb in a variety of published texts over three centuries brings to bear an unambiguous process of blackening of slaves. Blackening stains seeped into travel writing, contemporary popular histories, and public culture, leading to an overall loss of the complexity and historicity of the categories "slave" and "black" and at the same time a loss of a compassionate memory of slavery, an issue I will come back to in the final chapter.

Historical truths are understood here and sought out as "broad synthetic generalizations based on researched collections of individual facts. They may be wrong, but they are always amenable to verification by the methods of historical research."[16] What is significant to uncover as a historical endeavor is the way the Slave Island story and the origin of its protagonists acquired new meanings, as the events moved from the cloisters of academia epitomized by Anthonisz's account to the realm of popular history illustrated by Brohier.

The VOC's outposts at the Cape of Good Hope and in Mauritius are known to have been chiefly supplied with Asian slaves dispatched from Batavia or Colombo on the annual return fleets. From the fragmentary evidence available, the origins of enslaved people in Colombo were initially thought to be mainly from the Indian subcontinent—Coromandel, Tanjur, and Canara in South India—but there is evidence to suggest that from the 1660s, and especially after the fall of Makassar in 1667, slaves were also sourced from the Southeast Asian circuit encompassing Malaysia, Indonesia, New Guinea, and Southern Philippines.[17] Among the 1,570 company-enslaved people in 1685 and 1,741 in 1697, as cited by Remco Raben, or the 5,500 slaves in 1688 estimated by Matthias van Rossum, one can ponder on how many were from Southeast Asia.[18] Kate Ekama's evidence for the late eighteenth century disturbs Gerrit Knaap's view that most slaves in Colombo were purchased in South India in the late seventeenth century, although she warns that data on slave origins is very unreliable. Naming patterns and birthplace records suggest that many private and company slaves originated from Southeast Asia. This is most apparent in court cases and in records of the *materiaalhuis* (storage house, the old church in the castle) in Colombo, where deceased slaves were listed as "Bataviase" from Makassar, Ternate, Timor, and Boetin. This fact tallies with the origin of slaves who were involved in the fiscal's murder in 1723. In the December 1775 materiaalhuis list of nineteen deceased slaves, for instance, ten originated from Southeast Asia, with reference made to Bugis, Makassar, Mangarij, Timor, and Sumbawa. All ten were transported through Batavia. Others were transported through Coromandel, Tuticorin, and Malabar.[19]

While the evidence is tentative and limited, it helps explain the presence of enslaved Malay-speaking people in the British archive of the early nineteenth century, as the case of Valentin in chapter 2 will show. The narrative of the sentencing and punishment meted to the prisoners described in the criminal rolls has, interestingly, never entered the public realm. Yet such a story could have been appropriated by the popular domain where, more than in academic history, tales of extreme violence, domination, and subjugation are often sought out.

Punishment

Another metamorphosis happened in popular history: the violent punishment of prisoners by the colonial authorities became a story of a violent rebellion performed by an enraged crowd of Kaffir slaves. The prisoners, as reported in the criminal rolls (which unfortunately do not contain the court proceedings), pleaded guilty in different ways. Scipio, Wintura, Titus, and Rake prayed for forgiveness, Lotty asked to be hanged, and Tenna asked for pardon. The court declared that the main culprit was Kedoe. He and six of the accused identified as his accomplices would die for the crime they committed in the cruelest manner in order to deter others.[20] Kedoe as the leader was dragged to the execution place on a plank and bound to a cross by the executioner, who then scorched his bound arms, breasts, and thighs. Then he was cut open, his ear pulled out and his head cut off. The parts of his body and head were dragged around the citadel again and then hung on display with his head on a stick. The others would suffer a similar fate.[21]

Brohier's account of the suppression of the "Kaffir insurrection" does not include any public execution but a decision on the part of public authorities that all slave labor must be regimented:

> At the end of their days work in institution, or the households of the grandees in the Colombo of those days, they were massed on the "Kaffirs Veldt" and had to answer to a roll call. They were thereafter led along a narrow passage through the ramparts, called a "Sallypoort," and ferried across the lake to what was a jagged peninsula which came to be miscalled on old maps Ijemenaing "Island." They were concentrated here for the night in lines and shanties. Amid the changes of three centuries this name "Slave Island" has stood firm.[22]

As in most mythographies, cause and effect and temporal moorings are nebulous.[23] Brohier's narrative appears to merge a number of different events to create an explanation for the naming of the area as "Slave Island." Another borrowing of details is in the description of the gruesome murder by "dagger," which seems to be loosely inspired by another murder of a Dutch official by his slave at the end of the eighteenth century. In 1799 the last Dutch disava of Matara, Pieter Willem Ferdinand Adriaan van Schuler of Utrecht, as well as his wife, Wilhelmine Catharina Leembruggen, were both assassinated in their bed by a domestic slave. Anthonisz describes the events:

> The slave having secreted himself in the sleeping chamber for the purpose, and who used his master's own sword, which was hanging on the wall by the bed, for the perpetration of the deed. This he plunged deep into his victim's breast; and the lady, on being stabbed in the abdomen as she seized the assassin to prevent his making his escape. The husband expired immediately, but the wife lingered long enough to be able to identify the miscreant and to secure his conviction and execution.[24]

Thus popular memory seems to have fused the two stories of murder by a slave. The reasons behind the naming of the area as Slave Island—in particular its connection with a slave rebellion that may not have actually happened—need further exploration.

Slave Island

That the area was called Slave Island in connection with a past of slavery is not in doubt, but the nature of this connection and the dating of Brohier and others in his wake need to be scrutinized. A link between the name Slave Island and a violent Kaffir slave insurrection and its suppression in the early eighteenth century lingers on today in guidebooks and general works. A recent dictionary of historical places repeated the same formula:

> South of the fort lies Slave Island, so called because of events that took place during the time of Dutch rule. The Portuguese had brought slaves from east Africa to Colombo in the early 17th century, and the Dutch retained them as servants. Near the beginning of the

eighteenth century, the Africans violently revolted, killing some of their Dutch caretakers. After the insurrection was suppressed, the Dutch removed the rebels to a peninsula accessible only via the fort, and it is that peninsula *that ever since has been known as Slave Island*.²⁵

Earlier references to the "island of slaves" as the place where the Dutch company kept their slaves point, however, to an earlier date of naming in the eighteenth century. Catholic priests such as Father Manoel Miranda in his correspondence to the Superior of the Oratory at Goa in 1704 and 1707 already referred to "the island of slaves" where he began his mission and where there were two chapels.²⁶ Hence the naming of the peninsula most probably came from the fact that slaves employed by the VOC lived there at least since the early 1700s and seems to be unrelated to the murder of the fiscal in 1723 or any putative insurrection.

The term *slaveneiland* recurs in Dutch official documents in the mid- to late eighteenth century, as in the edict (*plakaat*) 307 of September 4, 1742, entitled *Advertentie verbiedende om tussen zonsondergan en opgang op het lak van het slaveneiland te varen* (Prohibition to sail on the lake of Slave Island between sunset and sunrise).²⁷ In the first British accounts there appears no reference to a Kaffir revolt in Colombo. In 1807 James Cordiner described Slave Island in a lucid and pragmatic fashion: "This peninsula divides the lake and receives the above appellation from having formerly been occupied by slaves, who were employed in the service of the Dutch government. The English on their arrival made it a station for the Malay regiment."²⁸

Each writer focused on what interested them most. James Selkirk, a man of the church, saw the area as a religious center in 1844. No reference to a revolt of slaves seeps through: "A lake almost insulates the fort. In the centre of this lake is a tongue of land called Slave Island being the place where the Dutch used to keep their slaves. It now contains several good houses, one of which the most handsome and most pleasantly situated is the residence of the present Archdeacon of Colombo, the Venerable JMS Glenie."²⁹

The events surrounding the murder of the fiscal point to the metamorphosis of an event over time and the dubious grounding on which authoritative knowledge of the name Slave Island rests. The deaths of de Swaan and his wife were caused by their domestic slaves, all originally from the East Indies, probably men and women who were in their employ in Kupang in West Timor, where de Swaan was the resident (*opperhoofd*) from 1717 to 1721. The slaves were brought to Colombo when their master was posted to Sri Lanka.[30] In 1723 the name Slave Island was already used for the place where the Dutch kept their company slaves. The equivalence between slave and African, which became internalized in the next centuries, did not work in the case of the fiscal's murderers.

This does not mean that there had been no slaves of African origin or free Africans in Sri Lanka. Even if his numbers cannot be trusted, Ibn Battuta mentions the presence of five hundred Abyssinians in the service of the minister and admiral Jalasti in Colombo in the fourteenth century.[31] Africans had fought in armies of the Portuguese and of the local kings of Sri Lanka, as testified in Sinhalese literary works such as the seventeenth-century war poems the *Parangi Hatana* (War of the Portuguese) and the *Rajasiha Hatana* (War of Rajasingha). The Dutch too used African slaves, acquired through privateers for hard labor in the port and fort as well as field labor in rice, cotton, and tobacco cultivation. There are, however, no records based on shipping lists or censuses of the number of African slaves during Dutch rule, apart from figures etched in reports of Dutch governors to their successors. The visual and judicial archives are more trustworthy. Africans together with slaves from India and the East Indies were employed as domestics in houses, as some Dutch paintings of Esaias Boursse testify.[32] On a number of occasions African slaves appeared in court cases in the mid- and late eighteenth century, as prisoners such as Louison, an African slave from Mauritius, or as witnesses to crimes committed by other slaves.[33] Ten years after the murder of Barent van der Swaan, the former governor Jacob Christiaan Pielat warned the fiscal about trusting Kaffirs:

> We cannot agree to the permanent appointment of two Kaffirs as assistants to the jailor for the guarding of the criminal prisoners. We consider that such an appointment should be made only in case of urgent necessity and even then, only temporarily; while they must never be allowed admittance to the prisoners alone but always in presence of the jailor, so as to prevent any conspiracies. The jailor alone must be held responsible, as the Kaffirs cannot be trusted.[34]

The term "Kaffir" has had different semantic trajectories in Dutch and British colonial settings. Kaffir was a census category in Sri Lanka's colonial censuses until 1911, but even as it disappeared from the bureaucratic language it continued to describe in popular culture a separate ethnic group of people of African descent. Unlike in South Africa, where Kaffir is today used as an offensive term to denigrate black people, in Sri Lanka the Sinhalese and Tamil usage of the term has no negative connotation. In South Africa during the early nineteenth century, the term would be used restrictively to qualify Xhosa people, while Khoikhoi and San, two other African ethnic groups, were referred to contemptuously as Hottentot and Bushman. The term Kaffir traveled to the metropole. The Xhosa wars from 1779 to 1880, fought between the Xhosa people and settlers of Dutch and British origin on the Eastern Frontier of the Cape of Good Hope, were unproblematically referred to as "Kaffir wars" in British parliamentary debates of the period.[35] Interestingly the term Kaffir, which once denoted "non-Muslims" at the Cape, later moved away from its original Islamic meaning and referred to slaves who performed police duties during the Dutch period.[36] Many Asians performed the function of "servants of justice" at the Cape, whereas in Batavia it was African slaves.[37] In Governor Pielat's text referring to a Sri Lanka case, we might be dealing with a more fluid, nonracial notion of Kaffir that describes the function of executioner's assistants or policeman and could also encompass convicts of many races, as in South Africa. Yet no other sources corroborate a broad, nonracial understanding of the term in Sri Lanka, which suggests a difference from the usage in Batavian or South African cases.[38]

Notions of Difference: Slaves, Blacks, and Free Blacks

The presence of enslaved people in Sri Lanka is documented through different types of taxonomical exercises that were practiced during European rule in the maritime provinces. The archive of numbers where slaves appear is composed of censuses of the population of the island, Blue Books, and slave registers, the last enumeration being the kernel of the British intervention to gradually abolish slavery. There are moments when slaves who moved from one place to another were counted, but Indian Ocean slavery never yielded the type of lists of passengers on ships that became the norm in the late nineteenth-century indentured labor migration. Little is known, therefore, about the origin and journey by sea of enslaved peoples. There are only a few instances of captain's logs, such as that of the ship *Delaware*, that refer to enslaved people in ships transiting in Sri Lanka. The voyage from Batavia to the Cape often with a transit in Galle or Colombo, is estimated to have taken seventy-eight days.[39] Many ships transported unfortunate unfree human beings under very difficult conditions as part of their cargo. The logbook of the *Delaware* refers to slaves only in quantities and as bodies, living or dead. On September 14, 1752, the ship was moored at Madras, and the captain's log mentions carpenters working in the "slave rooms" on the ship. On October 15, fifteen slaves "belonging to the Honourable Company" were brought on board, and the ship was ready for sailing. En route another thirty women slaves and two children were collected. They had to face the brunt of a hurricane, after which one slave woman was found dead between decks on November 1. Later in November, as they approached Galle, the log stated that one of the slaves "is delivered of a girl." On the morning of November 27 one of the enslaved women died.[40] In contrast to the practice in Atlantic slavery, where a slave gained a name in death owing to the need for accountability, her name and origin is not known or even mentioned.

Slaves and Free Blacks in Early Censuses

The idea of inventorying populations was not a feature unique to the nineteenth century or to British rule, but under successive European powers, taxonomies obeyed a different logic. The Portuguese and Dutch had each ruled over the rich and populous maritime provinces of Sri Lanka for nearly 150 years, with far-reaching social consequences.

Figures of enslaved people in the island dating from the Portuguese period and later accounts remained vague and anecdotal and mostly absent. A listing, for instance, referred to the Colombo population in terms of 900 families of "noble citizens" (*moradores nobres*) and some 1,500 other "Portuguese" families of artisans and merchants around 1650.[41] Slaves were not mentioned. Neither did they appear in the Portuguese land registers (*tombos*) of the late sixteenth and early seventeenth centuries, since such registers recorded only landowners and potential taxpayers.[42] The Dutch left various numbered accounts of the population, but with such differences that there remains much room for interpretation. There is thus considerable variation in the estimates of scholars and contemporary witnesses as to the number of slaves in the maritime provinces in the employ of the Dutch VOC or privateers. Remco Raben suggests that by April 1661 approximately ten thousand company and private slaves were working as cultivators on the land in southwestern Sri Lanka that Governor van Goens wanted to develop.[43] Other sources suggest lower figures for enslaved men, women, and children as company slaves in Colombo in the seventeenth century, but these figures, albeit tentative, give us an insight into the extent of slavery in the society of the day.[44] The sketches of Jan Brandes show us enslaved people in Dutch homes working as domestics, artisans, or cooks. A household in Colombo could have up to ten slaves working in various capacities.[45]

During the Dutch administration, a first census of the population of Colombo was held in 1684 that counted only the free Christians that encompassed four population groups, categorized as Dutch, Castiz (born of European parents), Mestizo, and Toepass. The last two categories comprised people of mixed descent. Other lesser humans, considered heathens, which included Sinhalese, Muslims, Tamils, and slaves of various origins, were left out. In 1694 a census of Colombo counted and divided the population into two categories: "Free" and "Slaves." The census revealed that over 50 percent of the population was enslaved.[46] Slaves played a crucial economic function in Colombo as in other VOC territories, and the census reflected the rulers' concern for an appraisal of the availability of labor. VOC officials were heavily dependent on slave labor for all matters, from domestic work—in 1694, 74.8 percent of Dutch households had slaves—to construction and public works.[47] Unsurprisingly, it was the governor of Ceylon, Thomas van Rhee, who was the largest slaveholder in the Colombo castle, with forty slaves, but in the town the widow of the commander of Malabar (Jaffna), Isaak van Dielen, held sixty slaves.[48] Ekama estimates the number of slaves laboring for the company in 1771 as amounting to 784, but in the absence of a census the figure is only tentative.[49] Numbers fell in the eighteenth century owing to the decline in a demand for labor, the return of Sinhalese people who worked the land as fulfillment of their caste obligations, and the company's preference for hiring private slaves rather than owning them as an economizing measure.[50] In 1789, by order of Governor Van de Graaf, the first census was made in Sri Lanka, covering all inhabitants in the Dutch East India Company, that is, the maritime provinces, and the population of free and enslaved enumerated was estimated at 817,000.[51] Before this census there had been other forms of counting people for specific purposes. Indigenous land records on ola leaf (*lekam miti*) and later Portuguese tombos had surveyed lands and were directly tied to the issue of taxation or service rather than to an interest in counting and categorizing population groups. In contrast, Dutch tombos of the late eighteenth century, though designed to provide a detailed inventory of land ownership, yielded some information on the composition of the population in villages in Galle, Colombo, and Jaffna districts. However, the temporal disparity in the registration of villages failed to provide "a credible census figure of individuals and holdings."[52] Moreover, the Dutch were only faintly interested in analyzing or classifying the island's population, and one looks in vain for accounts of writers of the period that describe in detail the people of Sri Lanka, apart from Philippus Baldaeus's early account and Francois Valentijn's later one in 1726. Yet both drew extensively (if without attribution) on the work of others, so there might have been descriptions in reports or manuscripts.

Baldaeus gives a detailed description of the inhabitants of Jaffna, whom he observed in his capacity as a Dutch minister who had learned Tamil and spent a number of years in the area: "In Ceylon are divers clans, or Families as well as on the Coast of Coromandel. The Generation of the Bellales is the chiefest here since Christianity has been introduced, the Brahmans challenging the first rank among the Pagans."[53] Valentijn's account that gives precedence to the Sinhalese in the Kandyan kingdom is not, however, based on a firsthand encounter with the peoples of the island: "The inhabitants," wrote Valentijn, "are in part Cingalese, in part Bedas or Weddas, but besides these there are also Moors, Malabars (already referred to) and very many Portuguese, Dutch, some English and French who are prisoners of the Emperor (King of Kandy)."[54] In both cases enslaved peoples were not referred to.

The division of the people into Sinhalese, Malabars (Tamils), and Moors was visible in the day-to-day bureaucratic accounts of the Dutch alongside the use of caste-like categories. Yet while these accounts did employ quantification, they differed from enumerations of the nineteenth century that followed a different rationale insofar as they led to a redirection of certain indigenous practices by affirming the value of particular forms of identity and consequent bodily distinctions. The colonial administrator E. B. Denham acknowledged this difference in 1911 when he wrote that "the Dutch were not ignorant of the value of censuses, but they regarded them as merely useful for taxation purpose."[55]

A DUTCH TERM?

The term "black" was commonly found in accounts of Europeans from the seventeenth century to describe people whose complexion was considered dark. Egidius Daalmans, a Belgian physician who wrote his impressions of Cape of Good Hope and Sri Lanka in 1687, uses the term to qualify "Cingalese" or "blacks of Ceylon."[56] There is also evidence that it was commonly used by the Dutch in Sri Lanka to qualify the subject peoples. The Dutch used the epithet *kakkerlak* for Portuguese descendants in the maritime provinces whose appearance was closer to that of the natives.[57] A graveyard in Galle divided into four parts points to the taxonomy based on color, religion, and freedom that prevailed: the inner churchyard was reserved for European Christians, and probably also mestizos considered European enough, while the outer graveyard was subdivided into three sections: one for black (*swarte*) Christians both free and unfree, one for free non-Christians, and one for enslaved non-Christians.[58]

CORYDON OF CEYLON, A FREE BLACK IN THE CAPE OF GOOD HOPE

The parallels between pre-British VOC taxonomies in colonies such as the Cape and Sri Lanka have seldom been foregrounded. The term "free black" is an obvious case in point. In Cape Town there is a curious and riveting story that goes back to the late eighteenth century about a "free black" called Coridon "of Ceylon" who was, it is believed, the first Muslim to own property in the Cape of Good Hope, then a Dutch colony. Intriguingly, the term "free black," used to describe Coridon, a man who was once enslaved and then freed in Cape Colony—just like the Dutch-inflected "Moor" and "Kaffir" as an occupation—finds its way across the Indian Ocean into censuses and enumerations of people in Sri Lanka until 1838. These terms hint at a more general mobility or resonance of words and their shifting meanings from one colonial territory to another, from metropole to colony, and reflect an empire-wide episteme of unstable racial taxonomies. "Free black" could thus be found as a descriptor not only in the Americas, the Caribbean, and Africa but also in Indian Ocean territories and in Britain, but it carried different meanings in different locations. While in South Africa it qualified a person who had overcome his captive self, the slave, and was free, in Sri Lanka free blacks were Sinhalese, Tamils, or Muslims who were neither slaves nor whites. Outside South Africa few people would know that in 1794 it was a manumitted slave of Salie van de Kaap, the free black called Coridon of Ceylon, who owned the property on Dorp Street in Cape on which the Auwal mosque still stands today. The mosque is recognized as the first one established in the country. 'Abdullah bin Qadi Abd al Salam, later known as Tuan Guru, born in 1712 and the son of a qadi, was a regal cleric from Tidore in the Ternate Islands of Indonesia and was appointed as its first imam. In 1793 Tuan Guru established a madrasa that operated from a warehouse attached to the home of Coridon in Dorp Street.[59]

While popular knowledge recognizes the geographical origins of Coridon as an undeniable fact through his description as being "of Ceylon," there is actually no evidence that he was born in Sri Lanka. It is far more likely that he, like many others, simply passed through a port of Sri Lanka before making the long voyage to the Cape of Good Hope. Yet many historians hold up written records of the colonial bureaucracy as testaments of a retrievable past made of the lives of men whose origins remain uncertain.[60] If Coridon's origins are opaque, they matter less than the story they symbolize. Coridon's incomplete and uncertain journey from Sri Lanka to the Cape is not only exemplary of that of thousands of other lives, it also brings to light the connections that existed between places. In the Cape and Sri Lanka, two former VOC territories that became British crown colonies in the early nineteenth century, there were resonances in the mode of ordering subjects using place and race as markers in the eighteenth century that continued in other forms during British rule. One can see at times an official focus on the individual as a colonial subject; at others or simultaneously, a desire for sharpening difference through the delimitation of broad collectives with ascribed common features such as color (whites and blacks) and people enjoying more or less liberty (free and enslaved).

During VOC rule, the term "black" (*zwart*) was equally used in Cape Colony for all manumitted slaves, exiles, and convicts who could be from Asian as well as African origin.[61] For this reason free blacks or manumitted slaves described as "of Ceylon" in Cape records are virtually impossible to identify by ethnicity or birthplace because they generally have only one name, together with the "origin tag." African, Malagasy, Indian, or Indonesian were all considered "Zwarten" at the Cape.[62] The term "black" was a former Dutch racial qualification for their entire empire in Asia and Africa. In nineteenth-century Sri Lanka the British understanding of the term was similarly inclusive of all nonwhite, nonenslaved colonized people, thus encompassing Sinhalese, Tamils, and Muslims alike. Yet it is difficult to imagine how the VOC ideas of blackness that pervaded in Sri Lanka would have been transmitted to British colonial officials who took over governing the colony and influenced their perception of difference. It is more likely that ideas of skin color and blackness were already influential in Britain from the late eighteenth century onward and traveled to the colonies from the metropole. Moreover, difference in color as a social category was a feature in the British Caribbean in the early nineteenth century, where no other colonial powers had preceded the British. As early as in 1799 the first governor of Ceylon, Frederick North, as he set foot in Sri Lanka, identified "different orders of inhabitants," and among the Burghers, a category of "Black Christians."[63]

British Notions of Social Difference

The emergence and disappearance of the slave as a category of identity in Sri Lanka is an intriguing feature that has until now not been scrutinized.[64] The slave as a category figures in the prehistory of the British census of Sri Lanka alongside many incongruous other categories that include large, all-encompassing terms. These terms contrasted with the flurry of social formations in the island that orientalist scholars and many colonial administrators in the island had observed and recognized during the same period. From afar, race in the guise of euphemisms such as black and white was the prism through which the population was seen and regulated from the metropole, even if the colonial state was a racial formation that "marked differences by other names."[65] Even with the waning of slavery as an institution, the absent figure of race structured the rule of colonial difference separating colonizer and colonized until the end of colonial rule. As slavery declined and more complex orientalist constructions of culture acquired prominence among rulers and elites, color-based racial categories "black" and "white" gave way to cultural-linguistic formations that first included Burghers, Sinhalese, Tamils, and Moors and later extended to other social groups.

Radically different notions of the people of the island circulated among administrators and officials in London who were often responsible for designing the enumerations. They also shifted in time and varied according to the instrument of rule. Officials on the ground attempted to carefully produce gazetteers and administrative reports from firsthand observation. They were often overwhelmed by what they encountered—the different "castes," "races," "mixed races," "half castes," "religions," "languages," and "classes of people" that Robert Percival described in 1803 with their own "manners, customs and language."[66] This led to a tendency to flatten difference. The penchant for gaining knowledge of the non-European world by making the unfamiliar familiar by reading it through grids of intelligibility was a common feature of most colonial regimes. Some of the census categories emerged from this logic. The seemingly illogical and confused categories reflect the multiple understandings of social difference that prevailed among officials in London as well as among administrators of the British state who were sent to Sri Lanka to govern on its behalf.[67] Alongside this tendency to simplify, there were other trends that led to a more localized reading of social difference.

The lives and work of men such as Frederick North, Eudelin de Jonville, Antonio Bertolacci, John D'Oyly, and Alexander Johnston suggest that many colonial administrators in Sri Lanka were aware that the people they ruled did not fall into the simple color-coded categories of the censuses. Efforts at understanding the culture and customs of the peoples were visible in important policies enacted in the first two decades of the nineteenth century with regard, in particular, to the protection of Buddhism and to the extension of jury duty to local peoples in criminal cases where Europeans were not tried. These measures that recognized difference based on ethnicity, region, and religion were coeval with census operations.

When Frederick North, the first governor of Sri Lanka, embarked in London on the *Brunswick* in 1798 to sail to Bombay, he was accompanied by an exceptionally gifted group of men speaking a number of languages and bearing expertise in a variety of fields. Among them was Eudelin de Jonville, clerk for natural history and agriculture, who would write in French the first account on the island under the British, *Some Notions About the Island of Ceylon*. Jonville sent a rough draft of his manuscript to the board of the East India Company as early as 1801 and never ceased to share his ideas with his paymasters, making many attempts at publishing his account but in vain. The account contains many glaring misconceptions, especially on the "religion of the Boudho," but it also conveys the eagerness that prevailed during the early nineteenth century, when the spirit of the Enlightenment easily merged with romantic notions, to understand the people of Sri Lanka, and the sense of curiosity that existed regarding the customs of the Sinhalese of the Low Country and Kandy.[68] Bertolacci, who came on the same ship with him and became controller general of customs and later acting civil auditor, divides the inhabitants of the island into "four distinct nations": "Ceylonese Proper," "Malabars or Hindoos," "Moors," and "Vedas."[69]

The two most prominent orientalists of the early nineteenth century were John D'Oyly, a key figure in the annexation of the kingdom of Kandy in 1815, and Alexander Johnston, who served as the island's third chief justice from 1811 to 1819. Both men and those who gravitated around them were intrigued by the cultures they encountered and made efforts to learn the vernacular languages. D'Oyly, who had been instructed by the high priest of Matara, Karatota Kirti Sri Dhammarama, excelled in Sinhala and became the chief translator to the government. He drafted the Act of Settlement after the fall of the kingdom of Kandy to the British in 1815, in which occurs the phrase "The religion of Boodhoo . . . is declared inviolable." William Tolfrey, who worked under D'Oyly in Kandy, translated the Bible into Sinhala and was the first Briton to master Pali.[70] Johnston's lineage prepared him for an exceptional career as a colonial official. He had encountered the most renowned orientalists of India while growing up in Madura, where his father was paymaster, and during his time in Sri Lanka studied with great care the customs and laws of the indigenous people. He believed in the capacity of the natives to dispense judgment and reason. Thus he was instrumental in introducing a Charter of Justice, which among other things introduced the jury system to the "natives of Ceylon." According to article 11 of the charter, the collectors were directed to prepare "lists of all persons resident in their Districts who by their Character and condition may be deemed qualified to sit upon juries distinguishing them into their respective Classes and casts."[71] Writing about this measure later on, Johnston referred to the grantee of this new right as "half caste Native" and "every other native of the country to whatever caste or religious persuasion he might belong."[72] The exoticizing gaze of the early orientalists on what they perceived as the different communities and castes of the island had little bearing on the making of categories of classification in the early censuses, where the rule of "colonial difference" founded on race and color still prevailed. Yet the recognition of groups based on language, caste, ethnicity, and religion in other affairs of the state, such as at the judiciary, lends credence to studies that adhere to a more multidimensional notion of difference in the colonial sphere.[73] Clearly, as far as governance was concerned, the grid of colonial power traversed the social order in its entirety rather than in binary terms.[74] The notion of blackness and the more complex reading of difference by orientalist scholar-administrators permeated in an uneven manner societies and bureaucracies in the metropole and the colonies.

The Idea of Blackness in Britain

Indian servants and Ayahs who lived in Britain in the eighteenth century were commonly referred to as "negro" or as "black." It was not uncommon to hear about "a black man from Bengal," "a black Indian boy," or an "East Indian Black from Bombay" who had been brought over from India to work in the households of former East India Company officials.[75] To what extent these words indexed an inarticulate color prejudice rather than a developed racial ideology is difficult to ascertain. Roxann Wheeler speaks of the "fluid articulation of human variety" and the "elasticity of race" in the eighteenth century. In particular, she warns against anachronistic and essentialist understandings of "race" as a set of fixed physical characteristics and suggests that diversity of human behavior and religious and cultural traits were more important as markers of difference than differences in color.[76] The presence of Africans in Britain was visible after the conquest of the New World, and they were seen serving in the court as trumpeters, or in the mansions of the gentry as pages or laundry maids. Rich planters, officers on slave ships, and seamen returned to Britain with African slaves.[77] When one looks beyond the statements of theorists of race and turns to the way race was practiced in late eighteenth-century Britain, the picture that emerges is somewhat different. The contrast between the eighteenth century and nineteenth century appears to be overstated. Later bigots could build on exclusionist and color-inflected policies of the earlier century. This is not to deny the break that occurred in the nineteenth century, when social status and religion ceased to be so explicitly important to Britons as the English increasingly constructed an imperial cosmology whereby skin color came to distinguish ruler from ruled.[78] In the first half of the nineteenth century, blacks were as ill-defined as a few decades before, when the plight of seamen originating in the American or Asian territories who had served on merchant ships or in the Royal Navy and were roaming without means in London led to the creation in 1786 of a Committee for the Relief of Black Poor by Jonas Hanway. This included all dark-skinned indigents, lascars from Mozambique to Malaya and Indian servants who totaled about ten thousand persons in London and other port cities.[79] This number increased with the arrival of free Americans after the American Revolution. Thus when the censuses for the colonies were being created at the very moment Britain was living its troubled transition to a society without slaves, blacks defined as nonwhites were already a familiar and inferior social group in the metropole. It is therefore not surprising that in British India and Sri Lanka the term "black" was used to describe Indians or Sinhalese and to label spatially segregated areas, as in the white town and black town of Madras and Colombo, where the British called the Pettah, the native area at the outer fringe, the black town.[80] Robert Percival explained in 1805 that the term "black town" came "from its being chiefly inhabited by black merchants and tradespeople."[81] Thus by the early nineteenth century the terms white and black seemed naturalized by British colonial officials on the ground.

It is in the late nineteenth-century imperial world that the term "blacks" ceased to loosely encompass all nonwhites and become reserved for Africans, and Africa was constructed as the other that needed to be civilized and uplifted. The belief in British superiority became the norm, as well as the acceptance of the cultural inferiority of all those with black skins.[82] A recent work on the census has argued that racial classification played a significant part in the way British people understood their empire, in contrast with German and Austrian predominant concerns with linguistic and cultural differences. For the British, the world was seen as one where different races competed, and in England this included a fear of Irish and Scottish immigration.[83] These ideas were then applied to the colonies. According to Christopher Anthony, throughout the British colonies the decennial metropolitan census initiated in 1801 and the U.S. enumeration conducted since 1790 served as models.[84] The first U.S. enumeration, for instance, made a distinction between whites, "all other free persons," and slaves, thus building a racial classification into a scheme that was initiated to determine who was free and hence taxable.[85] The framing of difference along the lines of whites, others, and slaves obeyed a logic unique to the United States. Yet it showed family resemblances with the language in use in Britain and its colonies.

Slaves and Blacks in Taxonomies of the Early Nineteenth Century

The census in colonized territories has generally been described as an instrument of rule in authoritative works dealing with colonialism and empire. What made it unique among other forms of statistical inquiry was its prerogative to gather information about a single territory. This could be a nation, as in Britain with the census of 1801, or a colony, such as Sri Lanka in the Census of 1824, which covered for the first time all the provinces under British rule, including the Kandyan provinces.

The enmeshing of knowledge and control has been the subject of a vast, multilayered, and vigorously debated scholarship on colonial knowledge, power, technologies of rule, and governmentality that I will only briefly deal with here. The argument that the census stood as a document whose manifest rhetoric was technical but whose subtext was disciplinary is indeed a well-established one.[86] The gist of it is that the act of enumerating subjects living in newly conquered territories was conceived as a guide for rulers to deal with their subjects by acquiring knowledge of the number of potential bodies that could be taxed or used for war and labor. The disciplinary argument, however, is less convincing in the early nineteenth century when methods of collecting data in Sri Lanka were amateurish and categories used in censuses to divide the "natives" were of a transient nature. In Sri Lanka the first British endeavors to count the governed were only a little more systematic than those of their premodern predecessors, the Portuguese and Dutch, and remained characterized by an appearance of factuality that hid the fiction of categories. As in other colonial territories, the process of gathering statistical information was often fudged by informants, enumerators, and commissioners.[87] Although the census was a policy requirement made in the metropolis, it depended on numerous intermediaries for its implementation. Pragmatic reasons guided the process of enumerating peoples in Sri Lanka as in other colonies. Early race-based enumerations contrasted with the later ones insofar as the clear-cut categories based on color and level of freedom were less protean in nature and conveyed less of an impression of confusion and ambiguity. There was some uncanny logic and order to the racialized view of society of the early nineteenth century. These early classifications were partly devised in London by ill-informed officials sitting in the Colonial Office who applied a single template to all crown colonies. They were not mirrors of society but rather revealed much about the interests and power relations of the counter and counted.[88] In this instance the census was partly answering a need that came from outside the colony: that of British parliamentarians eager to assess the success of amelioration policies with regard to the abolition of slavery in Sri Lanka, in contrast to the relative failure to end slavery in India. The presence of the slave as a category of census from 1814 to 1838 could be explained by an interest in numbers as evidence.

When a census was taken in 1814, there was still one independent Sinhalese kingdom in the hills of Kandy that remained, ruled by a dynasty that descended from South Indian Nayakkars. Antonio Bertolacci, a civil servant under Governor North, had undertaken a survey of the population of the maritime provinces between 1808 and 1810 based on food consumption and estimated the population at 700,000.[89] These were, however, uncertain times for the British, who were still not in full control of the island. In the census taken a few years later, in 1814, the population enumerated did not exceed 492,000, a much lower figure that has been explained by the incidence of a serious famine in the years 1811–1813.[90] Bertolacci himself mentions repeated droughts in those years that were detrimental to the cultivation of rice and led to famine and distemper, especially in the district of Matara.[91]

The General Abstract of the Population of the Maritime Districts of the Island of Ceylon in 1814 divided districts into ethnolinguistic regions, namely, Singalese districts that included Colombo, Caltura, Galle, Hambantotte, Chilaw, and Malabar, and Tamil districts including Batticaloam, Trincomalee, Jaffnapatam, Delft, Vanni, and Mannar. The categories used to classify the population of the Colombo district into collectivities are religions and "casts." Under the latter, however, one finds a variety of groups, ranging from ethnic groups such as Cingalese, Malabars, and Europeans to occupational groups including blacksmiths, wood-cutters, and barbers. In this long list of casts appear the two distinct categories of "free slaves" (numbering 209), and "slaves" (857). The enumeration in the Galle district only includes "free slaves," while in the Batticaloa district there were two different categories, "slaves" (92), and "Kovilan Slaves of the Pagoda" (477). This group probably accounted for slaves of Vellalas (the highest caste among the Tamils) working in the temples. In the Trincomalee district yet another variation could be found, with two categories, "slaves" (70) and "Dutch Company Slaves" (30).[92] The slave was thus omnipresent in this early census.

After the 1818 and 1821 acts of gradual emancipation of children of slaves (dealt with in chapter 3), counting slaves and their opposite, free people or "free blacks," acquired an additional function apart from that of offering the colonial government a picture of the peoples it was ruling, according to their occupation and their ability to be deployed for labor. Figures were indeed of crucial importance for the gradual abolition of slavery to be charted and proven by abolitionists before their many opponents in the British Parliament. Lt. Col. Colebrooke's report of 1831 upon the administration of the government of Ceylon, which was invoked in a parliamentary paper of 1838, testifies to the importance of census numbers as verifiable evidence: "Personal slavery, however is nearly extinct in the Cingalese provinces, but it still exists among the Malabars in the northern districts of Ceylon. The number of slaves in the district of Jaffna, *according to the returns of 1824*, was 15,350. The number of domestic slaves throughout the maritime provinces does not exceed 1,000."[93]

In the 1824 census mentioned in the parliamentary paper, slave categories are included in even more detail than in 1814. Descendants of slaves number 221; free slaves, 1,115; and slaves, 17,538, including 15,341 entered as slaves among the "Covias, Nalluas, and Pallas of Jaffna," 18 as "slaves of the Burghers," and 78 as "formerly slaves of the late Dutch government."[94] In the Colombo district, 610 slaves were listed separately according to gender and age (above or below puberty). The census also provides intriguing variations on the slave status of people: "descendants of slaves" are listed as numbering 221; "free slaves," 577; and "slaves," 610. The Galle district contains the same categories and includes a "Memorandum of the Slaves and Free Slaves," clearly emphasizing the importance of this classification.[95]

The reforms spawned by the Colebrooke-Cameron Commission (1829–1830) endorsed free labor and conceded a form of representation through the nomination of unofficial members in a newly formed Legislative Council, a forum for discussion of legislative matters, to local elites of different communities—Low Country Sinhalese, Tamil, and Burgher. Thus, from then on, communities began to be identified racially in the "enumerable sense," in contrast to the previous decades where there was a flurry of categories. The Ceylon Almanac of 1838 indicates that in a census of the population taken that year that did not cover the entire island, leaving out regions such as the Seven Korales, Nuwarakalawiya, and Bintenna, the population, counted and categorized, was estimated at 1,241,825 persons. These types of figures that were regularly published in almanacs and Blue Books were based on headmen's returns and birth and death registers.[96] Their doubtful accuracy was compounded by the fact that many people fled instead of submitting themselves to counts as they feared taxation as a consequence. The final appearance of the slave as a category of census and official classification was in 1838. By that time slavery had been abolished in the rest of the empire except in India, Sri Lanka, and St. Helena, and the commissioners of Eastern Inquiry had published the Colebrooke-Cameron Report, generally read as a key moment in the country's encounter with modernity.[97]

For historians of colonialism, the truth of numbers is less important than the mirror, even partial and warped, that the census holds on a colonial understanding of indigenous society. The difference from India is striking. Intriguingly, in sharp contrast to similar enumerations in gazetteers and early censuses held in India during the nineteenth century where caste and occupation were the markers, in Sri Lanka the census categories until 1838 were not only based on skin color (whites and blacks) but also indexed freedom or lack of freedom.[98]

In a practical sense, the arrival of notions of white and black conjoined with slaves and free blacks in the bureaucratic language of Sri Lanka during British rule could be linked to a template that was being applied to the empire at large and began with the Blue Books in 1822. The colonial Blue Books appear to have originated in a request from the Commons Select Committee of Finance in 1817 for returns of offices in the colonies. A book asking for the return of statistical information was first sent to each governor in 1822; this seems to have increased to three blank books by 1828. Lord Bathurst was the colonial secretary who inaugurated the issue of Blue Books on colonial affairs for all the colonies from 1822 onward that purported to give for each colony "a species of comprehensive budget."[99] A colonial publication succinctly summed up the history of Blue Books:

The Colonial Office, in Downing Street, has received annually for a series of years a "Blue Book" in manuscript from each Colony, containing a variety of commercial, financial, ecclesiastical, and general information for the use of Government. The "Blue Books" were commenced about the year 1828. Three blank books, with ruled columns and printed headings, are sent to each Colony every year; the blank columns are filled in by returns from the different departments, under the authority of the Colonial Secretary in each settlement; these returns are then sent in duplicate to Downing Street, and one of the three copies is retained in the Colony for the use of the Governor.[100]

In Sri Lanka, as in other British colonies such as Grenada or British Guiana, the population section of these annually produced colonial Blue Books of the early nineteenth century referred to "White," "Free Black" or "Free Coloured," and "Slave."[101] These were the printed headings that formed a common grid of legibility to deal with the diverse peoples under British rule. This empire-wide system constituted a forerunner of the modern, scientifically conducted censuses, but this uniformity was lost after the 1840s when each colony sought an individual form of categorization.[102]

On page 127 of the Blue Book of 1825, the governor would read this directive sent to him from London: "Insert population according to last census, and if none has ever been taken according to the last means of information that may be accessible."[103] These orders were diligently followed. The figures in the Blue Book of 1827 were based on the first official census that was made in 1824 under Governor Edward Barnes. They set the stage for a division of the people into imperial categories based on skin color and freedom.

In the enumeration of 1838, the final one where slaves were counted, blacks could be either "free" or slaves, unlike whites, who by definition enjoyed freedom.[104] As the nineteenth century proceeded, the grid of the table began to form the core of census reports and supported all official missives from Colombo to London discussing the matter of slavery.[105] With the table, a taxonomy was produced together with a hierarchy and positions of things or people in relation to each other. The idea of certain groups being the numerical proportion of a whole (the total) was a new and revolutionary concept. The table brought legitimacy to figures that were far from reliable.

TABLE 1.1
Population of Sri Lanka Based on Ceylon Almanac of 1838

	Males	Females
Whites	2,912	2,929
Free blacks	622,842	565,246
Slaves	14,108	13,289
Total	639,862	581,464

Source: H. N. S. Karunatilake, "Social and Economic Statistics of Sri Lanka in the Nineteenth Century," *Royal Asiatic Society of Sri Lanka Branch*, New Series 31 (1986/87): 45.

For censuses carried out in the 1820s and 1830s, the count of slaves in households was based on headmen's returns. How was information collected? Were enslaved people spoken to? If the head of household was indigenous to the island, as the main informant, did his answers reflect the variety of words and meanings that existed in the vernacular languages for "slave"? The *Sinhalese-English Dictionary* of 1830, compiled under government patronage by William Tolfrey with the help of two local informants, Cornelis de Saram and Don Jacobus Dias Bandaranaike, and taken on by Rev. Benjamin Clough upon the death of Tolfrey, lists a variety of words that are translated as slave, which brings into light the vagueness and pliable nature of the category:[106]

Bhritiya: servant, slave
Cheti: female servant or slave
Das: slave, skill, ability, sight, seeing
Dasaya: slave, bond servant
Desi: female slave
Goyu: freckle, slave
Karmakara: hired labor, servant, name of Yama, regent of the dead, slave
Kella: female slave, little girl, lass
Midya: female slave
Parichara: guard, attendant, companion, slave, servant
Pataraturu: slave, bond servant, menial, dependent
Pessa: servant, slave

Piliyana: slave, dependent, servant, menial
Sevakaya: slave, servant, menial
Vidupa: slave, servant, menial
Wala: a slave, dependent[107]

The words *dasaya* and *pataraturu* convey most sharply the idea of being bonded rather than working as a free (*nidahas*) servant in a household. Yet other words, such as *pessa* or *vidupa*, suggest an overlap between the status of slave and servant, which might have had some bearing on census figures. These words reflect, as in the Indian case, "the range of labour arrangements that could be termed slavery, each involving slightly different patterns of servitude and ownership."[108] Trust in numbers and figures among British officials was not a constant, and the imperfection of the data was clearly acknowledged. In 1838 the extraordinary variations of the number of slaves in the statements of the population caused some anxiety in Justice Jeremie, who read them as a sign that slaves had been imported to the island. But this interpretation was quickly dismissed by Governor R. W. Horton, who claimed that "such statements are of no authority and are compiled from very imperfect data."[109]

The flourishing of census making and enumeration in Europe arose amid the context of the rise of statistics and new tools of analysis. Interestingly, it was at Haileybury, home to the East India College, that census-making officials and enumerators for the British Empire were trained in statistics.[110] The census had many genealogies. In Norbert Peabody's argument, the genesis of Indian census categories and modes of knowing based on caste can be traced to enumerations of households taken in the kingdom of Marwar between 1658 and 1664 under the direction of the kingdom's home minister. It was, he suggests, not a purely European episteme since colonial discourses often built on indigenous ones.[111] His argument challenges a long tradition of scholarly production on the census in India and Sri Lanka that foregrounds its unique generative feature. The census of India, in B. S. Cohn's seminal work, in particular, is shown not only casting an external gaze but also creating many of the social forms, as categories of practice through a process of classifying and objectifying.[112] Arjun Appadurai has referred to the "colonial imaginaire" produced by these inaccurate and unscientific "colonial body counts." "Numbers," he contends, "gradually became . . . part of the illusion of bureaucratic control and a key to a colonial imaginaire in which countable abstractions, both of people and of resources created the sense of a controllable indigenous reality."[113]

In retrospect, and in contradistinction to the view on the modern census (1871), a very different argument could be made with relation to the early British modes of enumeration in Sri Lanka. In India, caste, in spite of the absence of any form of consensus on caste or caste hierarchies, became entrenched and the norm. In Sri Lanka, however, there was a much longer phase of experimentation, contest, and flurry of categories. In fact, the census categories that were in use in the early decades of the nineteenth century completely disappeared, to be replaced by others that remained, nonetheless, equivocal.

The reality of colonial rule was, however, an uncontested relation of power where the rulers exerted coercion over the indigenous peoples of the land, encompassed in the racial term "free blacks" to distinguish them from the category of slaves. In the Sri Lankan case, the necessity of counting the enslaved population kept alive the category of free blacks until the late 1830s.

On August 13, 1838, Governor J. A. Stewart Mackenzie sent the secretary to the colonies, Lord Glenelg, a missive with numbers of slaves formally manumitted since the meeting of the Legislative Council on June 28, 1838, the number of slaves registered under Ordinance No. 3 1837, and a return of the number of slaves according to the latest census. The census of 1838 and its categories of classification clearly served a distinct function: that of charting, in the words of the governor himself, the "happy advance to abolition of slavery in the island."[114]

After the slave disappeared as an identifiable social entity, the orientalist idea that the social body was an aggregation of collective and communal bodies would gradually gain ground, as it already informed the first forms of political representation based on group difference granted to the islanders in the 1830s following the Colebrooke-Cameron reforms.

Slave Names in Nineteenth-Century Slave Registers

The slave register, unlike the census and Blue Book, offers data about named individuals rather than groups. The most comprehensive registers are those of 1818–1832, but there are earlier slave registers in the British period that have been either destroyed or lost in the process of creating an archive. In 1798 Brigadier General de Meuron, who exerted military power over Sri Lanka after the Dutch capitulation, recommended the gradual abolition of slavery and the establishment of a register to secure to proprietors of slaves their property subject to a certain tax. Private property—which included slaves—had been guaranteed in all the capitulations. Governor North issued a proclamation in 1801 according to which all slaves were to be produced with their bonds and registered by May 1, 1802, or else they would be considered free. Governor Maitland, his successor, ordered the registration of slaves within four months of his regulation of August 14, 1806. There were delays, however, and the registration was never completed. The Maitland registers have never been read or cited in the historiography of the island. In 1818 two new regulations (nos. 9 and 10) were passed in Sri Lanka, which led, inter alia, to the creation of a registry of slaves in all areas of the maritime provinces. The registers for the northern districts of the island, where the majority of slaves lived, were divided into two kinds: those for domestic slaves and those for Nalavar, Pallar, and Coviyar slaves, who were indigenous to the island. The slaves listed in the registers of the southern districts were city dwellers who worked in homes as domestics or artisans and whose ancestors generally came from other VOC territories. Their names offer some insight, although very tentative, into the possible origin of the slaves.

In the slave registers for the Colombo district, for instance, different clusters of names appear: slaves who were given names from classical mythology, others who were given biblical names, names from the months of the year or days of the week, and Dutch- or European-sounding names. A fair number of slaves had names that were clearly Asian in origin, even when written down phonetically by the hesitant hand of a British official. These names, which take us back to those slaves who died in the pillory in 1723, merit some mention.[115]

SRI LANKA NAMES

Caronchy, Rascowella, Pooncha (3), Apu, Araliya, Kediramere, Champokke (2) (Champika ?), Mootowa, Caloewa (kalu), Pantchi, Suman (Saman)

INDIA

Apu, Sarvel (Sharvil), Mallati (Malathi) (2)

MALAY

Lucho (Lucu), Achamatus (2), (Ahmatus), Bentan (Bintan), Zamida, Ontong (Untung), Teija (Teja), Pooncha (3), (Puncak), Norifah (2), Zuraidah (2), Sele (Sallay/Salih), Champokke (3), (Cempaka), Seewa (2), (Sewa), Muskin (Miskin), Andika, Mawar, Jelek, Melati (2), Nuufiah/Nofiah, Norifsa (Norfizah), Seya (Zaidah), Suman (Saman), Satu

JAVANESE

Sewo

BALINESE

Puto (Putu), Bugu, Lakaay (Lakaag), Lafoor

NORTH INDIA

Zulfia, Seema, Zamida, Assani (Asani), Packreen (Pakhreen), Kutheria, Afsana, Afsen (Afshin), Jafar

TAMIL

Kethan, Ayyapan, Jehel Covia, Sinne Pulle, Letchemi (2), (Latcumi), Moettoe (2), (Muthu), Namasivagam, Savery Mooto, Sinnacathy (Sinnakutty)

MUSLIM TAMIL

Mootoosamat (Muthu Samath)

MALAYALI

Karuppa (2), Calle Cottal, Arathi, Cutthoor Kitto, Palliadal (Palliyadiyil), Narapore Patcha, Markan (Marakkan)

The limited data from slave registers suggests a predominantly South and Southeast Asian origin of around 10 percent of the names. Allowing slaves to keep their birth names is a unique phenomenon that is not found in slave registers of other Indian Ocean colonies. The vast majority of slave names in the registers, however, are unidentifiable in terms of origin. In the majority of cases, slaves were renamed in a dehumanizing act of erasure. James Scott has famously argued that a significant aspect of maintaining relations of domination consists of the symbolization of domination by demonstrations and enactments of power, such as erasing the past of a person through renaming and cutting family ties.[116] Renaming was essential to enforcing domination and creating powerlessness. "Slaves differed from other human beings," writes Orlando Patterson, "in that they were not allowed freely to integrate the experience of their ancestors into their lives, to inform their understanding of social reality with the inherited meanings of the natural forebears, or to anchor the living in any conscious community of memory."[117] The trajectory of the notion of blackness, the metamorphosis of the Indonesians accused of killing a Dutch fiscal into African Kaffir rebels, is understandable only in relation to the shifting official and popular perceptions of slavery in the long nineteenth century.

Over the first half of the nineteenth century, the census was a bureaucratic instrument that charted the collective through the delimitation of people along color lines and a simple grid that separated free and unfree peoples. Its purpose was both disciplinary, insofar as it was used by colonial functionaries on the ground to rule their subjects by extracting taxes from them, and justificatory, as it provided numerical data crucial to negotiations with their interlocutors in the metropole.[118] It was, for instance, possible to use numbers to suggest initiating reforms in the labor regime or for parliamentarians in London to add fuel to their campaign for the abolition of slavery in the empire by arguing that slave labor was still a significant feature in the island. Numbers provided evidence in spite of their often dubious accuracy. The disappearance of the slave, black, white, and free black as categories of enumeration firmly entrenched the transformation "of the census as an instrument of taxes to an instrument of knowledge."[119]

Reading the enumerations of the early nineteenth century along the grain allows a reflection on the xenologies of the day and on what determined the choice of unstable taxonomies based on color and freedom and what led to their end. The presence of the categories of blacks and slaves stems from different and connected anxieties of a new colonial power in the island: the establishment of firm and uncrossable boundaries between colonizer (white) and colonized (free blacks), defined in a binary, must be conceived as deeply connected to the imperial demand for charting the successful decline of slavery.

The life and death of categories reflect, as this chapter has shown, what is at stake at a particular moment in time: in this case, the necessity for colonial officials to manage the transition from slavery to its abolition. The disappearance of the categories of slave and free blacks saw the appearance of racialized categories to describe the various collectivities that formed the subject population of the crown colony. With the formal and definitive Ordinance of Abolition of 1844, the category of slave began to fade from the memory of people in the island and undergo the metamorphosis or blackening described in the first part of this chapter.

In the popular realm, however, notions of slave and black traveled in time, acquiring their own garbs of meaning. Slaves were increasingly associated with Africans, as memories and records of slaves hailing from other parts of the colonial world faded away. The term "black" has a similar history as "slave," disappearing from public documents in the 1830s but remaining as an invisible signifier until the departure of the British from the island. As late as 1942 a Sri Lankan mutineer against British rule in the military settlement of the Cocos Islands explained his motive for mutineering in terms of a war between blacks and whites.[120]

The next chapters will explore the lives of individual slaves in Sri Lanka through a range of documents where the enslaved is a name or belongs to a collective, where she sometimes has a monetary value attached to her, and where, on occasion, she appears alongside a master whose life is given some prominence. These stories will bring to light the partial nature of our knowledge of events and people of the past and the logic of the procedures through which information is collected, stored, conserved, and utilized as well as memorialized or forgotten.

CHAPTER II

From Colombo to Galle

Enslaved Bodies in an Archive of Violence

Your craft is to conjure a social system from a nutmeg grater.
—CAROLYN STEEDMAN[1]

The archive is, in this case, a death sentence, a tomb, a display of the violated body, an inventory of property, a medical treatise on gonorrhoea, a few lines about a whore's life, an asterisk in the grand narrative of history.
—SAIDIYA HARTMAN[2]

In 1703 a vessel named *Ter Eem* left the port of Colombo to Batavia carrying as cargo 38,000 pounds of cinnamon valued at 11,814.12 Indian guilders and twenty-six humans described as "slaves" and "Malabars" valued at 1,041.88 Indian guilders.[3] Many other ships transported a similar mixed cargo, a clear demonstration that enslaved people in the Indian Ocean basin were considered incidental goods, quite unlike the Middle Passage, where ships built or refashioned exclusively for the purpose of slave cargo transported enslaved Africans across the Atlantic to a life of forced labor on plantations.[4] Yet throughout the seventeenth and eighteenth centuries thousands of enslaved people in the Indian Ocean world, including Sri Lanka, made the journey out as cargo on ships, traveling with large quantities of pepper, cinnamon, myrrh, coffee, olibanum, salt, and silver-plated horse-riding gear to faraway destinations such as Batavia or the Cape of Good Hope.[5] Others from India, the East Indies, and Africa made the journey to Sri Lanka, where their lives left few traces in the colonial archive. In 1796, when the British took over the maritime provinces of the island, which had once been under the control of the VOC, they introduced new laws that led to an irreversible movement toward the abolition of slavery in a legal sense.

This chapter follows four enslaved people in the southern part of the island in the first decades of British rule, from Colombo to Galle, at moments of acceleration when their lives suddenly become less "insignificant" and draw a faint sign on the wall of recorded history. It listens to the murmurs of these enslaved people hidden in the legal archive and to "the object we have come to call violence."[6] It is an "archive of translations" in need of forcing and prying, an archive of fragments that opens a hesitant story that often has no closure.[7] It is indeed because violence was both committed and experienced that the lives of the four enslaved people were even reported. Violence is present in multiple and cruel forms in a life so unbearable that an enslaved woman, Selestina, killed her newborn child in 1820; an enslaved man, Valentine, running away from servitude, died murdered on a Maradana road; a woman from Cochin sold in Galle made a strong claim for freedom; and a child kidnapped for the Arabian slave market was saved by diligent neighbors and the British collector of Galle.

These stories come to us only in the fragments that the official records yield. What the historian has to work with are not verifiable facts but incomplete narratives and nonconforming structures that call for a different mode of history writing. We need to tell the story of the lives of the enslaved from their own perspective, follow them as they navigate the terrain of early nineteenth-century Sri Lanka, and remain attentive to the limits of historical representation. These shreds of stories give us a sense that slavery was characterized by both direct forms of domination, where the brutal asymmetry of power comes to light in regular and quotidian exercises of violence, and indirect forms of violence, more difficult to capture, that fall under the rubric of paternalism. In all four cases one gets a fleeting glimpse of the refusal to accept the terms set: infanticide could be read as protest, a refusal of sexual violence and being objectified; flight was a way of resisting, though in this case it was interrupted by murder; and the appeals to colonial justice in the final two cases signal a desire for moving out of enslavement or the conditions that come with it. A decolonial reading of archival traces allows us to challenge the authority of records produced under conditions of domination. Before I relate the stories of these four individuals who represent the condition of enslavement and reflect on the way they acted in their own particular circumstances and within the restraints of the time, it is necessary to set the stage, for the condition of enslavement could exist only if proprietors practiced and condoned it.

Slaveholders in the Southern Maritime Provinces

When the British took control of the southern maritime provinces (fig. 2.1), they inherited a society of subjects bestowed with different degrees of freedom and autonomy from their predecessors, the Portuguese and Dutch, who traded in humans across the Indian Ocean. As the tentative understanding of the origins of slaves discussed in the previous chapter indicates, in VOC-held territories it was customary not to enslave the indigenous populations but rather to bring slaves from elsewhere. The northern province in Sri Lanka was an exception to this rule, as chapter 3 will demonstrate.

The fact that Sri Lanka became a crown colony rather than an office of the British East India Company (EIC) in 1802 resulted in abolition procedures for slavery that were quite different from those in India. Uniquely for South Asia, forms of slavery across the island were included in empire-wide gradual abolition and emancipation procedures mentioned in chapter 1.[8] While the British abolished the slave trade in 1807, slavery continued to be practiced in Sri Lanka until its formal abolition in 1844. The majority of slaveholders in Colombo in the first decades of the nineteenth century were of Dutch descent or Burghers, as shown in the data from slave registers (fig. 2.2). C. C. Uhlenbeck's life and afterlife provide us with some insight beyond numbers.

C. C. Uhlenbeck: Slaveholder and Abolitionist

Among the list of subscribers to the Address to His Royal Highness of 1816 is a person called C. C. Uhlenbeck, whose name appears fourth on the list of 107 Dutch inhabitants and Burghers in Colombo.[9] The Uhlenbeck family, who trace their roots to Germany, became well established in the Netherlands and appear prominently in a published account of famous Dutch families. The life of C. C. Uhlenbeck is recounted by his grandson, who was a professor at Leiden University. C. C. Uhlenbeck was born in Colombo in 1780 and died in 1845. His father, Captain Johan Wilhelmus Uhlenbeck, was originally from Prussia. It was then quite common for Germans to join the Dutch armed forces and serve as mercenaries in the

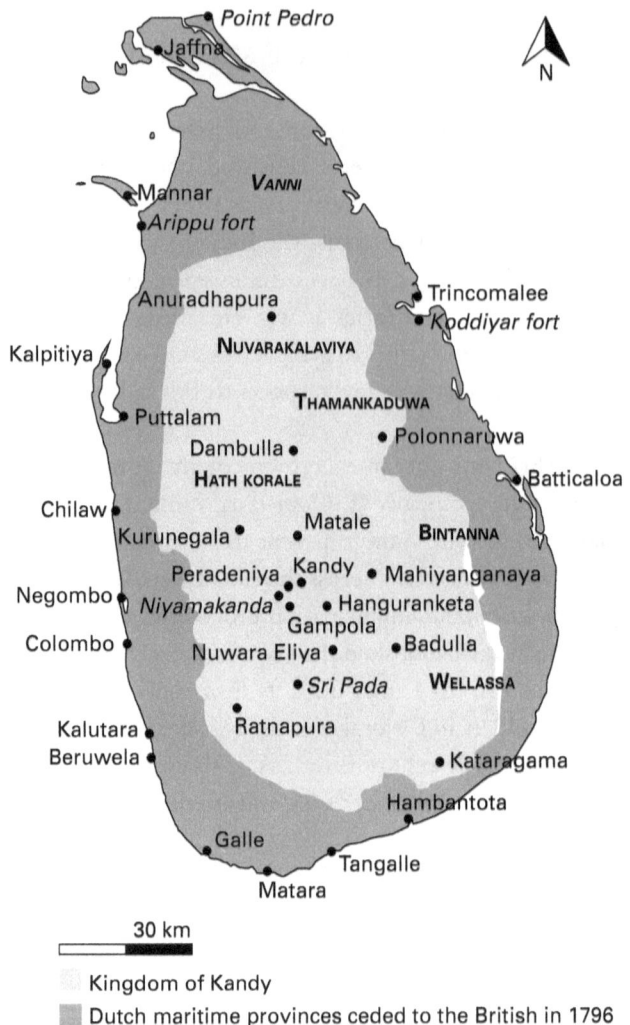

Figure 2.1 Sri Lanka in the early nineteenth century. Capital letters indicate disavas or districts. Italics indicate mountains and forts. Others are cities.

Dutch East India Company. Johan Wilhelmus Uhlenbeck entered the service of the VOC as a soldier in 1768, rose to major, and ended his career as commandant of Galle. He died in Colombo in 1810.[10]

Christianus Cornelius Uhlenbeck would have grown up in Colombo in a house where slaves performed a number of domestic tasks. The will of Maria Wilhelmina Gildemeister, his widowed mother, contains an explicit mention of a slave: "To the male slave of the testatrix by name January an

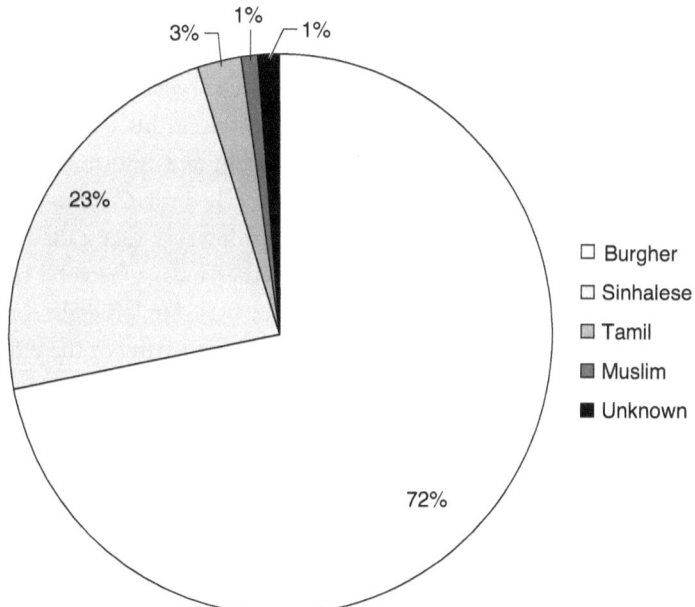

Figure 2.2 Ethnic distribution of proprietors (author's data from NA UK CO T71/663)

amount of thirty rix dollars, and the testatrix declaring further to emancipate him from slavery and desired therefore that the said legacy and the slave certificate of the said male slave should be given to him one month after the decease of the testatrix."[11]

Christian Cornelius became a cadet at the age of eleven and remained in the military until 1796, after the surrender of Colombo to the British. Later, rather than returning to the Netherlands, he worked as a civil engineer under British rule, but after some years he left this function to work as a wholesaler in Colombo. From the documents relating to his life in The Hague National Archives, he appears to have mingled with both Dutch residents and English authorities and acted as an effective spokesperson of the Dutch when they had grievances to be put forward to the government. His grandson wrote that his greatest merit was that together with "his friend Rajepakse," the mudaliyar of the Mahabadde (cinnamon peelers caste), he was instrumental in bringing about the liberation of slaves. During his time in Colombo he owned four slaves—Jacob, sixty-five years; Jans, twenty-one years; November, twenty-four years; and Susannah, sixteen years.[12]

Other records indicate the presence of domestics in the household, among them Celestina, who was baptized as a Roman Catholic in 1805.[13] For the "education and promotion in life" of his children, however, he thought it desirable to leave the island with nine of his children, his wife, Catherine Elizabeth Andringa, and his sister, Mrs. Gratien, and informed the chief secretary of his intention to take a ship in Galle called the *Cerberus* to return to the Netherlands via England.[14] In spite of a shipwreck that stalled him in the Cape, he eventually returned to the Netherlands, where he became burgermaster of Voorburg. He died in Delft in 1845. He left eight sons and four daughters; all sons enlisted in the Dutch colonial army or the navy.[15]

The source of C. C. Uhlenbeck's alleged activism regarding the abolition of slavery in Sri Lanka is possibly the farewell address of eighty notables in Colombo dated December 30, 1820, in which he is praised as one of the most virtuous and beloved men in his hometown, Colombo. The text of the address is worth quoting as it refers to his involvement in emancipation through his action to ensure "that the newborn of enslaved people are freed from the yoke of slavery."[16] Slavery was considered an evil while colonialism was implicitly construed as a liberating ideology that kept the enslaved in a sort of tutelage until they were ready to become subjects of the empire, devoid of any "free" voice but endowed with a limited "free" choice in the colonial labor market.

The Dutch Burgher Union Journal of 1933 gives us some insight into the way Uhlenbeck's act was remembered and projected by his descendants for posterity. They emphasized a single fact in his life—the performance of a benevolent act of liberation—neglecting to explain the possession of slaves until then, something that in the case of less generous proprietors perdured until 1844. Under the heading "Slavery in Ceylon" comes a snapshot view of Uhlenbeck's life in a British crown colony:

> Slavery was abolished in Ceylon on the 20th December 1844. It is however very much to the credit of our Dutch ancestors that they voluntarily liberated their slaves in 1817 or 27 years before they were compelled to do so by law.
>
> Dr C. C. Uhlenbeck, retired professor of Leiden University, states that his grandfather, who was son of Major Uhlenbeck Commandant of Galle, was one of those who interested themselves in the liberation of slaves in Ceylon, and that a document relating to this event, signed by eighty notables of Colombo, is treasured among his family papers.[17]

Upon his return to the Netherlands in 1820, Uhlenbeck did not play a role in a fledgling antislavery movement that was creating waves in Britain and the United States. This was not unexpected. In many ways the Netherlands stood out as a place where there was hardly any interest in the plight of slaves, and only rare antislavery rhetoric was heard in the Dutch public sphere. A few well-known personalities, such as Betje Wolff, had expressed opposition to the slave trade and slavery in the late eighteenth century, but these isolated voices failed to spawn an abolitionist organization until the 1840s, when informal circles and liberal clubs emerged in Utrecht and Amsterdam.[18] On the whole, Dutch abolitionism was small-scale, cautious, and late as compared to the British and American movements.[19] W. R. van Hoëvell's *Slaves and Free Men Under Dutch Law* (1854), the most read abolitionist publication in the Netherlands, failed to claim political or social equality for slaves and continued to conceive of black people as less developed than whites.[20]

The son of C. C. Uhlenbeck, C. H. Uhlenbeck, who was born in Sri Lanka but returned as a child to the Netherlands with his father in 1820, became minister of the colonies in a liberal government from February 1, 1862, to January 3, 1863. During this short period he passed the law of August 2, 1862, to abolish slavery in the West Indian islands of Aruba, Bonnaire, Curacao, Saba, St. Eustacius and St. Maarten, and Surinam. The law took effect almost a year later, on July 1, 1863. In Suriname, owing to the large population of enslaved peoples employed in the plantation system, the law mandated state supervision of the emancipated slaves, a form of apprenticeship, for a maximum of ten years. Slaveholders received compensation money that amounted to sixteen million guilders, ironically financed from the profits earned from the cultivation system based on forced labor in the Dutch East Indies.[21] Slavery was abolished in all directly ruled territories of the Netherlands East Indies (Indonesia) in 1859 without much noise, as convict labor gradually replaced slaves in the workplace. In the cities, freed slaves often continued to provide domestic services, albeit as free workers.[22]

Indigenous Slaveholders

The ethnic distribution of slaveholders in the slave registers of Colombo indicates a large proportion of local slaveholders. Other sources confirm that indigenous people employed enslaved men and women in various capacities, thus emulating the way of life of Burghers.[23] In many testamentary cases of indigenous wealthy landowners and businessmen in the nineteenth century, enslaved people appear amid jewelry, land, and household items as moveable property, either passed on to inheritors or sometimes emancipated and endowed with a parting gift.[24] Yet the presence of slaves in the lives of indigenous households in the southern maritime provinces is invisible in the historical rendering of the nineteenth century. Wickremaratne states categorically that the majority of slaves who lived in the towns of the southwestern seaboard were owned by Dutch Burghers.[25] Wills and deeds of transfer, however, show a sizable number of enslaved people in local homes and mansions (walauwas). In the late eighteenth century Moor and Sinhalese elite in Galle owned slaves. As Kate Ekama has demonstrated, emancipation deeds provide evidence of Sinhalese holding of slaves, if surnames such as Perera, Rodrigo, and Fernando are interpreted as evidence of Sinhalese ethnicity.[26]

Don Francisco Dias Abeywickrema Bandanaraike from the Matara district diligently registered his domestic slaves and their children in 1818. His antecedents are most probably traced to Don Francisco Dias Wijetunge Bandaranaike, born in 1720 and mudaliyar of Hewagam korale, and Don Christoffel Henricus F. Dias Abeyewickreme Jayatileke Seneviratne Bandaranaike, who was mudaliyar of the governor's gate and of Siyane korale East.[27] The slave register of 1818–1832 gives the following list (F and M stand for the gender, and the number is an indication of the age):

Amilia otherwise called Sebela F 58 emancipated by owner
Babby F 27.7 child Catistery not free
Camba M 14.7
Callua M 20.1
Celesteny F 21.7
Cethy F 26.7—Sabina F, Adirizema M
Calloo 23.7—Catharina F (died)
Cartha F 17.7—Juama M, Wattoemaide M
Castury F 10.7
Collondy F 17.7—Saberidi F, Sancha F, Juliana F, Adirra M (emancipated by proprietor)
Calloo otherwise named amma F 47.7 (emancipated by proprietor)
Dingy F 37.7—Ramassua F not free
Isacua M 20.7

Jacostria M 23.7
Paatma F 25.7—Sankindy F, Sarah F, Sanchia M, Mitto F, Senkindy F
Rosina F 7.7
Sompania M 7.7
Seekka F 8.7[28]

We can learn very little from these names. Were they local pauperized people compelled to sell themselves or their children to the landed proprietors at times of famine or crop failure, or were they bought from across the coast or from even further? What type of work did these slaves perform for their proprietor?

The wills of slaveholders provide some clues as to the labor that was extracted from slaves in the late eighteenth and early nineteenth centuries. The will of Nicholas Dias Abeysinghe Amarasekere (no. 1343, May 21, 1792), head mudaliyar of the gate in Dutch Ceylon, begins with a detailed explanation of what should happen to his slaves upon his death: "The testator desires that his slave maids Kaluda and Amelia shall remain with and serve his youngest son Abraham until he become of age or attain any qualified state when it is his desire they should be made free and at the expense of the testator's estate and their deeds should be delivered over to them such expenses being paid to the Deacon's Fund."

The church played an important role, as in the Cape, where fees for manumission were paid to the church. Freedom was not evenly distributed. The mudaliyar listed the names of slaves that should not be sold but would have to remain and serve his children for their entire lives: "Sumi Mira, the girl Sapra, the maid Amaldie and her daughter Rabja and Manchey, the children of the deceased Madalena named Katrnecha, Peena, the maid Ano and her son and one daughter, Abraham, Salman, Abea, Adena, Natto, the slave boys Antho and Phillipuwa, the maid Marco with her son and daughter Joan and Royattah."[29]

In an earlier, handwritten version of this testament dated November 23, 1783, in the National Archives of The Hague, two of the eight pages are dedicated to the future of the slaves, thus revealing their importance in the household of their owner.[30]

Nicholas Dias Abeyasinghe lived in Dangedera near Pokunawatta in the Galle province but also owned a walauwa at Silversmith Street in Colombo and a walauwa at Katunayake, so his slaves could have been domestic slaves—"maids" and workers in the "gardens" of his rural abode are referred to in the will. As the governor was encouraging native headmen and others with capital and an entrepreneurial spirit to engage in agriculture, in 1784 Dias Abeyasinghe had come to an agreement with the VOC that he would develop an estate in the northwest of Galle called Diviture, planting paddy, cinnamon, coffee, and pepper. He was given an investment from the company, which he was supposed to return after five years.[31] The mahamudaliyar had succeeded in attracting to his estate a labor force of poor and lower-caste people to whom he gave land to live on and till. But after the initial five years there appears to have been some compulsion exerted for them to continue working for him.[32] There is nothing, however, to prove or disprove that these were slaves or emancipees.

The will of Claudina Perera Ekanayaka, widow of Seneviratne Illangakon Kodituwakku Mohandiram, who died on September 27, 1816, and the joint will of herself and her husband were filed in the provincial court of Matara, as Case No. 3359. Both wills were written in Dutch. The translation reproduced by P. E. Pieris shows that the enslaved remained in an antechamber of freedom for two generations after the death of their masters, as though complete autonomy was not conceivable:

> The testatrix declares to be her desire that the above said the slave Catto with her three children Leno, Bale and Dingy Baby, should be obliged not alone to remain and serve by the survivor of the testators, but also to be subjected to serve under their above said children, Dona Anna de Zaa and Don Matthys de Zaa, with the restriction that they should be treated as faithful free declared slaves in the manner the equity did appertain.[33]

Deeds also indicate that slaves were purchased in southern India and brought to Sri Lanka. Louis de Saram Maha Mudaliyar of the Governor's Gate bought a boy called Maden, renamed Lourens, on December 30, 1728, from a vendor called "The Chetty Joan" for the price of 12 rix dollars in Tuticorin.[34]

The account of Dona Ana's estate of the Illangekoon family in 1780 lists the slaves with their names and value: Rosetta female, 50 rix dollars; Kaliestie, 60 rix dollars; Mado and child, 60 rix dollars; Pinne, male, 100 rix dollars; Katto and daughter, 170 rix dollars; and Wattoe and daughter, 344 rix dollars, between the lands she owned and the jewelry.[35] In 1835 emancipation of slaves was already a near fait accompli, as the will of Don Petrus

Abeysiriwardena Ilangakoon Maha Mudaliyar testifies. In this she refers with affection to her faithful emancipated slave woman Baby and bequeaths to the latter's children, Saarchy, Kaatchy, January, Siripinay, and Francina, a field of one amunam in the Girway Pattoe and six coconut trees from the garden Jamboeghahwatte at Noepe, for which Baby would receive the profits until the children were of age to support themselves.[36] Little more is known on the relationship between enslaved and slaveholders. In contrast, it has been the subject of a lively debate among historians of South Africa, with Robert Ross, for instance contending that there was no sense of being part of a "family" in a slaveholding household.[37]

In the early nineteenth century a class of new rich hailing from all castes and ethnicities and who had acquired wealth and education began to emulate the lifestyle of a new rich class, who in previous centuries had been the interpreters for colonial rulers.[38] For their collaboration they had been rewarded with land and honors. Both these groups enjoyed a "feudal" lifestyle aptly described by, inter alia, Patrick Peebles, Kumari Jayawardena, Michael Roberts, and Anoma Peiris.[39] The old rich group was epitomized by the Bandaranaike-Obeysekeres, who were committed to retaining their status based on landed wealth and loyalty to the British.

During the first decades of British rule in Sri Lanka, the economy "remained precapitalist and rudimentary with some export of natural products, a low level of trading and shipping activity, low productivity in agriculture and few manufactures."[40] European merchants did nothing more than adapt to existing structures, and no major innovations in the economy or society were apparent during this period of mercantilism. The British held on to the cinnamon monopoly until 1833, and the need for revenue compelled them to abide by the system.[41] There was little change in the sources of revenue from the early nineteenth century to the early 1830s: land rents, cinnamon, grain tax, pearl fishery, duties on spirits, fish rents, capitation tax, stamps, salt monopoly, and tolls were the main earning mechanisms during this period. Corvée labor was used to build the roads, and then a road tax was introduced.

While the Dutch East India Company was not favorable to an accumulation of property by Ceylonese, which it saw as a challenge to its own mercantile enterprises, the final years of Dutch rule and the beginning of the British witnessed a growth in the titles acquired by Ceylonese. Peebles suggests that during these years and in the confusion of Anglo-Dutch wars, the Dutch sold land for revenue and to increase the production of cash crops while Ceylonese made a grab for government-owned spice "gardens" in the Colombo district.[42] The first governor of British Ceylon, Frederick North, was hopeful that granting land to the natives would develop agriculture and make the colony viable. He created a Survey Department, abolished service tenure, ceased to enforce corvée labor, and introduced a tax on rice cultivation. Thomas Maitland, North's successor, reversed most of these policies but made new ones that consolidated the rights and obligations of private property. The governor could issue free grants of land at his own discretion, and before 1833 more than 50,000 acres of land, mostly areas that had been Dutch "gardens" planted with spices in the late eighteenth century, were partitioned into small plots and issued to Ceylonese. The recipients of these plots were both large landowners and villagers. From the list of grantees of more than 50 acres of land, it is clear that the majority were traditional local officials of high family status. The British believed that these grantees would be able to enlist agricultural laborers to work on their lands and develop them. This period saw the creation of a category of landed proprietors with large landholdings where laborers were called to work in the name of *rajakariya* (corvée), according to witnesses heard before the Colebrooke-Cameron Commission.[43]

Among the list of large landowners in the first decades of the nineteenth century compiled by Patrick Peebles, six were signatories of the 1816 declaration to emancipate the children of their slaves (see table 2.1).[44] There is a possible correlation between slaveholding and land utilization for

TABLE 2.1
Large Landowners in Early Nineteenth-Century Sri Lanka

Grantees	Number of grants	Acreage
P. Perera	5	264.2
C. de Saram	1	104.0
M. Perera	6	212.0
D. H. Dassenaike	3	88.6
A. de Saram	2	56.2
D. S. Ameresekera	5	52.0
M. Gomis	2	63.7

Source: Patrick Peebles, "Land Use and Population Growth in Colonial Ceylon," *Contributions to Asian Studies* 6 (1976): 70.

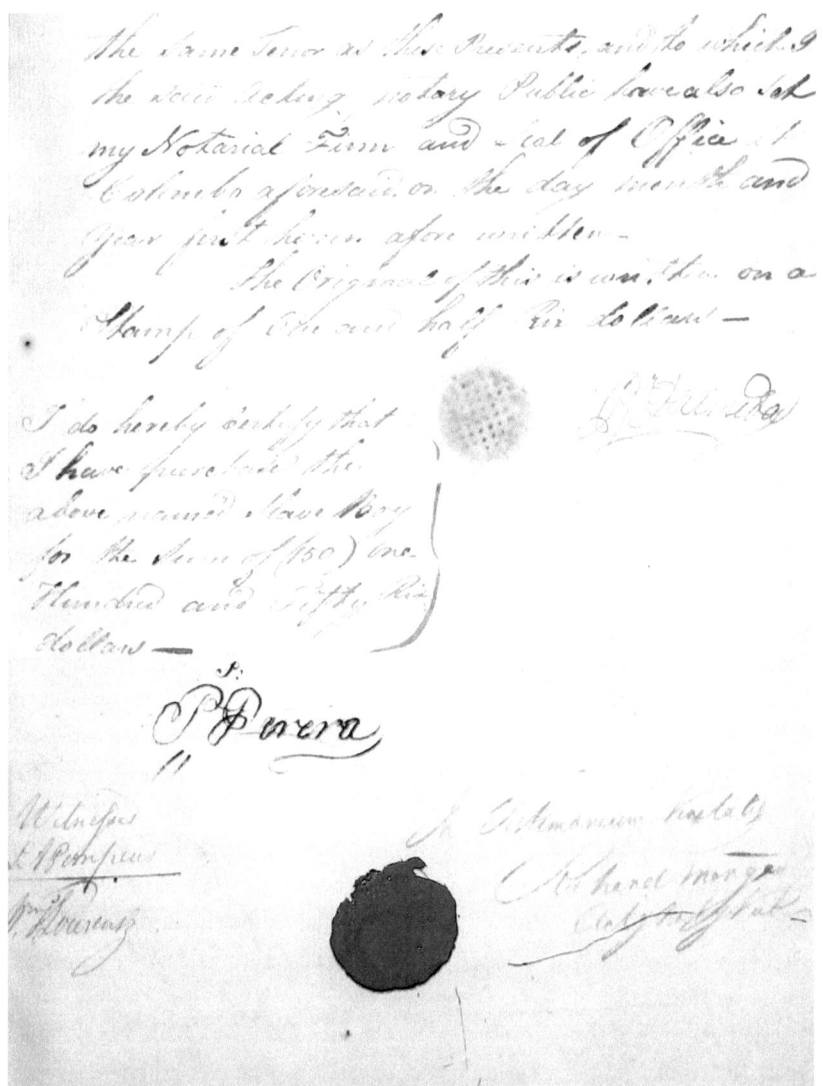

Figure 2.3 Deed of transfer of slave, June 30, 1809 (SLNA Lot 7/2133 with permission of Sri Lanka National Archives)

agriculture, but clear evidence of the use of slave labor in the spice gardens is yet to be discovered.

During the first fifteen years of British rule, slaves continued to be sold and bought in the presence of notaries, such as Adrian Vandort or Richard Morgan. Just as for any property, it was necessary to sign an official deed of transfer sanctioned by a notary that traced the past proprietors of the slave. A "certain slave boy named Abel" was held by Pieter de Almeida "as appears in the Notarial assignment made to him by J. C. Koelman dated at Bentotte the twenty eighth day of March One Thousand Eight Hundred and Six." In a subsequent deed drawn up and sealed by Notary Richard Morgan, the slave boy was legally transferred to Paulus Perera for the sum of 150 rix dollars in the presence of a witness J. H. Lourenz.[45]

The stories that follow relate to enslaved men and women like Abel, who accidentally enter the official archive for a segment of their life.

The Murder of Valentine, a "Malay" Runaway

In 1797 an enslaved man called Valentine went to the market a little outside the Colombo Pettah to buy some flowers. There he met his wife or companion Clara, also an enslaved person, and together they set out on the high road to Mahradan (Maradana) to the house of someone described in the court records as "the Malay sultan." Some men were waiting for them in the hut next door. Clara and Valentine had left their bundle of clothes and Clara's two rix dollars in the hut as they and another runaway male slave were planning to flee to Galle with the help of these men. The slaves and the men left together, walking in a row in the moonlight. Suddenly the men asked them to stop walking as they wanted to chew betel. On this road, surrounded on both sides by the jungle, Valentine was killed and Clara fled into the jungle. Three years later, when the Supreme Court tried two men for the murder of Valentine, the fate of the other runaway would be revealed.

The period is of some importance. The year 1797 was a time of trouble for the British in Sri Lanka as they encountered resistance to their rule from the local people. In September 1795 the British had captured the strategic harbor of Trincomalee in the east of the island, and in 1796 they proceeded to expel the VOC from the parts of the island that had been under their control since 1658. The government of the maritime provinces was then vested in the government of Fort St. George (Madras), and control in Sri Lanka was handed over to the military, led by Colonel James Stuart.[46] The headmen deemed responsible for the troubles were dismissed from administrative office, with the probable exception of those from the Salagama (cinnamon peeler) caste, and replaced by the Amildars and their assistants, known in popular parlance as the "Malabar Mudaliyars." This and other changes led to the revolt of 1797.[47]

The reading of the acts of 1796–1798 as a single rebellion and the need to locate them in a longer continuum of resistance against the colonial state and link them to the abolition of service tenure and imposition of a new tax on coconut gardens has been dealt with elsewhere.[48] What is important to understand here is that these disturbances provided a context for Valentine to consider running away from Colombo and starting a new life. Robert Percival described Colombo as a European city, "built more in the European style. . . . The interior of the fort has also more the appearance of a regular town." The houses are "regularly built, less than one story high," and the windows have glass panes, Venetian blinds, and shutters. Most houses have verandahs as a refuge "from the sultry rays and people spend much time in this space."[49]

Running away and providing help to runaway slaves was a crime under Dutch colonial rule under ordinances issued in 1663, 1674, 1677, 1757, and 1786. The regulation of May 31, 1757, in Colombo and July 4 in Galle—"Plakkaat waarbij de Straf-Maatregelen tegen het weglopen van slaven uit de Vier gravetten en het verlenen van hulp aan weggelopen slaven bekend gemmakt worden" (Declaration announcing the punishment for runaway slaves from the Four Gravets and for providing help to runaway slaves)—was translated into Sinhalese and Tamil.[50] There is little information on the number of slaves in Sri Lanka who fled by foot and the extent of their success during the transition period from Dutch to British rule, although unsuccessful runaways appeared in criminal records of all Dutch territories from Sri Lanka to the Cape.[51] In Sri Lanka, for a slave whose appearance was that of an indigenous person, it was sufficient to run away to a distant place where he or she was unknown and begin a new life there. If their destination was Galle, Valentine and Clara were probably planning to travel by boat with the help of the assassins. We do not know what triggered the escape—perhaps a chance meeting at the market, since both Valentine and Clara appeared to be free to wander in the city of Colombo, or simply the window of opportunity offered by a change of rule. In 1797, one year after the fall of the Dutch, did Valentine know that he was no longer subject to the draconian rules of the VOC concerning escaped slaves?

The court case of February 1800 surrounding Valentine's murder three years before discloses little about the victim. Was he courageous, reckless, or simply seizing the occasion of a loosening of power? His body is described as that of a young man below the age of thirty. He was possessed by Captain Olke Andringa, who appears to have had a large staff of servants and at least three slaves, Primo, Sooco, and Valentine. Andringa's life is better known than that of his slave. He was born in Kuinre, Netherlands, in 1741 to parents dealing in wood and building supplies. In 1764 he married Geesje Stam, with whom he had eight children. After he joined the VOC as a sailor in 1759 he went on seven voyages to the Dutch colonies. Going up the ranks, by his final voyage to the colonies in 1779 he was master (*schipper*) of the *Hoogkarspel*. By 1785 he was working as a sea captain in Colombo, until he was discharged from service in 1795 and became harbor master of Colombo. After his first wife died in Colombo, he married Magdalena Strobach, a widow who possessed a large group of slaves. Two daughters appear in the records. The elder daughter, Catharina, born in 1789, was probably the daughter of Magdalena's first husband. Catharina later married C. C. Uhlenbeck. The younger daughter, Agneta, was born in 1801 and was more likely Olke Andringa's daughter.[52]

Olke Andringa, according to Clara's testimony, was the first to be informed by Clara of the events, and he immediately went to the jungle in search of Valentine. Once Valentine's body was found, it was brought back to the fort.

Clara describes Valentine as talking in the "Malay" language with his assassins. Her statement comes to us in translation. What term did she use to qualify Valentin's language in the language she herself spoke, which could have been Sinhalese, Tamil, or Portuguese? The British used the term *Malay* in a loose and unqualified manner to describe people who they believed had roots in the East Indies. The Dutch had used the term *Oosterlingen* (Easterners), together with the term *Javanese*, to describe people who had been living in Batavia before migrating to Sri Lanka. People from Southeast Asia were far from strangers in Sri Lanka. Reverend Philippus Baldeus mentions in 1672 the presence of Bandanese and Javanese soldiers on the side of the Dutch and Sri Lankan rulers. Apart from being soldiers in the colonial armies, they were often anti-Dutch political exiles and convicts sent from the Indonesian archipelago.[53] The lives of political exiles from ruling families, such as the Javanese king Amangkurat III of Surakarta, exiled with his retinue in 1704, or the sultan of Gowa, in 1767, have been discussed in numerous publications. The close connection of the Malay people with the Dutch and then the British army, as well as the Ceylon Rifle regiment formed for Malay soldiers by Governor Frederick

North, is evidenced in military histories. Yet the presence of enslaved people from Southeast Asia in the maritime provinces of Sri Lanka since the mid-eighteenth century is scantily addressed and remains generally little known.[54]

By the early nineteenth century, most enslaved people in Colombo who had lived in the island for a number of decades generally spoke Portuguese. Percival remarks that Dutch ladies spoke a vulgar Portuguese probably due to "their frequent and familiar intercourse with their slaves."[55] Valentine, however did not converse in Portuguese. Since slaves were still traded and brought to the island until 1799, it is probable that he had been brought there recently enough for him to remember his mother tongue, a language spoken in the East Indies that the court translator described as "Malay." According to Percival, "The Dutch, to avoid the expense of keeping coast servants, introduced the practice of rearing slaves of the African casts, and employing Malays who made excellent cooks and gardeners, and indeed good servants in every respect, although they were kept for a trifle in comparison of the others." He contrasts the dress of the slaves with the attire of the Malays of noble descent. "While Malays of a higher rank wear a wide Moorish coat or gown which they call Badjour . . . most of the slaves in the service of Europeans, instead of the piece of cloth, have breeches of some coarse stuff given to them by their masters."[56]

Together, as the court account suggests, Valentine and Clara went to the "house of the Sultan" in Cinnamon Gardens and left their small bundle of clothes. The name of the sultan remains unknown, but he would have been a member of the noble families exiled by Dutch rulers from one of the Spice Islands. Official documents of 1792, for example, list 176 individuals belonging to 23 families of royalty and nobility exiled together with their families from Java and Sumatra to Sri Lanka.[57] The Indonesian exiles lived in the prince's quarters (Kampung Pangeran) in an area close to the Wolfendhal Malay quarters. It is possible that the sultan's house was the residence of the former sultan of Gowa, who was deceased. His widow, Siti Hapipa, remained there at least until 1807.[58] The exiled sultan Fakhruddin Abdul Khair al-Mansur Baginda Usman Batara Tangkana Gowa, the twenty-sixth king of the Gowa Sultanate of South Sulawesi, reigned from 1753 until 1767 and was banished by the Dutch VOC to Sri Lanka in 1767 on a charge of conspiracy with the British to oppose the VOC trading monopoly in eastern Indonesia. Might Clara and Valentine have visited the sultan to seek redress from some injustice? Might the Malay assassins have been connected to the sultan? The motivation for the murder might have been more complex than understood at the time.

Clara, for her part, was the slave of a Mr. and Mrs. Bruckner, the former appearing as a witness in the case against the two assassins, Bankanna and Dannah, for the murder of Valentine. A servant of Andringa mentions that Clara was previously called Cornumba, which suggests she was bought recently by Bruckner from another slaveholder and renamed. After having initially recognized the accused, Clara later retracted her statement, which she claimed she made "for want of sense." She did, however, claim that the three assassins were Malays. Once again the term is vague and perhaps lost in translation—we do not know what term she used in her testimony.[59]

Clara's account of the events three years after they happened is inconsistent and frayed, a feature that the reasonable mind of the judge was quick to point out. Clara describes the weapon as a "stick as long as her arm and as thick as her waist." Yet both victims appear to have been stabbed. The other person who joined Clara and Valentine to flee was a slave of Sergeant Bahre. Clara describes seeing Bahre's slave hit by a Malay man and dying, but she also states that she ran away as soon as Valentine was attacked. Her claim that she informed Olke Andringa himself is contradicted by his statement when he asserts that he missed Valentine at night and, feeling sick at the time, had sent off two servants, David and a gardener, to look for him. They, rather than Clara, informed Andringa that his slave had been murdered. Clara, it seems, never recovered her clothes and money, for as she had returned to collect them from the sultan's house, she was, according to David, "threatened with unbecoming terms in the Malay language." After that she had fled into the jungle.

Less is known about the other victim. His owner, Gerhard Hendrick Bahre, appeared before the criminal court on February 12, 1800, and testified to the murder of his slave on June 23, 1797. He confirmed that the men charged were not suspects at that time; instead, an old Malay man had been taken in by Provost Marshall Sutherland.

Of the accused, too, little is known, except that they were "Malay" and soldiers. It appears that Bankanna was a soldier in the company of Lieutenant Langvalle. Many Malays served in the Dutch army and thereafter joined the British forces. Some of the soldiers were emancipated slaves. The Dutch government sometimes gave freedom to slaves in its employ in exchange for joining the army. A Malay company made of deportees and thirty-one slaves was thus created in 1763, blurring the lines between slave origin and army military lineage of the Malay community. In the same manner, freed slaves formed a large contingent of the expedition of 1781 to invade the Kandyan kingdom during Governor Van de Graaf's term, and in 1786 "Eastern slaves" were emancipated and made into a company of militia.[60] When Colombo fell to the British, it was decided that the Malay prisoners of war, rather than being sent to Java as suggested by the Dutch, would be sent instead to Madras to be part of the British military establishment. After the Treaty of Amiens, when Sri Lanka became a crown colony, Governor North took measures to absorb Malay troops into the island's military.

Pinning murder on Malays was quite common, as Malay men were believed to be naturally disposed to violent acts. Percival speaks of the "ferocity of the disposition" of the Malays and their propensity to take opium, get involved in murders, and run amok for revenge.[61] Furthermore, Malays were perceived as murderers in Sri Lanka, owing to the murder in 1799 of the last Dutch disava of Matara, Pieter Willem Ferdinand Adriaan van Schuler, and his wife by a Malay, who was a "servant" according to Hussaimiya and a "domestic slave" according to R. G. Anthonisz.[62] Anthonisz notes that the slave "had secreted himself in the sleeping chamber for the purpose, and . . . used his master's own sword, which was hanging on the wall by the bed."[63] This type of incident only confirmed, for those in positions of authority, the Malay people's propensity to violence, a deep-seated orientalist and psychologized reading of their character.[64] The case of the Slave Island murder of 1723 described in the first chapter may have also contributed to the creation of this stereotype.

In the end, the court found Bankanna and Dannah not guilty but put them on remand to be tried for other offenses. The archive thus gives only part of the story and leaves many gaping holes on the motives of the murder of Valentine and the role played by the sultan in these events.

Selestina

The story of Selestina is similar to that of many other enslaved women who experience violence in the bedroom, the workplace, or the field. These stories have been forgotten by the historiography pertaining to early nineteenth-century Sri Lanka, even by gender historians. There is a sense that one has to respect the limits of what can be known. Yet there is a duty to report these counterhistories as scandals revealing the excesses of colonialism as everyday practices. Though the colonial archive reports the life of subaltern women only at moments of aberration and Selestina is a failed witness who utters only a few words, her story betrays a certain familiarity. Excessive violence in the small hut where she lived was the norm. The ordinary was a continuous life of pain and humiliation. It was only the death of a child that made it worthy of being recorded. The archive is made of other matters—matters of state that involve the men who commit the violence—so the pain and oppression Selestina and others suffered has to be pried out of texts produced by the oppressing powers of state and patriarchy. It is in court cases and reports on court proceedings that these voices can be heard, albeit faintly.[65] The layered nature of the colonial archive and the possibilities it offers in reading echoes and whispers and silences have been explored in a rich body of work that is an inspiration to force the archive and capture the precarity of Selestina's life.[66]

Women of color belonged to two marginalized groups. Gender and race combined to make them invisible. In the colonial archive they appear through the prism of the voice of male slaves or slaveholders; in the registers they appear as names often distorted by the hand of a culturally insensitive colonial scribe, as a gender encompassed in the letter F, and as an age.

The gender ratio among the population of enslaved people as it appears from the slave registers of Colombo points to an imbalance between women and men: there were 348 slave women and 284 slave men.

This was a patriarchal society where social and economic powers were concentrated in the hands of the slaveholder. Added to this vulnerability, women were also exposed to the pressures of male slaves who came from similarly male-dominated societies. Imposed nonconsensual sex was a natural condition in a household composed of masters and enslaved people. Scholars have often linked sexual violence and homosexual activity by slave men in Cape to the ratio of men to women among enslaved people which, was approximately 4 to 1.[67] Feminist historians have disputed these conclusions and asserted that sexual violence is about domination rather than fulfilment of a libidinal need.[68]

Selestina of Colombo was, according to the words of the sitting magistrate of Colombo on January 21, "charged with having murdered her child."[69] On January 18 Gabriel, the servant of J. L. Cramer, secretary of the sitting magistrate in the Colombo district court, informed him that

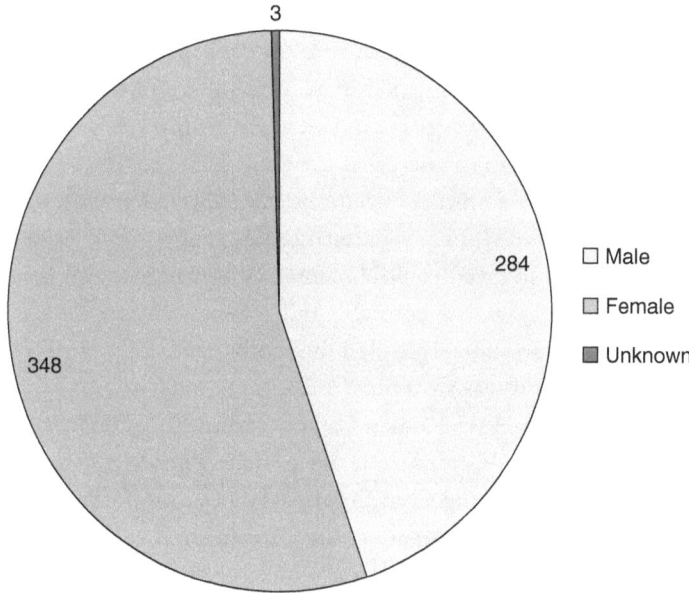

Figure 2.4 Gender distribution of slaves in Colombo (author's data from NA UK CO T71/663)

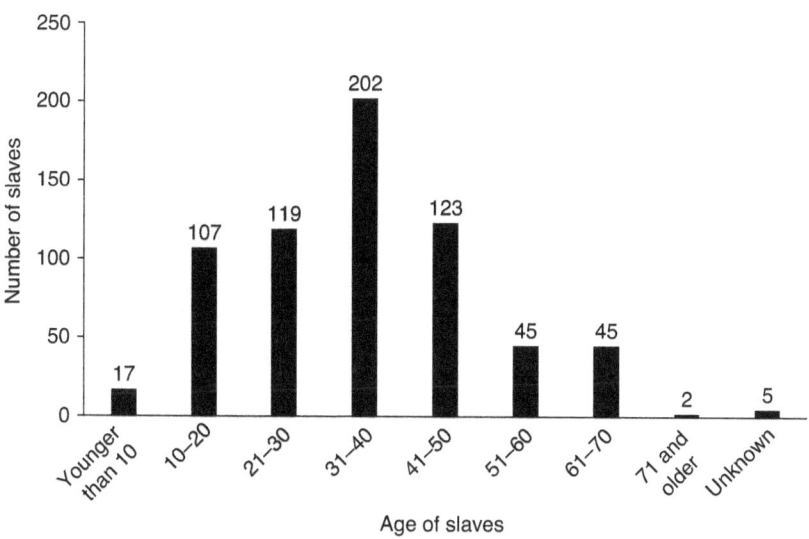

Figure 2.5 Age of slaves in Colombo (author's data from NA UK CO T71/663)

"his slave girl Selestina had been brought to bed of a child which she had thrown into the necessary," a euphemism for the toilets. These words testify to the confusion between a narrative version of an event and a literal version. Clearly Cramer was narrating an event he had not witnessed, yet he was confident enough to assert that the child had been "thrown." Upon the return of Cramer from the Pettah, he claimed he had instructed the child to be "extricated," but later testimonies suggest that his staff had already acted to try to save the child before his return. Selestina was taken into custody by J. Ebert, the constable of St. Sebastian Street. A medical attendant who had presumably visited the mother and child in jail testified in court that the child was alive but "in a weakly state."

Constantia, described as a Roman Catholic, whose function in the household is not indicated but seemed to be one of some authority, stated that at 7 p.m. she saw Selestina going from the necessary to a room detached from the house, and that from her "manner" she suspected that she had delivered a child. Constantia had entered the room, where she found Selestina "with her cloth drenched in blood." Selestina had first claimed that the blood came from her period, but then Constantia had sent Maria Silva to the necessary to check. Maria returned and stated that a child was crying at the bottom. Sarviel and Maria took a light and found the child and, "having collected people," a person called Noor—a Muslim name—descended into the necessary, took the child, washed it, and gave it to its mother. The child was covered with excrement and there were traces of blood on the planks of the seat of the necessary. Blood was flowing from the navel and the top of the head prior to the child being cleaned. The child had been dropped nine feet and fallen on the filth, which "was not very deep as it had been cleared six months since." There were no marks of violence except a scratch on the nose. The child seemed at that point to be very weak and appeared unlikely to survive.[70] The afterbirth was found in Selestina's room, so it seemed that Selestina had delivered herself. She was examined by the medical officer, M. Mack, to ascertain whether she was fit enough to go to jail.[71]

The child, a boy, died at 4 a.m. on the morning of January 20. He was examined by Mack and midwife Sittee—possibly a Malay Muslim—who filed reports on the death.[72] The secretary of the court reported the statement of Sittee, described as a Mahomedan in the court record. She had gone to Cramer's house at the request of Constantia around 7 p.m., and Selestina and the child were brought to the room. Selestina explained that "something like a ball had dropped from her into the necessary." Sittee confirmed that the child was full term and the birth was natural.[73] The doctor, however, stated that Selestina would have delivered herself "by forcible means" since the navel string was broken, and the child must have died from loss of blood. Upon his first examination, however, he had confirmed that there were "no violent marks on the child's body" and only "a slight blue mark on the chin."[74] Cramer expressed surprise at any suggestion that "his slave girl" had the intention of getting rid of the child.[75] Noor, who had rescued the child, stated that the child was then alive and covered in filth so no blood could be seen. He surmised that injury would have been caused by the fall.[76] Selestina's testimony as it was reported confirmed the narrative of the others, including her description of feeling something like a ball drop and then losing her senses until she went to the room adjoining Cramer's house. The magistrate brought to the notice of the court that Selestina had already had two children. Selestina added she did not do this "intentionally."[77] She then was committed for trial before the Supreme Court for having murdered her child.

The trial, which would have taken place before Chief Justice Sir Hardinger Giffard, did not actually take place, as Selestina appears in a list of prisoners as a female slave, of twenty-two years, Roman Catholic (fig. 2.6). Below her name is scribbled "discharged without prosecution," dated February 1822.[78] Selestina's life thereafter is unknown.

Figure 2.6 List of prisoners, Supreme Court circuit for Colombo, February 1822 (SLNA Lot 81 with permission of Sri Lanka National Archives)

Before the tragic events of 1822, Selestina's name appears in the slave register for Colombo, which diligent slaveholders used to confirm possession of human beings. In 1818 she was eighteen years old, and no children were registered under her name. We do not know what she looked like or the color of her eyes. Her master, Cramer, owned two other slaves, Jisabelle (female, twenty) and Spadetje (male, thirty-eight).[79] When were Selestina's other children born, who fathered them, and what happened to them?[80] The unsaid is revealing. At no moment in the proceedings does the magistrate question Selestina on the paternity of the child, which would be a natural concern. Was it to avoid the embarrassment of hearing the name J. L. Cramer? At no moment is there any sense of surprise or consternation that a twenty-two-year-old slave woman would have given birth to three children out of wedlock. The relationship between male slaveholder and enslaved working in the home is not alluded to, but in 1803 Robert Percival, in *The Account of the Island of Ceylon*, describes the Dutch women he encountered and their relationship with enslaved women. He touches on the cruelty displayed by them on occasions:

> Dancing is the principal amusement of the younger women: while the chief pleasure of the married and elderly ladies consists in paying formal and ceremonious visits to each other. To these visits they go attended by a number of slave girls, dressed out for the occasion. These girls walk after them carrying their betel-boxes, or are employed in bearing umbrellas over the heads of their mistresses, who seldom wear any head-dress, but have their hair combed closely back and shining with oil. Their chief finery consists in these female attendants, and their splendour is estimated by the number of them which they can afford to keep. These slaves are the comeliest girls that can be procured and their mistresses in general behave very kindly to them. With that caprice however, which always attends power in the hands of the ignorant and narrow minded, the Dutch ladies frequently behave in a very cruel and unjust manner to their female attendants, upon very trifling occasions, and in particular on the slightest suspicion of jealousy.[81]

Dutch paternalism vis-à-vis slaves was also subject to doubt by Percival when he noted that Malay slaves to the Dutch had "on account of ill treatment made their escape to the Candian territories."[82]

J. L. Cramer's name was listed among the Dutch inhabitants and Burghers of Colombo who were subscribers to the address to the prince regent for emancipating children born of slaves after August 12, 1816.[83] Little is known about Cramer and his relationship with his slaves. It was, however, not uncommon during the early years of British rule, when few British women traveled to the colonies, for European men to marry or have liaisons with local women or women of mixed descent. This continued the policy of Portuguese and Dutch colonizers who on occasion promoted mixed marriages. After the fall of Jaffna and Colombo, two hundred Dutchmen were reported to have married women of Indo-Portuguese origin. Whether these unions were coerced or free is not known.[84] The presence of Indian domestic slavery under company rule in the subcontinent has been revealed in studies of inventories and wills written by Anglo-Indians. Slaves appear, sometimes unnamed, under the designation of "slave boy" or "slave girl," reduced to itemized objects, and at other times as slave-concubines and intimate parts of British households.[85] Had Selestina's child survived, he would have been freed from enslavement upon reaching the age of fourteen and joined the mixed-race community of Burghers or Eurasians.[86]

The fact that Selestina had already had two children makes it difficult to accept that she did not know she was carrying a child. The fact that she had cut the umbilical cord herself shows that she saw that what she described as a "ball" was a child. We do not know if the child was dropped intentionally, but other, similar slave narratives lead one to speculate that the child may have been the product of rape. Rape was until 1855 a crime punishable by death in Sri Lanka as in any other British colonies, together with forgery, arson, sodomy, carnal knowledge with a child under ten, and abortion.[87] Just like many violated and enslaved women, Selestina may not have wanted to bring a child into a world where he would not be free and would surely suffer bodily harm. Slavery was antithetical to family, womanhood, and motherhood. The juridical narrative is blank on her motives but hints toward a strategy of survival. When Selestina claims that she had lost her senses and makes the point clearly that the child was not dropped intentionally into the necessary, she is in effect putting forward her defense.[88] In many ways, historical fiction such as Toni Morrison's *Beloved* or Yvette Christianse's *Unconfessed*, a fictionalized account of the story of Sila van den Kaap, who was sentenced to death in April 1823 for killing her nine-year-old son Baro, fills in where the archive falters.[89] Turning to fiction means veering toward subjectivity and trespass on the boundaries of the conventional archive of professional historians. For this reason we have no accounts of subaltern women under colonial rule, although accounts of the construction of native women's sexuality by colonizers and local elites have been scrutinized. In general, native women were circumscribed by colonizers and local elites in a domestic sphere where their main duties were childbearing and looking after the home.[90] This is why infanticide was seen in the society in which they live and labor as the most horrendous crime, the ultimate perversion. For Selestina to kill her own child meant facing the opprobrium of her entourage, which leads one to imagine that she felt a sense of complete desperation and absence of hope in the future if she committed such an act where she risked prosecution. Her defiance was not covert, oblique, or symbolic, as was often the case in more repressive slave societies.[91] Selestina's act must be looked at as part of the ordinary life of an enslaved woman rather than an interruption of it or an aberration.

Two Stories from Galle

Ameensa from Cochin

On July 26, 1800, Ameensa appeared before the Supreme Court at Point de Galle, the city that lay on the coast in the lush, wet southern province of the island, where Valentine and Clara were hoping to reach. She stood there on behalf of herself and her daughter to claim freedom from a Galle merchant, who affirmed that she and her daughter were his lawful slaves. The court declared that Walle Odiar Tirewa Nainde Markar had unlawfully kept her in slavery and was called to appear before the Supreme Court together with another merchant called Mapola Tambi of Colombo and a Galle resident called Lebbe. Lebbe was under arrest as he was the last person who claimed ownership over Ameensa.[92]

For over five hundred years before the arrival of the Europeans, Galle had been a place of trade for Arab merchants who sailed along the coast of Lanka. The Portuguese established a small trading post in Galle in the early sixteenth century and eventually, pushed away from Colombo by King Rajasingha I, had to withdraw there and build a fort to guard the harbor. In March 1640 the town succumbed to the attack of the Dutch and became the VOC's first administrative base. Galle was the most important port for the VOC, the seat of the first Protestant church and for some time the headquarters of the Dutch government, with a sizable population of Dutch officials, settlers, and clergy.[93] After the capitulation of Colombo in 1796, only nine hundred Dutch inhabitants remained in the entire island. British forces took Galle a few months later in a peaceful manner, with the Dutch commander Fretz having made arrangements to disarm the Dutch garrison and receive the British troops at the fort. Captain Lachlan Macquarie, who led the military conquest of Galle, describes it in this manner: "The Dutch Garrison paraded, presented their arms and piled them afterwards with the utmost regularity and order, on the Grand Parade within the Fort, fronting the British detachment which was formed on the same Parade opposite to them."[94]

On August 1, 1800, Ameensa, also called Afsnoema, began telling her story to the court. She was born in Cochin, in Arne in the dominion of the Nawab, and remained there for ten years, then went to various places on the coast. She was married to a Patan—a term generally used in South India to refer to Deccani Muslims—named Afsinga from Dasoo in a territory also under the Nawab. She lived with her husband in Seringapatam and had many children, of which only one remained with her, a daughter of eleven years called Khadirtah. Her husband was, in her own words, a commandant under Tippoo Saib (Tipu Sultan). He was wounded in the wars and died in the service of Tipu Sultan at a place called Kneculmallee. After his death she remained for a month at Serangipatam and then left. She had no support. She walked for fifteen days to a place called Palghat, also in the dominion of Tipu Sultan, where she remained three months.[95] There she stayed in the house of Syed Mookheiden but provided for herself. From there she moved to Cochin. A woman called Cundooma "invited her to live there." For twenty days she supported herself and her daughter but lived at Cundooma's. Ameensa's voyage to Galle would begin here.

Ameensa had found herself caught in the last wars that the kingdom of Mysore was waging against the British East India Company. Her origins were, however, in Cochin, a coastal town that since 1760 had been under the suzerainty of Haider Ali and from 1782 of his son Tipu Sultan. In 1794 or 1795, if her own sense of time is correct, her husband, an officer in Tipu Sultan's army, had died in a place called Kneculmalee. A few years later Tipu Sultan himself would be killed fighting at the Siege of Serangapatam when the British, helped by the Nizam of Hyderabad and the Maratha forces, stormed his fortress. The British took large parts of the kingdom and ended the Mysorean power in the southern Deccan. This event spelled a complete change in Ameensa's life. As a widow without resources except probably her savings, she was gradually becoming destitute and feeling the precarity of her life.

In Cochin Cundooma "gave her in charge" to her son Mapola Tamby, who was then in turn "in charge" of taking Ameensa to Colombo. Ameensa describes how she and her daughter were escorted to a ship by Cundooma and from there sailed to Galle. Before leaving her, Cundooma had promised that in Galle Ameensa would "get everything she needed" and also that she would visit now and then. Ameensa declared that she had not signed any papers. This was, she said, "seven months before the English took possession of this place, full six years ago." The dates are important as they indicate that Ameensa reached Galle when the island was still under VOC rule, seven months before the 70th Regiment of the British Forces led by Captain Macquarie took control of Galle on February 23, 1796. She was then brought to the house of one of the accused in the case, referred to as the prisoner Lebbe. Before that, she mentioned to the court, she had appeared before a magistrate, presumably a Dutch official, who had ruled that since she was a subject of Tipu, she should be sent back "over the waters." But Mapola Tambi took her again to his house and the same day on board a ship. No explanation was given as to what happened on the ship. Ameensa lived in the house of Mapola Tambi for two months as his guest. After that he had delivered her to Lebbe, whose house was in the fort, introducing him as the "son of a brother," and said that he himself was going back to Bellingham. Two years later Ameensa appeared before the magistrate to complain that her daughter was being punished by depriving her of "victuals." Furthermore, when she had complained about her daughter's treatment to Lebbe, he had threatened "to have her hair cut off and her head shaved."

Ameensa had heard with astonishment that Lebbe had bought her daughter. On an occasion when he had beaten her daughter, she asked him to give her back and get back his money from Tambi. He told her he had bought the daughter for 150 rix dollars and that when she paid that, she would be free.

Claims and counterclaims followed in succession. A year and a half after she had been left in the home of Lebbe, Ameensa had requested and obtained that Tambi be brought before Commandant Agnew (Major Agnew).[96] His (presumably Tambi's) eldest brother was then put in prison. Six months later Ameensa was herself put in jail for a day, and when released again she was "offered for sale." The court then moved on to assessing whether Ameensa was a slave, asking for proof of enslavement from those making claims on her, and calling other witnesses as well. The accused then produced in court two translations of slave bonds.

The renter of the sea customs was called in to testify about the boat on which Ameensa arrived in 1795 with Mapola. He recalled that fourteen or fifteen slaves came onshore and Mapola paid the duty; they came in a company ship and had regular papers from Cochin. He did not recognize the woman and daughter because "they were all so lean" and only took an account of them. Jan Jacques David D'Estandin, fiscal of Galle in 1795, explained the procedure:

> It was reported to the fiscal that slaves were imported and they were subject to a duty of 10 rix dollars per head then the proprietor was at liberty to sell them. It was the custom to transfer them by endorsement on the same paper. If there was only a certificate in the Moorish language it was necessary to have the slave brought before the magistrate and that he should declare himself a slave and a new act made out. . . . The permission of the Cochin government was required but the Captain in the Company ship was supposed to check papers before boarding a slave.[97]

The extent of slavery in the Galle district is known to us from the list of signatories to the 1816 statement, although under the Galle listing are included slave proprietors from Matara, Tangalle, and Hambantota, which does not allow any analysis relating to the city of Galle. Among the signatories there was still a majority of Dutch inhabitants and Burghers in spite of the fact that in 1807–1808 many of them returned to the Netherlands or sailed back to Batavia following the Prediger mission, which was sent to the island by the Batavia authorities to pick up the remaining VOC employees.[98] The following list is an emic taxonomy that reflects the self-perception and location of individuals in ethnic categories of the period.

DUTCH INHABITANTS AND BURGHERS

E. De Ley
J. H. Brechman
P. A. De Moor

J. P. Rabinel
J. S. Augier
J. A. Wittensleger
J. Rose
J. H. Roosmalecocq
P. H. Roosmalecocq
J. Poulier
J. H. Meurling
A. V. D. Brocks
W. Aldons
D. Loret
W. Stroef
E. M. Degen
J. J. Engelbregt
J. Waltzell
H. A. Bogaars
P. Z. Andriessens
C. Hollebeek
H. Puttenaar
C. V. Houten
A. De Silva
L. H. Anthonietz[99]

CINGALESE

D. A. Dias
T. S. D. Abeysekere
Harmanus
J. D. Silva
Bacobus Jansz
Floris Jansz
N. R. Keuneman
Amelia de Meis

VELLALES

D. B. Illangakoon
D. B. Wandigediwakere
D. S. Perera

D. B. Illangakoon
G. J. Illangakoon
Don Simon Sammerewicre Kaamewickreme
Don Philippoo Bandernaike

MOOR

J. Miracando

The slave registers of 1818–1832 do not provide information on the ethnic identity of the proprietors. The ethnic categories I have used in the list are purely based on the surnames provided and are for this reason very tentative. They do show, however, a certain pattern: while the number of Dutch inhabitants as slaveholders is predictably much smaller, one sees a much larger group of local slaveholders. The names of the slaves are difficult to decipher as they were handwritten. The age of some slaves was not included. In the list below, "M" indicates male, "F" indicates female, and the number indicates the slave's age.[100]

SLAVEHOLDERS IN GALLE AND MATARA

Muslim/Moor
Ahlamon Lebbe Markar: Alalia M 39; Bebee F 48; Miran M 42; Miran M 34; Pakival F 35; Pakivoal F 35; Sinnevel F 37
Afsin Naynna Canacapully
Ismael Lebbe Markan Sultan Suybar: Palleadun
Secadi Markar Sedder Lebbe Markar: Castorie F 35
Mianagna Markar Udouna Lebbe Markar: Maira Candoe M 12; Pakeer M 30; Pakiervel F 14
Alema Nataka: Mambey F 40
Samsee Lebbe
Slema Lebbe F 4
Mira Nayna Larkar Noocana Lebben Markar: Jummabaronmoer M 30
Audoes Lebbe Sinne Lebbe Markar: Mathem Candoe M 56; Sinnevel F 45: Salem M 44
Ahamadoe Natechiea: Harithoe F 35
Mira Nayna Larkar Noocana Lebben Markar: Jummabaronmoer M 30
Audoes Lebbe Sinne Lebbe Markar: Mathem Candoe M 56; Sinnevel F 45; Salem M 44

Sinhalese
>Don Bastian Jayatilleke Attapattu, mudaliyar: Casandra F 45; Dingey F 28 and 3 children; Loesa M 27; Samelie F 44 and 5; Sinne F 40 and 1 child
>Don Abraham Dias Guard Modl: Libina F 60; Anthony M 35
>Mevan Pirknan: Afsnenna M 30
>Lem Fernando Lindo Miked Canden: Slematie F 43 and 5

Burgher
>Mr J M Anthonys: Selphia F 45
>W de Vaas: Philida F 22; Rosina F 8, Selvia F 58
>Mrs Wegen: Jesmine F 40; Malathi F 36 and 2; October M 40; Sophia F 68
>Mr van Hek: Margues M 40
>Mrs Ludivice: July M 47
>M Engelbregt
>Cannega F 35

SLAVEHOLDERS IN MATARA

Muslims/Moors
>Ibrahim Lebbe Mihideen Lebbe: Allema F 15; Coongy Umma F 37; Patchier not free—declared free by Prov. court; Handgy F 17; Rukutty F 10
>Moottokoddy Lieene Atchi Hema Lebbe Udiema Abbemar kan: Cartha F 38
>Sadhakho Lebbe Markar Segoe Abul Rasy Lebbe Markar: Calindar M 34

Sinhalese
>Henrick de Saram Mudaliyar; Andia M 14; May M 50
>Don Francisco Deza Abeywickrema Bandaranaike: Amilia otherwise called Sebela F 58 emancipated by owner; Babby F 27.7 child Catistery not free; Camba M 14.7; Callua M 20.1
>Celesteny F 21.7; Cethy F 26.7 – Sabina F, Adirizema M; Calloo 23.7—Catharina F (died) ; Cartha; F. 17.7—Juama M Wattoemaide M; Castury F 10.7; Collondy F 17.7—Saberidi F, Sancha F, Juliana F, Adirra M (emanc. by propr.); Calloo otherwise named Amma F 47.7 (emanc. by propr.)
>Dingy F 37.7—Ramassua not free; Isacua M 20.7; Jacostria M 23.7; Paatma F 25.7—Sankindy F, Sarah F, Sanchia M, Mitto F, Senkindy F; Rosina F 7.7; Sompania M 7.7; Seekka F 8.7

Don Constantin Wickremesinghe Ameresekere Mudaliyar; Babea M 25; Dinga M 38

Upon the testimonies of all the witnesses, the court was cleared and the prisoner, Lebbe, found not guilty. Signing in the "Malabar language," however, he renounced all claims on Ameensa and her daughter, who were declared forever free. With this sentence and their newly regained freedom, the rest of their lives remains unknown to us. Ameensa's appeal to the court system in British Ceylon at the precise moment she felt that her situation was no longer tolerable shows that her resistance to the status quo was motivated by something akin to moral outrage rather than a wish for freedom.[101] Clearly, notions of justice and injustice born out of societal religious and ethical values of the limits of permissibility permeated enslaved people's attempts to deal with their condition. What is evident is that participants in these struggles invoked no universal principles, which invites historians to shift the frame from one that supports the emancipation process by abolitionists, one embedded with imperial notions, to the frame inhabited by the actors involved. We need to remain sensitive to the fact that exerting one's personal choice need not be understood as an index of freedom, as it is conceived in liberal thought.

Ameensa's story points toward little-known migration patterns of subalterns between India and Sri Lanka in the early nineteenth century, a movement caused by landlessness, war, crop failure, and famines in South India that preceded the large-scale migration of labor with the opening of coffee and tea plantations in the following decades. From the turn of the century, the colonial state in Sri Lanka had made use of an immigrant workforce from South India for public works, mainly roads. Indeed, Governor Frederick North's pioneer corps in the early years of the nineteenth century consisted of Indian immigrants.[102] The proximity of the island to the subcontinent suggests a regular flow of landless agricultural laborers from India before the coffee planting years. Ameensa's story is thus unique only insofar as it has been recorded.

Louis Badgamege, Kidnapped in Kallehe

The outcome of the case of Louis Badgamege, age nine, kidnapped in Kallehe, near Galle, in 1813, tried by the Admiralty Commission in

Colombo on May 17 of that year, is closely related to the adoption of a Slave Trade Felony Act by the British Parliament in 1811. This act was passed a few years after the act abolishing the slave trade in 1807 because it was felt that the penalties under the Abolition Act were not commensurate with the crimes committed. The Abolition Act relied on a system of fines for its enforcement. The Slave Trade Felony Act, instigated in Parliament by Henry Brougham, member for Camerford, made the removal or assistance in the removal, transportation, and shipment of slaves by British subjects or in British territory a felony. The legislation also provided increased penalties of imprisonment and hard labor to between three and five years or transportation for fourteen years.[103] In terms of the number of prosecutions, however, the impact of the Admiralty court system was negligible.[104]

Vice Admiralty courts were established in various ports of the Indian Ocean from 1801, including in Colombo, Calcutta, and Bombay. More scholarly interest has focused on the mixed commissions for the suppression of the transatlantic slave trade, in particular the Sierra Leone court, as a precursor of an international human rights court, as it was composed of judges from different countries who attempted to apply international law.[105]. In Sri Lanka the Felony Act had a negligible impact, but the single slavery case brought before the Vice Admiralty court in Colombo in 1813 is interesting in its own way as a descriptor of the times. Rarely does history record the voice—even filtered—of a frightened nine-year-old child under colonial rule.

The Admiralty Commission comprised Governor Robert Brownrigg as chief commissioner and Supreme Court judge Alexander Johnston.[106] A grand jury of twenty "gentlemen" was sworn in, among them some familiar names, including Anthony Bertolacci. The twenty men were English, as it was decided that only Englishmen could perform the duty of indicting British subjects.[107] In 1813 Dutch Burghers were already sitting in juries, a measure that had been suggested by Sir Alexander Johnston in 1806 when he was Puisne justice and eventually adopted in 1810–1811 following the Return Orders and Regulations Touching the Supreme Court of Judicature in the Island of Ceylon in Pursuance of His Majesty's Charter dated August 6, 1810, and 1811. In accordance with Governor Maitland's insistence, the jury was to consist wholly of Europeans in the trials of Europeans and "persons born of European parents."[108]

The hearings were held in Colombo. The people who "were summoned from Galle" to attend them were paid a batta (a small fee in cash) to compensate their travel, and seven hundred rix dollars were required by the advocate fiscal to this effect.[109] The grand jury, after retiring to deliberate, presented several bills of indictment since more than twelve jurors were convinced that there were grounds for a trial. The six indicted (three of whom were British subjects) hailed from a variety of Indian Ocean locations: an officer of an Arab ship, who was a native of Mocha in Arabia; a Malay priest from Malacca; a lascar from the Malabar Coast; and two Muslim men, Lebbes from Galle and a Burgher from Galle. The first proceedings took place with double interpretation, in Tamil for Ahmed Cassim Patchiren, accused of having carried on board the ship *Johan Banny* in the harbor of Galle the child Louis Badgamege, and in Dutch for the jurors of the "petit jury," who were all "Dutch gentlemen of Colombo."[110]

The vessel was sailing from Malacca through Bengal and was bound to Mocha, an important slave market.[111] For dhows sailing the Indian Ocean, it was a common practice to collect a few slaves bought by sailors or fishermen and trade them in markets at Mocha or other Indian Ocean ports such as Zanzibar. These slaves could be sold for work on coffee plantations or as household servants, dockhands, tailors, pearl divers, or soldiers in the Persian Gulf or, from then on, sold to merchants who might take them to Arabia or Bombay.[112] In southern Sri Lanka it was a time of scarcity. The father of Louis, called Simon, living in Kallehe near Galle, had sent his son to the bazaar to buy "tobacco, salt and fish with one fanam and a half." En route Louis was enticed by a man who offered him cakes and sugar, locked him up, and promised to take him to a ship where he would be fed with rice and sugar and then brought back home. Instead, the child was clad in a "Muslim costume" and kept below deck. His father searched for him for three weeks, traveling from Galle to Matara and Colombo. The child in his "Mussulman dress," described as "trousers and a muslim cap," was spotted on the ship by a fisherman, Omoor Lebbe Lakkier Tamby, a neighbor of Simon, who upon the request of the child informed his father. Simon called on the collector, Mr. Hooper, for help; Don Abraham, an *arachchi* (headman), and two *lascarins* (soldiers) were sent to the boat with Simon and rescued him. Hooper then went on board himself to verify the information that other children were also captive and discovered fifteen Sinhalese children, "many of them concealed under fire wood and cables" and all except two clad in "Mussulman dress."[113] The defense put forward the argument that abduction was in fact an act of compassion toward starving children whom they intended to send back ashore before departure.

The witnesses hailed from a variety of communities. The man who saw the boy on the ship was himself a Muslim. His testimony showed his solidarity with the father, whom he accompanied when the boat was searched. Don Abraham, the arachchi of the collector of Galle, was also present during the search and provided matter-of-fact testimony, unlike the emotional neighbor, who mentioned that the boy pointed to the accused and said he had received ten rix dollars from the captain for providing him. Don Abraham, on the other hand, said he heard nothing of any money exchange.

The testimony of the boy is illuminating in many ways. We learn that Ahmed Cassim Patchiren was a frequent visitor to his home and that he enticed him with the promise of "a great quantity of biscuits, rice and jaggery." Louis saw the owner of the ship, whom he calls Moyedeen, giving the prisoner ten rix dollars. The boy had then boldly asked the reason for this transaction, thus showing his lack of fear and grasp of the situation in which he had fallen. He clearly understood that he had been "purchased by a lascar belonging to the ship." Tamil was spoken between the prisoner and the owner, a language the boy did not comprehend. Louis knew he was sold into slavery, but his imagination created other fears of the unknown: "I understood I was to be carried to the country which the ship was going, which was inhabited by giants and cannibals." He noticed that he was the only boy who was not allowed to go onshore and deduced that in his case there was a risk that someone would recognize him. He continued describing his change of identity: "I wore a particular dress: I fancied by putting it on that I was to change my religion: I do not know what religion I was to assume. The people onboard told me that we had become their slaves and then we must profess the religion which their slaves professed. A Cingalese lascar onboard told us we were to be slaves and no longer to be Cingalese."[114]

Louis understood parts of the conversation between the accused and Moyedeen. They spoke, he said, in "Maurs," and some words were "Hamien Jaga Ranera Jaga," which he thought meant that he was not to get much rice. The child had asked Ahmed Cassim Patchiren to take him back onshore. We learn that the prisoner might have had a pang of guilt, as he had tried to take the child onshore, even offering to give the money back to his buyer. What were then his intentions? But Moyedeen was adamant about keeping the boy.

Simon confirmed that Ahmed Cassim Patchiren was in the habit of coming to his house with another Moor "to buy jackfruit, and other things of that sort, as there was a great scarcity of food." The fact that Simon suspected that someone had stolen and sold his child suggests that this was a common occurrence. He had then made secret inquiries so as not to give prewarning to the parties involved. Ahmed Cassim Patchiren, who gave his version of the story of the boy willingly following him and wanting to remain on the ship, was found guilty.

On May 18 the trial of Jacob Pieters, "a Portuguese Taylor" indicted for carrying away two of the boys found on the ship and sending them into slavery, took place in Colombo. One of the boys, Appuhamy, related how he and his brother Babay had gone to meet their older brother Andries to get some food—rice and maldive fish—when they were accosted by the prisoner. Pieters had offered to employ them to carry toddy for three rix dollars a month. For three days they were kept in his house, fed, and given toddy, before being taken to a ship. There they were left in the charge of a man called Maline, from whom Pieters had received five rupees. The accused, Pieters, was found guilty on both indictments.[115]

Ephemeral moments in the lives of Valentine, Clara, Selestina, Ameensa, and Louis snatched from an archive of violence open a rare window into a hidden world and what it meant to live as a colonized and enslaved person in a port city such as Colombo or Galle in the early nineteenth century. They offer a counterpoint to sterile state narratives replete with edicts and figures. These individuals, when confronted with situations that took them to police stations and law courts, encountered collectors and magistrates who were probably also slaveholders, as well as Burghers, Sinhalese, Malabars, Moors, Toepasses, males, and females, a collection of people who harbored many identities that overlapped and relentlessly combined, thus challenging the uniformity of "being" that is so sharply inscribed in colonial official documents. From the acts of resistance performed by our protagonists, ideas and practices of race, sexuality, equality, justice, freedom, or rights were similarly differentiated in the realms of labor and home. Reading the acts of the runaway Valentine and the enslaved Ameensa, Louis, and Selestina does not allow much more than speculation on what motivated their individual struggles. Louis's story provides a counternarrative to the common descriptions—especially in European travel accounts—of desperate natives selling their children at times of great scarcity, revealing the actions of a grieving and loving parent, searching for his child and succeeding in liberating him from the clutches of slave traders.

How was freedom conceived in the minds of the enslaved? What were the limits of the permissible for an enslaved violated woman? On what terms, on what turf did they resist? Was a yearning for freedom the trigger or something else? Owing to the difficulty in culling such stories, few historians have tried to unearth singular struggles of enslaved people, more frequently turning their attention to collective attempts at flight or resistance. These are read as a move from unfreedom to freedom, something out of the ordinary for scholars of both Southeast and South Asia who highlight the prevalence of bondage as the norm in the societies in which the enslaved lived.[116] The unfreedom-to-freedom continuum as an analytical device is perhaps not the most suitable to think with. It encapsulates a liberal vision of an ideal society where freedom is conceived as autonomy and a lack of social bonds and assumes that people in non-Western societies accustomed to bondage were not generally susceptible to aspire to freedom in the liberal sense. It also ignores the possibility that an individual could display a unique form of agency motivated not by a dream of freedom but by a perception of being unjustly or unfairly treated. What the fragments of the lives of these individuals gesture toward is the need to turn to the particular if one wants to grasp the complex nature of being colonized and enslaved in the Indian Ocean world.[117]

CHAPTER III

Slave in a Palanquin

Jaffna in the Early Nineteenth Century

I presume that you have a large number of dead serfs whose names have not been removed from the revision list.
NIKOLAI GOGOL[1]

Tout pouvoir, y compris celui du droit se trace d'abord sur le dos des sujets.
MICHEL DE CERTEAU[2]

In 1819 a Coviyar slave named Cander Wayreven was whipped under orders of the collector of Jaffna, the highest British official in the area, for traveling in the palanquin of his master, thus going against what was conceived as the prevailing law and allegedly overstepping his position and status. Interestingly, this punishment was immediately contested as illegal by the Supreme Court sitting in Colombo. Prudence, however, was in order. Exposing evidence of human injustice and an act of cruelty was never at stake. The epistolary debate among collector, governor, and Supreme Court judges revolved solely around the just interpretation of the law rather than around issues of morality or right and wrong. While these legal luminaries purported to represent and uphold the sanctity of their own reading of the law, they did not question the violence of the law against colonial subjects or the rooting of the moral project of law in the everyday violence of caste and social hierarchies.[3]

This event is a window into the governmentalizing form of colonialism of the period, when the main aim of British rule was to consolidate its grip on the island and devise strategies to police its new subjects. Wayreven's punishment brings to light the corporality of colonial power, evidenced in the need to leave enduring scars on the back of a young man for a crime that today would seem incomprehensible. It also illustrates the complicity of certain colonial officials with the local dominant groups, whose power over slaves and others rested on "age-old" customs. It finally reveals that in spite of the ambivalence displayed by British officials in Sri Lanka to defend and uphold antislavery and proabolition policies initiated in the metropole since the beginning of the nineteenth century and endorsed by a few liberal colonial officers, small spaces of resistance were opening in Jaffna society in many different and unusual ways. A bold young man riding the palanquin of his master, fearless of the whip; a family of slaves wearing jewels and standing proudly in front of the Nallur temple, where they were prohibited from entering owing to their status; female slaves taking their masters to court for failing to register their children's birth and freeing them under the Act of 1818; and men like the Nalavar slave Minjen fleeing Jaffna to take refuge in the Vanni in order to join the rebel Pandaram Wanni were all events that occurred in response to a muted message of freedom that was slowly reaching even the least fortunate people of Jaffna. This awareness of British liberalism's rejection of slavery gave enslaved peoples the psychological thrust to act. People's dreams of justice were clearly caught up in the law. The regime of compensation to slaveholders that was put in place with the Act of 1821 and the manner in which this act was put into practice are a fascinating and until now an unwritten chapter in Sri Lanka's encounter with British colonial liberalism. However, the way in which the law reworked normative worlds and imaginations of justice is less our concern than the effects of abolition acts on people's lives, desires, practices, and actions.

A Place in Time

The Jaffna peninsula is mostly surrounded by the sea and connected to the rest of the landmass by a small strip of land. A string of islands pepper the waters of the Palk Straits reaching out toward India. This location permits the peninsula to rule the waterway between the eastern and western coasts of India. The vital force of the sea that Fernand Braudel described when referring to the Mediterranean drew "into its orbit all regions that look seawards" and gave the region its particular coherence.[4] Its history is one of a coastal region that looked seaward for its commerce and trade and attracted people from overseas as diverse as merchants, priests, travelers, corsairs, fishers, conquerors, and slaves. Borrowing from the words of J. C. Heesterman, however, it was not a frontier zone that separated and enclosed the Jaffna peninsula but rather its "permeability" that allowed it to develop in this particular manner, sometimes flourishing owing to a thriving maritime and commercial activity driven by the annual monsoon winds and other times falling into decline, as during a destructive Portuguese rule.[5] Europeans, defined Jaffna by the sea, as were the two other maritime provinces, Colombo and Galle, that were conquered between the sixteenth and eighteenth centuries. Unlike these two maritime areas, which were peopled essentially by Sinhalese, Jaffna was recognizably the land of Tamil or, as they were called then, Malabar people, in the same way as people of the southern coasts in the Indian subcontinent.

Across the sea was India and the Coromandel Coast, the root of the word itself being from a corruption of "Cholomandalam," a region that was part of the Chola Empire. It encompassed more specifically the eastern coastline that stretched from Point Calimere in the south to Ganjam in the north, dotted with significant ports such as Bimlipattinam, Masulipattinam, Armagon (where the British established a factory in the 1620s), Pulicat (under Dutch control), and Fort St. George, or Madraspattinam.[6]

James Cordiner's *Description of Ceylon* (1807) refers to the garrison town of Jaffna and its surroundings as "fruitful" and benefiting from "a regular trade with the opposite coast of India." The country around Jaffnapatam, he wrote, "is flat, the scenery rich and the rides delightful. Fields of waving green, enriched with luxuriant groves, and enlivened by purity of air.... The soil is fertile and the constant verdure allays the heat."[7] Emerson Tennent, who was colonial secretary of Ceylon from 1845 to 1850, described the scenery of the peninsula: "The sand, which covers a vast extent of the peninsula of Jaffna, and in which the coconut and Palmyra palm grow freely, has been carried by the currents from the coast of India . . . and thence washed on shore by the ripple, and distributed by the wind." He further admired the arable soil, which was endowed with "a deep red colour, from the admixture of iron," and signals the fertility of the land: due to the "lime from the comminuted coral, it is susceptible of the highest cultivation, and produces crops of great luxuriance."[8]

The Vanni

Jaffnapatam, as it was called by the Dutch, covered the entire peninsula up to Trincomalee in the East and the island of Mannar in the West (fig. 3.1). To the south was the large province of Vanni, a flat land of dense jungles,

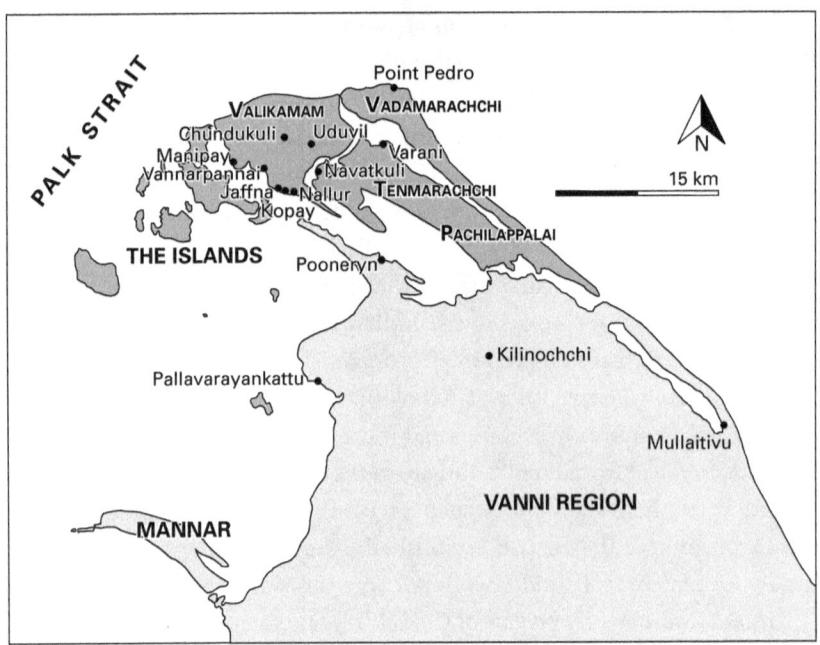

Figure 3.1 Jaffna and Vanni

small rivers, and lagoons, which under the British was composed of the district of Vavuniya and part of Mullaitivu. Colonial officials marveled over the scenery of the Vanni, and J. P. Lewis referred to the way "the atmosphere seems to dance and sky and water to merge into one in the far distance."[9] The area was ruled by semi-independent chieftains called Vanniyars. These chieftaincies, located between the kingdoms of Jaffna and Kotte, emerged in the fourteenth century as a result of the collapse of the Polonnaruwa kingdom.[10] Under the Dutch, the local chiefs were nominally subordinated to the commandment of Jaffna and required to pay a yearly tribute of forty elephants to the company. Yet they were autonomous in many ways, and as the eighteenth century came to a close, obligations to pay the Dutch their tribute became less enforceable. After rebellions and punitive actions, the Vanni provinces were forcefully conquered by Lieutenant Thomas Nagel, to whom the colonial government leased the district for five years.[11] The Vanni was very much a frontier region where escapees could lose themselves in the forests, but it was also the victim of raids by rival kingdoms in the north and south.

If a Palanquin Could Speak

The Archaeological Museum in Nallur, a small building nestled behind the Arumugam Navalar cultural hall in Jaffna, displays side by side two nineteenth-century palanquins. One of them is described as "An Ancient Ladies Palanquin" made of wood and dated ca. 1820 (fig. 3.2). The caption says it was used by Mapana Mudaliyar in Atchuvely, Jaffna, and donated by his grandson Thikkam Selliah in 1948. Mapana Mudaliyar and his descendants were from early eighteenth-century Dutch rule in Jaffna, the main administrators of the Kandasamy temple in Nallur. I realized with some trepidation during a visit to Jaffna in July 2018 that the palanquin in the museum belonged to the same mudaliyar who was at the center of the palanquin controversy examined in this chapter. Was it the same ladies' palanquin or a similar one, also belonging to the mudaliyar, in which a young Coviyar slave had traveled in 1819, causing a furor among Vellalars and unease among jurists?

If a palanquin could speak, it would give a testimony of the violence perpetrated against unfree people, the challenge posed to injustice, and the ethical compromises of the new rulers, upholding values of liberalism yet eager to maintain a status quo and avoid "disturbances." As Talal Asad

Figure 3.2 Palanquin ca. 1820 (Jaffna Archaeological Museum with permission from the Department of Archaeology, Sri Lanka, copyright Abhijit Wickramasinghe)

brilliantly points out, a symbol is "a set of relationships between objects or events uniquely brought together as complexes or as concepts, having at once an intellectual, instrumental, and emotional significance."[12] The slave/palanquin nexus of hierarchy and inequality of status is unique as something that facilitated symbolic action. In other contexts the actual size of the palanquin also mattered to establish one's privilege to a certain honor or disdain. In princely Mysore, gurus, heads of religious institutions called Mathas, traveled in an *adda palaki* (cross-palanquin), which had an axle that was horizontal and long, compared to the axle of an ordinary palanquin, which was shorter and parallel to the street.[13] The slave in the palanquin episode illustrates the way things "recruited" a person into politics as much as a person recruited things in an intertwining with users.[14]

This case of a palanquin and a slave may seem trivial at first, an epiphenomenon in the scheme of events of the century. For the historian, however, this episode allowed colonial archiving to happen and valuable testimonies of all the parties concerned—slave, slaveholder, collector, judge, governor—to be recorded and give hints to future researchers on how to reconstruct the ambiguous power relations and politics that shaped those decades. Yet there are many things that cannot be known, as we lack accounts by enslaved persons about their feelings and emotions at the moment they became free. We have only a sense of the monetary cost of freedom, something measurable since what was paid for freeing an enslaved person as well as the sum of money received by a free person for labor performed after liberty have been recorded. An understanding of a slice of a person's life when the cusp of freedom was grasped can only come through examining what enslaved people did, how they acted, and how they performed, keeping in mind that the description of their acts come to us sifted through the words of the dominant men of the time.

Castes as Slaves

Many of the early ethnographies on social stratification in Jaffna dating from the 1960s and 1970s show the resilience of a system based on purity and pollution, where the Vellalars, the dominant landowners, employed a number of castes to service their various needs.[15] There were, however, important differences between the degree of attachment between caste groups in predominantly agricultural villages, on the one hand, and in artisan and fishing villages, where people had nonbound intercaste relationships, on the other.[16] According to Prashant Kuganathan, all people on the Jaffna peninsula, not only Vellalars, lived their everyday lives "through the lens of what they perceived to be clean and unclean."[17] Being a Vellalar acquired much prestige over time, as illustrated by the increase of the Vellalar caste designation as 37 percent of the population of Jaffna in the early nineteenth century to over 50 percent today.[18] Over time, people belonging to other castes were incorporated into the operative caste system of the Vellalars in a fashion similar to the process that has been explored with relation to the Goyigama caste, the dominant caste in the Sinhalese areas. There Brahmin migrants were assimilated into the Goyigama caste, with some placed in its aristocratic segment while others converted to Sinhalese-speaking priests.[19] Ethnographies of the Jaffna peninsula indicate that castes that served the Vellalars were divided into the *kutimai* (service) castes, similar to the "right-side castes" of South India, who could not be bought or sold but had to perform various ritual and secular occupations, and the *atimai* (bonded) castes. Early scholarship on agrarian bondage in South India has revealed the variety in the forms of agrestic slavery and how widespread it was in the early nineteenth century.[20] But while the presumed specificity and uniqueness of a "South Asian slavery" has been critically examined, less so the specificity of the Sri Lankan case, where local forms of bondage entangled with Dutch Indian Ocean slavery were dismantled by British regulations on abolition.[21] Indeed, during Dutch rule, by sanctioning and tapping into a perceived local practice of slavery, colonial rulers constructed and legally constituted Chiandos, Coviyar, Nalavar, and Pallar castes as "slave castes." The reconfiguration of these caste groups as slaves was done through legal codification, administrative empowerment of local Vellalar elites, and litigation practices.

Portuguese and Dutch Rule in Jaffna

For two hundred years before the arrival of the Portuguese, apart from the first half of the fifteenth century, the Jaffna peninsula had little political contact with the Sinhalese kingdoms in the south of the island. While the Portuguese had spearheaded various punitive actions from Goa against the king of Jaffna in response to his intolerance and repression of Christians in

Mannar (notably Parava fishermen), it was a decisive moment when, in 1591, the king of Jaffna was dethroned and a Portuguese nominee installed in his place.[22] Portuguese rule in Jaffna lasted forty years—from 1618, when Jaffna was annexed, to 1658—and was mainly characterized by violence perpetrated by the army and high taxation of local people. The peninsula's numerous temples and the Nallur library were razed to the ground while the population was compelled to convert to Roman Catholicism. This was often only a nominal conversion since most reverted back to Hinduism once the Portuguese were routed by the Dutch, but for the members of the fisher caste conversion had a more lasting effect.[23]

Dutch rule followed from 1658 to 1795. A firm and controlled administration was put in place that aimed less "at transforming the social system than at extracting from it as much as possible."[24] Under Dutch rule, the status of subjugated castes, especially the praedial castes Nalavar and Pallar, was defined as "slavery" in the Justinian sense, as the complete opposite of freedom. In what Alicia Schrikker describes as an "act of bold ethnographic-legal interpretation," the Dutch applied their own rigid notions to the way the Nalavars were treated by their Vellalar high-caste masters.[25] The seventeenth-century Dutch minister Baldaeus describes the Vellalars as agriculturalists in "verdant fields where grazed their cattle" and for whom worked "nasty" and "filthy" folk of inferior standing, among them the "Nallouas" (Nalavars), described as "slaves of the Bellales" (Vellalars).[26] With the Dutch presence came an intensification of labor imported from India in the first instance, and from Southeast Asia in the eighteenth century. There was also a business interest in forced labor, as the company owned enslaved people, trafficked them, and taxed the import of these people by other traders. At the same time, the VOC appropriated service labor in Jaffna just as in other parts of the country. In Jaffna, however, slavery and caste-based service labor become closely intertwined. The company identified four castes as slave castes: the Chandios, Coviyar (Covias), Nalavar (Nalluas), and Pallar (Palluas).[27]

A seventeenth-century governor's instructions regarding Jaffna provide us with some understanding of the Dutch reading of caste hierarchies and difference: "The Wellales or highest caste must be treated with more consideration than the others: these are also the most obedient. . . . The Nalewas Chewias have been slaves from remote times; they are employed as water carriers, house servants, palanquin bearers etc. . . . Labour is provided by free men of the 'Bellale and Madapally castes' one day each month for the lord of the land."[28]

When the Dutch took control of the Jaffna peninsula, they had to put down a rebellion in September 1658 led by the two other influential castes, Karayar and Madapalli, who had converted to Christianity under the Portuguese. This served the Vellalars, who emerged as loyal supporters of the Dutch, sharing with them their knowledge of the revenue-collecting machinery.[29] A distinction was made in the eighteenth century between the Nalavar and Pallar castes, essentially praedial castes, and "the new coast slaves," who were presumably employed as domestics by Vellalars and whose presence in Jaffna was more recent.

> All other services must be rendered by the Nalewas and the Pallas (Nalavars, men of the climber or toddy drawing caste and Pallars or Pallas outdoor servants of the Vellales, as Koviyas were their domestics). These are slaves of the inhabitants who do not live with their masters, but apart with their wives and children, and only have to serve them during the time of ploughing, harvest, etc. . . . The *new coast slaves* live with their masters, and are clothed and fed by them and are therefore not called upon to do any labour for the Company.[30]

Apart from castes such as the Nalavars and Pallars that served the Vellalars, other caste groups who could not be bought or sold had to perform various ritual and secular occupations. They were skilled people, such as the goldsmiths, carpenters, blacksmiths, temple carvers, coppersmiths, potters, masons, washers, barbers, and Paraiyars.[31] These castes were associated with the household of the Vellalars.[32]

The transformation of castes into slaves in the Roman sense led to "a monstrous growth of a slave-based export economy."[33] Jaffna was endowed with productive garden lands known as tottam, which were irrigated by fresh groundwater and thus independent of the vagaries of rainfall. The Dutch strategy was to develop tottam agriculture rather than rice, basing it on the labor of certain caste groups that they redefined as slaves and unfree labor imported from South India, adding to the number of slaves. Rice was imported to Jaffna, while the Dutch made large profits through the export trade of food crops and tobacco. The result was the growth of a slave-based export economy in which Jaffna produced intensively cultivated palmyra products as well as onions, gourds, chilies, turmeric, pumpkin, and eggplants, in addition to tobacco. The Dutch profited from this import-and-export trade and made no attempt to curtail the social abuses it encouraged. Although tobacco was grown in Jaffna before the arrival of the Dutch, mainly for export to India and the kingdom of Travancore in particular, peasant farmers increasingly shifted to tobacco growing since they were guaranteed good sales and advances on the crop.

Castes and the Law

The story of the Coviyar slave riding in a palanquin is closely related to the prescriptions contained in Dutch ordinances that were collected into the Jaffna Compendium in 1704 under Governor Cornelis Joan Simons (1703–1707).[34] Taxation and litigation combined with oppression were central to Dutch colonial rule, which was founded on social control and revenue extraction. Yet control could not work without a deeper understanding of the natives. There had been continuous requests by the rural court (*landraad*) for detailed knowledge of local customs. It was in this context that, in addition to the collection of ordinances, the Thesawalamai (Jaffna customary law) was drawn up by a Dutch administrator, disava Claas Isaaksz, in 1707.[35] His report, translated into Tamil, was commented on by the twelve major chiefs in the region. It acquired the status of a foundational text for the Tamil population in the British period and became the source of much controversy during the ethnic conflict in the twentieth century.[36] In Sri Lanka, as in other territories under colonial rule, Europeans gelled indigenous customary laws through close cooperation with local elites. In India, however, orientalists believed that ancient texts, the Sastras and the Koran, were the source of authentic knowledge about an age-old custom and tradition. In Jaffna, by contrast, since there was no written text, the code was the outcome of the practical knowledge gained by Isaaksz in courts in Jaffna and the insights given to him by Vellalar chiefs. The outcome was naturally a text that consolidated the dominant status of the latter. The ascent of the Vellalar during the Jaffna kingdom from the thirteenth century onward is, according to S. Arasaratnam, charted in a sixteenth-century chronicle called *Kailayamalai* (Mount Kailash), which describes their appointment as officials in the kingdom.[37] In the later colonial period their rise and consolidation as a distinct landowning community was closely related to shifts in their economic power, founded on the profitability of growing and trading in rice, tobacco, and palmyra. There were, however, a number of other landowning castes that counterbalanced the power of the Vellalars, the most notable being the Madapalli, whom the Dutch appointed as collectors of revenue and mudaliyars. In 1760, of a total of 516 mudaliyars in the four provinces of Jaffna, 317 were Vellalars and 127 Madapalli. Gradually the Vellalar caste was able to absorb into its fold a host of other castes, including the Madapallis.[38] The *Yalpana Vaipava Malai* (History of the kingdom of Jaffna), undertaken by Mayivakanan at the request of the Dutch governor in 1736, remains a valuable source on the period in spite of its lack of dates and its mythical elements. While it focuses mainly on Jaffna kings, the tale of kings is punctuated with references to the migration of different castes within Jaffna, in particular the Nalavars.[39]

The Thesawalamai code had sections dealing with inheritance, pawning, and transfer of property where explicit references are made to slaves and the slave trade. Slaves are described as transferable property that could be bought, sold, inherited, and manumitted according to the will of the slaveholder. In a single section, usufruct of cows, sheep, and slave women is dealt with, confirming a chattel-like feature of slavery. The legal position of slaves in Jaffna society was more ambiguous though, as demonstrated by the separate section devoted to the legal rights and obligations of slaves.[40] Here the Thesawalamai code identified four slave castes—Coviyar, Chiandos, Pallar, and Nalavar—under the category of slaves of Jaffnapatam, with each holding different historic foundations, rights, and obligations.

The first paragraph of the slavery section in the Thesawalamai explains how the Dutch appropriated service labor: the company would by custom be entitled to one out of five or six children—boys and girls—born of the marriage between a Nalavar or Pallar slave owned by the company and a slave woman from the countryside. These company Nalavars and Pallars would have presumably lived in circumstances similar to those of other slaves kept by the VOC in the island. For those Nalavar and Pallar slaves who lived in the countryside, the situation would have differed. They lived separate from their proprietors and made their living from agriculture. In these circumstances, it is possible that the slaveholders did not impose a continuous demand on their labor, even though they were in control. According to the Thesawalamai, young boys could be taken out of the household to perform long-term duties for the masters, such as keeping herds.⁴¹

The end of the section in the Thesawalamai that discusses the rights and obligations of the slaves shows that the Dutch preferred to equalize the legal status of the Nalavar and Pallar to the enslaved they imported from overseas. Here the relationship of manumitted slaves and their former masters is discussed, and whereas the mudaliyars claimed the right to punish manumitted slaves if they publicly insulted their former master, the VOC stipulated that such cases were to fall under the provisions (slave code) of the Batavian Statutes.⁴²

The changes in the law in the eighteenth century reveal a process whereby the lower strata of Jaffna society became even more rigidly controlled. Anthony Mooyaart, commander of Jaffnapatam, described the power dynamics in the following manner: "Those who have the power and are held in estimation by the authorities are like birds of prey who strip their victims to the bone of everything they have and leave them hardly their toes."⁴³

In 1829, in a petition written in Tamil and translated into English, a widow in Jaffna called Amarapati and her sister Cetupati wrote to commissioners Colebrooke and Cameron to complain that their two slaves, named Kattai petti and Tampiyan, were usurped by an adigar of Karaveddi. The petition is not unusual in its nature, as it calls on the commissioners to check in the Dutch tombos for the true owners of the slaves in question. This, however, is a rare case when the petition in Tamil is also available, which allows us to see that the English translation is more a summary than a word-for-word translation. What is interesting is the language used to describe the "slaves" in the original Tamil petition. The Tamil used by their master was "Parai Siraik Kudi" in Tamil, which means Paraiya and other Kudi (chattel) who are confined in a "Sirai" (prison) or compound. When compared with the English version, it is clear that additional words were introduced in the translation: the English version refers to Nallua slaves, while the Tamil mentions Paraiya but not Nalluas. Why was this piece of information added? The language of "transfer" present in the Tamil version of ancestral *siraik kudikal* also conveys the uncontested notion of ownership of human bodies in a manner similar to material goods. Thus it appears that notions of ownership of human bodies as property that were present in Simons's code had by the nineteenth century been truly absorbed and naturalized by Jaffna Vellalars and had superseded earlier ties that existed between bonded laborer and landowner based on dependence and attachment.[44]

Much Ado About a Palanquin or Andol: Law and Justice

In Colonial Office documents preserved in the National Archives at Kew, a singular event that took place in 1819 is reported in the following manner. An individual named Cander Wayreven, described as "of the covia caste," was apprehended by Cadirgamar Mylen Bellale (Vellalar) and the police *vidane* of Nallur for using a palanquin.[45] The documents report the statement of Cander Wayreven, who alleged that he was sent by Mapana Mudaliyar with a palanquin—presumably carried by palanquin bearers—to Malluviel village for the purpose of bringing a sister-in-law of Mapana, but "finding himself unwell he was induced to get into the palanquin." Even if the translation has muted their edge, these were defiant, insolent, perhaps willingly mischievous words of a young man who knew what would attend him. Cadirgamar refutes Wayreven's claim, stating that "this covia had no appearance of being unwell that he started from his master's house in the palanquin and had gone some distance in it before he stopped him."[46] This episode signals a disquiet affecting the very foundation of Jaffna society. A Coviyar, during Dutch rule, was forbidden from traveling in a palanquin. Wayreven's act was a rebellion of a sort that spelled a complete rejection of the status quo. There were similar caste disputes over honors and ceremonial symbols such as umbrellas, horses, spears, and drums in early colonial port cities in Southeast India.[47] The palanquin case was not a singular or uncommon event, as other incidents of contestation by caste groups described and categorized as slaves appear in the archive during the early decades of the nineteenth century. Jaffna society appears to be, then, the theater of generalized caste unrest created by the arrival of the British, a new colonial power in the land, and the often contradictory measures taken to address the hierarchical social system among the Tamils of Jaffna. Until the early nineteenth century what was perceived as custom "from times immemorial" had been sanctioned by the Dutch and encouraged by the ruling Vellalar elites. In the case of the palanquin, British jurists in their newly conquered crown colony of Ceylon were faced with a dilemma of a sort regarding the applicability of the code of former Dutch governor Cornelis Joan Simons to the inhabitants of Jaffna in the north of the island.

The magistrate's court declared that Wayreven should be punished with eighteen lashes and further committed to hard labor for a period of fourteen days. W. H. Hooper, the same man we encountered in the previous chapter as collector of Galle, in the hope of proving the validity of his judgment and the acceptability of the punishment meted out to Wayreven, put forward the statement by a number of Vellalar mudaliyars written on ola leaf as evidence that it was the prerogative of Dutch officials in the eighteenth century to grant a license to mudaliyars of Vellalar caste to use palanquins, and that the entire procedure was described in the license in great detail. The details included the type of palanquin, sometimes described as a "crooked palanquin," the number of Coviyars who would carry the palanquin, which varied from six to twelve, the permission to use elephants, and the attendance of tom-tom beaters, kachcheri arachchis with peons, and flags.[48]

There was, however, much dissension within the administration of the colony. One argument by Lusignan, deputy to the governor, in favor of hard labor rather than flogging was based on clause 51 of Governor Simons's code: "No native officers nor individuals shall be entitled to be carried in andols/palanquins through the country or the fort much less to take any coolies from the country for that purpose except those who are authorised by the successor of governors and Commodores on the pain of being out to hard labour for the period of six months and such persons as may procure coolies for the service of those unauthorized to employ them shall also incur the said punishment."[49] The commissioner of revenue, on the other hand, offered arguments in favor of the Jaffna collector's decision to inflict flogging on the Coviyar slave as punishment. First he invoked "the custom that has in this respect notoriously prevailed in Ceylon" as sufficient to warrant the punishment inflicted. Second, he warned that the decision of the Supreme Court that the use of a palanquin was common to everyone might lead to "breach of the peace" and be "productive of very serious disturbances."[50] Clearly, the British saw the maintenance of presumed customs based on hierarchies as a safety valve against any potential antisocial act perpetrated by dominated people.

When confronted with these arguments, Chief Justice Harding Giffard and Judge Henry Byrnes responded with some degree of irritation, finding flaws in two areas of the arguments made by the governor and his supporters. The first related to their doubt whether the cited regulation, Simons's Code, was still in force in Jaffna, and the second related to the punishment of whipping that was pronounced by the collector of Jaffna and that was, in their view, "'wholly unsupported even by the document now produced."[51] Indeed, the judges pointed out that the Regulation of 1706 mentioned a punishment of six months of hard labor rather than whipping. The Supreme Court was then composed of two officials who had some degree of independence vis-à-vis the governor since they were appointed directly by the Crown.[52] They could take a dissenting position, as in the case of the palanquin under scrutiny.

There was no anxiety or change in sensibilities among members of the judiciary as far as whipping and flogging were concerned. Indeed, tattooing, branding, and flogging of slaves, criminals, and prisoners were age-old practices in Europe aimed at stigmatizing and identifying marginalized groups and "criminal classes."[53] In British India and Burma, the name, crime, date, and court were branded on the forehead of certain classes of offenders to enable easier identification. British ideas about punishment were enmeshed with what was seen as local practices and spawned penal interventions that were in many ways unique to the Indian subcontinent.[54]

The case of Sri Lanka was somewhat different, as the British inherited a land that had been colonized and disciplined by a Dutch Calvinist understanding of crime and punishment. Significantly, the Ceylon governor's proclamation of September 23, 1799, abolished torture and what was referred to as "barbarous modes of punishment," such as breaking on the wheel and mutilation, which were commonly practiced under Dutch rule.[55] Legal punishments were severe in Europe at the time, but by the end of the eighteenth century they were most often practiced after the *coup de grace*.[56] The colonized and enslaved body was subject to a high level of torture and pain much longer than for citizens in the metropole.[57] John Rogers contends, however, that early British courts did not abandon the practice of "branding, the pillory, banishment, and the confiscation of property" together with sanctions of fine, imprisonment, and whipping.[58]

A list of prisoners accused of selling free persons as slaves (fig. 3.3) provides us with some insights into the type of punishment that was handed out for various infringements of the law. In the first case listed, two of the prisoners guilty of stealing a "Vellale boy" were sentenced to receiving 101 lashes and imprisonment for two years, and in the second case the

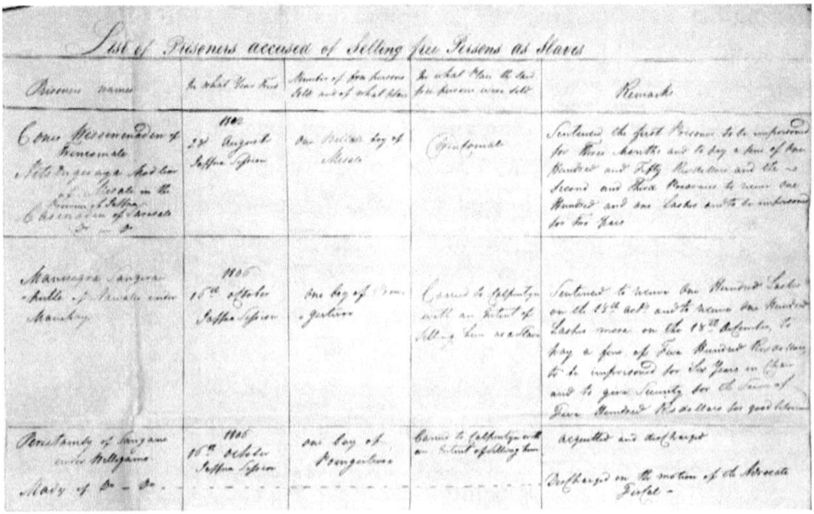

List of Prisoners accused of Selling free Persons as Slaves

Figure 3.3 List of prisoners accused of selling free persons as slaves (SLNA Lot 25.1/19 with permission of Sri Lanka National Archives)

prisoner, seemingly guilty of the same misdemeanor, got a very severe sentence: 100 lashes on two occasions, a fine of 500 rix dollars, and imprisonment for five years.[59] Flogging slaves and prisoners was a common practice in British colonies as well as penal settlements such as the Moreton Bay Penal Settlement in Southeast Queensland, where it was not uncommon to sentence convicts to up to 200 or 300 lashes, but more common sentences averaged 45 lashes for offences such as disobedience or absconding from work.[60]

The process of colonizing the body was found "across a whole range of interlocking colonial discourses, sites and practices: from penology to anthropology, from the army to the plantation and the factory."[61] The outcome of the case was the quashing by the Supreme Court of the "illegal proceeding" of the collector who had ordered the flogging of a man traveling in a palanquin. The governor eventually had the last word when he passed Legislative Act 2 of 1821 that aimed at defining the meaning of the world *andol*—a type of litter similar to the palanquin but without a tent and with a straight pole—and at giving magistrates discretionary power to inflict corporal punishment, instead of a fine and imprisonment, on slaves who were convicted of misdemeanors, thus complying with the wishes of slaveholders, for whom imprisonment of their labor force was a huge impediment.⁶² The legal wranglings, however, are of as much interest as the manner in which this episode illustrates the social tensions wreathing Jaffna in the early nineteenth century. The timing of Wayreven's individual revolt in 1819 was not accidental; it happened precisely at the moment abolition acts were being put into application in Jaffna and the edifice of slavery was beginning to erode.

Abolitions Acts and Compensation in Jaffna: Negotiating Registration

The early nineteenth-century context was an enabling one where even the least literate people were increasingly aware that the institution of slavery as it existed during Dutch rule was being dismantled by the abolition laws passed a year before the palanquin incident. This process of gradual abolition of slavery started in the early nineteenth century when the British conquered the provinces in Sri Lanka that were then under VOC rule, including Jaffna. Frederick North brought about a number of reforms in 1799–1800, the most important being that slaves who had belonged to the VOC were set free, and the import and export of slaves was forbidden. This was very early compared to other British colonies. For slaves who were not owned by the VOC, other measures were passed that included forbidding the purchase of slaves (children) during famine. Slaves could not be ill-treated by masters, and if they were they would be set free. These regulations would have created a feeling among slaves that the end of slavery was near since the government had to issue a warning that "any act of disobedience against the 'just authority of their masters and mistresses' or false and frivolous complaints against them would be punished severely."⁶³

The bedrock of the reforms that followed after 1806 under Governor Maitland was the creation of slave registers in all areas under British rule where slavery was still practiced. Regulation 13 of 1806, dated August 14, made it mandatory for slaveholders to register their slaves "classed under the denomination of Covias, Nalluas, and Pallas" within a period of four months on the penalty of forfeiting the title to those who were not registered. After expiry of the period another regulation, Regulation 3 of 1808, suspended the penalty of forfeiture and extended the term for another six months.⁶⁴ This was known as Maitland's registry and was quite an innovation in the newly acquired crown colonies of the empire. While the registries remain lost to historians, Supreme Court records refer to specific cases of emancipation of Nallua slaves that took place through litigation, as in the case between the "Sovereign Lord the King" as plaintiff and Supermaniam (Subramaniam) Seagen Chitty as defendant. The slaves Naatchy and eight others were declared free according to the Supreme Court decree of February 24, 1807. Freedom was bestowed so that "they and their descendants would enjoy the rights immunities and privileges of free born persons." It was also declared that their names should be "expunged" from the tombos (a type of census that registered adult persons and their services due to the VOC, on which they had been entered as slaves).[65] This regulation, like the previous one, was not complied with, as the penalty of forfeiture was never exacted. For the next ten years little progress was made. In the British Parliament, however, under the influence of William Wilberforce and other abolitionists, there arose a call for the registration of all slaves in the West Indian colonies for the avowed purpose of preventing an illicit importation that violated the Abolition Act. Yet more covertly it emanated from a concern for improving the condition of the enslaved peoples. Colonial legislatures reluctantly passed acts instituting the registration of slaves—first in Trinidad in 1812, conceived as a test case by abolitionists, and then in Jamaica, for instance, where there were six triennial registrations between 1817 and 1832. In Barbados, after quelling a slave rebellion, the Barbadian planters passed a Slave Registration Act in 1817.[66] Other colonies, such as Mauritius and the Cape of Good Hope, followed suit in making registration part of colonial law. The laws enacted in Sri Lanka were significantly different from those in British plantation colonies as they dealt with a population that was not socially alienated, that belonged to the land they worked on, and whose status had been modified from bonded labor to slave during Dutch rule. The purpose of the new regulations in Sri Lanka went beyond those of establishing an official slave census and monitoring illegal smuggling.[67]

In 1818 two new regulations (nos. 9 and 10) were passed in Sri Lanka, one effecting a complete registry of slaves in all areas of the maritime provinces and abolishing the joint tenure of slaves, this being particularly applicable to Coviyar, Nalavar, and Pallar castes in Jaffna. The other established the procedures to enable registration to be done in an effective manner. This entailed appointing commissioners in Jaffna, namely, the collector, provincial judge, sitting magistrate, and assistant collector of Jaffna, to oversee the registration process. The costs would be covered by the stamp duty on the certificates of registration. Every detail was considered, including the amount and cost of stationery—"about 40 reams of royal and 30 reams of foolscap paper"—that would be needed for the various forms and certificates to be issued.[68]

According to Regulation 9 of 1818, the prince regent accepted the voluntary emancipation of all children born of female slaves on and after August 12, 1816, whose proprietors had signed a declaration. This compromise, which entailed freeing the children but releasing them from service only once they reached the age of fourteen, was hatched by Chief Justice Sir Alexander Johnston, who encouraged slave proprietors who had been given the right to sit on juries to display their high moral values through a voluntary emancipation of the newborn children of their slaves. A phased process was always envisaged. "A sudden and total abolition of slavery," according to the Dutch gentlemen members of the juries, would indeed subject "both the proprietors and the slaves themselves to material and serious injuries."[69]

The impact of this regulation was immediate as slave proprietors were expected to register their female slaves and the children at the provincial court within three months of the regulations being issued. Furthermore, death or birth of a slave or child of a slave had to be registered by the proprietor within eight days of the event. Similarly, a newly acquired slave had to be registered. A number of forms were created for this purpose, and severe fines were stipulated for failure to register slaves. Under certain conditions, slaves who wished to be emancipated could appear before the provincial court of the district. The British kept a close watch on slaves in the same way as they did over other forms of property in their colonies as well as in Britain. Article 24 empowered the court to "by order in writing assemble five respectable persons, of whom two shall be chosen by the proprietor and two by the slave, and the last appointed by such court, and those five persons, or the major part of them, shall by a writing under their hands, recorded in court, fix a fair price to be paid by the slave to the proprietor, on payment of which . . . the said slave shall be free."[70]

Very few holders of domestic slaves in the northern province had subscribed to the Address to His Royal Highness Regent for Emancipating Children born of slaves after August 12, 1816: in Mannar, eleven Dutch inhabitants and Burghers, seventeen Chitties, and one Moorman, while in Jaffna, only nineteen Dutch and Burghers. Jaffna Vellalar proprietors were reluctant to abandon the privilege of keeping humans under bondage and saw no advantage in complying with British directives. There might have also been a certain degree of willful uncertainty among Jaffna proprietors about whether Nalavar, Pallar, and Coviyar slaves were included in the provision.[71] As far as domestic slaves in these areas were concerned, the slaveholders were exclusively Burghers and Europeans, as revealed from the names of the proprietors. The slaveholdings in 1818 varied, from one or two as in the case of Widow Tussaint or Gerret Frankena to twenty-two in the case of Widow Saalfelt.[72]

The colonial administration set about establishing an office in each district and nominating bureaucrats in charge of overseeing the application of the new procedures. According to Regulation 9 of 1818, a registry would be opened by the provincial court in each district in the maritime provinces, where proprietors of slaves were required to register the names, ages, and sex of the children of the female slaves in order to determine if the children were born before or after August 12, 1816. The time allowed for registration was three months from the date of the regulation. The colonial state would issue a stamp of six fanams[73] for each certificate issued to the person registering, who would then have to pay this amount to the colonial state (article 10). Commissioners were expected to take a weekly tour of duty while sitting singly in weekly rotation at the kachcheri (cutcherry) together with a secretary, a clerk, an interpreter, a Malabar writer, and two peons. As part of their duty, they would send a report on the first of every month with the lists of slaves from each district and other matters pending to be carried to the next monthly account.[74]

The entire process as envisaged by the colonial administration of Sri Lanka if it were applied to all districts of the maritime provinces could earn the following revenue for the government through the issue of stamp duties: 1,000 rix dollars for 2,000 domestic slaves at six fanam each, and 5,000 rix dollars for 20,000 Coviyar, Nalavar, and Pallar slaves at three fanam each.[75]

The 1818 regulation built on the notion of penalty to slaveholders that was introduced in Maitland's registry of 1806. The antecedents of the idea of penalty can be traced as far back as Thomas Cromwell's official injunction of September 5, 1538, to every parish incumbent in England and Wales to make a written record in a book of all ceremonies—christenings, marriages, and births—conducted in a parish. Failure of an official to undertake such a recording was monetarily penalized. The idea of a potential danger of tampering was visible in the injunction to keep all registers under lock.[76] But there was a singular difference. In 1818 there was clearly a desire to school slaveholders in adopting better practices through an exercise of power that was "a mode of action upon the actions of others."[77] Going much further than the simple act of forfeiture present in the regulation of 1806, the 1818 regulation provided in great detail the list of fines for omitting to register, for omission or willful misstatement, and for omitting to give notice of the birth of a child. The fines ranged from twenty rix dollars for failing to give notice of the death of a slave to two hundred rix dollars for omitting to notify of a birth. Failure to pay would lead to imprisonment and hard labor for a term not to exceed twelve months (article 11). A schoolmaster or headman neglecting to certify or withholding a certificate of registry from a proprietor would have to pay a fine of ten rix dollars (article 23). As such, the exercise of government was never simply an act of repression or of granting freedom, but fundamentally an act of intervention and production; there was an intrinsic effort to restructure, re-create and act upon the social reality by making it intelligible and thus malleable. Corporal punishment remained as traces of the old world, for crimes such as fraudulent erasure or false entries in the registers.[78]

The registers for the northern districts of the island were divided in two sorts: those for domestic slaves and those for Nalavar, Pallar, and Coviyar slaves. The latter, compiled in the 1820s, dealt with Coviyar, Nalavar, and Pallar slaves from Jaffna, Mannar, Tenmoratchie, Patchelapalla, The Islands, Trincomalee, Waddemoratchie, Walligammo, and the Vanni.[79]

The process of registration and issue of certificates of freedom entailed the production of a number of precise forms (A–H) and fourteen different types of certificates under a colonial "regime of verification."[80] The issuance of these documents was instrumental in binding people to a certain version of social reality, thus creating "paper truths" through bureaucratic documents.[81] For instance, form B was the "Return of Slaves Belonging to an Owner Who Was a Subscriber to the Address to His Royal Highness the Prince Regent, in Favour of Emancipating Children of Slaves." It listed the date; slave's name, sex, and age; how the slave was acquired (purchase, gift, bequest, or inheritance); name of children of female slaves; age and sex of children; and whether born on or after August 12, 1816. Form G included the name and caste of deceased slave, name of proprietor, date of death, and parish of original registry. Certificate no. 1 was for registration of domestic male slaves, and no. 2 was for domestic female slaves.

The slave registers listed domestic slaves in alphabetic order for province, district, and parish covered by the regulation, and separately slaves of the Coviyar, Nalavar, and Pallar castes and domestic slaves in the North, thus differentiating between the situation in the southern maritime provinces, where slavery involved domestics, and in the North, where it varied considerably between domestic and other types of labor, such as work in the gardens and fields.[82]

Regulation of 1821 and Compensation

Another regulation was passed in 1821 for the emancipation of all female slave children by purchase at their birth. With this regulation, the concept of compensation was introduced in Sri Lanka more than a decade before the Slave Compensation Act was passed in the British Parliament in 1837. The question of compensating slaveholders was debated among UK abolitionists and not endorsed by all. Thomas Clarkson, for instance, protested that men and women would receive "compensation for abstaining from iniquity."[83] The issue was that a compensation regime upheld the legitimacy of owning human beings, erasing possible readings of slavery as a mortal sin or a heinous crime. As Susan Thorne has argued regarding compensation under the 1837 act, "compensation, in short, contained abolition's implications within the amoral economy of free market capitalism."[84]

The regulation issued in 1821 is important and unique in many regards. It was designed as an "orderly bureaucratic process with published rules and regulations and governmental procedures" and further strengthened the instruments of governmentality put into place in 1818 with the slave registers, a decade before the Colebrooke-Cameron reforms. In light of the slavery reforms of the preceding decades, the reforms enacted in 1832 after the visit of the Eastern Commission of Inquiry seem less of a break in the nature of state-subject relations in colonial Ceylon than a stage in a longer continuum.[85] In 1821 W. H. Hooper, the collector of Jaffna instrumental in whipping a slave for traveling in a palanquin, was already convinced of the advantages of free labor: "we must rather imagine, that people born free and capable of acquiring, in common with their

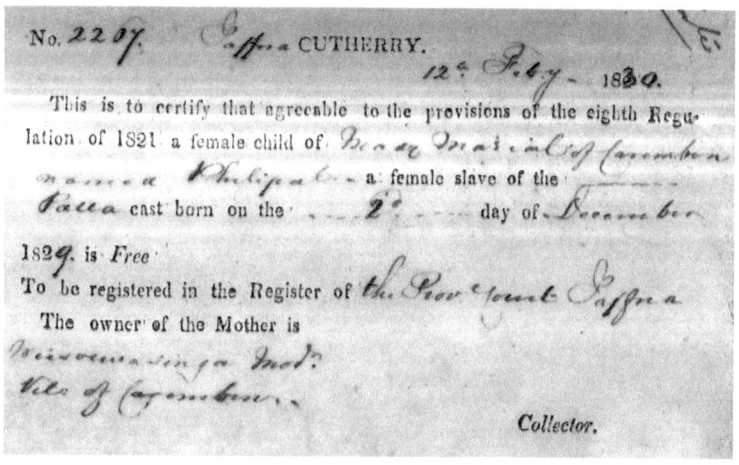

Figure 3.4 Slave certificate, Jaffna kachcheri, 1830 (SLNA Lot 10/41 with permission of Sri Lanka National Archives)

neighbours, property of all kinds, are much more likely to become an industrious and in every respect useful set of persons than when laboring under the same disabilities that the slaves of the present day do."[86]

Regulation no. 8 of 1821 improved on the Regulation of 1818 by introducing the principle of monetary compensation to the owner who willingly registered the child of a slave. The amount received from the collector by the proprietor depended on the "present value of grown-up female slaves and the chances of life." Thus if the mother was of Nalavar or Pallar caste, he would receive the sum of two rix dollars, and if the mother was of the Coviyar caste, the sum of three rix dollars. The rationale was that bodies had monetary worth according to their labor value. The fact that Coviyars were used as domestic slaves in the home might explain their higher value as compared to the Nalavar and Pallar slaves, who were employed outside as workers in the fields, tending cattle or collecting produce from trees. A certificate of freedom would be issued and given to the mother and a duplicate sent to the officer holding the registry of slaves in the district. A unique and curious deviation from the norm of compensation in place in British colonies resided in the payment of two rix dollars to the mother for every child who was registered as free. Governor Barnes estimated the full cost of paying compensation at no more than 11,000 rix dollars annually, a cost that would have to be covered with the approval of "His Majesty's Ministers."[87]

The passing of this act provided an opportunity for the colonial authorities in Colombo to clarify issues regarding the work and life of slaves and to obtain information from the collector regarding this issue. Lusignan reminded that "the number of children born who die before the age of 14 is reckoned at six in ten" and wanted to find out if emancipated slave children would be supported by their masters. He was informed that there was a custom that the slaveholder provided five fanams and a piece of cloth six cubits in length at the time of the confinement. The collector and judges in Jaffna also revealed that slaves could belong to one master and work for another landowner for their own individual interest, thus obtaining a share of the produce (paddy, coconut, tobacco) or even of the land. One doubts, however, that "'many of the slaves" were "very opulent," even if "the demand for labour" was seen as "high in the region."[88]

British records that chart the "success" of abolition procedures invariably convey quantitative rather than qualitative results of the various regulations of 1806, 1818, and 1821. Lieutenant Colebrooke thus summed up their effects purely in terms of the number of persons who were emancipated. In 1829 the number of female children who were made free under the 1821 regulation was 2,211; the number of children who had been registered as free by the signatories of the address to the prince regent in 1816 was 96. There were still 15,350 slaves in the district of Jaffna according to the population returns of 1824, and 1,000 domestic slaves mainly but not only belonging to Dutch inhabitants or their descendants.[89] In 1829 the government had purchased under this regulation 2,211 children, while 501 slaves had purchased their own freedom under the Regulation of 1818 either by labor on public works or otherwise.[90] The registration of enslaved people by their proprietors continued well into the 1830s, as testified by the continued presence of officials dedicated to registration of slaves: there was a "malabar writer" employed in the slave registry at the provincial court of Jaffna until 1833.[91] Tables of sums paid to Coviyar, Nalavar, and Pallar mothers and to the proprietors show that these regulations were actually enacted on the ground. The lists of emancipated children born of slaves further indicates that a sum was indeed disbursed to the mother of each child. The archive has a near complete record of the amount of money disbursed to mothers, as well as to officers, including the salary of clerks and Malabar writers employed in the commissioner's court and the house rent for holding sittings under Regulation 10 of 1818—a total of ten rix dollars for the month of December in the Jaffna kachcheri.[92]

Just as in other societies that had slaves, the contempt of slaveholders for registration laws was revealed through delays, fraud, and passive-aggressive attitudes. In Mauritius, the Order in Council of 1826 requiring a slave surname as well as first name in the census led to proprietors registering their slaves under absurd or demeaning names, such as Vache, Capricieuse, La Sourde, Salade, or Asperge.[93] In Trinidad, where registration of slaves took place in 1812, owners had only a month to file slave returns and pay the registration fee. The stipulation that any slave found unregistered after that time would be freed led most owners to comply.[94]

In Jaffna, some slaveholders who failed to comply with the regulation ended up in jail. Weler Taanduwen, Vellalar of Carrewilly, wrote to the Commissioners of Enquiry in 1830 begging for his release from jail, claiming old age and that, having been absent from his village, he was unaware that his Coviyar slave, Maria, had three children who needed to be registered. Upon his return to the village in 1825, as he recounts, "one Mapana mudaliyar made a complaint before the Sitting Magistrate" and the court fined him sixty rix dollars. Since he did not pay, he was sent to the jail of Point Pedro, where presumably he remained at the time of writing his petition.[95] Other slaveholders used the visit of the commissioners as an occasion to protest against what they described as the unfairness of the

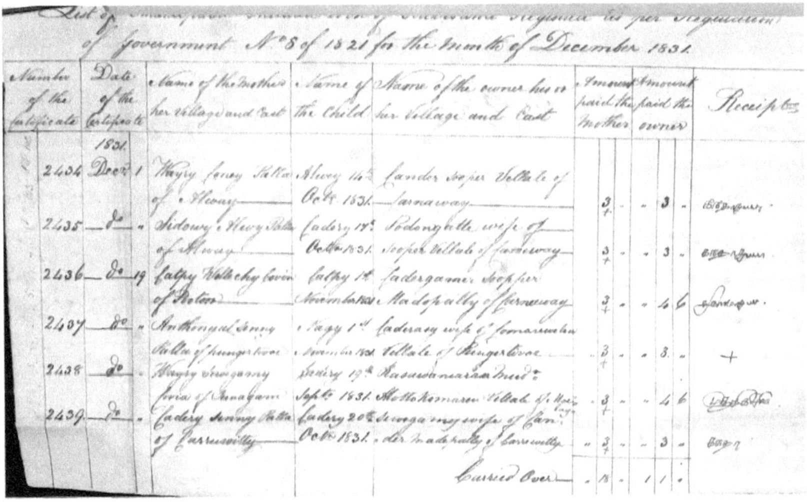

Figure 3.5 List of emancipated slaves under government regulation no. 8 of 1821 (SLNA Lot 6/974, February 3, 183, with permission of Sri Lanka National Archives)

Regulation of 1821.⁹⁶ This regulation covered only slaveholders in the northern maritime province, but on occasion a proprietor in the western province would try to obtain compensation for loss of slaves by order of the Supreme Court. Renaldus Hendricks de Ortha, a resident of Colombo, complained that the three slaves he had bought thirty years before from a Dutchman, Lieutenant Fenenkamp, had left him. The slaves, however, made a complaint in court after the promulgation of the 1821 regulation, and the court ruled against the proprietor, dismissing his documents. Hence he petitioned to get justice for his loss of property: "the 'slaves left the house," he wrote sadly.⁹⁷ But in Colombo there was no regime of compensation put in place. Other slaveholders in Jaffna sent in petitions in 1830 asking for restitution of money paid as a fine for not registering slaves in 1820 owing to ill health or young age and orphan status. One slaveholder claimed that a person who had only a share in the slave had received the entire value for registering.⁹⁸

Slaveholders or other tricksters were also quick to make use of the situation to extract money from the colonial state under the pretext of registering slaves. The sitting magistrate at Point Pedro reported: "I have the honor to inform you that I have discovered that frauds have in instances been committed by persons obtaining payment for female children under the Regulation No. 8 of 1821 whose mother's name was not inserted in any slave registry and consequently are free." He called for measures to prevent future fraud—in particular for the kachcheri to issue a certificate to proprietors certifying that the mother was actually registered.⁹⁹ Denouncing slaveholders who had failed to register the birth of children of their slaves within the stipulated eight days was also a way of earning money for zealous officers and sometimes a way of settling old scores. In the case of Savesiar Chinnatamby against Cadergamar Chieftain Bellale of Inoville, taken prisoner for a breach of clause 23 of the Regulation 9 of 1818, the motivation of Chinnatamby to appear for a Nallua of Inoville, Siduwy Nagy, was clearly not humanitarian. Clause 23 of the 1818 regulation stipulated that the fine of ten rix dollars that the proprietor would have to pay would be divided between the informant—that is, the person prosecuting— and "our Lord the King."¹⁰⁰ In her petition, Siduwy Nagy claimed that neither her ancestors nor herself were slaves to anybody, and that Cadergamar, her employer, was wrongfully trying to sell her off. The sitting magistrate, George Speldewinde, eventually ruled in favor of allowing Siduwy Nagy to purchase her freedom but stated that she needed to work for her master until such time as a certificate of slave registration was produced in court. The rest of the decisions regarding the freedom of the child born in 1829 were sent for further advice and remain unknown.[101]

The day-to-day difficulties of the registering process appeared in the letters of the commissioners and magistrates of Point Pedro, Kaits, Chavaganerry, Mullaitivu, and Mannar and the provincial courts of Jaffna and Trincomalee, who complained that they lacked sufficient stationery to regularly issue the lists of registered slaves as stipulated in Regulation 10 of 1818. They asked respectfully to be supplied with "three quires and sixteen sheets of foolscap and one ream and 14 quires of China paper."[102] The system that was put in place was quite draconian insofar as every three months a letter had to be sent from the commissioner to the deputy secretary to the governor with the number of slaves registered.[103]

The number of children of slaves emancipated as per Regulation 8 of 1821 was significantly lower in the 1830s than in the early 1820s. In September 1833 a single Coviyar mother was paid 3 pounds sterling and the proprietor 4.6 pounds sterling.[104] The accounts for October were only marginally higher: two Coviyar mothers and four Pallar mothers were paid their due.[105] The registration of slaves in the North gradually came to a halt. Yet figures in the Ceylon Almanac of 1838 still showed over 25,000 enslaved persons in the northern maritime province.[106]

Symbols and Power: The Ambivalence of Freedom

It often happened in battles around material culture—a palanquin, jewelry—the existing power structures were challenged by people at the bottom of the hierarchy. By acting in a certain way—traveling in a palanquin or wearing gold jewelry in public at the feast at the Nallur temple—they claimed for themselves honors that had until then been denied to them. While the palanquin case was a fait accompli where the harm done to Wayreven could not be undone, in the decade that followed members of less privileged groups, cognizant of the reluctance of the local authorities to go against Vellalar privilege, overrode this hurdle and sought to gain direct redress from the governor in Colombo. A petition written in 1830 to the Commission of Enquiry relates the long process and eventual defeat of a group of Nalavars trying to obtain the right for their women to wear earrings. The signatories of the petition, whose names were written by a petition writer since the petitioners were most probably illiterate and had little room for self-representation, were thus named: Poroijy Paulo, Wiryasi Morgan, Poroijy Sawery, Poroijy Santiago, Welen Nagen, Siviame Welen, Canden Sinnesen, and Perrian Canden. Their names suggest that their ancestors were converts to Catholicism during the Portuguese rule of the peninsula but had clearly reverted back to Hinduism or practiced both in congruence since they attended the feast at Nallur temple.[107]

The petition begins with an acknowledgment of the caste hierarchies prevailing in Jaffna. Vellalars were recognized as a "higher cast of people" and their people, the Nalavars, as an "inferior cast" in a discursive strategy of praise and deference that resembles what Francis Cody, using Arjun Appadurai's formulation, has in the Tamil Indian context identified as "coercive subordination."[108] But unlike the case described by Cody, where deference is performed in order to compel the receiver to bestow kindness and compassion, the petition of rights-bearing colonial subjects bypasses the Vellalar masters to reach out to the bureaucratic realm of the colonial state. The petitioners were using the formulaic and prosaic language demanded by the listening state. The issue revolved around "the females of the petitioners" wearing gold earrings and the anger this provoked among Vellalars, who, together with headmen, convinced the collector to order the women to remove them. According to the petitioners, the collector was unaware that the governor had allowed them the privilege to wear earrings and to "remit the fine imposed against them." This last point referred to the joy tax imposed by Governor North on personal jewelry ("Joys and Jewels") and promulgated on April 4, 1800. This tax had initially led people to rise against it, one of the three areas where disturbances took place in the early nineteenth century being Mannar.[109] It seems, however, that the right to be taxed was for Nalavars a right worth claiming rather than fighting for, since making such a claim incorporated them into the circle of reasonable subjects. It also gave credence to the claim that the governor had granted them permission to wear jewelry. So paradoxically, being taxed even without representation in an oppressive colonial situation was a ritual of affirmation, a way for less privileged groups to assert their individual freedom as subjects of the state through a direct relation with its representative outside the parameters of custom. While their acceptance of the social contract by paying the tax brought legitimacy to the colonial state, it also had the more socially threatening effect of leveling differences between locals, all subjected to the same regime of extraction.

The petitioners used "hatred," a strong term, to qualify the sentiment expressed against them by both Vellalars and Chitties. They also alleged that because they refused to pay twenty-five rix dollars to the police vidane who was attempting to raise money to cover a fine that the magistrate had compelled him to pay, he too "became much displeased" with them. They asserted that they had paid, as they did every year, the expenses for attending the "heathen temple of Kandaswamy," and on the night of the seventh of the previous month, the first and second petitioners, their sisters (perhaps their wives?), and their children went to watch the feast, standing at a distance on the public road. The use of the term "heathen" by the petition writer, translating his own biases vis-à-vis non-Christian religions into the text, shows that petitions were not written in a context-free, abstract language that characterizes the field of bureaucratic administration in an ideal rational Western model.[110]

Nallur is a town in the Jaffna district about three kilometers from the city of Jaffna. It was the historical capital of the old Jaffna kingdom. The temple where the events that led to violence against Nalavar people happened, whose presiding god was Murugan, was not the ancient temple long destroyed but one constructed in 1734 by Don Ragunatha Mapana Mudaliyar, *schroff* in the Dutch kachcheri and whose descendants continued to serve as administrators of the temple. The owner of Wayreven, the slave in a palanquin, belonged to this family of temple officials.

According to their rendering of the event, the petitioners were beaten and assaulted by the brother-in-law of the temple superintendent. He was assisted by a crowd of people who tore off the jewels worn by the female members of the party. The police vidane discharged one of the persons who stole the jewels while promising to restore them to the petitioners. During the attack the petitioners were stoned. But witnesses belonging to the caste of the police vidane and the superintendent accused them of assault, not only the first two petitioners but also six others who were not even present. The petitioners, as they explained in the petition, were then brought and convicted before the Supreme Court, where their witnesses who could have proved their alibi were not examined. Finally, the petition appealed to the humane consideration of the commissioners, thus attempting to establish a community of affect through accepted codes of communication.[111] The petitioners never pleaded as subordinates nor performed subordination. The entire petition was written to frame injustice performed against respectable and tax-paying colonial subjects, in the expectation of a just ruling.

Whether the petitioners obtained justice is unfortunately not known, but this episode lucidly illustrates the determination of the Nalavar people to brave the possible wrath of the police vidane by refusing his extractive demands and displaying their jewels in public, thus performing their right. It is interesting to note the continuing centrality of jewelry in the rituals of domination and subordination. Jewelry was also a way laboring women were able to represent their status and erase conditions of poverty and labor exploitation, as studio photographs of jewelry-clad Indo-Caribbean indentured women in the early twentieth-century Trinidad testify. A century earlier, before the advent of photography and commercial postcards, there were no records of the visual style of the jewels worn by the Nalavar women who stood in front of the Nallur temple.[112] Silver or gold, bracelets or chains, jewelry carried the ideology of resistance or was conceived as a challenge to the order of things. Until the 1950s, depressed castes in Jaffna, known collectively as Pachamars, were not allowed to wear jewelry.[113]

Was it because lower castes had a reputation for disorder and were perceived as unruly that the Dutch felt compelled to issue orders forbidding them to desert, carry weapons, or divest themselves of other imposed features? In 1806 the British, just as the Dutch, made hierarchies clear in an ordinance stating that "all persons of the lower castes shall show to all persons of the higher caste such marks of respect as they are by ancient customs entitled to receive."[114] In 1830 a letter from a person called Caatty Chasin Cooronader Pulle suggests that the practice of people of lower caste contributing to a "poor fund" "whenever a person from the low caste wishes to obtain that honor ('spreading white cloth at their wedding')" was no longer followed. Usurpers "without permission began to take upon themselves all the honours without distinction." Clearly, the aim of "keeping casts in peace" was not being fulfilled.[115] A Jaffna assistant government agent's report of the late nineteenth century pointed to the symbolic nature of wearing jewelry, riding in carriages, and using tom-toms for marriages and other social functions for Nalavar, Pallar, and Coviyar caste people who were getting wealthier and hence refusing to abide by old prohibitions that demarcated them from the Vellalars.[116]

Religious conversion and preaching by missionaries could also have played a role. The imbrication of caste and slavery in Jaffna bears some resemblance to "caste slavery" in Kerala, where most Dalits, mainly Pulayas, Parayas, and Kuravas, were agrestic slaves engaged in agricultural production for upper-caste landlords and temples. More than in Jaffna, though, oppressed castes in places like Travancore saw in conversion to Christianity in the mid-nineteenth century a way of reclaiming a place in the modern polity and reformulating their self-image. The role of missionaries in introducing the concept of equality among enslaved peoples appeared to be less significant in Jaffna, where enslaved individuals dealt directly and in an unmediated fashion with state institutions.[117] Furthermore some accounts of missionaries in Jaffna point to a more conservative stance by Christian preachers toward challenges to the given hierarchies. Father Roberts of the Wesleyan Methodist Church described his preaching in these terms: "Last Sunday morning I preached in Tamil at the village of Washermen. I was surprised to see a Brahmin present and in the evening I preached in the village of silversmiths and the Brahmin was again present. The people began to laugh at him and asked him: 'are you coming to be taught' but as they saw that I disapproved of their speech they desisted."[118]

Other rare sources from the 1820s describe domestic slavery in Jaffna. One of them points to a relationship between a slaveholder and an enslaved woman who worked as a domestic in a Jaffna household that is less based on fear than on a seemingly unswerving loyalty of slave to master. Her life under the patriarchal authority of a Vellalar proprietor resembled in many ways that of a domestic slave such as Selestina in the southern maritime province or of enslaved domestics in Indian port cities under East India Company rule.[119] This Coviyar slave appeared in the background in a criminal case in Jaffna involving the death of a Vellalar woman and her child in 1821.[120] Mother and child were found dead, drowned in a well close to the compound of the house. The testimony of the "maid servant" Cadery Wayrewy lucidly explains the circumstances of her missing her mistress and the infant in the morning and hence going to wake up her master. Cadery lived in the home and had been working there for the past six years. She had access to the bedrooms of her master and mistress. One senses some familiarity between the servant and the couple. She painted a rosy picture of the relationship between husband and wife, asserting that the husband, Poodetomby, never beat his wife or quarreled and that there was no strife between them the night before the death occurred. Her story differed completely from that of other witnesses. What kind of intimacy or ties of dependence existed between master and slave to warrant such loyalty? A Pallar slave also belonging to the household was sent to call the brother of the dead woman upon discovery of the drowned bodies. The brother's testimony suggested a history of domestic violence and that his sister wanted to leave her husband. Other witnesses, two travelers from Point Pedro staying overnight in the house, corroborated that the husband had abused his wife that night, calling her names and beating her. After that there had been a silence, and then sounds of people whispering while doors were shut and opened. It soon became clear that the child and mother were tied together in a cloth before drowning and that the husband was having a relationship with another woman. The case was referred to the Supreme Court by A. G. Speldewinde, and the prisoner, despite the testimony of his loyal slave, remanded to jail until further notice.

From an archive of fragments, the historian is left with an ambivalent picture of caste relations in Jaffna in the early nineteenth century, at a moment when slavery was gradually being dismantled. While there are cases that show that the refusal to accept an unjust social system gained momentum, others point to compliance. Later developments, however, may offer some insight. Writing in the 1950s, Michael Banks commented on the rebellious nature of the Pallar, who were believed to be fallen Vellalars who had suffered a loss of status due to landlessness and poverty imposed on them. "Pallas," he wrote, "always shout, even standing beside the person they are speaking to; they make no effort to look humble or smile ingratiatingly."[121]

Running Away

Unlike the rich literature on runaway slaves in places like Cape Colony, little is known of the scale of runaways from Jaffna besides an occasional mention in records pertaining to other matters. Judicial records from the 1800 onward seldom refer to runaways. There is reason to believe, however, that this phenomenon that was present and reported during the Dutch occupation of the land would have continued until the formal abolition of slavery in 1844. For enslaved people from Jaffna who occasionally ran away from the oppressive lives they were caught in—in acts of defiance against the repressive labor apparatus they had been born into—the Vanni was the obvious destination.[122] Nigel Worden has referred to a "slave geography" to qualify the areas that in the slave worldview were the ideal spaces of refuge and meeting. While in Cape Town it was Table Mountain, for the Jaffna runaway the thick forests of the Vanni and beyond them the Kandyan kingdom provided the most inviting option.[123] They belonged to this wider family of deserters insofar as they were permanently absconding from work and breaching an unwritten agreement between them and their master. In the past, running away from Jaffna was punished severely by Dutch law, as various plakaats relating to runaways clearly state. The case of the runaway Wany Minjen illustrates the experience of many others whose lives were not recorded.

In 1812 in the court of Jaffnapatnam, a prisoner named Wany Minjen was tried in the High Court of Justice in a murder case dating from 1804. The account that comes to us through the report of the judge on court cases tried in Jaffna in 1812 illustrates the typical feature of the prose of counterinsurgency: that is a primary discourse of officials who either belong to the colonial apparatus or are affiliated with it. The account of the case has a quality of immediacy and involves direct participants. Statements that Ranajit Guha describes as "from the other side," in this instance of the accused insurgent, appear only as "enclosures" to the larger truth claim.[124] The picture one gets is hence from a "distorting mirror" through which one can only seldom read subordinate intentions through the veil of official rhetoric.

Minjen was apprehended by Mr. Turnour in Mullaitivu in 1809 and acquitted but brought back before the court owing to certain circumstances that the chief justice deemed important. In his initial trial it was stated that he was born in Jaffna, was a Nalavar slave, and that "in the year 1803 or 1804 he joined a man well known by the name of 'Pandara Wannian.'" Pandara Wannian was described at the trial as "a coast man" who "came over to this country as early as 1783 as Pandaram or travelling mendicant" and who then settled in the Vanni. The character of Pandara was vilified in the account of the court, as a man who assumed a rank he was not entitled to by being carried in a palanquin, as well as ordering and judging people. Popular history remembers him, however, as he is described in J. P. Lewis's *Manual of the Vanni Districts* (1895), as "one of the dispossessed Vanni chiefs" from the northern part of the Vanni who married into a prominent southern Vanni family, the Nuwara Wewa clan. His battle against the British was fought using conventional warfare and guerilla tactics in Mannar and Trincomalee, and he earned himself the support of the Kandyan kingdom. He was successful in seizing the fort of Mullaitivu and driving the British out of the area, capturing their cannons, and spreading his power up to the Jaffna peninsula. Pandara's troops, however, were taken by surprise a few months later, and after a battle where many died and forty-three of his men were taken prisoner, the power of the Vanni chiefs was effectively destroyed. Although Pandara's death is commemorated as having happened in a battle with Lieutenant von Drieberg on October 31, 1803, when the British launched a three-pronged attack from Jaffna, Mannar, and Trincomalee, Lewis gives clear evidence from the account of Turnour that Pandara, after a period of seven years during which no overt acts were committed, began raiding villages again in May and November 1810. Lewis was probably unaware of the earlier raid of 1804 where Minjen too was involved, which led to the death of an inhabitant but where Pandara was clearly described as well and sound. In May 1810 Pandara was reported to have attacked a village a mile away from Vavuniya and a Sinhalese Tavalam (resting place) with a party consisting of "fourteen men, and their arms of one sword, four creeses, two large knives and bludgeons."[125]

The temporal referents of the report on the case are ambiguous and the descriptions loaded with animosity. Pandara, it states, was driven out of the Vanni by Turnour in 1790 and sent to Mullaitivu, from where he escaped and then took refuge in the area between the Kandyan kingdom and the British territories. The British rendering of Pandara is that of a hated man who, together with his gang of "persons of the worst description," began from 1803 to make "irruptions in the British Wanny." The military battles are not recounted but rather acts of violence and marauding committed against inhabitants. His gang allegedly attacked a village for the purpose of stealing the women but was repulsed: the description states that five Malays of his party were killed and three villagers died "defending their women." Pandara's insurgency against the British was unequivocally equated to acts of pure violence for loot and personal gain rather than motivated by any kind of anticolonial stirrings.

The account of the character and acts committed by Minjen, the Nalavar runaway slave, and his companions in 1804 comes to us through the voice of a witness from the Vanni who had been sent by Malay soldiers in the British army to a village to collect fowl and other goods. The witness recounts that he was caught in the midst of an attack. The warning came to the village that "the caffree (a deserter from Admiral Suffren's fleet) Wayreven and Minjen were coming." This led all the villagers and their families to flee into the woods. But one man (the deceased in the court case) was caught and brought back severely wounded by a sword, and the witness was caught "by the caffree and others and . . . marched on about

200 yards." There, by order of Wayreven, "the deceased's head was struck off." The witness then described the behavior of Minjen: "armed with a pike and calling out to cut and kill," thus contradicting Minjen's allegation that he had been compelled by his two companions to take part in the killing. The witness was then taken in front of the Pandara Wannian, "who threatened to cut off his nose and ears and send him in that state to the Gentlemen for having endeavoured to procure supplies for the Malays," but his life was spared and he was miraculously able to escape from confinement. Minjen, appearing in court, alleged that he was ordered by the Pandara to "join his Pallas," that the killing was done on Wayreven's orders, and that "he had no hand in and could not prevent it."

When the puisne justice summed up the evidence for the jury, he strongly argued to convict the prisoner for murder, saying that there was little evidence that Minjen was acting as a person in the service of another government such as the Kandyan kingdom but that everything pointed toward him being "a private person committing lawless depredations and cruelties upon defenseless people." The only issue that needed to be discussed was whether he was there by his own consent, as suggested by the witness, or by fear for his own life, as he tried to argue. The jury gave a verdict that went contrary to the wishes of the judge, who thought "he ought to have been convicted," but he decided not to impeach their decision as the jury system had just been introduced in the country. The judge recommended, however, that owing to the nature of the crime committed, Minjen "was a partaker"and was a "fit subject both morally and politically" for "removal to another country."[126] The life of the Nalavar runaway slave years after the case is not known, but one can surmise that he was deported to India as a measure of security and ended his existence there.

In this chapter enslaved people in Jaffna expressed their discontent with social hierarchies through a variety of transgressions. This was a period of increasing colonial governmentalization of society when everyday interaction between people and the state was expressed through processes of registration, legal codification, and petitioning, as well as individual revolt and rebellion. The fragmented bureaucratic legacy of these interactions reveals the complicity of certain colonial officials with the local dominant groups over slaves and others vested in "age-old" customs. Cander Wayreven publicly challenged the repressive customs that had been upheld

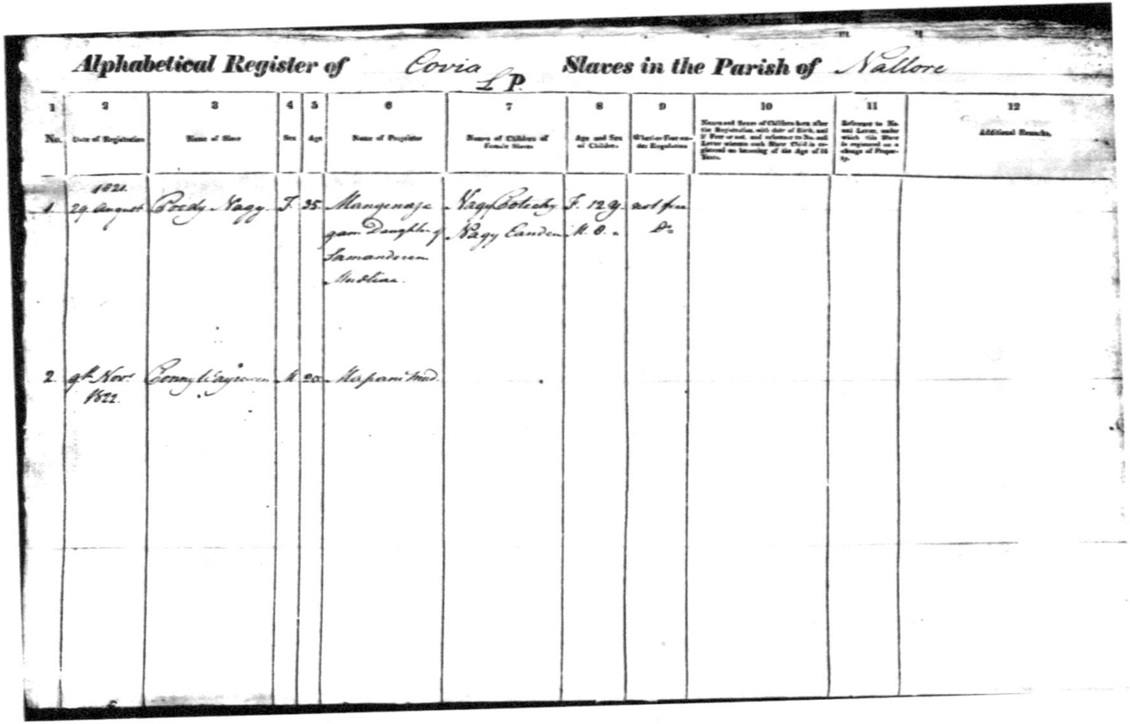

Figure 3.6 Slave register, parish of Nallore, 1818–1832 (NA UK CO T71/664, with permission of National Archives, UK)

by the Dutch and Vellalar elite for so long, only to find out that the British officials were reluctant to take a stand that might lead to disorder.

A similar phenomenon occurred in India under East Indian Company rule, where slavery was perceived as an indigenous, religiously sanctioned institution that was so closely entwined with Indian sociability and domesticity that it was considered beyond the reach of British reformers. The difference between the Jaffna and the Indian cases is that the early Dutch framing of the Nalavars, Coviyars, and Pallars as slaves in the legal sense allowed for their later registration and inclusion in an abolition process and compensation regime.[127]

This chapter shows that small spaces for personal maneuvering and resistance were opening in unusual ways. Poroijy Paulo, Wiryasi Morgan, Poroijy Sawery, Poroijy Santiago, Welen Nagen, Siviame Welen, Canden Sinnesen, and Perrian Canden petitioned for the right of their wives to wear jewelry, a right they claimed on the basis that they had paid taxes on them. Minjen chose to flee to the Vanni.

In individual cases, bureaucratization provided grounds for negotiation and resistance and the potential to take control over their individual lives. Publicly, however, registration practices confirmed the presence of slavery and hierarchy in society, and it was on such premises that the assaulters of the Nalavar women wearing jewelry to the temple acted and where freedom was publicly denied. What happened to Wayreven, the slave who rode in his master's palanquin, is difficult to fathom. All we have about him is his name in the slave register of the parish of Nallore (fig. 3.6) and a date of registration, 1822. His master remained Mapana Mudaliyar, and he was registered as a Coviyar slave.[128]

CHAPTER IV

The Chilaw "Experiment"

Labor for Freedom

The Chilaw experiment in slave emancipation that began in 1820 has gone unnoticed by historians of slavery and historians of Sri Lanka alike. This is not surprising since, as an event, it did not shatter the economy of the colony nor provoke any incidents of violence or social unrest. Yet it deserves to be inscribed on the wall of history for the part it played in the long journey of people who, through bold acts and practices, reclaimed the right to be treated as humans. It is in a sense a prelude to better-known experiments in freeing labor in the British crown colonies of Mauritius and Trinidad.[1] It displays some uncanny and striking resemblances to later labor systems of the nineteenth century commonly defined as indentured and contractual and/or free wage-based labor. This singular episode contributes to shoring up the nineteenth-century reality of labor in Sri Lanka as an uneven and irregular temporal sequencing of a variety of modes of labor organization.

The Chilaw experiment applied a seemingly simple equivalence: emancipation of enslaved people in exchange for their labor in public works. According to this scheme, which ran for over ten years, hundreds of Coviyar, Nalavar, and Pallar slaves from Jaffna whose freedom was purchased by the colonial government from their proprietors were sent over three hundred kilometers away to Chilaw in the southwestern part of the island in the early decades of British rule to perform hard labor on canals and other public works.

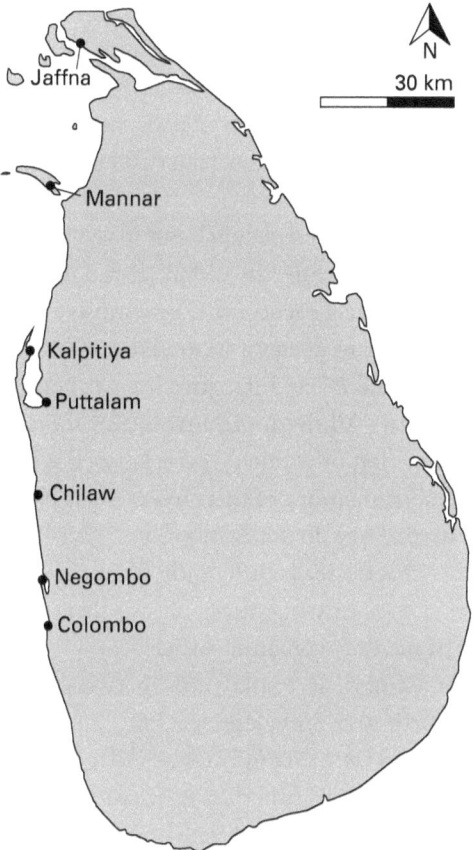

Figure 4.1 West coast of Sri Lanka

The impetus for the enslaved to work in such hostile conditions may have been the hope that their status in Jaffna's hierarchical society would change. Upon their return, they were told, they would become free subjects. This freedom, they were not told, was conceived purely in a legal sense since it would not shield them from other forms of economic duress based on landlessness and lack of capital. Later developments show that emancipated slaves became free only insofar as the constraints limiting their choice of employment were economic factors rather than coercion on mobility enforced by the state or the social environment.[2] The colonial decision to introduce this scheme of freedom for labor was motivated by the labor exigencies of the day rather than by the moral and legal reformist aims that underpinned the antislavery movement in Britain.³ While the idea that some aspects of slavery were inhuman or un-Christian was present among a few judges, most notably Justice Alexander Johnston, in the early decades of the nineteenth century, it was not until the arrival of the Colebrooke-Cameron Commission in 1829 that evidence of the ills of slavery was systemically sought out.

Traces of the lives of enslaved people loom in the bundles of correspondence between the zealous collector of Jaffna, the main protagonist, and his counterpart in the Chilaw kachcheri. These missives often take the form of a litany around a constant need for more slaves, for more or better quality rice to feed them, and of cold statistics listing their deaths, flights, or sojourns in the hospital. While the archive yields some details about the men—there is no mention of women—who labored under painful conditions, there is no public memory of their lives. Their elision from modern historiography is total. They do not exist even as "facts" or representations. For this reason this chapter reads differently from the others in this book. The individual stories are tiny fragments of lives that come to us as lives of labor rather than of men or women in society.

The district of Chilaw, a coastal area between the predominantly Tamil-speaking North and Sinhalese-speaking South, was described in the *Universal Geography* as "a comfortable village, lying between two branches of a large river. Pearl fishery was occasionally carried on here. It was a frontier area where 'the inhabitants begin to consist of Singalese instead of Malabars.'"⁴ A few years later, Simon Casie Chetty mentioned that the opening of the new canal between Chilaw and Colombo had "proved very beneficial to the inhabitants of Calpentyn (Kalpitiya) and the trade by inland navigation is rapidly advancing," and that the inhabitants of Calpentyn were "composed of Malabars, Burghers, Javanese and Moors."⁵

Sri Lanka's system of waterways dates back to the fifteenth-century reign of the king of Kotte, Parakrama Bahu VIII, when it was necessary to transport goods such as cinnamon and other spices from the interior to the bustling seaport of Negombo, where ships were anchored before sailing to China, Burma, Rome, and Greece. The Dutch had built on the older waterways and had joined several of the lagoons in the South by canals, forming an inland navigation from Puttalam to Negombo that is still navigable for small vessels. In the decades that followed, the British colonial state would engage in the work of clearing many of the canals that had been filled by sand and restoring the capacity for inland water communication that extended more than 150 miles from Kalutara to Kalpitiya. The British colonial state's concern for canals was apparent in early legislation passed to encourage people to look after the infrastructure. For instance, according to Regulation 9 of 1821 for preventing obstruction of navigation from the Grand Pass to Colombo Harbor: "Any person who is convicted of throwing any dirt, rubbish or dead animals into either of the said canals shall be liable to pay a fine not exceeding fifty rix dollars and to be imprisoned till such fine be paid."[6]

The migration of hundreds of emancipated slaves from Jaffna who lived, worked, and died in Chilaw is an absent event that has a disturbing side to it. It seems to conform to a logic that freedom was a privilege that only able-bodied men capable of hard manual work could aspire to, rather than a right shared by all. The equivalence of work and freedom as it was conceived by the colonial mind was reminiscent in some ways of an older notion of freedom as a status that only some deserving bodies would be bequeathed with. What were the moral and political assumptions that underpinned the design and implementation of a scheme that quantified freedom in terms of work hours and aptitude for labor? What, then, was the monetary value of being a free man? Of course slavery had naturalized the idea that enslaved human bodies were commodities. This notion, coupled with the spread of a free labor ideology, of which Adam Smith, in his *An Inquiry Into the Nature and Causes of the Wealth of Nations* (1776), was the most distinguished exponent, made the Chilaw experiment possible to conceive.

Since the mid-eighteenth century many British colonial thinkers believed in the rationality of a social scientific exercise that aimed at assessing whether free wage labor was comparable or superior to slave labor. In Chilaw, however, there was little to compare with the "mighty experiment" of West Indian emancipation that British policy makers conceived as a quasi-scientific experiment that, if successful, might be replicated all over the world. There the fundamental question that was put to test was whether, and under what conditions, freed people would work for wages, quite unlike the issue in Chilaw, which was borne out of a pressing need for a labor force of any sort—coolie, convict, or emancipated slaves put on a fast road to freedom.[7]

The Chilaw experiment also begs some questions about the reasons that led Coviyar, Nalavar, and Pallar people to leave their homes in Jaffna for an uncertain life of labor in a relatively distant district. Can we ever know how voluntary this choice was, and under what conditions it was made? Was the idea of freedom or justice so powerful that desire for it could empower men to act in unexpected ways, or was their life so unbearable that they signed on a blank sheet, making a decision that was devoid of self-reflection?[8]

More broadly, this forgotten episode of labor migration also has the power of unsettling some of our assumptions about the pairing of the premodern and the modern and constructed temporal divides. The accepted narrative of the coming of modernity in Sri Lanka is that it unfolded as a natural consequence of the Colebrooke-Cameron reforms of 1833. These reforms, hailed as a key moment in Sri Lanka's trajectory, are believed to have put a sudden end to what David Scott describes as the Old British Colonial System of Empire that was dependent on "the application of a mute physical force" on the bodies of dominated people. The ensuing New Colonial System of Empire supposedly brought in "techniques of subjectification, surveillance and discipline."[9] This neat pattern of social change based on an old replaced by a new reflects an unlikely Manichean situation rather than what seems to resemble much more a messy past of colonial experiments and roads half taken. There is much evidence that the Colebrooke-Cameron reforms were not, as mentioned before, such a crucial pivot. The Chilaw episode brings to light transitions, periods that complicate and mediate bondage and freedom taken in their most prosaic sense and indicate the need to examine the longer historical duration and to question a putative freedom to unfreedom continuum. We know little of the way postemancipation actors and subjects thought of coerced and free wage labor in an island that was on its way to transforming into a labor-intensive, export-oriented plantation colony. Were the emancipated slaves conscious that the freedom they gained, as Marx argued, was nothing more than a freedom to work and choose between a set of ever more oppressive employers?[10]

This chapter will show through a bricolage of the lives of labor of these emancipated slaves in Chilaw that modernity and liberal thought were ever present in the procedures informing a gradual abolition of slavery, decades before the Colebrooke-Cameron reforms. Much earlier than is generally conceived, colonial administrators as children of the Enlightenment relied on a concept of universal reason, albeit inflected by racial considerations, to devise practical responses to issues of insufficient labor for public works and the inadequate revenue generated by the new crown colony. It was precisely these liberal free market concepts that were employed to extract labor from the Coviyar, Nalavar, and Pallar slaves of Jaffna in exchange for their own freedom or that of their kin. Liberalism was clearly not purely the pursuit of an extension of individual rights.

Beyond a few petitions written by enslaved men calling for a change in their contract, their voices are absent. The historian is left with a discursively reflexive task of translation that involves filtering the occasional moments of the lives of emancipated slaves hidden in letters and reports penned by colonial administrators and reading against their representation.

Leaving Jaffna

By 1820 the colonial government was concerned that it was in dire need of labor to work on the opening of a canal in Chilaw and informed the Jaffna collector that labor from Jaffna was to be tapped and encouraged to serve the state. The first reference to this measure came in a letter dated June 6, 1820, in which the Chief Secretary's Office gave permission for "the slaves who may be emancipated at the cost of government" to be given a *seer*[11] per day in addition to their ration of rice from the moment of their departure from Jaffna.[12]

The precise reason for opening up the canal in Chilaw does not appear explicitly in the correspondence between collectors and Colombo officials. It was perhaps too obvious to even mention that the function of the canal was to create a mode of facilitating the flow of goods to and from Chilaw and Colombo, transporting in "ballams" to the Colombo market "copperah (coprah), salt fish, fish roes, dried shrimps, ghee, deers horn, in return for the Chinaware, English cloth, sugar, dates, jackwood planks, tiles, bricks, iron, lead."[13] Yet this episode in infrastructure building for trade was also aimed at bringing about improvement to the region in order to prove British advantage over their Dutch predecessors, renowned for building canals and other waterways. The Dutch had constructed a canal system that connected Negombo, Chilaw, and Puttalam lagoons, thus providing transport by water from Colombo to Kalpitiya. For the British, a relatively new colonial power in the island, work on canals and roads was endowed with a value beyond the purely economic. As environmental transformative technologies, canals and roads served political and ideological imperatives too, that of representing for colonial subjects the efficiency of the new colonial power, its ability to enlist a docile army of coolies and emancipated slaves, and their mastery of the scientific tools to transform a hostile natural environment into a triumph of what would later be called "colonial science."[14] Infrastructure development was a way of appropriating and claiming ownership of the land and stabilizing authority and power over the people. By intervening in transport and trade, the colonial state could enter and intervene in the intimate domain of everyday life, linking its project with the lives of the local people.

More directions regarding the procedures to be put in place were sent by the Colombo authorities to the collector of Jaffna in September 1820. Recruiting labor from Jaffna meant taking away men from their existing work and occupation. A monetary compensation was offered to slave proprietors to remedy the loss of labor that would inevitably affect their production units, but there was a sharp concern on the part of British officials about the reaction of the headmen toward their bonded labor earning their freedom and moving away. Less slave labor signified not only a loss in terms of manpower but also a loss of prestige and status for proprietors. British officials were aware of the mounting opposition. In a letter to the sitting magistrate of Point Pedro, the collector of Jaffna mentioned that "all others interested in retaining them [the slaves] in bondage will no doubt thwart the intention of government." The method of recruitment was uncomplicated. Unlike later forms of labor recruitment that involved, in various colonial settings, intermediaries known as *sirdars* in eastern India or *maistries* and *kanganis* in southern India, in this situation, where migration was internal and organized by the state, it was the magistrate who initially played the role of recruiter.[15] The magistrate's task as defined by the collector of Jaffna was to assemble the Nalavars and Pallars of his magistracy at different times for each caste and "earnestly explain to them that the measures now proposed are most positively to their advantage." He was also asked to appeal to their sense of duty by stressing that "their services were needed." The enslaved were not given much information about their future destination except that they would work on the canal that was being made between Negombo and Chilaw.[16] It is difficult to know if they had a sense of distance and if they had ever left their district of birth. The call for labor was issued and made public in the same way as other state regulations. The court was the public arena where people were assembled to hear about the rules, needs, and wants of a remote state nested in Colombo. In a similar fashion, a year later the magistrate of Jaffna was reminded to make "the contents of the same [Regulation 8 of 1821] as generally known as possible through the country by causing the same to be read in Tamil every Saturday in his court."[17] Three hundred copies in Tamil of Regulation 8 were sent to Jaffna to be distributed among the people.[18] The literacy of the population in Tamil would have been quite high owing to the early efforts of Dutch missions among slave children in particular. In 1786 the total number of schoolchildren in the northern province was 35,963, of which 2,180 were slave children.[19] Even if these figures are only estimates, they suggest that literacy in Tamil was fairly well spread among the people and that educated enslaved children in 1785 would have been adults in the 1820s. In 1816 the first American missionary school in Tellipai had already opened its doors, paving the way for a long-standing involvement of American missionaries in Jaffna.

It is difficult to know if the initial system of recruitment was later replaced by a more informal one where returnees or runaways from Chilaw would play a role in providing positive or negative information on the labor conditions there. The difficulty in persuading people to move to Chilaw suggests that rumors that generally flourish at times of tension and change would have reached people in Jaffna regarding the sickness and mortality that accompanied the journey to Chilaw and the concomitant dream of acquiring freedom. There is, however, no trail for the historian to follow, no "documentary debris for historians to sift through," as rumors constructed in the vernacular of the people have not been recorded for posterity.[20]

For slaveholders, letting go of their slaves would have meant a considerable loss. The labor for Chilaw was recruited among Coviyar, Nalavar, and Pallar slaves but mainly from the two last caste groups, which had been involved in tobacco cultivation since the Dutch period and can be identified with agricultural labor castes from the Coromandel Coast, referred to as "coast slaves" in Dutch reports of the period. In the late seventeenth century, 3,589 such slaves were brought from Coromandel (today's Tamil Nadu) by private individuals to be employed in Jaffna as domestics and as agricultural labor.[21]

Tobacco cultivation was described by Emerson Tennent as "the grand staple of the district, and that on which the prosperity of its agriculture is chiefly dependent."²² It was grown on what was called "garden lands" and on paddy lands after the harvesting.²³ As Tennent explained, the soil is prepared and manured to an extent that, after that, two or even three crops can be grown on the land. Tobacco cultivation "causes new land to be broken up for its growth," thus leading to an improvement of all inferior land.²⁴ Writing two decades later, in 1830, Casie Chetty mentioned the tobacco of "very superior quality raised in large quantities, particularly in the district of Pachellepalli," one of the four districts exclusive of the islands, the three others being Wadamarachy, Tenmarachy, and Waligamme.²⁵

Cash crops such as tobacco had been introduced in Jaffna by the seventeenth century but were more widely cultivated in the eighteenth century as an article of export to the kingdom of Travancore. Merchants from Travancore provided credit to farmers in Jaffna to purchase the forthcoming crop, and middlemen often bought the leaves and sold them to Malayalee traders at a profit.²⁶ Tobacco spread to new areas in the Jaffna peninsula, such as Wadamarachy and East Valikaman villages, as well as Mannar and the Vanni. In 1783 more than a million pounds of tobacco leaves were exported from Jaffna. The Dutch imposed an export duty of 20 percent.

Sinappah Arasaratnam alleges that tobacco plantations "benefitted a wide segment of the community," a qualification that stands to be tested.²⁷ Tobacco cultivation was indeed one of the most labor-intensive crops: it involved preparing the land, planting the seeds, watering, weeding, laying fertilizer (animal manure), harvesting, stringing and hanging the leaves for curing, and carrying the harvested leaves from the farms to the curing. While figures for Jaffna are not available, it is useful to compare the labor rendement in Virginia during the seventeenth and eighteenth centuries, where each slave or indentured servant working on a tobacco plantation may have planted and weeded about two acres of cleared land with nine thousand to ten thousand plants a year. In 1901, according to Tennent, more than fifteen thousand acres of Jaffna were under tobacco, which would explain why seventy years before, there were, according to slave registers, over seven thousand slaves in the Jaffna population.²⁸ However, the figures for Nalavars and Pallars, who generally worked in cultivation, bring the number of slaves potentially working on tobacco farms to approximately four thousand (fig. 4.2).

The figure of fifteen thousand acres may be excessive, as a sessional paper of 1912 on tobacco cultivation estimates the area under cultivation at seven thousand acres.²⁹ The same paper gives an estimate for the early twentieth

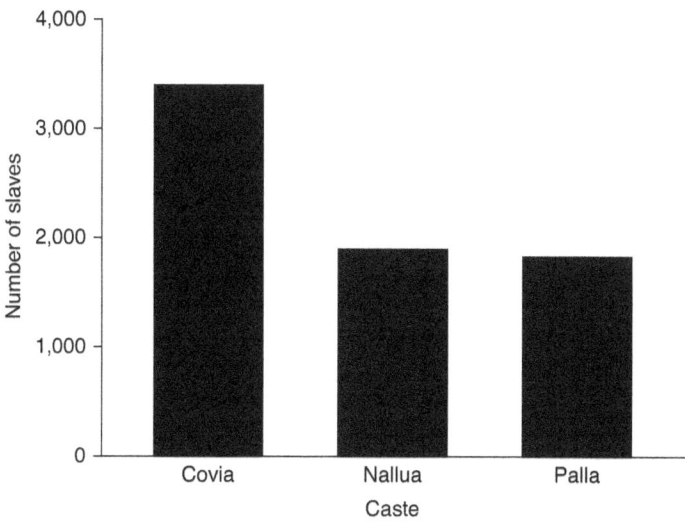

Figure 4.2 Number of slaves per caste (author's data from NA UK CO T71/664)

century of the costs of production of an acre of tobacco and includes some details of the labor force involved:

40 coolies for hoeing
40 coolies for burying the leaves and arranging and transplanting
2 men for watering for 60 days
40 coolies for hoeing
1 man for topping for 16 days[30]

Apart from tobacco and rice, palmyra palms were ubiquitous around the villages and provided an important resource in the northern parts of the peninsula. The fruit, leaves, toddy, and timber were an integral part of the lives of the people in Jaffna. Enslaved people also worked in palmyra gardens, drawing toddy from January to August and digging palmyra roots. A criminal case in Jaffna where a Nalavar caste man, Mody Winsy, stabbed to death his fellow worker, Pody Podien, for allegedly mixing water with his toddy, gives a rare insight into the life of Nalavars who are seen in the account, drawing toddy with two knives, rooting out palmyra side by side, and occasionally getting into murderous disputes that lead to conviction and hanging.[31]

The Nalavars were deeply connected to the land they worked on and tied to their proprietors through a bundle of rights. Thus freeing enslaved labor engaged in working in tobacco, palmyra, and other forms of cultivation for the Chilaw scheme could be done only at considerable cost to proprietors.

Terms of Employment

Unlike laborers utilized for public works, working under rajakariya or convicts, the Chilaw workers were issued a written contract, which they signed. This piece of paper created a bond between employer and employee based on written conditions rather than on custom as in rajakariya or even state disciplinary practice such as convict labor. The rajakariya system, which combined land tenure and caste service, underwent many changes during the precolonial and successive colonial domination of the maritime provinces; the British inherited a "metamorphosed system in 1796."[32]

Rajakariya involved the performance of two kinds of duties: the first related to services based on caste with respect to lands, and the second, to unpaid services rendered by people for the repair and maintenance of the roads and bridges of their district. The British appropriated this traditional form of labor extraction specifically for public works, quite unlike the Portuguese and Dutch, who had used it to their benefit without altering its character. The form of military government that prevailed in the first two decades of British rule permitted the governor to serve direct orders relating to the making of roads or canals and issue military orders to requisite labor. There had been attempts to abolish rajakariya during British rule: first during the short period of East India Company rule (1796–1802), when freeing labor and abolishing the service tenure failed to receive the support of the people. It was reintroduced after an upheaval and once again abolished by Governor North, who replaced it with an obligation to serve on public works against payment. Governor Maitland (1805–1811) was extremely critical of this procedure as the "lazy native" could not be compelled to work, nor was he interested in monetary compensation, "for there being no penalty, there is not an inhabitant in this island that would not sit down and starve out the year under the shade of two or three Cocoa Nut trees, the whole of his property and the whole of his subsistence, rather than increase his income and his comforts by his manual labour."[33]

Maitland reintroduced the right of the state to extract service on the basis of caste. The performance of duties in connection with public works was made, as under the kings, a gratuitous service.[34] Owing to their higher status, the farming castes, the Goyigama in the Sinhalese areas and the Vellalar in the northern Tamil areas, were exempt from the obligation of service. Other castes that performed the duties that were specific to their caste were increasingly called for service on public works and building roads and bridges, these "icons of colonial rule" that Governor Barnes and his successors saw as central to consolidating British rule in Kandy, the last kingdom to fall to the Europeans.[35] Rajakariya was mainly used for public works in the districts that belonged to the former Kandyan kingdom. The extractive and unfair nature of this system of "unrecompensed compulsory labour" came to an end in 1833 when Commissioner Colebrooke, sent to Sri Lanka as a member of the Royal Commission of Eastern Inquiry (1829–1832), recommended its "entire abolition."[36]

Native convict workers were used as early as 1806, for instance, to transport salt from the beach to the salterns of Magampattu in Hambantota, in the south of the island. There salt lakes formed in the dry season. Not only was the labor cheap, it was seen as a way of punishing criminals further and reforming them morally as the work involved was extremely hard and physically demanding. In some ways their plight resembled that of the Chilaw slaves, as they too were moved from their places of abode to far-away destinations. The convicts of Magampattu were used for other work too, repairing roads and clearing canals alongside laborers paid by the day when work in the salterns was sparse.[37] Alongside convict labor, wage labor was already common in the early nineteenth century, coexisting with rajakariya, slave, and other forms of bonded labor. In the minute of November 16, 1825, a "Schedule of rates of daily Pay to Coolies or Labourers employed in the Service of Government on the Public Works" listed rates per day for the nine districts in the maritime provinces. A worker in the saltern in Hambantota would receive 6d (VOC duits), while a laborer in Jaffna would receive half of this sum. "Boys" would be paid one-third or two-thirds of the pay of an able-bodied laborer and were very much sought after.[38] Wage labor was in existence in spite of the compulsory services system that would have had the effect of draining the supply of laborers. It had been and was used by the government, missionaries, and local inhabitants—the Salagamas employed wage labor to avoid serving in the Cinnamon Department.[39] In Dutch Ceylon there is evidence of wages being paid by VOC officials to unskilled laborers such as craftsmen's servants and coolies and skilled laborers such as carpenters, masons, and smiths, although the majority of the population was not working for wages under early VOC rule.[40] The circulation of coins as early as the sixteenth century in trading centers on the coast and in the hinterlands as well as occurrences of "hired labour i.e. labour working for money wages" in the Kandyan areas further testify to the availability of wage labor before the nineteenth century.[41] R. N. Dewasiri suggests that in the late eighteenth century in the areas under VOC rule, the rajakariya system had mutated into a "quasi wage-labor system," where instead of getting accommodessans for their services, carpenters, sawyers, and other workers were often given monetary payments.[42] Another illustration of the existence of a widespread concept of wage for labor in the eighteenth century was the common practice of people in Jaffna, and to a lesser extent in the Sinhalese areas, to buy themselves out of their rajakariya service by paying a fine. In 1695 it is estimated that 24,641 people paid fines to avoid rajakariya in the Jaffna area.[43] While these figures are revealing of a transformation in labor relations and the distribution of labor time in the island between caste-related labor, wage labor, and subsistence agriculture that had begun long before the onset of the Colebrooke-Cameron reforms, for the purpose of this chapter the figures also shed light on the strategies deployed by enslaved people to navigate the routes toward an end of enslavement.

It is obvious, then, that Jaffna in particular had been a money economy long before the arrival of Europeans. Government revenue was collected in cash, and it was common for the king of Jaffna to pay for his administrators, soldiers, and headmen in cash.[44] The value of money and what it could buy was not an unknown fact in Jaffna in the 1820s when the Chilaw experiment was mooted.

Before the Chilaw experiment, other schemes had been tested and tried. The labor shortage during the first decades of British rule had led to various plans to introduce Indian and Chinese migrant workers, whose believed sense of industriousness would, it was hoped, contrast with the indolence of the natives. Governor Maitland's term of office saw two unsuccessful attempts from 1810 at settling Chinese workers from the Malay peninsula near the naval base of Trincomalee in the eastern part of the island. Under Governor Brownrigg in 1813, Indian Christians from Tanjore were more successfully settled in the island. Throughout the 1820s the idea resurfaced but was not implemented. The Chinese workers/settlers soon became "a burden to Government without benefit," taking up "gambling, and profligate pursuits or idleness."[45]

The Contract

Enslaved men who were leaving for Chilaw were issued certificates of emancipation that would be deposited at the kachcheri office in Jaffna until they had completed their term of labor. An agreement was signed by them and kept by the collector of Jaffna. This constituted a significant departure from the past, when only slave masters were entitled to sign legal papers on matters relating to the lives of enslaved people. The signature, even if a cross or a fingerprint, was a symbolic performance of personhood. The collector of Chilaw in turn was to be sent regular and correct lists of the names of enslaved people dispatched for labor.

The agreement signed did not have the feature of a labor contract, as the later indenture/engagement contract would have in plantation colonies such as Mauritius, Reunion, or Guyana, nor did it resemble slave bonds that proved ownership of a slave by a master and transfer to a new proprietor. The indenture/engagement contract that came into place in British and French colonies after the abolition of slavery derived from and conjoined other existing contracts, namely, those of sailors and agrarian laborers.[46] It was even more probably derivative of indenture contracts issued to Europeans who moved as bondsmen or bondswomen to the Americas in the eighteenth century. Such a contract stipulated that the master pays for the voyage and maintenance of the contracted servant in exchange for his or her labor for a determined period, generally five or six years.[47]

The contract issued for the Chilaw laborers was quite singular in its content and form, and could have also derived from a preconception among its creators of what constituted a labor contract in Britain in 1820. In the metropolis, contracts were regulated by statutes dealing with masters and servants, and the law made it a criminal offense for a worker to break his contract, whereas any breach by an employer was considered a civil offense only. These terms were codified in the Master and Servants Act of 1823.

The agreement was signed by a collective, a batch of enslaved people, and the terms enunciated upon which emancipation was granted according to Regulation 9 of 1818, which revealed the nature of the labor that would be performed and what the slave would receive in return. To a certain extent, but in an extremely loose manner, the agreement codified labor relations. It stated that the signatories would have to work as a laborers for the term of one year, "receiving during that time a seer of rice and five pies daily."[48] Furthermore, the enslaved people could work for the emancipation of their families serving a time "as shall be proportionate to the sum advanced calculating at the rate of seven and a half rix dollars the month." To extract as much labor as possible, the agreement ended with the ominous clause that "male children shall give their labor to government during that period gratuitously."[49]

The contract did not stipulate the amount of hours of work that each emancipated slave was expected to serve, which suggests that all his time was provided to serve his employer. Unlike contracts issued to sailors, there was no penalty for desertion in the agreement. The suggestion made by the collector of Jaffna to the magistrate of Point Pedro in 1820 that upon completion of the term of work, which he refers to as "servitude," and if the slave had "behaved well and wishes it," he would be settled on government lands and grants and assistance provided to him to bring these lands into cultivation is not inserted as a condition in the contract.[50] In Brazil in the 1850s–1880s, a system of conditional manumission was introduced in which, upon signing a labor contract, the slave was nominally free and at the same time subject to a form of compulsory labor.[51] This agreement thus bore some resemblance to an indenture document of the later decades but with the conditional aspect of freedom attached to it and with some notable differences, as, for instance, the final clause about labor extraction from children of slaves. The indentured worker of the late nineteenth century signed a contract as an individual, unlike the cohort of emancipated slaves.

The collective signatories of this sort of contract all belonged to the so-called slave castes, the Coviyar, Nalavar, and Pallar, whom Dutch colonialism had redefined as slaves in the eighteenth century (chap. 3). Even among them, there were perceived hierarchies that were reflected in the monetary value of their laboring bodies. The commodification of the bodies of enslaved people was naturalized by colonial officials who determined the rules governing the value of a slave in the Regulations of 1818 and 1821. The idea of placing a value on a human as a market product was implicit in the centuries of slave trading. Yet after the abolition of the trade in 1807, the British in Sri Lanka continued to abide by this notion by differentiating between the compensation given to Coviyar mothers, on the one hand, and Pallar and Nalavar mothers, on the other. By agreeing to compensate slaveholders in Jaffna for their losses incurred according to a putative value of the enslaved, British rule was in effect accepting the commodification of bodies and that enslaved bodies had differing pecuniary values. We do not know the value enslaved people placed on their own personhood since, in order to become free, they went along with the terms set.[52] The manner of establishing the value of a slave who wished to be emancipated was enunciated in clause 21 of Regulation 9 of 1818. Any slave had the right to apply to the provincial court, which would then summon the proprietor in writing. Five valuators, of whom two would be chosen by the proprietor and two by the slave and the last appointed by the court, should fix a fair price to be paid by the slave to the proprietor. The slave would then be issued a certificate of emancipation.[53] In June 1820 fifty slaves had been emancipated by government purchase for a total sum of 2,497 rix dollars, for an average per man of 50.9 rix dollars. "The average value of the Nallua and Palla slaves of about 30 years of age has not been found to exceed 30 or 35 rix dollars."[54]

Nalavars and Pallars were the preferred group as far as purchase of freedom was concerned, as Coviyars were believed to not be "at all well adapted for labour" and "being rated at much higher value."[55] The collector mentioned a few instances when the "valuation of the Covia slave conjointly with his family had nearly tripled the amount authorized to be expended by Government." He had on those occasions not followed through with freeing the slave. However, he was ready to pay more than the amount stipulated if the slave had family members who were "capable of rendering efficient service," and if the slave engaged himself to extend his term of service.[56]

The cost of the emancipated bodies was enunciated as an "aggregate sum paid for the freedom of themselves and their families" to the proprietors. This sum was a matter of concern for the authorities in Colombo. In 1825 the collector received a letter from the governor's office questioning the "large sum of eight thousand eight hundred and ten Rix dollars advanced to the proprietors of emancipated slaves."[57] Another missive further dwelt on the issue of the cost of purchasing Coviyar slaves in particular, which was seen to considerably exceed that of the two other castes, and the fact that Coviyar, who were chiefly employed as domestics in Jaffna, were not suited to hard labor in Chilaw. The governor was favorable to their emancipation as long as it cost no more than that of the Pallars and Nalavars.[58] A parsimonious colonial government was vehemently upholding an equal monetary value for all slaves.

Flow of Workers, 1820–1829

The Jaffna kachcheri issued a circular to all magistrates in the area impressing on them that the "government was extremely desirous of obtaining the emancipation of as many slaves as possible, particularly those of the Nallua and Palla castes," according to the government advertisement of July 15, 1820.[59] On August 2 thirty-one emancipated slaves were dispatched to Chilaw.[60] On August 31 the collector of Jaffna informed the governor's office that another "64 persons who have been emancipated from slavery" had been dispatched to Jaffna. He included a list of their names and added that it had been necessary to advance "batta" to each individual in the proportion of eight seers of rice and four fanams in cash.[61] The language of the officials in the otherwise bland and dry missives is revealing in one respect: emancipated slaves were referred to as "persons," a quality that was not recognized in them as long as they remained the property of someone else. From being a traded commodity, they had by virtue of signing a labor contract graduated to personhood. The belief that enslaved people were capable of reason, morality, and diligence was not explicit in the official correspondence in the island. Yet across the seas such ideas were becoming more acceptable among Christian reformers and antislavery proponents. Enslaved persons were given numbers, as, for example, the four deserters who were sent back and were listed as numbers: No. 33, No. 38, No. 86, No. 88.[62]

In October another batch of fifty to sixty persons of the Nalavar and Pallar castes were sent to Chilaw, and a few weeks later parties of thirty-two and eleven followed.[63] In November a list of sixteen emancipated slaves sent to Chilaw was shared with the government in Colombo.[64] In 1820 approximately 191 emancipated slaves were sent to Chilaw. This number was clearly insufficient in the view of the government, and the governor sent instructions to cease advancing money for the purchase of emancipated slaves, publicly announcing that no further applications would be attended to.[65] In response, the collector attempted to redeem the scheme by stating its effects: not only were 191 men emancipated, but 348 others—wives, children, and relatives—had benefited from the scheme. The main obstacle was, in his view, the negative influence of the proprietors, who were actively dissuading their slaves from engaging in this scheme.[66]

The collector seemed to have convinced the authorities, since the following year saw another case of labor consisting of emancipated slaves in March 1821, with the construction of a new canal in Chilaw between Jagampattoo and Meddapalale in the Pettigal Korale. The expenditure for the canal was 19,935.10½ rix dollars. The work was completed in 1828 with the use of various types of labor. The remarks in the Blue Book are revealing: "This work was originally intended to be performed by slaves from Jaffna with a view to gain the emancipation of themselves and families, as requested by the Governor's Dispatch to Lord Bathurst no 64 of 11 March 1821 and of Sir James Campbell no 46 of 23d Dec 1823, and approved by his Lordship under date 17th June 1821 No 41." There seems, however, to have been a dearth of slaves willing to work on the canal under the conditions laid out: "as the work advanced and the number of slaves that came forward to be emancipated by these means were less than expected, it became expedient to employ other labourers from time to time."[67]

During the early years of British rule, a pioneer corps of Indian laborers, composed of bricklayers, carpenters, and artificers paid on contract, had been constituted for petty irrigation works. Unlike the emancipated slave workforce, who received only a batta or special allowance, these men were paid salaries. They were placed under the collector of each district as a corps of pioneers. In 1804 the pioneers were diverted from civil to military control and attached to various regiments fighting the war against the Kandyan kingdom. After the fall of the kingdom, the pioneer corps was once again diverted to public works under the supervision of European officers. They worked in divisions of four hundred to eight hundred men alongside customary laborers.[68] In 1821 Governor Barnes recruited pioneers from the Coromandel Coast.[69].

In 1822, according to the minute of February 5, 1822, the governor approved the purchase of the emancipation of 300 slaves of Nalavar and Pallar caste and their families, a measure that would "permanently benefit that class of people and the government," and moved that the collector of Jaffna be authorized to advance sums necessary for purchasing their emancipation.[70] In 1824 there were still more than 15,000 slaves in the northern province. That year large groups of emancipated slaves left Jaffna accompanied by a "peon" to work on the Chilaw canal. In August and October,

30 and 101 emancipated slaves, respectively, were mentioned in an official communication as having been sent to Chilaw.[71] A month later the collector of Jaffna referred to sending 46 and then 62 men to Chilaw, forming "a party of slaves who have accepted emancipation on the terms offered by the government."[72] A group of 22 followed shortly thereafter.[73] It was clear that emancipation was given in exchange of labor, but it remained unclear what type of arrangement was made, or if it was different from the initial scheme.

A letter of August 16, 1825, from the collector of Jaffna helps us piece together the reasons for a decline in numbers. He stated that 1,323 slaves have been emancipated under the minute of the September 3, 1824, but then referred to "a few deaths at Chilaw among the slaves" as a possible reason for the decrease in the number to be procured. He remained optimistic, however, that the required number will be attained, as many Coviyars appeared to wish to "work their emancipation," but from the letter it seems that he was not allowed to recruit them. He now asked permission to use this source of labor.[74] Coviyar slaves were generally household slaves in Vellalar homes and hence not deemed suitable for the hard labor of building a canal.

Notice of slaves emancipated by purchase by the government appears again in 1826 in a letter from the then collector of Jaffna in which he referred to the auditor general's remarks in civil warrant no. 130 for November 1825. The auditor's query concerned the voucher of C. Scott, collector of Jaffna, for an amount spent between March 20, 1823, and October 31, 1825, for the purchase of slaves for the use of government "as authorised by Minutes of Council dated 28 October 1822 and 23 September 1824." The auditor general asked to specify the number of slaves purchased and in the absence of "acquittances of the proprietors" imposed a surcharge. The collector contended that the large part of the money mentioned in the voucher had been spent, and that "it is impossible to procure the signatures of all the proprietors of the slaves emancipated on account of government many of them being dead or others absent from the district." He requested that the auditor "accept the bonafide of the transaction of purchase of slaves and withdraws the surcharge."[75] On July 18, however, the collector made clear in a letter that the governor was not ready to dispense with the acquittances, and he therefore asked the auditor general for a delay of six weeks to assemble the proprietors of the emancipated slaves on account of government.[76] Ten days later the collector was able to provide some accounts: the amount of 140.17 pounds "was expended for the purchase of Palla and Nallua slaves as authorized by the Minute in Council of the 28th October 1822 and 23d September 1824."[77]

Again in 1826, the purchase of slaves for use by the government was authorized by minutes of Council dated July 4, 1826.[78] That year there was a trickle of slaves going to Chilaw, and it seemed that more Coviyars were engaged, in spite of their high value—seventy rix dollars—perhaps due to the lack of Nalavar and Pallar workers.[79] Work was going on in the Chilaw district, with the deepening of several parts of the inland navigation connected with the canal. Emancipated slaves and other laborers were deepening the canal between Puttalam Lake and Andepana Lake.[80] The soil was "found to be of so firm clay" that it required more labor. During the rainy season, when the area was underwater and the work was interrupted, emancipated slaves were used to raise the road between Thabbowa and Tommodera Bridge, which ran the risk of being washed away due to the floods.[81]

Registers of slaves sent to Chilaw indicate that until November 1829 the system of emancipation in exchange for labor was still functioning.[82] Work on the Chilaw canal was over, however, and instructions were sent to the collector at Jaffna to use labor that had been "purchased" either to collect materials, to burn lime, or to help in the digging of the proposed tank at Poolonne. More purchase of slaves would be discontinued until "public work of sufficient magnitude and importance" would make the recourse to that measure useful.[83]

The work on the Chilaw canals led to an increase in the value and future value of the lands surrounding them. In the early 1820s the British gave a few members of the Sinhalese elite land grants with the hope that they would continue to grow cinnamon. To the government's distress, most Sinhalese landowners were more interested in coconut plantations, which required a relatively small labor force and low maintenance. Adrian Jayewardene, known as "tambi mudaliyar," was rewarded for his services to the British in the war against the Kandyan kingdom with a large landholding in Chilaw that amounted to 2,612 acres at his death in 1830.[84] He seems to have appropriated much more land than the government intended to give him, and his landholding was exceptionally large. Others also received grants, but from March 1824 land had to be purchased. The Corea family, whose ancestor Christoffel Corea had supported the king of Kandy, became the leading family and landowner in the Chilaw area. The evidence of

Johannes Corea Wijesekere Abeyratne, mudaliyar of Alut Kuru korale and Negombo, in response to questions posed to him by the Colebrooke-Cameron Commission on March 8, 1830, gives some interesting insights into the expansion of cultivated land in Chilaw in that decade. In 1830 Johannes Corea's lands consisted of 107 acres in the Chilaw district and 110 acres in Alut Kuru Korale between Negombo and Colombo. Of this, 100 acres were paddy and 117 high ground: 25 acres of coconut, jackfruit, and areca, 90 acres of young coconuts, and only 2 uncultivated. He had purchased 10 acres of cash crop land under the Proclamation of March 2, 1824, and governor's address of June 24, 1825. His lands, he wrote, were cultivated by "servants" who were fed and clothed and whose "parents are now and then, supplied with Paddy, Money, and Cloths, in consideration of the Services of their children." The status of these servants remains unclear. Could they have been children of debt-ridden parents in neighboring villages, loaned temporarily for labor and services? We also learn that agricultural labor received a share of produce, while laborers were paid three or four fanams a day. Johannes Corea had 1,500 bearing coconut trees and nearly 5,000 young trees and had transplanted his cinnamon plants to the government garden.[85] While colonial rule blunted potential dissent by providing occasions for local elites to establish themselves in the new role of coconut plantation owners, they enforced harsh conditions on the labor force that was opening up the Chilaw district with the construction of a new canal.

Chilaw: Lives of Labor

The workforce employed to open the canal from Kudawewa to Thabbowa constituted by emancipated slaves was supervised by representatives of the state. Statements of expenses sent by the collector of Chilaw to Colombo provide some insight into the various groups involved. The overseer of the canal work was, in 1828, a man named Goldlieb. He was supported by a superintendent called Don Adrian de Silva, mudaliyar. Different worlds of labor coexisted until the mid-nineteenth century, more or less coerced, more or less free, working in conditions "analogous to slavery," to borrow Frederick Cooper's expression. Alongside the emancipated slaves were a large contingent of "coolies" who were part of the pioneer corps. In July and August 1821, for instance, the number of paid laborers/coolies working on the canal varied between 285 and 426.[86] They seem to have performed specific tasks, such as carrying the mammotties necessary for the work from Colombo to Chilaw and transporting the sand from Maracaly to the canal. They were paid in copper money. A coolie was sent to Colombo to bring the weights used to weigh the money dispensed to the laborers.[87]

The line between coolie and emancipated slave gets blurred as the decade comes to an end. In October 1829 emancipated slaves were employed at Natandy and paid a daily pay of nine pence. A *kangany* was going to be recruited to supervise their work. Unfortunately there are few details as to the type of person that the collector intended to recruit and the roles he was expected to perform. The distribution of responsibilities was as follows: the collector would inspect the work done on a weekly basis, while the kangany, "a trusted person," would be with them on days the collector was not present.[88] Familiarity with labor management would suggest that the foreman would have had some authority over the workers and hence was most probably a headman. Colonial officials would have thought that incorporating a traditional figure of authority in a new context was a viable managerial strategy. The kangany would become a familiar face in the next decades when plantation labor on coffee and tea estates had to be managed by an intermediary who was also an insider. This function, as it is mentioned in the Chilaw labor context, announces the future labor regime where the kangany emerged as "an indispensable part of labor organization in mills, ports and plantations . . . in the tropical colonies where Indian emigrants went for work."[89]

In the Register of Slaves Emancipated by Government on the Conditions Stated by the Deputy's Secretary of September 24, 1824, and sent to Chilaw on May 12, 1829, one gets a glimpse of these individual lives (see fig. 4.3). The twenty-seven slaves were numbered from 367 to 394, and their names indicate their caste. Nagy Wayreven Pallu was one among six Pallars, and there were seventeen Coviyars and four Nalavars. They came from different villages—Pallaly, Poottore, and Mandowila—and their ages varied from sixteen to forty-five. The time of service indicates more than one year and up to two years, five months, and fourteen days. The table included in detail the amount of money paid for the emancipation of the men and the amount paid for the family to the slave proprietors either to let them go to work for a limited period of time or for their actual liberation. For instance, the freedom of Wally Cadiren, a Coviyar from Pallaly, would have

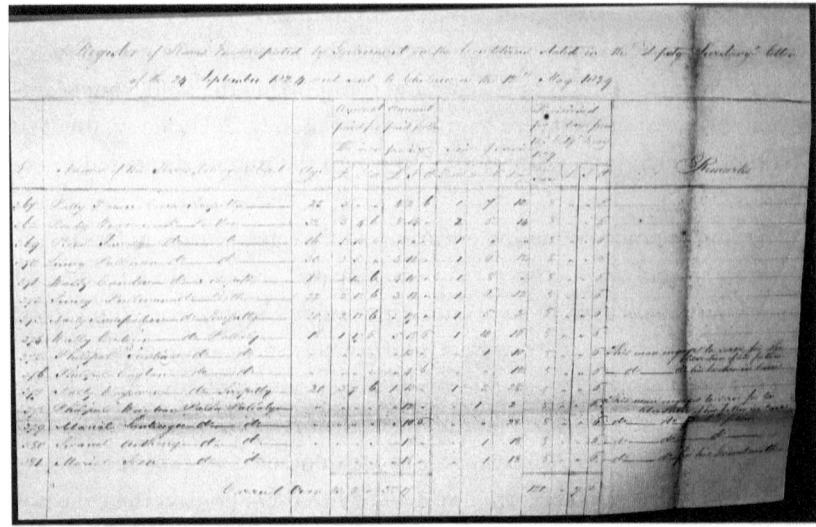

Figure 4.3 Register of slaves emancipated by government, September 24, 1824 (SLNA Lot 6/971A, September 24, 1824, with permission of Sri Lanka National Archives)

cost the government one pound, seventeen shillings, and six dimes, and of his family five pounds, eighteen shillings, and six dimes. Most interesting are the appended remarks: many of the slaves were "serving" not for their own liberation but for that of a father, father-in-law, their family, wife, or children, and even grandmother in the case of twenty-year-old Marial Soosa from Pallaly.[90]

Of their lives after work, little is known except through the lists and tables compiled by the collector accounting for the subsistence of emancipated slaves. In 1821 there is no mention of food consumed other than rice.[91] A year later the collector of Chilaw sent a letter to Colombo asking for authorization to buy 213 cans of arrack at three fanams per can for the emancipated slaves, the total value being 53.2 rix dollars.[92]

Sickness and Death

The deaths of emancipated slaves in Chilaw appear in the archive in an anecdotal fashion as the collector of Chilaw sends notice of deaths to Colombo. There are no reliable statistics regarding mortality rate on such public works, and no reference to funerals or cemeteries. Were the corpses thrown into unmarked graves or tossed into the sea without any religious ceremony? On June 29 Perial Siwelly, a Pallar of Odepitty, died, and on July 9 and 10 Sinny Colenden and Cotty Canden passed away. The deaths of two emancipated slaves named Perial Weelen and Anditchy Sinneven on July 24 were reported.[93] Five men had died within a month. What were the causes of these deaths, and could they have been prevented? Lives seemed expendable. On October 10, 1824, Cadiren Canden, whose village or caste is not mentioned, also "departed his life," and in December another two men died.[94] Men continue to die in the following year—nine in the single month of January 1825.[95]

Chilaw hospital was host to many ill emancipated slaves during the 1820s. Governor North had established hospitals in the early years of British rule, essentially to inoculate people against smallpox. In 1802 vaccination against the disease had been introduced, and by 1805 more than ten thousand people had been vaccinated, especially in the Southwest and Colombo, where Buddhist Sinhalese were less hostile to vaccination than in the northern areas.[96] In the four large districts of the island—Colombo, Jaffna, Galle, and Trincomalee—there were full-fledged hospitals, while the twelve smaller ones initially had only a medical overseer visiting people in houses.[97] In the 1820s the hospital was probably not large enough to accommodate large contingents of sick people.

One escapee slave from the hospital was described in an official letter as suffering from a "sore mouth."[98] This might have been a symptom of scurvy, where ulceration of the mouth and bleeding accompanies fatigue and pain in the limbs. A starch-based diet without fresh meat and citrus was bound to lead to such sicknesses. Feigning illness, too, was possibly a strategy used to avoid excruciating work; hence the high proportion of "hospital stoppage." These were the less serious types of illness when compared to the epidemics that ravaged large numbers in the 1820s.

In 1819 a cholera epidemic that emerged out of the Ganges delta stemming from contaminated rice, traveled along trade routes, and broke out in the island, reaching Jaffna in December. It "produced dreadful devastation on the western coast of Ceylon."[99] There were insufficient numbers of surgeons—only five in Colombo, Kandy, and Trincomalee, and one assistant surgeon each in Trincomalee, Badulla, Alupota, and Jaffna. There were no private practitioners. During the epidemic one medical officer had to oversee patients in Chilaw and Puttalam, thirty miles away.[100]

The work conditions would have been extremely harsh when one looks at the hospital bills of the emancipated slaves in Chilaw from February 23 to March 23, 1821, submitted by the medical subassistant. One does not come across any reference to housing or sanitation facilities, and bringing laborers from Jaffna with inadequate prior planning and enforcing strict labor regimens would have weakened them considerably and worn out their energy. During this month alone, seventy-one slaves were admitted to the hospital, and some of them, such as Nadie Kaderen, remained there for twenty-four days.[101] The nature of the illnesses was not included in the accounts, but the "dark horrors" of cholera as described by Emerson Tennent would explain the long periods spent by the workers in the hospital apart from the usual food-related diseases due to the poor quality of the rice and wounds and sores of all kinds due to the heat and working conditions. Like enslaved workers throughout the Indian Ocean world from the Ile Bourbon to the Cape, workers in Chilaw would have been vulnerable to endemic diseases such as cholera for which they had no immunity.[102] For cholera there was still no cure or prevention measure available. In the years that followed, emancipated slaves continued to be admitted to the hospital under the charge of a medical subassistant named J. H. Vansenden.[103]

Petitions

Emancipated slaves on occasion made demands concerning their living conditions as they were probably aware of the shortage of labor available for public works owing to the reluctance of people to comply with rajakariya. This provided them with some room to negotiate better terms of employment. Their claims took shape either in the form of a petition addressed from the slave to the governor or in a letter from the collector to the chief secretary "on behalf of the slave." They complained, in 1826, that sand was mixed with their rice rations and demanded better quality rice, a demand that was supported by the collector, who admitted the rice grains were of bad quality.[104] Other petitions related to possibilities of sharing the burden of labor. A man from Jaffna named Weerawen asked to be permitted to serve one year on behalf of his brother as an emancipated slave who was working at the canal and had two more years to complete his term. The collector of Chilaw wrote a letter to the governor on behalf of Weerawen, supporting the request as the man was "strong and able bodied."[105] The only petition signed by an emancipated slave was a similar request by Sinnacanden of Jaffna written in the obsequious and self-demeaning language typical of the genre, addressed to Governor Barnes. He used words such as "with due veneration" and "humbly" in order to approach "the worthy feet" of the governor. His plea was to be allowed to serve for eight more months in order to reduce the period of his aunt's son. The petition bears only a cross as a signature, the mark of Sinnacanden.[106] It shows the strength of familial ties, where a man is ready to work for the freedom of the son of his aunt, the reason given being "so as to reach their Country in time." In time for what is not revealed. Was his translator, whose name appears in the corner of the petition, A. Solomon, using this overly self-deprecating language because of his own reading of the inferior status of the petitioner? In many ways the petition resembled in its form, style, and codes those written by professional petition writers for indentured laborers in other contexts, such as Mauritius or South Africa.

Running Away

The first emancipated slave to run away from Chilaw was Coty Waireven of Pallali, who absconded on September 11, 1820. He deserted Puttalam in the night and appeared to have returned to Jaffna. The fear of the collector of Chilaw was that unless he was apprehended "in all probability others will follow his example."[107] Indeed, fourteen more followed on September 28.

LIST OF EMANCIPATED JAFFNA SLAVES WHO DESERTED
FROM [WORD ILLEGIBLE] ON THE NIGHT OF
SEPTEMBER 28, 1820

33 Nagy Tawesy Palla of Poetter
36 Natty Sinncwcvy ditto
37 Sinnie Wayreven ditto
38 Nagie Wayreven ditto
56 Modelie Andie Palla of Pallalie
58 Pattie Caderen Palla of Poettor
60 Pattie Modelier Palla of Sirapetty
68 Harie Canden Palla of Poettor

69 Sandie Weenasy Palla of Anerencal
85 Pocken Nielen Palla of Pottoer
86 Canden Andie ditto
87 Madie Canden ditto
88 Maroedie Tawesi ditto
89 Poedecal Wayreven ditto[108]

They were all Pallars and came from four villages, mainly Pottoer but also Pallalie, Sirapetty, and Anerencal. In October Cotty Piriam, an emancipated slave who had deserted but whose name was not on the list, was apprehended and "punished for his conduct." He was sent back to Chilaw with a new batch of emancipated slaves.[109] Others followed and were often caught in Jaffna and sent back to Chilaw. Nally Wayreven and Aynal Nallauwe were escorted by a detachment of sepoys proceeding to Colombo in April 1821. Each laboring man counted enough for such effort in recapturing them and forcing them to work for their freedom. Over the decade there was a regular movement of runaways to and fro, punished and sent back.[110] The record on runaway slaves, however, is haphazard and incomplete when one compares it with the rich material available for Mauritius, where "marron" registers of the late eighteenth and early nineteenth centuries provide a host of information on fugitive slaves, including date of desertion and capture and return.[111]

On October 2, 1821, Wallheoff informed the government that "on the morning of Saturday last" two emancipated slaves had fled from their workplace. They were identified as Nienievel Tawisiel, a Nallua aged thirty, and Poedial Caderen, a Palla aged twenty-five. Both men came from the same village of Wasawolaanse. The only remark is that they deserted on the evening of September 10, 1821. Within two days of receiving notice of their flight, the Colonial Secretary's Office (CSO) informed the collector of Jaffna that these two emancipated slaves had "deserted from Coddeweeve in the Chilaw district while they were employed agreeable to their engagement." They were to be apprehended, "punished," and sent back to Wallheoff.[112] A few weeks later, on October 30, two more slaves ran away from the same location supervised by Wallheoff—a Palla aged forty-five from Mottuwil and a Nallua aged twenty-two.[113]

What awaited runaways returning to Jaffna was probably a new situation where power had shifted away from the hands of the proprietor.

Reading through the case of Sedoowy Poody, the wife of an emancipated slave still working in Chilaw, one sees new lines of confrontation come to the fore. Sedoowy asked for redress for a "certain case of oppression" done to her by her former proprietor in Jaffna. There are no details except that it relates to land and produce, which the proprietor is presumably trying to deprive her of. There are no records of families joining the men working in Chilaw, nor are there details of the lives of the families of emancipated slaves who remained in Jaffna and worked with the former proprietors of the emancipated worker. Grief and despair in particular are absent from the source material available to historians.

Emancipated slaves continued to desert their workplace in Chilaw to run away back to Jaffna. Poodie Castan of Poetoir in the Jaffna district was one of them in 1825 to be sought after by the collector of Jaffna.[114] The fact that many were apprehended and sent back shows that they were probably not aware that the collector of Chilaw would notify the chief secretary to give necessary orders to his colleague in Jaffna to react to the disappearance of a single slave. Communication among the different officials in Chilaw, Colombo, and Jaffna was fast enough to take the runaway by surprise, once he returned to his village.

By 1829 the collector of Chilaw had a more systematic method to apprehend fugitive emancipated slaves. The case of Seduwy Maylow, who deserted from the Puttalam canal, exemplifies a slightly more detailed taxonomic apparatus. There is a certain incongruity in informing the governor of the island of the escape of a single emancipated slave, but it is perhaps understandable since the collector appealed to the governor to publicize a description of the runaway in the Gazetteer to supplement his prior correspondence with collectors of Mannar and Jaffna. The description of the emancipated slave gave details of the name, caste, village, age, complexion, and height of the man: No. 403 Seduwy Maylow, Palla of Caydaty, thirty years of age, pale color, and short.[115] Thus caste and complexion came out quite predictably as important markers that defined the colonized in the eye of the colonizer. What specific measures were taken to find and apprehend the fugitives is not known, but given the small numbers involved it was probably not a system comparable to the *chasseurs de police* or slave patrols employed in Mauritius as special forces charged with hunting marron slaves (runaways) who took refuge in the forests and mountains.[116]

Amelioration in Ceylon and Other Colonies

The Chilaw experiment needs to be read in the context of amelioration policies introduced in British colonies. In the 1820s the British Empire witnessed a quickening of a legal transformation that had begun in the previous century. The Society for the Mitigation and Gradual Abolition of Slavery Throughout the British Dominions Throughout the British Empire, which was formed in 1823, still had a small membership of five lords and fourteen members of the House of Commons. The registration of slaves that had been pressed for since 1812 by James Stephen Sr. showed some success with slave registration acts passed in all the Caribbean colonies by 1820 and the setting up of a central registry dedicated to the maintenance of colonial registers by act of parliament.[117] The first legislation for ameliorating slavery was introduced in 1824, a year after the founding of the Anti-Slavery Society. It was in Trinidad that the first experiment was made with the introduction of an office of the guardian of slaves that was supposed to adjudicate between slaves and their masters. The legislation permitted slave marriages, allowed slaves to give evidence in court, and forbade the separation by sale of mothers and children as well as the flogging of slave women.[118] It was expected that local legislatures and legislative councils in the various colonies would pass their own version of the order. As Secretary Canning in the House of Commons said: "It is hoped that other colonies will follow an example so set, without the apprehension of danger."[119]

Ceylon was an example of a sort. During the debates in the House of Lords pertaining to the West Indies, Earl Bathurst, secretary of state to war and to the colonies, rhetorically asked, "Where were instances to be found of a transition from servile to free labour, in circumstances similar to those of our West India colonies?" "Ceylon," he said, "had been appealed to, where the same kind of slaves existed, and had been manumitted; but in that island they were a minority."[120] Legislation in Ceylon regarding emancipation of children of slave women had indeed been passed in 1818 and 1821, seemingly independently of directives from London. Much of what was suggested in the Trinidad order had already been achieved in Ceylon. In Cape Colony, Ordinance 19 of June 1826 realigned amelioration with the Trinidad model, albeit with a few changes. While Christianity was no longer required for slaves to marry, children under the age of ten, rather than of sixteen as in Trinidad, could not be separated from their mother, and all slaves could testify in court. Most important, a guardian of slaves was established to adjudicate on cases brought out by slaves against their masters.

On the whole, in all British colonies, colonial assemblies and councils were slow at implementing the amelioration orders. Finally, the British government abolished slavery in the West Indies and Cape Colony in 1834. A number of other schemes were put forward in 1833, including a plan drafted by Henry Taylor that proposed a system where slaves could purchase their freedom by installments. His recommendation that the British government partly buy a slave's freedom was reminiscent of the Chilaw system. Slaves would employ some days of the week to earn money to purchase their freedom and in the process acquire qualities such as industriousness. This was seen as a gradual introduction to wage labor once full freedom was granted. The calculation was that a strong male slave would be able to be free in three years. Naturally this system was detrimental to frail and weak people.[121]

The culmination of these debates in Britain was thus a compromise: the Slavery Abolition Act of August 28, 1833, provided for the award of twenty million pounds sterling to the owners of "slave property" in the British colonies but exempted Ceylon, St. Helena, and the territories under East India Company rule, such as India. Furthermore, the slave was bound to unpaid labor for a further four to six years from August 1, 1834, through a system of "apprenticeship." The compensation regime established by this act led to the creation of a Slave Compensation Commission, which handled "forty-five thousand individual claims from owners of eight hundred thousand enslaved." Statistical work on a number of the colonies involved has thrown much light on slaveholding, revealing that more than half of the compensation was paid to metropolitan British masters, and half of that went to a rentier class.[122]

In many British colonies, such as Trinidad, the legislation relating to slave registration and the idea of compensation for slaveholders were key policy initiatives by abolitionists who were looking to reform slavery in the short term while viewing abolition as a long-term goal. These measures acted as a prelude to full emancipation. During this period compensation—generally understood as a financial indemnity in the form of monetary payment, land, or forced labor (apprenticeship)—was paid to slave proprietors not only in Britain but also in France, the Netherlands, Denmark, Sweden, the District of Columbia, and countries in South

America as well as to resident slaveholders in the colonies concerned.[123] As Susan Thorne has argued in an insightful discussion of the 1833 act, "compensation, in short, contained abolition's implications within the amoral economy of free market capitalism."[124] The Ordinance of 1844 finally brought the emancipation of slaves in the British crown colony of Ceylon, ten years after the abolition of slavery in Britain's Atlantic and Indian Ocean colonies.

There was, however, a particular moment of "amelioration" or gradual abolition of slavery shared by Britain's three new colonies, Ceylon, Mauritius, and Cape Colony, that took very different shapes owing to a number of factors, including the difference in the organization of the economy and consequently the different type of labor needed at the moment of abolition.[125] In the case of Mauritius, apprenticeship schemes described so fittingly by the abolitionist James Stephen in 1832 as a "transition from the brutal to the rational predicament" were introduced to respond to the continuing need for labor on plantations.[126] Apprenticeship taught former slaves no skills; rather, it was intended to teach them a discipline that would prepare them for the rationality of the market. Yet the goals of apprenticeship in Mauritius were severely compromised by the introduction of thousands of "free" Indian laborers between 1834 and 1839, giving former slaves few options to negotiate with estate owners and leading to their effective marginalization.

The Chilaw experiment can be read alongside other, similar labor-related experiments that were tried out in the British Empire in the period preceding the Abolition of Slavery Act of 1833. In 1823 George Hibbert suggested in the House of Commons that experimenting with manumission of slaves ought to be tried out on small numbers first: "Surely in an experiment of this kind . . . it were most prudent to attempt it on 10 000 or 30 000 people, who are to be found perfectly isolated than at once to try it on . . . near a Million."[127] The early abolitionists, such as Wilberforce, believed that slave labor was wasteful and inefficient and that free labor was inherently superior according to both natural and Christian law. But until the first decades of the nineteenth century, parliamentary abolitionists remained cautious toward any practical experiments in the slave colonies. One idea put forward by Earl Percy that was brought down virulently by Wilberforce himself the day after the Slave Trade Abolition Bill of 1807 was passed was to "declare every negro child free, who shall be born in his majesty's dominions after the 1st of January."[128] As mentioned in earlier chapters, a variant of this scheme was implemented in Sri Lanka a few years later when Alexander Johnston, chief justice of the Supreme Court, convinced slaveholders to liberate the children of their slaves voluntarily in 1816. This was implemented by legislation in 1818 that brought effective liberation to the children at the age of fourteen.

According to the free labor ideology propounded by Adam Smith, the extension of freedom was the primary moral and political goal of human progress. Labor, however, was the principal theme of his *Wealth of Nations*. If the property of every man in his own labor was "the most sacred and inviolable foundation of all property," slavery was in complete violation of the values of individual autonomy and social justice. Of course the principle of labor freedom was not purely founded on sentiments of morality, sacrality, or inviolability. At the core of the argument was the importance of labor freedom to maximize economic utility. Smith made his argument about the economically defective nature of slavery: "A person who can acquire no property, can have no other interest but to eat as much and to labour as little as possible. Whatever work he does beyond what is sufficient to purchase his own maintenance can be squeezed out of him by violence only, and not by any interest of his own."[129]

This chapter has shown the implicit understanding by colonial officials of enslavement of Jaffna Nalavars, Pallars, and Coviyars as the "other" of free labor. In the view of colonial administrators, in the 1820s free labor/wage labor was congruent with the liberal promise of emancipation. The fact that so many enslaved men partook in this scheme in the early 1820s indicates that there was an aspiration for a change in the status quo among the most humble subjects of colonial Sri Lanka; that freedom as it had been offered to them by the colonial state was a value, a quality worth the exchange of hard labor. What they imagined would follow is not known. One can only assume that their long walk from Jaffna to Chilaw shows a shared hope that, through economic industry, a person's passage to freedom would be enacted. For today's observer, it is clear that their passage was one simultaneously entering the being of a colonial subject, another form of oppression. As Frederick Cooper has suggested, apostles of abolitionism would never have accepted the idea that slavery and colonialism were on par in terms of evilness. Other forms of coercive colonial practices were given an "aura of normality" that slavery had shed by the early nineteenth century after long centuries of having been naturalized.[130] The question of the nature of the freedom that the emancipated slaves who worked in Chilaw acquired at the end of their term is difficult to measure. Their situation bears much resemblance to that analyzed in Bihar by Gyan Prakash, where abolition of slavery by the East India Company in 1843 in effect reformulated as debt-bondage the *kamia-malik* relationship that had been earlier classified as slavery and serfdom. Slaves reconstituted as bonded labor would "voluntarily" move into a debt-bondage based on lease and contracts with their masters.[131] As mentioned in the previous chapter, the singular difference between the Indian and Sri Lankan situations was that the reconfiguration of certain castes of Jaffna as slaves was a condition inherited from the period of VOC rule in the island and thus a fait accompli for the British. British crown rule could present itself as the bearer of freedom, eliminating in one stroke practices sanctioned by Hindu tradition and VOC rule.

In the early period, before the first slaves left Jaffna for Chilaw, the then collector viewed their potential for full moral and legal subjecthood and described their future in rosy terms: "After their time of servitude has expired such as have behaved well and wish it, will be settled in government lands and grants of the same made to them with whatever assistance may appear necessary to enable them to bring such into cultivation."[132]

How many of these emancipated slaves were awarded land of their own to cultivate is not known. Was it in Chilaw or in Jaffna? What does the ethnic crucible in Chilaw mentioned by Casie Chetty reflect? It is possible that emancipated slaves joined a newly formed pool of wage labor that would have been needed for the clearing of lands belonging to the growing group of local land magnates such as the Coreas or the Jayewardenas who had been given land grants or bought land and were opening vast areas for planting coconut, paddy, and other produce.

When, in the early 1840s, John Scoble wrote to the secretary of state to the colonies on behalf of the British and Foreign Anti-Slavery Society, warning him that "the extended culture of coffee and sugar which has taken place within the last two years, will necessarily extend the evil (of slavery)," he believed that enslaved people from the North would, in the future, fill the needs for labor on plantations. He also displayed the preconceptions of his time about the superiority of wage labor over servile labor.[133] Coffee needed seasonal labor from the mid-1840s onward. Yet only a few of the emancipated slaves of Jaffna would join the migrant labor on coffee plantations that was mainly brought from South India, where there was a constant pool of landless peasants in search of work.[134] Perhaps emancipated slaves, having escaped from legal bondage, sensed that Vellalar domination was still more acceptable than becoming subjects to a finely attuned repressive labor code, the precursor of which they had experienced working in Chilaw. In the plantation era built on "free labor" that thrived in the mid-nineteenth century, the constituents of coercive social discipline rather than disappearing would assume a new configuration.

CHAPTER V

The Plaint of an Emancipated Slave

A Play in Two Acts

The Slave of MH S6 first stepped upon the stage of modern history in 1942.
AMITAV GOSH[1]

Nothing further took place in this cutchery.
G. DEANE[2]

In 1826 Packier Pulle Rawothan, a resident of the city of Colombo in the British crown colony of Ceylon, applied to the headman of the Muslim community (known as the headmoorman) of the district of Colombo to obtain permission that his son be circumcised.[3] This act of a father belonging to the small Muslim community of the island would not in any way have been unusual or exceptional and hence enter the colonial archive if not for the fact that it led an entire section of the Muslim community of Colombo to rise up in opposition, seeking to preempt the possibility of Rawothan obtaining the permission he sought. This spawned a war of reports, petitions, and complaints, one of which went up to the governor of Ceylon and others to three successive collectors of Colombo, and led to a court case filed by Rawothan in the provincial court of Colombo against eight members of the Moors, the largest Muslim community in the island.[4] The issue was spelled out quite simply: Rawothan was described by members of his community as someone "of slave extraction," further castigated as "a cooly and the son of a maid slave of Pakkeer Pulle," and thus in their opinion not eligible to perform "such honorary ceremonies the respectable Moors are only entitled to perform."[5] This encounter of slavery and Islam on an Indian Ocean island illustrates the importance of looking at the way Islam was practiced in specific acts and performances rather than as abstract principles. As it developed in Indian Ocean rim states, in settings far away from the Arab heartland, Islam as a set of beliefs, legal norms, and social practices was transformed through its interaction with local societies.

Somewhat like Amitav Ghosh's celebrated Slave of MS H6, this chapter is the product of a fortuitous discovery in the Sri Lanka National Archives.[6] The lengthy correspondence between British officials and the group of irate Moormen who describe themselves as "respectable Moors," as well as reports regarding the court action brought by Rawothan against these Moors and later against the headmoorman, spanning a period of two and a half years, have until now escaped the eye of historians of early British rule.[7] These rediscovered documents reveal aspects of the forgotten lives of slaves and emancipated slaves and enable us, albeit only very partially, to reconstruct the contexts in which they lived. They are invaluable as records of a human story of revolt motivated by a strongly felt sense of injustice and a desire for equality. Sadly, the lack of an outcome to the plaint of Rawothan shows the gulf between legislation and quotidian colonial practice.

The thirty-two handwritten pages filed in the records of the Colombo kachcheri (public office) exist as a testimony of the legitimate strategies of claim making that were available to and used with some confidence by disgruntled subjects of the colony: these ranged from writing petitions to court action in the provincial court. In both instances, relations between people were mediated through sheets of paper, exemplifying that the crown colony was not dissimilar to what has been aptly called the "Document Raj" across the Palk Straits.[8] These documents constitute a large bundle of letters dated from 1825 to 1827, organized in no particular chronological order. They occupy a quarter of a single bound file of the Colombo kachcheri records, attesting to the careless and disordered documentary regime that had been put in place in the kachcheri. Insofar as legibility permits, they have been identified as the following and reordered in a chronological manner.

1825

- The Humble Petition of Packier Rawothan Naynia a Moorman of Colombo to Thomas Eden Esq, Collector of Colombo, July 1825
- Letter by G. Deane, Collector, on September 4, 1825: Packier's petition is dismissed

1826

- Petition by Moor inhabitants to E. Layard, Collector of Colombo, April 1826
- The Humble Report of the Headmoorman of Colombo, Arbitrator and Priests of Colombo, April 5, 1826
- Complaint made by Packier Pulle Rawothan to the Respectable Headman, Arbitrators and Aliem Saib or High Priest, May 29, 1826
- Report of the Arbitrators Muhammed Lebbe Seccado Mira Lebbe, Headmoorman of the district of Caltura as senior arbitrator, chief priests, priests and arbitrators to C. L. Layard Esq, Collector, June 8, 1826

1827

- Provincial Court 7262—Packier as Plaintiff and Magadoes Nayna Packier Bawa and 7 others as Defendants
- Enclosed letter/certificate with signatures of 14 people in support of Packier, January 25, 1827
- Letter from Commissioner of Revenue to Collector of Colombo, February 9, 1827[9]

Rawothan, although a free subject in colonial Sri Lanka, soon came to the realization that his freedom was illusory if he was not recognized as free by his community, the Moors of the island, and as equal by the colonial authority, embodied in the person occupying the function of collector of Colombo. The inherent injustice of being free albeit unable to act as a free man triggered his long battle. The acts that followed his application for the ceremony of circumcision of his son, petition writing and appeal to the law, can be read as a performance in freedom that led to a claim for equality. From being an object of regulation and law, Rawothan, by asserting his freedom in court and by acting on his anger, became a wielder of power. It is through this "breaking and entering in play" that he challenged the denial of equality meted by his community.[10] The colonial state and the legal system were perceived less as potential instruments of justice than as a stage to make claims for social equality in a public arena.

This chapter will first set the stage where Rawothan acted out his claim for equality, namely, the Moor community and the city of Colombo. Then it will examine the two acts in Rawothan's performance: first, his claim to a form of religious humanity and Islamic equality with the Moors of Colombo, who in turn refuted his argument with allusions to the virtue of respectability; and second, his claim to juridical and political equality as a free colonial subject to colonial authorities, who responded with prudence as upholders of the prevailing social order. As we will see, his performance of selfhood was mirrored by that of his opponents' claim for respectability, a claim made to the colonial state at a particular moment of history.

Setting the Stage

The Moor Community in Colombo in the 1820s

When the Portuguese set foot in Sri Lanka in 1505, a country that was already extremely diverse ethnically and religiously with an elite culture that was anything but monolithic in its modes of civility, technology, allies, and rituals, they encountered a community of Muslims whom they dubbed as "Mauros" or Moors. The Muslims of Sri Lanka appear to have referred to themselves as Sonahar, which in the pure Tamil form of Conakar denotes a connection to a native of Arabia or their descendants.[11] The presence of this community identified as Moors is part of a complex picture of Islam's long-standing presence in the Indian Ocean region as well as pre-Islamic seaborne trade, Arabic and Persian, among South Asia, Southeast Asia, and the Middle East. By the mid-eighth century, under the Umayyad Caliphate (661–750), merchants from the Gulf region were sailing the seas in search of markets along coastal eastern Africa and western India. In the centuries that followed, as the Abbasid Empire (750–1258) became more prosperous, the demand for luxury goods led Muslim merchants to explore markets even further. Gradually Arabic became the language of trade and Islamic law and "provided a legal framework for regulating trade" in the western Indian Ocean.[12]

As in other islands and coastal area trade, travel and sufi brotherhoods played a central role in the dissemination and formation of local communities claiming Arab descent, who today see themselves as communities founded by Indian Ocean commerce. These include the "Moors" of Sri Lanka and the Maraikkars of Tamil Nadu. Muslim communities settled in various parts of the island, and by the seventh century large populations of farmers were established on the east coast of the island. Archeological evidence also points to seventh- and eighth-century Muslim settlements in the north of the country.[13]

In this precolonial period, Buddhist kingdoms in the island permitted Arab merchants to establish themselves in port settlements such as Colombo, similar to their settlements in places like Calicut, India, where they often had local wives and children.[14] Over centuries, strong commercial, cultural, and migrational links developed between Tamil-speaking Muslim communities in Sri Lanka and the Muslims of the Malabar and Coromandel Coasts. Iranian merchants, who had dominated the seas in the pre-Islamic era, continued to play an important role in the Indian Ocean from China to East Africa. Persian continued to be one of the lingua franca in the western Indian Ocean alongside Arabic, as the fifteenth-century trilingual tablet installed by the Chinese Admiral Zheng He in Sri Lanka testifies. Rather than Arabic, the tablet was in Persian, Chinese, and Tamil.[15] In the fourteenth and fifteenth centuries Indian Muslim communities grew along the coasts of the island, fed by regular streams of migrants from port settlements of the Indian subcontinent. The Sri Lanka Moors, like the coastal Muslims of South India, were Sunni Muslims of the Shafi'i legal school, residing on the eastern coast of the island owing to the Kerala connection, which has also influenced Tamil Hindu social structure in Sri Lanka, to a large degree following matrilineal and matrilocal family patterns. Engseng Ho refers to a "new world" for Islam created along the long-distance trade routes of the Indian Ocean, symbolized by a common allegiance to the Shafi'i school and stretching from Sri Lanka to Timor. The Moors of Sri Lanka belonged to the "enlarged Islamic ecumene" traversed by numerous Muslims, including the Hadramis from Arabia.[16] This particular form of Islamic thought and practice that was shaped by merchants rather than sultans, soldiers, or scholars is evocatively encapsulated in the term "Monsoon Islam," which encompasses the borderless maritime world of precolonial East, Southeast, and South Asia and East Africa.[17]

When the Portuguese encountered people they called Moors in Sri Lanka in the early sixteenth century, they were a well-integrated group that had been given royal permission to collect custom duties and regulate shipping in the major southwestern port settlements then under the control of Sinhalese kings of Kotte. According to Markus Vink, there was a flourishing trade in areca between the Madurai Coast and Sri Lanka that was dominated by "Muslim Maraikkayars, along with significant numbers of Hindi Chetties and some Christian Parava merchants."[18] During Dutch rule the status of Moors worsened, and from 1665 their trading and shipping was subject to differential and discriminatory duties, not only because of their faith but also because of the threat they posed to the European monopoly of overseas trade. As a result, many Moors, fleeing persecution, migrated to the central Kandyan kingdom from the coastal areas, where they diversified their occupations from purely trade to paddy cultivation, fishing, tailoring, and other crafts and were often enlisted in the local army or as royal guards.

According to Ameer Ali, Sri Lanka's link with the interconnected Islamic world of the precolonial era was cut off with the presence of the Portuguese in the Indian Ocean.[19] Pilgrimages to Mecca and the movement of Islamic scholars and clerics were severely hampered, and Portuguese rule inadvertently contributed to the formation of a community of Muslim people more and more rooted in the island.[20] While early Dutch rule systematically restricted the economic and religious life of the Moors, in the latter half of Dutch rule Governor I. W. Falck introduced a number of measures that showed a more cordial relation with Muslims: he was instrumental in having a code of customary laws drafted for the Muslims and another for the Mukkuvar caste, the Tamil-speaking Muslims in the Batticaloa and Puttalam districts who had a special customary law of intestate succession.[21] In the case of the Muslims of Sri Lanka, Governor Falck in 1770 obtained the code relating to marriage and inheritance from a chapter entitled "Special Laws Relating to Moors or Mahommedans and Other Native Races" in the New Statutes of Batavia of 1766. This exercise in social engineering was rationalized as a measure especially important to protecting Muslim people, supposedly ignorant of their own laws, against potential abuses by headmen.[22] During the same period Falck was instrumental in nominating Muslim headmen and employing Muslims as assessors.

The self-identification of Muslims of Sri Lanka with Arabia was accompanied by attempts, from the nineteenth century on, at proving a racial connection with people from Arabia through ethnological, cultural, and textual sources that were subject to contestation.[23] Yet more important than their veracity or falsity, they showed a determination among members of this community to claim difference vis-à-vis the Hindu Tamils and, unlike Muslim communities in other parts of South Asia, to assert an ethnoreligious identity rather than a purely religious one. From the 1830s, when the idea of political representation in the newly established Legislative Council based on ethnic community (Tamil, Low Country Sinhalese, and Burgher) was introduced with the Colebrooke-Cameron reforms, it became imperative for Moors to play up their uniqueness as a community. Claims to ethnicity were claims for political recognition, and it was crucial to fend off attempts to absorb Muslims into the Tamil community. This issue became acrimonious in 1885 when the Tamil representative Ramanathan argued at the Legislative Council that the Moors of Ceylon were actually ethnologically Tamil and hence not eligible for a separate seat in the Legislative Council. In 1889, however, Muslim and Kandyan Sinhalese members were added to an expanded Legislative Council.[24]

The events described in this chapter took place in the city of Colombo, the capital that had grown out of a small migrant settlement adjacent to the seaport, Kolonthota. In Deputy Surveyor General R. L. Brohier's accounts of the city under three successive colonial regimes, the Portuguese lived in the residential area or the Pettah (*pita kottuva* meaning outer fort) where they established churches and married indigenous women. The city they established marginalized Muslim traders and indigenous people in a predominantly white Christian city. Their progeny were known as Toepasses (Tuppahi, children of mixed marriages). The Dutch (1658–1796) housed their entire administration in the main citadel, where they accommodated Hollanders, Toepasses, and other Europeans working for the VOC, known generally as Burghers. Outside its walls to the north lay the Pettah, and beyond it the suburbs of Wolfendaal, Hulfsdorp, St. Sebastian Hill, and the Moorish quarter, and to the east Slave Island, which is believed to have housed the Kaffir (African) slaves.[25] A commission appointed by Governor Simmons allocated specific areas in the immediate vicinity of the fort to Muslims, Chetties, and Paravas who had settled there during the Portuguese period, and each community was under the charge of a headman.[26] During the early British period five hundred families who were the descendants of Dutch and Portuguese were kept in a marginal position and confined to the Pettah, outside the fort.

According to the census of Ceylon in 1814, there were 31,618 Muslims and 166,242 Sinhalese in the maritime provinces. In Colombo, of a total population of 134,507, there were 6,382 Moors, which accounted for about 5 percent of the population. Ten years later, in the census of 1824, the number of Moors in Colombo had increased to 13,421 in a population of 213,930 for the city. These figures give an approximate sense of the presence of Moors in Colombo, a small minority able since 1799 to practice their faith freely yet unable to establish places of worship or schools without obtaining licenses from the governor.[27]

A few years before the events that concern Rawothan, a petition was signed by the slaveholding inhabitants of Colombo, as mentioned previously. This address to the Prince Regent for Emancipating Children Born of Slaves after August 12, 1816, gives an interesting breakdown of the ethnic distribution of slaveholders in Colombo in the early nineteenth century and belies the common assertion that they were only Dutch and Burghers.[28] For a small community, the Moors had a rather high proportion of slaves, which comes as an anomaly given the interdiction that prevailed during Dutch times for Muslims to purchase slaves from Christians, as stated in the Statutes of Batavia of 1749[29]. This fact was pointed out in 1800 in an official communication to the Marquis of Wellesley, governor general of India:

> The manner in which the unhappy persons, whom it is the principal object of the proposed regulations to protect, are treated in general by their masters and mistresses of every nation, cast, and religion, within these settlements, render it a positive duty of Government, to delay as little as possible, the adoption of strong measures for their relief. Those which I propose are taken chiefly from the statutes of Batavia, particularly from one published in the 1770, and which recurred, in some instances to the civil law, on which the jurisprudence of Holland is founded; and, as the principal class of proprietors of slaves are of the Mahomedan religion, I have adopted, and made general some of the regulations by which the Khoran and its commentators have softened the rigours of slavery, at the same time that they established its lawfulness.[30]

The breakdown of proprietors of slaves, signatories of the 1816 statement, shows a proportion of Moor (Muslim) proprietors higher than their number would warrant, though they do not appear to form the "principal class of proprietors":

Dutch Inhabitants and Burghers: 107
Vellales (Goyigama caste Sinhalese): 38
Fisher cast: 17

Washer cast: 24
Mahabadde (cinnamon peelers): 20
Malabars (Tamils including Chettiars): 30
Moors: 29[31]

Some names appear twice in the following Moor proprietors list:

Slema Lebbe Markan	Nayna Markan
Secadi Markam	Ossena
Sego Mira Lebbe	Kooskanie
Aliar Markan	Slema Lebbe
Ibrahim Lebbe	Segoe Mira Lebbe
Oedoma Lebbe	Seesma Lebbe
Katte Lebbe	Secca Markan
Wappoo Markan	Oedoema Lebbe
Pakkier Tamby	Mahadoen Pulle
Seesma Lebbe Constable	Pakier Pulle Segoe Lebbe
Alpiers Sinne Lebbe	Hadjie Marikan
Packier Tamby	Ahamadoe Lebbe Markan
Secadie Markan	Sinne Loawppoo
Alchoe Markan	Seesma Lebbe
Omer Lebbe Markair	

The list of names displays a very strong influence of Tamil on Moor names of the period. The Tamil phonetic influence can, for instance, be seen in a name like Ahamadoe Lebbe Markan—Ahamadoe for Ahmed, or in the use of Tamby in the name Packier Tamby, which means younger brother in Tamil. Many of the names also bear the two suffixes Marikkar (Markan, Markair) and Lebbe. For Simon Casie Chetty, Marikkar was a name especially applicable to headmen. In southern India the Labbais were a Tamil-speaking Muslim group said to be descendants of Qur'anic scholars. In Sri Lanka the term Lebbe appear to have been used as an honorary affix as well as to describe "priests officiating in their temples."[32]

The proprietor named Pakier Pulle Segoe Lebbe was possibly the former master of Rawothan's mother. In the decades that follow, one loses sight of most of these proprietors. Slave registers of the period 1818–1832 list only two names of Muslim slave proprietors in Colombo: Markar Mira Lebbe, owner of two female slaves and one child; and Mamo Atcha, widow of Sisma Lebbe, owner of four slaves, two males and two females, and three children.[33] The small number of Moor slaveholders who registered their slaves does not necessarily reflect the patterns of slaveholding that continued throughout the nineteenth century. Other sources suggest that even after the formal abolition of slavery in 1844, it was common for Moors to purchase boys from Sinhalese parents who were too poor to maintain them, for the purpose of bringing them up as Muslims, and that these converts were known as Maulas, a term that connotes "freed slave" in other Muslim societies.[34]

Rawothan, Son of an Emancipated Slave

The folio gives us only a few details about the main actor in this story, Rawothan Packier Pulle. He enters the story marked by his inheritance as the son of an emancipated slave woman, whose father is not alluded to. His name, however, is perhaps a claim of a sort that his father was someone called Packier. Pulle or Pillai means son in Tamil or Malayalam. Rawothan's story happened before the formal abolition of slavery in 1844 but during the decade when an act (1821) enforcing a gradual abolition of slavery through registration of slaves was introduced in the maritime provinces. Rawothan's lineage from his mother's side was unknown and also never alluded to. After the 1840s, mention of slavery was expunged from British colonial documents, and seldom was descent from slaves claimed or remembered. In popular consciousness, slavery is connected to the African continent and evidenced by the progeny of Africans, who were brought during Portuguese, Dutch, and British colonialism for hard labor and military service. This ethnic group called Afro–Sri Lankans remains a visible connection to a past where some Africans at least were used in the island as slaves. Known as "Kaffirs" in colonial times, they were and still are easily identifiable in villages in the Puttalam and Batticaloa areas of the island and have been the object of studies by ethnolinguists and musicologists.[35]

Rawothan's ancestry may be from Africa or from elsewhere; his name, however, points to a southern Indian origin. His mother or her parents would have been brought from either a VOC territory or a slave-sourcing location outside Sri Lanka since the custom in the VOC empire was not to enslave people from the region. Slaves often moved around VOC territories with their owners. Rawothan's story and that of his mother were thus intrinsically linked to the two centuries of Indian Ocean slave trade that involved capturing, buying, selling, and transporting unfree labor from one locale in Asia or Africa to work in homes or fields or construct forts and factories in another.

Once Rawothan ceased as a child to be a slave, he would have joined the world of free wage labor. We learn that he worked as a coolie for Markar Mira Lebbe, the head coolie, a function that entailed recruiting labor as a contractor and providing their service to labor-seeking businesses.[36] From the replication of Rawothan as the plaintiff in an 1827 court case against eight Moors of Colombo who opposed his application to have his son circumcised according to custom, we patch together some meager details of his personal life. We learn that he was married to Attachchy Oemman and had several children by her. One of the witnesses even remarked that Rawothan was the natural son of Packier Pulle, his former proprietor. Another witness pointed out that Rawothan's sister's name on her marriage registry does not register a father, and that she is hence not "borne to Packier Pulle." Other witnesses, too, confirmed that there is no evidence of Pakier Pulle having declared that Rawothan was born to him. What was established was that his mother, Slamathy, was the maid slave of Packier Pulle's deceased wife. There is a silence on the nature of the relation between Packier Pulle, his wife, and Slamathy. However, in a household with slaves and master, one can surmise that the imbalance of power was such that a maid had no option but to acquiesce to sexual relations. There was no element of choice in a situation when one party had control and ownership of the body, although such a situation could also have resulted in ties of affection forming between master and slave.[37]

Rawothan was not a man without friends or supporters of a certain standing. These included two priests and a constable, who signed their names on a certificate to the collector in order to convince him that "in the time of the former headmoorman, barbers were allowed to attend marriage and funeral ceremonies of several persons of equal rank with Rawothan Packier Pulle Naynia." They are, with license given to an execrable transliteration of their names: Seyyedoo Omar Ebonoo Mussettoo, Moor priest; Seyyedoo Alepe Ebonoo Agammaolo, Moor priest; Mamina Lebbe, constable; Setia Marikar; Seesma Lebbe Samoo doorey; Oodoma Lebbe; Samoo Lebbe Markar; Casy Lebbe; Seesma Lebbe Tamby Naina; Rattoo Bava; Pathier Alloor; Segoo Ismael Lebbe; Samsie Lebbe Marikar; Pakkier Pulle Samsy Lebbe; Asy Lebbe Marikar; Isboo Lebby.[38]

But was this letter actually supporting Rawothan's plea for equality given that barbers, the Osta, were themselves a socially marginalized group among Moors and were largely endogamous? The fact that barbers had attended ceremonies of people of equal rank as Rawothan was a far cry from an acknowledgment of Rawothan's respectable status.

Manumission

Building on the insights of Marcel Mauss in particular, Orlando Patterson's pathbreaking work has described and analyzed the rituals of redemption, where unfree people are ceremonially released as a ritual process that "amounts to a classic instance of the anthropology of gift exchange" between master and slave. Through this system defined as "prestation," a new social compact is put in place.[39] In the report of arbitrators to Collector C. L. Layard, witnesses described the process of manumission of Slamathy and her two children Rawothan and Koonjal: "the wife of Packier Pulle in her deathbed had asked for her husband Packier Pulle and requested him to emancipate the maid slave Slamathy, her children Rawothan and Koonjal after her death by making them pass under the bier of her dead body."[40] It was a ritual passage where the body emerging from under the bier came out newly born to a different status. Such a manumission of a slave mother (*umm al-walad*) was not according to the Islamic custom that prevailed among Muslims of the Shafi'i school of jurisprudence, where a slave woman was free upon the death of a master who had cohabited with her and rendered her pregnant.[41] The classic manual of jurisprudence does not mention manumission upon the death of the master's wife. There are, however, no other descriptions or scholarly studies of the way manumission took place in Sri Lanka and more specifically in a Muslim household in the mid-1820s. One searches in vain for similar description in other societies where emancipation of slaves was carried out and for textual sources that refer to the ritual rather than to the fact of manumission.

Islam was born in societies where slavery was a fact of life. Freeing a slave was considered a pious act in Islam. Manumission was endorsed in the Qur'an, which "directs Muslims to write contracts of emancipation when slaves seek them and encourages Muslims to bestow a portion of the God-given wealth when they free slaves."[42] It served as expiation for a number of ill deeds, such as manslaughter or violation of a solemn oath, and was accepted as a means to draw closer to God.[43] Yet there was a clear hiatus between the normative scriptural precepts and social reality that determined the response to slavery in different societies. There was no uniform or monolithic Islamic viewpoint on manumission.[44] The description of the ceremony involving Rawothan is exceptional, as rituals of manumission have not been explored in any depth in the Indian Ocean world, in contrast to the ancient world. In Roman society in late antiquity, the most common method was the *alapa* or slap on the side of the head of the slave by the master. It was performed in front of witnesses and a magistrate and resulted in freedom after a final act of violence.[45] In the premodern world, ceremonies of release were common. Among the Langobards, freed slaves were passed from lord to other freemen until the fourth, who then led them to a crossway and handed them weapons, from where they could then go wherever they wished. What these ceremonies from Babylonia to Germanic societies shared was the communal nature of the act of manumission performed to symbolize transition to a new self for the liberated slave.[46] In the Indian Ocean Islamic world, sources generally stressed the reasons that led proprietors to engage in manumission. In Morocco, for instance, it was a way of securing a better place in the other world, hence the frequency of manumission in the testamentary mode and at the death of the owner, or motivated by the wish to expiate a sin.[47] One can surmise from these examples that at the deathbed, as in in the case of Slamathy and her two children living in a Muslim/Moor household in Colombo, manumission was "a pious act that was good for the master's soul" and "enhanced the master's good name and honor."[48]

Years later, Rawothan, a free man, laid a claim to equality on the basis of two forms of entitlement: first, as belonging to the ummah, the community of believers, and second, on the basis of being a free subject of the colonial state.

Being Muslim and Religious Humanity

The Emancipated Slave as a Religious Subject

Prophet Muhammad and his immediate successors advanced a pietistic egalitarianism. The ritual of the Hajj, the pilgrimage to Mecca, illustrates the egalitarian ethos in Islamic belief and practice. When asking to be treated as an autonomous subject who as a Muslim was endowed with the same rights and duties as the collectivity he belonged to, Rawothan was inspired by his knowledge of the Qur'an. The Qur'an and the Sunnah asked of the believer that he act to "bring about a state of equality in human affairs" and viewed equality as "an action-virtue."[49] However, in the Qur'an the distinction between slave and free was used as an example of God's grace and thus considered part of the natural order. Slaves were considered members of the private household though of a status lower than that of a free family member and more consistent with the view of slaves in the ancient Near East. The Qur'an emphasized society's responsibility toward the slave and recognized the humanity of the enslaved.[50] Yet there was no explicit injunction to encourage the community—and former masters—to accept an emancipated slave or her descendants as equal members and treat her as such. In the case of the Moors in Sri Lanka, the fact that their community was in the process of defining its boundaries using the trope of "respectability" founded on birth, wealth, and occupation as features for inclusion led to a further challenge to the egalitarian orientation of the Islamic religious ethos. The extension of an egalitarian religious ideal to the social sphere was not a given in many stratified societies where forms of discrimination persisted after formal manumission. Talal Assad and others have addressed the complexities of "the phenomenon of inequality in Islamic society."[51]

Rawothan, as a devout Muslim man, wished the ceremony of circumcision to be performed on his eldest son, Awoor, and applied to the headmoorman, Oedema Lebbe, for permission and for the barber to attend to the ceremony and invite the guests "who are in a habit of frequenting and taking their meals" in his house.[52] The British recognized the importance of circumcision as central to being a Muslim. A British official, in a curious mimicking of the language of the "respectable Moors," wrote of circumcision as an "honor" that Rawothan was applying for, or as a "prayer."[53]

The behavior of the various parties involved in scuttling the possibility of a religious ceremony for Rawothan's child needs to be scrutinized as much in terms of religious motives as in casting light on a field structured by its own institutions, relations of authority, instilled dispositions, and representation of symbolic capital. More than the operation of circumcision itself, it was the practice of using the barber to invite guests that was deemed unacceptable by the Moors of Colombo. This was the practice that bestowed distinction on some and denied it to others. While the folio in the archives gives no detail of the ceremony of circumcision in the early nineteenth century, Mudaliyar Casie Chetty provides us with a lively description of a circumcision ceremony that happened a few years after the event involving Rawothan:

> According to the ordinance of Mohammed, a boy ought to be circumcised on the eight day, as among the Jews (Gen xvii, 2); but they commonly defer the performance of this rite to the tenth or eleventh year and sometimes longer.
>
> It must be observed that great show attends the performance of every thing connected with the native character, whether joyful or otherwise, and that pomp is the first thing thought of in the celebration of all that relates to them. In the case of circumcision it is announced as a great event; a pandal is erected, friends invited &c. and on the day appointed, the head moorman and priest also attend, when the boy is dressed up and placed on an elevated seat, early to display his clothes. His first visit to the mosque, to say prayers, whither he is taken in procession, under a canopy, with such appendages of honor and distinction as may be due to his rank; he is then taken through the streets in procession, and should he pass the house of a relative is regaled with bruised plantains and milk while the women shout. This perambulation generally takes place at night by torch light, and as it would be inconvenient to circumcise the boy then, it is deferred until the next evening, when the same persons assemble and the operation is performed by a barber. Loud shouts and discordant music is continued during the time, so as effectually to drown any noise the boy may make. A plate being set before the assembly money is collected, which, with the babilliments of the boy, become the requisite of the barber, besides what the parents may also give him. No entertainment is provided on this occasion, but some days afterwards a small repast is spread in commemoration of the event, consisting chiefly of rice puddings, grule and sesamum oil.[54]

Thus circumcision that was a rite of passage for the child, considered compulsory among Muslims of the Shafi'i school of Islamic law, became for Rawothan a symbol of acceptance and recognition within the wider Islamic community of himself and his kin. It was, after all, believed by all that Abraham was the first man to be circumcised on God's instructions.

A Play in Respectability

The events that unfolded around Rawothan's claim became a play in respectability performed by members of a community that had only very recently begun to be considered as part of the charmed circle of colonial allies. When the Moors staged their outrage as respectable subjects, it was clearly for a larger public than Rawothan and his family. By excluding Rawothan, the Moors of Colombo were presenting themselves to the colonial authorities as a community that was cleansing its less honorable aspirants and that would have to be reckoned with in the future. Drawing the boundaries of inclusion in the community through rituals was essential for a group still in need of legitimacy and eager to project itself as equal to the Sinhalese and the Tamils but different in spite of being Tamil speakers. How they did it, however, is "largely outside the vision of historians," as Robert Ross so sharply reminds us, because written sources can only give us an impression of what really went on. Physical postures, rituals, languages, dress, and food are ways in which people marked their status or claimed a status they felt they deserved.[55] In the mid-1820s Muslims remained absorbed in customary means of livelihood. English-language education, still in the hands of Christian missionaries, was not open to them, nor was it attractive.[56] There was still no explicit language of affirmation of a racial identity based on an Arab lineage, but what was emphasized was a certain claim of respectability by traders who wanted to display their distinction from the world of hard labor.

Rawothan's plaint and the response of his opponents need to be located within the space of a community in the making. His encounter with headmoormen, priests, and arbitrators sheds light on ideas of status and class that pervaded among the Moors as well as other communities that had similarly fluid boundaries during this period. A semiotic history of the early nineteenth-century Colombo needs to be written for the light it would shed on groups such as the Muslims and the Burghers, who showed a similar feeling of unease vis-à-vis any form of common inheritance with formerly enslaved people.[57] The cleansing of the Burghers of any connections to enslaved people had begun a few years earlier during the discussions that eventually led to admitting local people, or, in Sir Alexander Johnston's words, "natives" and "half-castes," to sit in juries in criminal trials. Respectability for Burghers was not only the ability to present oneself in European dress. There were certain other criteria that permitted respectable Burghers to purify their group, one of them being to disclaim any person who was connected to emancipated slaves. In 1809 a list of names compiled by a group of Burghers based on "the information given by the constables of the different divisions," divided in three categories of "the present inhabitants of Colombo who go in European dress" was sent to the governor to offer advice on suitability for jury duty. Predictably, the letter was signed by a number of prominent Dutch Burghers of Colombo, among whom were Andringa, Van Dort, Francken, Giffening, Hofland, and Wickerman. The two main criteria of distinction that underlined the creation of separate lists were lineage and occupation. The first category was of "Europeans Descendants of Europeans by the father or the mother's side without any distinction." Among these were the familiar names Olke Andringa, J. H. Uhlenbeck, and Jacob Burnand, and amounting to 432 males and 805 male children under sixteen years. The second category was entitled "Malabar and Cingalese Descendants that earn their bread in the same manner as the Europeans." They numbered 96 males and 310 male children under sixteen. The third category is the most intriguing: "Descendants of free slaves that earn their bread in the same manner as the Europeans": a much smaller group of 35 males and 106 male children under sixteen. The three lists provided for each name the employment of the person. The first list was an example of respectability and distinction since the majority of the men listed, from the most important employs to the most humble, were either in the army, in the colonial administration, or employed as bookkeeper, proctor at the Supreme Court, shopkeeper, writer, or dancing master, with an occasional but rare carpenter or tailor; only the last pages of the listed Europeans included names of seamen, coopers, and blacksmiths. The occupations of the Malabars and Cingalese were as diverse, starting from Malabar and Cingalese preacher to writer, sailor, schoolmaster, surgeon, interpreter to the magistrate, blacksmiths in large numbers, bookbinder, tailors and carpenters in large numbers, soldier, hatmaker, painter, tanner, lacemaker, lanternmaker, hairdresser, gravedigger, musician, and servant. The majority of descendants of slaves were listed as tailors, with a few blacksmiths, shoemakers and fiddlers and a hatter, glassmaker, and carpenter. It was clear that the third list only had men who performed manual labor. It was not necessary to even point this out to the governor, as it was self-explanatory for the signatories of the letter that this factor and their slave ancestry disqualified them from being selected to sit on juries.[58] There was, however, another factor involved. Respectability was also imbued with a very specific class ideology among the Burghers as well as the Moors that was an appropriation of a British notion seamlessly naturalized by colonial society.

To be an equal partner in colonial society with the Sinhalese and the Tamils, Muslims needed to make visible the accoutrements of respectability. Among these, clothing was a marker of status. A simple rule applied: the more the body was covered, the higher the status. Weddings, like circumcision ceremonies, were an occasion for Moors to claim status through clothing and elaborate rituals. Bridal clothes of a Moor groom were described as an "outer garment being a white gown with long sleeves, reaching from his collar bone (where it fits close) to his ankle; the waist is confined by a richly embroidered sash, in which is placed on one side a silver sword or dagger; a scarf is loosely thrown over the shoulders, and he has a turban on his head, formed by a ribbon worked with gold thread."[59]

High status and respectability were the prerogative of headmen. During the Dutch period, native headmen had enforced service obligations on behalf of the government, enjoyed wide judicial authority at the local level, and had overseen all agricultural activity as well as the maintenance of irrigation facilities. There were many complaints on the part of the people against their excesses and corruption. Land, through a traditional form of payment known as accommodessans (the grant of revenues of productive land in villages), was given to the headmen by the Dutch, thus enhancing the power of the native chiefs. They often served as translators. Muslim headmen were present in Dutch-controlled areas such as Colombo, Galle, and Matara, and their main role was to ensure that uliyam service was performed by Muslim inhabitants for the Dutch. In 1762 Uduman Kandy Meestrie Aydroos Lebbe Marikkar was headman of Colombo.[60] With the end of Dutch rule, the power of native chiefs was curbed. During Governor Maitland's term, "all native headmen of the rank of Mohandiram and upwards were to be appointed only by the Governor, the inferior officials being appointed solely by the Commissioner of Revenue on the recommendations of the Collectors."[61]

It was about this time that the British appointed Moors as local headmen for the first time. One of the earliest of these was Hadjee of "Velassy," a distinguished, though little-known, Moor. A more popular individual was Uduman Lebbe Marikar Sheik Abdul Cader, the grandfather of the late I. L. M. Abdul Azeez, who in his day was a prominent member of the Moorish community. He was better known as "Shekady Marikar," and was appointed headmoorman of Colombo by Sir Robert Brownrigg on June 10, 1818. Several other appointments soon followed, and the Moors not only were made chiefs in different parts of the maritime provinces but were also admitted into the public service. The Ceylon Calendar of 1824, which was an official publication in book form, listed the headmoorman of Colombo as Uduman Lebbe Marikar Sheik Abdul Cader.[62] This same name appears in Rawothan's case in 1826. In March 1825 Sir Edward Barnes, governor of Ceylon, appointed the first Moorish notary public, the "Shekady Marikar," "for the purpose of drawing and attesting deeds to be executed by females of the Mussalman religion."[63] Thus by the time Rawothan made his claim in 1825, Muslims were already affirming a new status, which involved respectability as headmen through colonial patronage and entrance into public service, a field traditionally dominated by Burghers and Tamils.

The headmoorman of Colombo was first approached respectfully by Rawothan to obtain his permission to hold the circumcision ceremony. He appears to have considered this option positively until eight members of his community got wind of this and "interdicted him from granting permission on the plea of his [Rawothan] being of a slave extraction" by sending petitions to the governor and the collector of Colombo.[64] The attitude of the eight Moors toward Rawothan was most apparent in the language of their petition to Collector Layard: "That your honor's humble petitioners have been given to understand to their greatest surprise that Rawothan a cooly and the son of a maid slave of . . . Pakkier Pulle has presented a petition."[65] Rawothan's status was immediately made clear. He was a working man, a coolie. His origins were suspect and considered low. He was therefore not eligible to "perform the ceremony of circumcision to his son with such honorary ceremonies the respectable Moors are only entitled to perform." The Moors used the language of the law, "eligible" and later "illegal," when qualifying Rawothan's application to the headmoorman to present their case to the collector. The exclusion of certain people from the community of Moors reflected the Moors' own anxieties as a community in search of consolidation that was for long treated with little respect by the former colonial rulers, Portuguese and Dutch, who marginalized them from the confines of the city and on occasions even persecuted them. Under the Dutch Resolution in Council of February 3, 1747, Moors and Tamils were prohibited from owning property or residing within the Fort and the Pettah or Colombo. Up to this time, according to the old order of things, groups defined communally had separate residential areas allotted to them. For example, the Moors were confined to Moor Street, which is designated Moors Quarters in old maps of Colombo; the Colombo Chetties lived in Chetty Street or Chekku Street. With the change of fortune that came with the British, Moor traders began to acquire the trappings of a middle class, claimed more forcefully descent from Arabs, and distanced themselves from Muslims who had connections to the Indian Muslim coastal communities and by extension people who were brought as slaves from the subcontinent.

The headmoorman's position was ambivalent, as pointed out in the petition of the eight Moormen. They accused Rawothan of having "combined with the headmoormen and arbitrators of Colombo" and the latter of aiding and assisting his application. The arbitrators were also castigated as belonging to the same family as the headmoorman, and hence their ability to be impartial questioned.[66] In the headmoorman report to C. L. Layard that prompted the irate reaction of the community, Sekkady Markar adopted a compromising attitude, listing names of individuals "of such class as the said Rawothan" who had a ceremony performed by the barber: "the undersigned know of their own knowledge that several people who were slaves and who obtained emancipation had performed circumcision for their children through barbers without any objection whatever and therefore the petitioner may in the like way perform the circumcision to his son through Barbers but if he wishes to perform any other ceremony than the circumcision he must then himself invite the guests and perform such ceremony."[67]

The reasons for the headmoorman's partiality vis-à-vis Rawothan's plea were revealed in another "complaint" written by Rawothan to the headman of Colombo, arbitrators, and the high priest in May 1826. He alleged that "about two and a half years ago in order that the Headmoorman, Arbitrators and Priests may attend at the ceremony of circumcision to my child, they asked for a fifth of five hundred Rix . . . and [illegible]." He pleaded further, "This is known to God Allah Prophet and I have paid this with my own hands."

The list of "gifts" appeared in detail:

I paid the headmoorman Rix 150; 10 Parrahs of rice for 20/170
   To the Arbitrator Ahmad Lebbe Marikar: Rix 125; in pots and chatties 3/120

To his brother Arbitrator Mohamed Lebbe Marikar: Rix 25
To the other Arbitrator P. Sekady Markar: Rix 25.[68]

The Priest

The priest appears to have played an important role in convincing the headmoorman to go back on his initial openness to Rawothan's request. In a report on the case written in 1826 by the headmoorman of Caltura (Kalutara) as senior arbitrator, Rawothan, the complainant, alleged that he was asked by the headmoorman of Colombo to produce the "Raddotam" or registry of his marriage. The priest claimed the registry was mislaid. Rawothan then used his own resources to get a "registry made by the guests who assembled at the marriage before the Magistrate Council" in order to satisfy the headmoorman's request.[69] In so doing, he too made a claim for respectability based on the criteria of monogamous registered marriage enshrined by British Victorian society. Illegitimacy was Rawothan's own fate, but he could prove that his son was born to parents who were lawfully married, and he was eager to function within the codes of acceptable behavior. According to Casie Chetty, "among the Moors, the term marriage is usually expressed by the Arabic word Kavin and its synonyme Nihkka, and is by them considered the most essential of all objects."[70]

Rawothan complained about the "new priest" as "the cause by whom this case arose" in his own petition to the headman, arbitrators, and high priest for having "denied registry" of his marriage and disgraced him and his children: "moreover without any regards to this assembly and being himself a respectable man he called me a thief and slave," and for not following the instructions of the collector to the headmoorman "to permit the Priest and Mohideen to attend the House of Markar Mira Lebbe as the Head Calle . . . yet the Mohideen only attended but not the priest." The priest appealed to custom and usage as the main obstacle in granting Rawothan's request.[71] It seems that only the barber (Mohideen) attended the ceremony, but the text is silent about the circumcision of his son. Respectability was manifested by Rawothan in outward signs, such as his explanation that Head Coolie Mira Lebbe, a man of some means, was willing to host the circumcision ceremony in his house, thus bestowing on Rawothan recognition and respect.

The next section will analyze the working of colonial institutions in this dispute and the position taken by its agents when custom and traditional leaders are pitched against the claims of an individual for rights within a liberal discourse.

A Play in Institutions and Rawothan's Claim

What is particularly exceptional is the persistence and courage displayed by Rawothan to claim justice for himself and his family over a period of two and a half years. He made use of the colonial court system in so doing, displaying his relentless though misguided faith in that system and his posture of familiarity with the practices of the colonial state with regard to disputes, registration, and claim making through petitions.

Petitions and Legibility

The rarity of documentary evidence produced by enslaved people in the Indian Ocean world is atoned by the possibilities offered by criminal court cases. Court testimonies that entail written petitions, translated from a local language to English, and other types of correspondence produced by emancipated slaves such as Rawothan do not in any sense constitute truth claims. Historians are aware that testimonies, whether petitions or court appearances, can err toward bending the truth for various reasons, from forgetfulness to a deliberate wish to mislead. The very nature of testimonies makes them appeals to be believed rather than proof. What would one not say to convince?[72] Historians need to read testimonies with caution and suspicion in a near philological mode, not so much for insights into a truth of enslavement but, as in the case of Rawothan, to follow the tribulations of a claim-making descendant of a slave through the hazards and illegibilities of the colonial state, as he battled the prejudices of the Moors as a community, to recognize him as one of them. The statements made in court by the different parties concerned appear in the arbitrators' report through their mediated voice and that of a translator. Furthermore, the content of the petitions too may contain lies and inaccuracies. Yet for the historian, much can be learned from their form and their silences about the antagonistic parties, as well as about the bureaucratic logic of the colonial state.

Petitions and the court system were central artifacts in the making of political subjects in Colombo in the early nineteenth century because colonial subjects were disenfranchised in all other ways, except through these few channels given to them to vent their anger and distress. The frequent use of the colonial court system as a mechanism of dispute settlement by the least fortunate and the proliferation of scribes writing petitions and plaints on behalf of nonliterate plaintiffs tell us something about how government institutions were normatively perceived.

Moors were governed by their own laws, which were codified and proclaimed in the year 1806. These laws, promulgated by the British and based on the code of Muslim Law of the Dutch governor I. W. Falck, related to matters of succession, rights of inheritance, and other incidents occasioned by death and matrimonial affairs. In the case of contracts and all other affairs, the Roman Dutch Law or the Common Law applied. Among the nine documents in the folio, the key items are two petitions: one addressed to the collector of Colombo by local inhabitants and the other by the plaintiff.[73] Petitions were, in the early nineteenth century and before, the main mode of communication between subjects and rulers and were submitted by the humblest of people. There was much faith in the efficacy of written appeals and the sincerity of direct address. Just as in imperial India, preparing petitions was a thriving business where petition writers doubled as translators from vernacular languages to English and from spoken register to bureaucratic language.[74] The petitions of Rawothan and of his opponents open with a similar honorific language that summons up virtues of respect and good conduct: "The Humble petition of Packier Rawothan Naynia, a Moorman of Colombo" and "The humble Petition of the undersigned Moor inhabitants of Colombo."

The tone is deferential, one of humility or even supplication: Rawothan describes himself as the "humble petitioner" while referring to the collector, the recipient of his petition, as "your Honor" and ends with "Shall ever Pray," thus mixing linguistic registers.[75]

The petition as a form belongs to the precolonial political order, where a central feature of the regime was direct access to the highest authorities, then the king, but this practice endured during the colonial period. Before a system of representation or election was put into place from 1833 on, under British rule, local people continued to send their representations to Portuguese rulers and, more specifically when the maritime provinces came under Dutch company rule, to the commander or his representatives. This betrayed the widely held belief that power was concentrated at the apex of government. A petition from 1636, which was presented to the General Portuguese captain, contains a list of claims against headmen (mudaliyars) and other major Sinhalese and Portuguese officials. It was written by lascarins, village chiefs, farmers, and representatives of castes, Salagama and Durava.[76] The petitioners accused the Portuguese of failing in their duty to protect the law and the Sinhalese custom, a promise that was made by the conquerors and entered in the Convention of Malvana.[77] Although many petitioners were not familiar with the language of the colonizers, literacy in the vernacular language was widespread owing to instruction given in Buddhist temples. Most indigenous leaders were educated at least to a certain degree, and they soon became mediators between the rulers and the people. Petitions took different forms, though they were chiefly written collectively. D. A. Kotelawele mentions the petition of a group of persons belonging to the caste of "washers" who were converted to the Dutch Reformed Church and used myths about the origin of their caste to ask the Dutch authorities for permission for men to wear coats and women hats and stockings. In this text, some of the signatories were trying to deny the laws governing customs and traditions of Sinhalese and asking to wear coats, hats, and trousers, which were privileges originally reserved for members of the upper-caste Sinhalese. The petition was a direct way to involve those who would be able to change a social system rooted in century-long mentality. It was heralded by the British as an instrument of social transformation, progress, and claims based on a certain idea of justice that preceded the modern idea of rights. The petition was a way to voice complaints about abuses committed by officials. In 1801 Cornelis de Alwis Vidana and the muhandiram of Caltura (Kalutara) petitioned the governor, complaining of being hit by a British officer, Commander Short, the latter having broken his comb while hitting him on the head. Having been treated in public in this way had created in him a sense of humiliation. The result was that the officer was asked to resign from his official post in charge of finance in Caltura.[78] The British would artfully display their sense of justice and fair play in unimportant incidents, thereby giving the local people the impression that the colonial government was defending their interests. In Sri Lanka, as in India, the British sought to regulate and make petitions the "only legitimate mode of expressing grievance."[79] Before the idea of representation was introduced, the petition was also a means for the representatives of the colonial state, in this instance the collector, to gain information on the complexities and anxieties of the people they controlled. That a working man such as Rawothan would resort to petitioning was therefore not unusual. Yet his persistence and perseverance were exceptional.

From 1805, when Maitland became governor, until 1832, British rule under the Crown was manifested in the provinces and the city of Colombo in the position of the collector, the predecessor of the government agent, who was initially appointed with only the management of revenue in mind. As colonial rule progressed, however, his office concentrated the major administrative, financial, and revenue powers of the administration in the provinces. He had a supervisory role over all officials in his district.[80] In Colombo during the years that concern Rawothan's plaint, there were three collectors: John Deane, succeeded by Thomas Eden in mid-1825, and L. C. Layard, who was collector throughout 1827.[81] The collectorship of Colombo under Layard had a staff composed of two assistants, a head clerk, ten clerks, a clerk and salt storekeeper at Caltura, a keeper of the records of the late land registry, a tombo holder, a shroff, and a salt storekeeper in Colombo. From the names of the staff members, it is apparent that most were either Dutch or Burghers.[82]

None of the three British collectors who were approached by Rawothan for a decision on his case wished to go against what they believed was customary among the Moors. The last account was from the commissioner of revenue, Robert Boyd, whose judgment based on the correspondence sent to him about the case was indecisive: he wrote, "It is clear the person in question has no right to such honor," and he recommended only that he "prosecutes the parties accused for the restitution of the money stated to have been taken from him before the provincial court."[83] John Deane had a similar reluctance to interfere with tradition as he saw it: "It appears upon enquiry from the statement of the Head Moorman that according to their customs the person in question was not entitled to such honors."[84] Layard was the most interventionist of the collectors, asking two sets of arbitrators to make reports about the case by calling the plaintiff and witnesses before them and obtaining evidence. The first report was by the headmoorman, arbitrators, and priest of Colombo, and the second by the headmoorman of the district of Caltura and other priests and arbitrators. Both reports gave Rawothan permission to perform circumcision through the barber but did not permit him to perform "any other ceremony" or invite guests through the barber.[85] Instead of making a decision, however, the collector sent all the documents to his superior, the commissioner of revenue, who in turn bowed to custom and hierarchy even more deeply than the "respectable Moors" by advocating that any form of ceremony performed by Rawothan would be unacceptable.

Provincial Courts, or the Emancipated Slave as Juridical Subject

The court and the judiciary appear in the documents relating to this case as oscillating between "a rational mode of being and a magical mode of being."[86] The judiciary was an arena of arcane rules and regulations, yet it provided a stage for ordinary people to enact their anger and anxieties. The law was seen as the sign of a distant power, but also as a resource for seeking justice. Through the court system, the state was present in the everyday life of the community. The performative aspect of "stateness," with its spectacles and public legal processes, was mirrored and mimicked by Rawothan's use of the court as a stage on which to perform his play on equality and freedom.

A few years before Rawothan appeared in the district court, the judiciary had shown its willingness to uphold the right of the individual, often against what the government conceived as the customs of the local people. One instance was in 1818, when the puisne judge of the Supreme Court, William Coke, ruled against a mudaliyar of the Durawa caste for illegally beating a laborer who had deserted work. Governor Brownrigg, however, in fear of subverting the social order, enforced Regulation 5 of 1818, which authorized headmen to arrest and employ deserters who went against caste obligation. The second example, the case of the slave in a palanquin, is described at length in chapter 3. Here again, the arguments made by the Supreme Court resting on clause 82 of the Charter of Justice of 1801 were set aside by the governor on the basis of respect for tradition.[87] While these cases have generally been read as instances when the judiciary upheld individual freedom against caste society, they could offer another reading where social class comes into play as the determining factor and issues of equality rather than freedom are foregrounded. In both cases, coolie and slave represent the most subaltern groups in society in terms of status, as well as the coercive unpaid labor extracted from them. Were these examples known by people who were, like Rawothan, coolies in the city of Colombo?

Rawothan as a plaintiff represented by a proctor, G. G. Milleband, filed case no. 7262 in the district court of Colombo against Magadoes Nayna Packer Bawa and seven others. His main complaint was that his application to get his son circumcised "was however not attended with any success because the headmoorman was (as he observed) interdicted by the defendants from granting the said permission."[88] Through this act of attestation, the emancipated slave became a juridical subject equal in all ways to his opponents in court. In the late 1820s there were eight provincial courts in Ceylon—at Colombo, Galle, Matara, Jaffna, Trincomalee, Kalpitiya, Mannar, and Batticaloa. In each of the courts, the provincial judge "was assisted by a Dutch Secretary and Clerks, and a native interpreter." The procedure and rules of evidence in court were similar to that in England, with pleadings by affidavit and litigants obliged to pay certain fees.[89] It was the successors of the first governor, Frederick North, who introduced changes in the judiciary. While continuing to enforce Roman Dutch law, they codified Tamil and Muslim law and created a series of courts. The Supreme Court had criminal jurisdiction over the entire island and civil jurisdiction over Colombo and all the Europeans. British judges ruled in the Supreme Court. Everywhere else it was courts of the justice of peace that had civil jurisdiction. Trial by jury was created in 1812, with juries initially selected on caste and class basis.[90] A few years after Rawothan's claims were made, C. H. Cameron, one of the commissioners examining the judicial system of the colony in 1832, commented on the litigiousness of the people who used and abused the system performing perjuries, hatching conspiracies, and forging documents. Apart from the alleged "lack of moral principle" among the natives, the reason for this flurry of judicial activity could be attributed to the feeling among the people that the land tenure system as well as social laws and hierarchies were now uncertain and could be contested.[91] Rawothan's claim for justice as an emancipated slave could be read in this light. It shows a certain courage to take on the Moor establishment and drag it to court. It is possible that he was the natural son of the slaveholder, and that using his name, Packier Pulle, may have given him the confidence to take on the challenge. Ten years later an action was brought for defamation where another plaintiff and his family were called slaves. The Supreme Court did not award damages, since no loss or injury had been incurred, but underlined the moral hurt inflicted on the plaintiff: the plaintiff's object appeared to be only to establish his right to freedom. It further decreed that the defendant should pay the costs on both sides and affirmed "that if a man took upon himself to call another his slave, he did so at his own risk, and if he could not prove his assertion, the least that the person whose freedom was questioned, had a right to expect was that he should be identified for the expense of publicly contradicting the assertion."[92] Was the court system delivering a form of justice less prejudiced by hierarchies and traditional values?

Rawothan partook in the theater of trial procedures, wherein individuals assumed the roles of plaintiff, defendant, witness, judge, and so forth, this theater being, as Hannah Arendt's work on trials shows so cogently, the only guarantee that guilt, culpability, or responsibility for crimes might be attached to individuals as opposed to groups, historical processes, or abstract concepts of good and evil.[93] In the case of Rawothan, the outcome of the court case is lost, so we will never know if he received compensation for the money he disbursed to the headman and arbitrators. Yet as Arendt further states, his accomplishment lies in the performance itself rather than in an end product. His action was effective insofar as he performed before an audience who will judge and remember him.[94]

"The act of manumission," Orlando Patterson argues cogently, "creates not just a new person and a new life, but a new status."[95] When reflecting on why Rawothan was so persistent and used all possible means available to him to demand justice, one reason may be that it was only through acts that he could establish in his community that he was a free man. His status had changed from son of slave to coolie. He was now a wage earner who could pay others—the petition writer or the proctor—for services. But his status remained fragile. Indeed, as long as institutions around him that had awarded him freedom continued to stand by old hierarchies and refused to go beyond deliberation, he would remain inferior in rights and status to those "ill-disposed persons" of his community. Rawothan's language, as it appears in translation in the petition, was based on claims for justice: his petition ended with the words "Grant me justice for the sake of God Allah and the Prophet," which is as much an appeal for rights in the liberal tradition as one based on faith by a religious subject.

His claim stems, we can surmise, from having reached the limit of the endurable where the burden of injustice comes to light. In the opening lines of *L'Homme révolté*, Albert Camus invokes the act of rebellion as that of a man who says "no" after having agreed to take orders all his life. But his act is not purely negative. His refusal is also saying "yes" in an act of affirmation that his life is worthwhile and that he will no longer be ignored. David Scott sums it up as a moment when "the rebel slave abandons the particularity that ties her or him to the imposed—slave—status and identifies with the universality of humanity" and is propelled into decisive action.[96] What, then, is the meaning of an act of refusal? Patterson's oeuvre has been described as a meditation on this question. He argues that while material or ideological conditions matter, it is the arriving at metaphysical crossroads, what he refers to as the "moral autonomy of self-determination," that leads to action.[97] Did Rawothan believe that persuasion through narration and colonial benevolence would answer his plea? His acts show that he relied on the power of the written word, and that propelled him into a particular type of action, framing his act of rebellion within the confines of legality, appropriating the Enlightenment discourse of rights, the outcome of which will sadly never be known. Yet his performance produced him as a free subject.

CHAPTER VI

Eclipse of the Slave

Traces, Hauntings

(Ghosts) . . . by nature they are haunting reminders of lingering trouble.
—AVERY F. GORDON[1]

The entire world is experiencing the process of creolization.
—EDOUARD GLISSANT[2]

This final chapter evokes the eclipse of the slave as a figure of history and her effacement from popular memory. I follow an intuitive path of inquiry that interlaces the past and the present and braids archival traces with their echoes. Memories, as I conceive them, and their absence are constructions of and for the present rather than stored truths, and the history I would like to write is made of the relation between the present and the past.[3] The eclipse of slavery in Sinhalese and Tamil societies is not complete, however, disturbed as it is by ghosts of different sorts. Among the Sinhalese, this chapter suggests, there is a repressed fear of any hint of creole pasts that disturb the comforting certainty of being and belonging and query the idea of unique roots. I consciously use the term *creole* and draw from the body of work that has sought out creolization's applicability outside of the Caribbean, as exemplified in the works of Françoise Verges, Stuart Hall, and especially Edouard Glissant. In recent works the term has been dislodged from its biologized and racialized inscription. I use it, as Glissant does, in a broader sense to describe "the entanglement" or what he calls "the relation between different cultures forced into cohabitation in the colonial context."[4] Among Tamils of dominant castes, invisibility is a symptom of a refusal to face the difficult past of enslavement of one's own people. Recent Sinhalese nationalist rhetoric makes ample use of the Tamil ambivalence toward its own suppressed past to delegitimize rival Tamil claims to a homeland in Jaffna. This chapter moves from traces to hauntings, summoning the ghosts, listening to the murmurs and echoes in the present. It aims to think with and through the end of enslavement.

This approach does not completely shy away from questions generally posed by Rankean historians in search of valid truths who would ask: What then *actually happened* to freed slaves after slavery was abolished in 1844?

By virtue of Ordinance 20 of 1844, slavery was abolished in Sri Lanka. Section 1 states: "Slavery shall no longer exist in the Colony, and that all persons at such time being slaves shall thereupon become free, and entitled in every way to all rights and privileges of free people, any other law or Ordinance to the contrary now in force notwithstanding."[5]

The census of 1837 gave the number of slaves as 12,605 males and 11,910 females in the northern province and a few hundred in other areas of the island. Ordinance 7 of 1843 made registration by proprietors imperative, with the clause that if any slave was not registered before January 1, 1843, absolute freedom was the consequence. Not a single slave was registered, and on the morning of the January 1 "the sun rose on nearly 23,500 freemen (and women) who were nominally slaves the day before."[6] The *Morning Star*, a semimonthly Tamil publication, summed it up: "The neglect of proprietors to attend to the registration of their slaves shows they have little or no desire for the continuance of slavery."[7] It was, however, with the Ordinance of 1844 that slavery in Jaffna officially came to an end.

Where did all these men and women go, if they existed at all? Although this question can be partly answered and will be addressed in a fragmentary way, I find it less central (if not to say futile) than to try to understand the presence and absence of enslaved people in the collective memory of people of Sri Lanka. We need more urgently to fathom the issue of a "repressed memory" about enslaved people. Why were slavery and the existence and manumission of slaves from the sixteenth century onward effaced from the narrative of history at all levels of explanation, comprehension, and representation?[8] What is the local ideological context that makes it possible for enslaved people to be seamlessly associated with "Kaffirs" in popular knowledge and the reality of enslaved people brought over from the East Indies and India to be ignored? Thousands of men and women in Jaffna who were enslaved and freed in the first decades of the nineteenth century appear today in the Sinhalese public discourse only to prove a polemical political point. Their lives, their pain, and their battles remain in the shadows. Why is the slave in the palanquin not celebrated in Jaffna?

I would like to suggest that the confluence of racial ideologies that began in the nineteenth-century imperial world and the ensuing reshaping of Sinhalese, Tamil, Muslim, and Burgher communities based on ideas of purity and authenticity made the slave an aberration or an object of shame. There was degradation or diminishing of the being in the contact and mixing.[9] In the South, as we have seen, the enslaved came from outside; if they had a genealogy traceable to the island, it was one full of mixity, mélange, and miscegenation. It was born of a migrant past that disturbed the official version of the peopling of the island. The inability to accept and celebrate creolization as a process that had been taking place over centuries in Sri Lanka led to a refusal to memorialize the individual that was the embodiment of creole pasts: the slave.

In the North other ghosts were at play. The history of slavery reminded of pasts that one wanted to forget: the potential presence among ancestors of many Tamils in Jaffna of enslaved men and women who were brought as labor by Vellalar landowners or by the Dutch as late as the eighteenth century; the reality of Tamil dominant castes as slaveholders working hand in hand with the Dutch to sustain regimes of bondage that denied equal humanity to thousands of Tamil people.

Deep roots and purity are crucial in islanders' sense of belonging. Sri Lanka's littorals, conquered by the Portuguese in the sixteenth century and the Dutch in the seventeenth century, shared some features with smaller Indian Ocean islands whose creole pasts are acknowledged and that suffered a similar fate of external conquest.[10] Yet the island of Sri Lanka differed from spice and plantation islands such as Mauritius or Réunion in a central manner. Sri Lanka's population was not purely the result of European expansionist needs for labor but a crucible of peoples, whose first traces appear in prehistoric archeological records that date back to 30,000 BCE. Continuous population flows from various parts of the Indian subcontinent over centuries, and other migrants crossing the seas from West Asia and Java or even filtering in from China, contributed to the peopling of the island, adding to and mixing with communities later described as Veddas and typologized by Europeans as the indigenous "primitive' inhabitants of the island."[11] Forgetting the past of mixings and mergings, nationalist ideologues since the nineteenth century tend to focus on the Early Historic Period (ca. 300 BCE) in order to imagine Sri Lanka as a space uniquely and mainly peopled by migrants from eastern India and their descendants, whose lives were only occasionally disturbed by conquerors from across the Palk Straits or beyond.[12] This specious reading of "journeys in" forms an integral part of national myths and dominates the official history of an island even today marred by disputes about who are the first, authentic, and legitimate inhabitants in the modern nation-state. In the foundation myth of Sri Lanka, the land itself is consecrated as a Buddhist land since, as the Mahavamsa recounts, Prince Vijaya arrived on the shores of the island on the very day the Buddha achieved nirvana.[13] The existence of the slave in the midst sits uncomfortably with the mythography of the island as made of clear-cut communities defined by "race" and religion and is a throwback to submerged and cacophonic histories of mixing and merging.

Traces

In an extract from a lost memoir by Johannes Arnoldus Christoffelsz dated January 28, 1851, that comes to us recopied in 1908 by the author's son, emancipation comes to life:

> As executor of my mother's estate I emancipated all our slaves which cost about Pounds 200 on an average of Pounds 15 each consisting of seven men four women and several children. Those born at home were all baptized and my brother and sisters became their sponsors. One of them, a brown girl named Kananga who died shortly after her marriage was brought up like one of us, was educated in the principles of Christianity and attended Church with my mother in a vehicle called tricycle pushed at the back by a strong well built slave and steered by the occupant of the conveyance (William Sperling Christoffelz).[14]

Such traces are rare. Written from the viewpoint of the master rather than the slave, they cannot be taken as more than they are, a single voice of a man writing from a position of power about dominated men and women. Looking at these occasional traces in the archive of former slaves who were emancipated may help us understand the reasons for this invisibility. Invisibility, we will see, is sometimes the necessary condition to create a new self. Rather than political institutions, cultural discourses, and racial categories that have been studied as structuring forces in the production of identities and communities, I turn my attention instead to people's acts, what they did to disappear, and their agency in making themselves something else. A combination of race, class, religion, occupation, chance, and misfortune came into play.

Emancipation in the Longue Durée

Invisibility of slave lineage or heritage did not happen suddenly in 1844 with the passing of the Abolition Act, as an act of cutting away and drowning the past. It was rather a process that unfolded in the longue durée. From the moment slaves were brought to Sri Lanka to work in fields and forts, there is evidence to show that some of them acquired freedom from their masters while others fled and merged into the indigenous population.

Most of the slaves brought to the port cities of Sri Lanka were in transit, as figures from the database Boekhouder Generaal Batavia (Bookkeeper General of Batavia) testify. Occasionally some additional information is inserted in the cargo lists of the ships. Slaves were qualified as quantifiable bodies. On June 13, 1704, a ship named *Matroos* arrived in Colombo with a cargo of forty-five male slaves from the Malabar Coast in transit to Batavia. We learn that "of the 45 slaves, 15 were shipped in good health and 25 others were to follow. One slave died in the Colombo hospital, while three others still lay sick in that hospital. One slave ran away."[15] The history of Colombo, wrote Remco Raben two decades ago, is still to be written. In many ways the silences of historiography on moving peoples makes this statement true even today. What happened to the runaway?[16]

Today people in Sri Lanka either deny that there was any form of slavery—even Buddhist monastic slavery described half a century ago by R.A.L.H. Gunawardena has faded into oblivion—or confuse it with the labor migration of the late nineteenth century to plantations, or immediately associate slavery with the small community of Afro–Sri Lankans who live in villages in Puttalam and Batticaloa.[17] The latter are indeed visible as outsiders insofar as they are seen as culturally and physically different from the Sinhalese majority and the large Tamil and Muslim minorities in the island. The current configuration of international scholarship on slavery does not help. In spite of efforts by historians to write global histories of slavery, it is perceived as uniquely the burden of African people, an idea partly generated or at least sustained by the global representation of slavery in popular culture as Atlantic slavery. It is not surprising that in Sri Lanka, too, only descendants of Africans are thought to be of slave descent. Literary works that point to an early presence of Africans in Sri Lanka confirm, however, that if some of the present Afro–Sri Lankans have a slave heritage probably dating to the Portuguese and Dutch period, not all Africans were slaves. This is quite clear from references to Africans in the Portuguese army in Sinhalese literary works such as the *Parangi Hatana* (War of the Portuguese) and *Rajasinha Hatana* (War of Rajasinghe) and in the British army in the *Kapiri Hatana* (War of the Africans).[18] The *Rajasinha Hatana*, a panegyric poem as well as a text written to embolden soldiers, describes Africans in a disparaging manner as "the worthless Kaffirs, like mountain cats fattened and on beef and steeped in drink."[19] Yet they were also used by local kings and fought alongside local people. Some of the African soldiers fighting for the Portuguese defected to the Sinhalese side and joined the army of Rajasinghe I of Sitawaka. Numbers remain uncertain, but Africans may have amounted to at least four hundred soldiers in the Portuguese army.[20]

After the Dutch defeated the Portuguese in 1658, most Portuguese officials left the island. Among those who remained was a group later known by the Dutch as Toepasses, Catholic and presumably of Indian or local descent. Kate Ekama suggests that African slaves of the Portuguese who converted to Catholicism had also been incorporated into this group once emancipated.[21] Many studies have foregrounded the ambiguity of the category of Toepasses, which is interpreted either as "people speaking two languages" or as "hat men." This one of the social groups the Dutch created to order their new territory according to their own rationality. They saw a world without complexity divided into Europeans, Sinhalese, or Swarte (blacks) and made of categories less well defined yet named as casies, poesties, mixties, and toepas (toepasses). Sources differ on the meaning of casties and poesties, which sometimes are seen as ethnic Europeans born in Asia and at other times as Eurasians.[22] M. Roberts quite rightly states that these classificatory schemes should be read as "statements of intent rather than effective instruments, as attempted modes of control rather than overwhelming ways of being."[23] The term *toepas* (or *topaz*) was used in the sea-lanes of the Portuguese Empire to qualify native Christians as well as the progeny of mixed marriages or liaisons. The Dutch adopted it to differentiate the Dutch ruling classes from the Portuguese descendants in the maritime provinces. The first Dutch census of the population of Colombo, dated 1684, displayed the mixed society the Dutch took over from the Portuguese, of which emancipated slaves of various regional origin were part. According to Lodewijk Wagenaar, under the category of Christian Toepasses one finds several groups, among which were descendants of manumitted slaves.[24]

Beyond speculations about number of Kaffir slaves who were brought to the island over three centuries, the use of categories like Toepasses confirms more significantly that mixings had taken place and were taking place, and that emancipated slaves were, by then, entering social groups by acquiring the trappings of communities that were based no longer on a freedom-unfreedom divide but on shared language, religion, dress, and appearance. Even the poorest of Toepasses were entitled to wear hats and thus, according to article 42 of the chapter on slaves in the "New Ordinances of Batavia," be counted as Europeans.[25] The hat was the insignia for mobility into the community of Europeans for numerous emancipated slaves, even if social status through attire alone was not immediately acquired and depended on many other markers. It was a way of erasing a slave inheritance and becoming another.

Throughout the seventeenth and eighteenth centuries, enslaved peoples were freed by their owners in a variety of circumstances. Manumission of individual slaves practiced by proprietors in Sri Lanka under Dutch rule has been studied through a detailed exegesis of emancipation deeds of the late eighteenth century. While deeds provide a wealth of information on the gender, age of slaves, and circumstances leading to emancipation, they are silent on the regional origin of slaves, except when names provide a clue.[26] What happened once freedom was given to emancipated slaves and their families is not recorded. Testaments of slave proprietors who promised to free their slaves upon their death offer occasional clues; for instance, as mentioned previously, the will of Don Petrus Abeysiriwardena Ilangakoon Maha Mudaliyar's wife bequeaths to the six children of her emancipated slave Baby a property of one anuman in the Girway Pattoe and six coconut trees from the garden Jamboeghahwatte at Noepe, for which Baby would receive the profits until the children were of age to support themselves.[27] An emancipated slave in an urban setting might have had totally different life chances.

R. G. Anthonisz describes in the prejudiced language of the local bourgeoisie in 1905 the emancipated slaves of the Dutch as a free town community occupying a *lower status* in the social scale and called "Libertines."

They were, he writes, "an ever increasing class because large numbers of slaves from time to time received their freedom on the death or the departure of their masters." Their distinctness as a community disappeared, he suggests, and, quite typically in an effort to draw a line between true Burghers and those of doubtful genealogies, he asserts that they gradually merged with the Toepasses.[28]

The early nineteenth century was a period in which the status of people was in constant flux. Individuals who had been enslaved under the VOC witnessed a number of measures that brought about formal freedom. According to Governor North's regulation, slaves who had belonged to the Dutch Company were set free.[29] These emancipated slaves would have then melted into colonial society, acquiring new names and identities. The fate of domestic slaves working in Dutch families who were still living in Sri Lanka under the British varied. In 1806 the Batavian government sent a mission headed by Commissioner Rudolph Prediger to Colombo to take to Batavia the remaining Dutch families and look into the needs of those who would remain. In 1807–1808 four ships, *Rusthoff, Resolutie, Goede Trouw,* and *Coromandel,* transported around a thousand people to Batavia, of which a third were slaves.[30] These enslaved men and women would probably have to await the formal abolition of slavery in Indonesia in 1862 to join the community of free people, unlike those who remained in Sri Lanka and were freed under the decrees of 1818 and 1821.

Some emancipated slaves who traveled to other VOC territories, such as Cape Colony, had the misfortune of being reenslaved. Thus slaves of Ceylon reappear in the papers of the office of the guardian of slaves in Cape Town at the moment of the dismantling of the Dutch Empire. Ordinance 19 of 1826 created a registrar and guardian of slaves whose task was to investigate whether complaints made by slaves were founded.[31] In the 1820s the guardian of slaves in Cape Colony kept a book of complaints that reports the testimonies of slaves in the first person. The women of Ceylon who appear in the book claimed they were illegally kept as slaves in Cape Town while they should have been free rather than be listed as slaves in the slave registers. In one case, case no. 52 of January 18, 1827, Marie, a grandmother from Ceylon, appears on behalf of her grandchildren Betje and Grietje, who were detained as slaves in Somerset and Swellendam. Marie appears to have come to the Cape with a man called Captain Stoll, with whom she had a child, Caatje. She was then left in the charge of another man, whose son Hendrik van Aas sold her publicly. Did the van

Aas household consider her a slave? The fact that Caatje had been manumitted previously and is described in proceedings as a "free woman" shows that indeed Marie and her progeny were treated as slaves, although Marie was born as a free woman in Ceylon.[32]

Another complaint was made on August 19, 1826, by Samida or Samila, held as a slave by the widow Jacob Vander Merwe. Samida complained "that she is illegally detained as a slave and states that she, together with her mother and two sisters, arrived here, in the year 1787, from Ceylon at which place they were free persons. . . . she stated that she came to this colony on the ship Hofter Linde." Their names, however, were not inserted in the list of passengers as in the case of Caatje and her mother. The Report of Proceedings stated: "The complainant is sister to Samida (see No. 11 this and former report); and it is the intention of the Guardian to take the necessary steps on behalf of these persons."[33] The guardian's office went to great lengths to check the status of Samida in Ceylon, but a last will bequeathing the four women to Matthezer by the widow of Egbert van der Veld, made on May 4, 1777, was brought forward by Matthezer's widow to prove that Samida, her mother, and her sisters were reenslaved in the Cape. The fact that in both cases the plaintiffs were not on the list of passengers could suggest that enslaved people were attempting to use the mechanism of the guardian of slaves in Cape Colony to wrench their freedom by inventing a history of free status in Ceylon.

Other emancipated slaves chose to lose themselves in a society where one was still not subject to identity controls. An emancipated slave named Babbea in Galle simply disappeared after he was charged in a murder case in 1802, accused of having stabbed a man who had confronted him about killing his hog. Although a free man, he was looked down on and not even considered free by the man he killed, who before dying of his wounds referred to him disparagingly as "a slave Babbea, a servant of Wannigesegere." Other court witnesses, however, refer to him as "the *emancipated* slave of Wannigesegere." Babbea fled and, like many others who carried with them the stigma of a slave identity, disappeared into the shadows of history.[34]

Locals and colonial officials alike looked down on those who were former slaves or descendants of one. British officials saw this as a sufficient reason for dismissing Pasqual, the Peshcar (revenue official) in the Batticaloa kachcheri, removed for being born of a slave mother. Had he remained in his post, he would, they believed, have created "disgust" among people of high caste, especially if he had been allowed to attend to any matters of ceremony.[35] Other sources show that Pasqual Mudaliyar was not a poor man but a Christian Podiyar, Podiyars being large landowners who were originally Mukkuvar and Vellalar caste cultivators. His slave ancestry had not proved to be a disability since in 1817, according to Canagaratnam: Pasqual Mudaliyar owned all the paddy fields of Buffalo Island, an "immense tract of paddy fields, about ten miles in circumference." Pasqual Mudaliyar is also credited by local tradition with the creation of the Catholic Christian community of Sorikalmunai and building the Holy Cross Shrine church about ten miles south of Mandur.[36]

Thus when the Acts of 1818 and 1821 were passed, the island's population had already gone through centuries of incorporating former enslaved people within the existing society. This phenomenon was similar to the incorporation of many low-country caste groups, such as the Karavas, Duravas, and Salagamas, who migrated from South India from the fourteenth century onward and were partially integrated into the Sinhalese social structure by the nineteenth century.[37] While these castes became sinhalized but distinct from the dominant Goyigama caste, Gananath Obeysekere provides evidence from palm leaf manuscripts (*vitti pot*, boundary books) that Brahmins, Hettis, and some Ksatriyas from India too were incorporated into the caste system as Goyigamas.[38] On the whole, by the early eighteenth century, the "littoral societies" of the Indian Ocean world, made up of communities living on coasts connected through maritime corridors and riverine arteries to hinterlands, were deeply influenced by their relationship with port cities such as Colombo or Galle and the constant flux of slaves, soldiers, convicts, exiles, and sailors.[39]

Another mechanism by which emancipated slaves and their descendants disappeared from scrutiny was by acquiring a communal and religious identity through conversion or marriage. The case of Rawothan shows that Islam favored the absorption of converts, although not all members of the "respectable" Moor community were as egalitarian as the scriptures. Malay-speaking emancipated slaves from the East Indies would have filtered into the Malay community of the island and into other communities that had their own prerogatives. If slave children were christened in the Dutch church with the consent of their proprietor, they immediately became free. The proprietor was then required to pass "an act called the Act of Adoption by which he is considered their guardian until they are of age."[40] The will of Peter Mellonius from 1821 is an illustration of the way christening and adoption were pathways to freedom: "I the testator," wrote Mellonius, "bequeath unto the two free children who are bought up by me called Daniel and Matthias all my clothing which I shall leave behind at my death together with a small chest to each of them. Requiring I the testator that the said children shall remain after my death under the guardianship of the above named Petronella Latour,"[41] who was Mellonius's daughter.

According to Lodewijk Wagenaar, slaves were never admitted as full members of the Dutch Reformed Church during Dutch rule of the island, although many enslaved domestics were baptized.[42] There are a few records of slaves owned by Governor Van Imhoff and Governor Lubber Jan van Eck in the mid-eighteenth century who married in the Dutch Church of Wolvendaal, which would suggest that they were accepted as part, in some way at least, of the Christian community.

APRIL DIAS of Bengal and ANGELIE of Bengal, both slaves of Governor Van Imhoff, married February 7, 1740

AUGUSTUS FERDINANDO and HELENA MACASSAR, both slaves of Governor Van Imhoff, married January 17, 1740

CAESAR FERDINANDO of Surat and AURORA DE ANDRADO, both slaves of Governor Van Imhoff, married January 24, 1740

ABRAHAM HENDRIKSZ of Bengal and TAMJON JANSZ of Bali, both slaves of Governor Van Imhoff, married January 24, 1740

SCIPIO JANSZ of Bengal and ROSETTA FRANSZ of Java, both slaves of Governor Van Imhoff, married January 24, 1740

CONSTANT PHILLIPSZ of Bali and GANGERIA ISAACKSZ of Bengal, both slaves of Governor Van Imhoff, married February 14, 1740

PYLADES, Slave of the Governor Lubber Jan Van Eck, and MARIA, married November 18, 1764[43]

The names and the origin of the slaves—Surat, Bengal, Java, Bali—are in themselves fascinating and confirm our contention that most slaves were purchased in and perhaps came from India or the East Indies. The fact that they have surnames—Ferdinando, de Andrado, Hendriksz, Jansz, Fransz, Philippsz, Isaacksz, Macassar—unlike slaves listed in the nineteenth-century slave registers is also a rare occurrence and perhaps explained by the fact that they belonged to the Dutch Reformed Church community. It is not possible to know whether they were emancipated or enslaved at the time they married. What is fascinating is that their names are today associated with completely different ethnic belongings. Ferdinando, whose origin is listed as Surat, is today understood to be a low-country Sinhalese name. Hendriksz, Jansz, Isaacksz, and Fransz (all slaves from or bought in Bengal and the East Indies) would suggest a Dutch Burgher lineage in present society, while Macassar, rather than a name, is probably the place of origin of Helena, which she then adopted as a surname. Thus surnames are not a trustworthy indication of the place of origin or ethnicity of the enslaved person since they are probably the names of their proprietors. A Jansz in the twenty-first century may actually have as an ancestor someone with origins in Bali rather than hailing from Amsterdam.

During early British rule, church records indicate that domestic slaves were sometimes baptized under the Dutch Reformed Church after being emancipated. A case arose in 1805 when a maid had been baptized by Rev. Kauwertsz following the prescription of her owner, Philippus Harmanus Helgers, before he mortgaged her and other bonded slaves to his guarantors (his son Harmanus Helgers and J. H. Lourenz) on account of his debts. Rev. Giffening and his council decided that the maid should be forbidden from making her declaration of faith and not be admitted as a church member, as this would enable her to be free since "according to the laws of the government of Holland (which are still valid), the slaves who declare their confession of faith and become members of the Church may not be sold." The maid's freedom would indeed cause a loss to the people she had been mortgaged to.[44] Fifteen years later, slave registers showed that J. H. Lourenz was still a slaveholder. His slaves Agustena, Azor, Apellus, Nurnerrot, Samuel, and Simira and her two children Maria and Jacob might have been the former slaves of Harmanus Helgers Sr. Giffening himself appears in the slave registers as a slaveholder whose estate was composed of seven slaves, Absolon, Amerinta, Betje, Dominga, Ismael, Mandaag, and Maro.[45]

Baptism certificates of the Wolvendaal Church can sometimes help us reconstruct the path to freedom opened up to slaves through conversion. The baptism certificate of Jacobus Balliers, born on August 4, 1830, suggests that his parents, Orantus and Castoria, were enslaved people since, like other slaves in the colonial city, they used only first names that had been given to them upon purchase or transfer.[46] The slave registers of 1818–1832 confirm that in 1818 a male slave named Orantus, age thirty-two, and a female slave named Castoria, age twenty, lived under the roof of their owner Romana Christoffels.[47] Questions remain unanswered. What led to

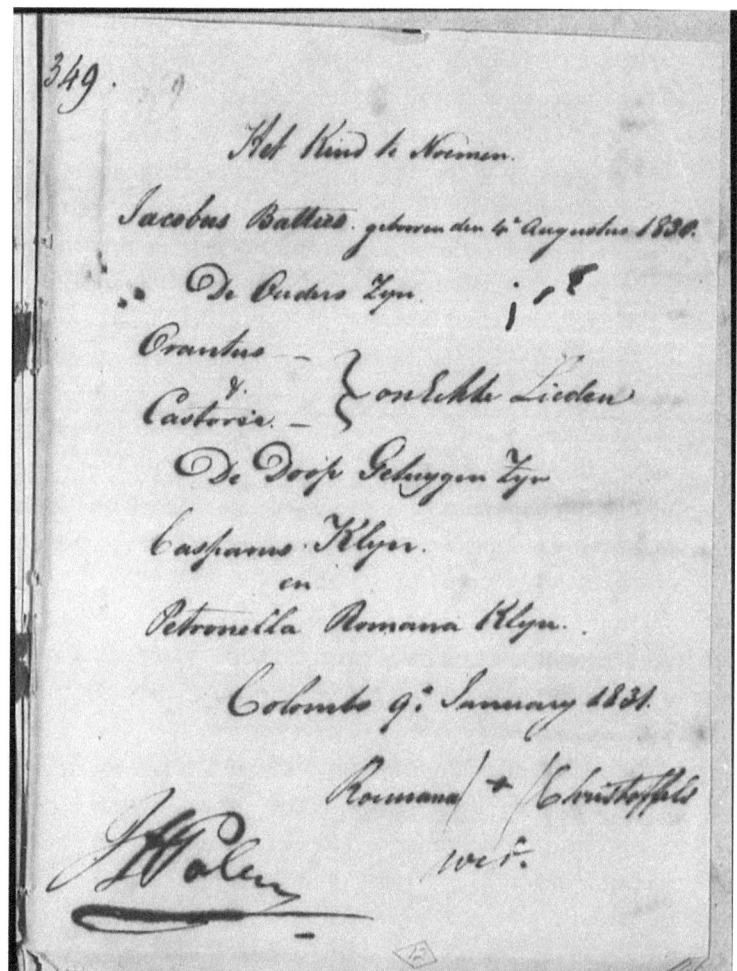

Figure 6.1 Baptism record, Dutch Reformed Church, Colombo District, 1831 (Dutch Reformed Church Records, 1677–1990, Colombo District, Sri Lanka)

their child being baptized twelve years later is not known. Were they later sold to the witnesses at the baptism, Petronella and Casparus Klyn, who then freed the child Jacobus by baptizing him? Why is the name of Romana Christoffels at the bottom of the baptism certificate (fig. 6.1)?

In 1815 a group of Burghers wrote to Chief Justice Sir Alexander Johnston to put forward two grievances regarding the new right and duty that had been granted to them and other natives in 1811, which was to sit on juries as a result of the introduction of a system of trial by jury. Their first grievance was that only some Burghers had been summoned to serve while others were passed over. Their second grievance related to the qualification and ability to serve of Burgher jurors. While they observed that in other denominations issues of class and rank were taken into consideration, in their case "Burghers from the highest to the lowest class have been promiscuously introduced in the list and in like manner panelled together including mechanics and artificers of all description, even this promiscuousness has been further acted upon by introducing the descendants of Emancipated slaves with actual Burghers."[48] A year later these jurors would agree to sign a statement voluntarily abolishing the enslavement of the children of their female slaves. Their prejudicial views on emancipated slaves would probably remain.

The same sentiment was visible nearly a century later when the issue of the selection of a Burgher member to the Legislative Council was discussed in 1909–1911. The vexed question of the true Burgher came to the fore. A commission chaired by Hugh Clifford (the colonial secretary) and composed of an ethnic mix of British and local notables heard evidence on the part of Burgher notables. One of them, Dr. W. G. van Dort, explicitly referred to emancipated slaves:

> At present [the Burgher community] is somewhat heterogeneous. First of all, there is the Burgher community proper, and then there is a large admixture—a number of different shades and sorts of people, composing the bulk, as it were, of the community. If you go by numbers, they are partly European descendants, partly Indo-Portuguese, partly "Portuguese" of the lower classes among whom are to be found the children of emancipated slaves intermarried into descendants of Portuguese who have married native women. These have been an accretion to the Burgher, but, properly speaking they have no legitimate standing here.[49]

Writers in the late nineteenth century shared the belief that Toepasses, later called Portuguese Burghers, encompassed most emancipated slaves of African or South Indian descent.[50] L. A. Wickremaratne is a rare modern scholar who refers to emancipated slaves. He claims, however, that descendants of slaves who had been with the Dutch "were designated as Burghers" in a formula that clearly fails to cover the variety of trajectories followed by freed men and women.[51]

Hauntings

Emancipated slaves and their descendants had to become other in order to gain acceptability in a status-conscious society. They had to erase their connection with slavery and become part of a community based on religion or ethnicity. Their own quest for invisibility has made it difficult to trace slave lineages. Why is there shame in being associated with this past, shame in having been forcibly brought to the island and having labored as an unfree person? The absence of roots weighs heavily in societies where belonging to a *gama* (village) defines your identity and status. Yet myths, narratives, rituals, or the cult for the Goddess Pattini provide a form of legitimization for incoming immigrants.[52]

The issue is that slavery poses troubling questions about race if one takes the latter to signify a flexible, ambiguous, and social rather than biological construct that was inflected by and can be rarely separated from other social categories. Accepting the reality of slave ancestry in our midst is akin to accepting that all races are mixed and impure. It is hence easier to refuse to remember or to lay over the past a protective layer made of Afro–Sri Lankans, and plantation "coolies" whose lives—witnessed and visible—permit us to turn away from the possibility of slave pasts. We see here a case of Paul Ricoeur's second type of amnesia, namely, *oubli de réserve*, in which case it is no longer oblivion that materiality begets, forgetting by the effacement of traces, but forgetting in terms of "a reserve or a resource."[53]

The inconvenience of the Portuguese language remains, too. Portuguese creole—creole used here in its more conventional sense for a vernacular language developed as a result of contact between groups that spoke mutually unintelligible languages—was the language of slaves. Up to the 1930s there was a memory of those days related in journals such as the *Journal of the Dutch Burgher Union*, when households had slaves. During the eighteenth century and up to the mid-nineteenth, the language of the household among Burghers was not Dutch but Portuguese. While English replaced Dutch as the language of governance, trade, politics, and polite society, Portuguese remained in the home of Burghers and in various pockets of the island where mixing had taken place. Writing in the *Dutch Burgher Union* in 1824, the writer very confidently asserted "the children spoke it with the slaves and used no other till they went to school and learnt to read and write." He then recounts his meeting with C. C. Uhlenbeck, professor at Leiden University, who "said that he remembered his grandmother, who belonged to a family in Ceylon, after she had spent a whole life in Holland, even so late as the middle of the nineteenth century, preferring to express herself in Portuguese rather than in any other language."[54]

The invisibility process functioned differently in the north of the island, where slavery disappeared as a category of governance but remained in a different form. Slaveholding by Europeans and Westernized Sri Lankans in which a person was the chattel property of another person was easily dealt with and abolished between 1818 and 1844. In Jaffna, however, the condition of the atimai castes proved to be more difficult to resolve. They had been unfree laborers dependent on Vellalars, but the Dutch had treated them as chattel slaves. Simply abolishing slavery did not change their status and in fact worsened their condition as they remained dependent on the Vellalars. After abolition in 1844, according to C. Rasanayagam, castes that had been enslaved did not experience a visible change in status. Pallars and Nalavars continued to work as tree climbers and agricultural labor. For Coviyars, there was change insofar as they became domestic servants and joined in the Pallars' occupation of cultivating their masters' fields.[55] H. W. Tambiah also concurs that depressed classes remained "de facto slaves of their masters" and provides examples of a continuation of service ties under another name. The continuation of battles for respect and temple entry rights by the Panchamars of the North from the 1950s illustrates the contention that after 1844 it was a travesty of freedom and equality that was bestowed on formerly enslaved people.[56] After 1844 most formerly enslaved in Jaffna fell back into caste servitude.

To understand the change as it affected people who had been considered material goods, one has to search for clues in novels about Jaffna or of similar transformations in Kerala. K. Daniel's novel *Mirage* relates the lives of Naniyyan, a landless laborer, and his family of Nalavar caste in Jaffna in the early twentieth century. In the past, Nalavars and Pallars in the village of Cinnakkalatti had been *atimaikal*, that is, Vellalar chattel slaves. After the abolition of slavery they became bonded labor to the same Vellalar landowners. Their day-to-day humiliations and the violence and rape by a Vellalar landlord of a young woman of Nalavar caste led the family to convert to Roman Catholicism. The novel describes in vivid detail the work performed by the Nalavar family on the tobacco land and their dispossession, conversion, and eventual exploitation by Catholic Karayyiar lagoon-fishing labor contractors.[57] Freedom and salvation end up being only a mirage.

The abolition of slavery in Kerala has also been described in three Malayalam novels dealing with the experience of slave castes in the nineteenth century: *Ghatakavadham* (The Slayer slain, Kottayam, 1865), published in Malayalam in 1877 by Mrs. Collins; *Saraswativijayam* (The Victory of knowledge, Kozhikode, 1893), written by a Tiyya autodidact, Potheri Kunhambu; and *Sukumari* (Cannanore, 1897), written by Joseph Muliyil, a Tiyya convert to Christianity. In these three novels, slavery is central as the authors locate the story around the time of its abolition of slavery in India in 1843 or just prior. They bring to light the rich, contradictory subjectivities of enslaved people. In India the Act of 1843 was limited in scope since the company as legislator was bound by a ruling of the Calcutta Sudder Court in 1798 that insofar as rights to property in slaves were recognized by Hindu and Muslim law, they were valid in the company civil courts. In Kerala there was no domestic slavery on account of extreme notions of caste pollution, and most of the slave population consisted of Hindus working in agriculture as field slaves. The government itself held slaves in Malabar, and thousands of them labored on plantations.[58] Where the archive falters and leaves us with holes, these novels address the densities of everyday life and questions of self, community, and society afresh.

As indicated previously, slavery in Jaffna, if absent from mainstream national political debates among liberal and progressive Tamils, has become a useful instrument for Sinhalese nationalists eager to attack Tamil critiques of Sinhalese domination. The past of slavery practiced by Vellalars on their own people adds fuel to a generalized desire to cast aspersion on Tamil claims for a homeland, or today on devolution or federalism in the North. The slavery story indeed gives much ammunition to counter Tamil aspirations on the basis of the trope of historical presence of Tamils and of internal violence among them. It casts doubt on the idea of an immemorial attachment of all Tamils to the land since many Dutch sources cited by Sinhalese ideologues provide evidence that Tamils of depressed castes were brought to Jaffna from India in large numbers as slaves throughout the Dutch period. It is then simple to claim that Tamils are little more than migrants in the island.

Slavery among Tamils, perpetrated by the Vellalars, is thus a useful trope in the Sinhalese nationalist discourse to attack elite Tamil people: Sinhalese nationalists use this argument to advance that Tamil Vellalar leaders since the 1950s had no legitimate claim to speak on behalf of the Tamil peoples, since they were their oppressors. H. Mahindapala, on the occasion of the publication of Daniel's *Mirage*, explicitly referred to slavery in Jaffna:

> The horrors of the Vellala crimes against their own exploited people condemn the Vellalas as a brutal caste/class that showed no mercy to the non-Vellala Tamils of Jaffna. Worst was when the Vellalas, quoting Hindu texts, assumed the divine right to oppress and exploit their fellow-Tamils as slaves. Their contempt for their own people was displayed when they categorised a segment of their own people as pariahs who were kept out of high-caste Vellala society. Some of them were forbidden to walk even in daylight. The Turumbars, for instance, were allowed to walk only in the night just in case they should pollute the purity of Vellala eyes. No other community suffered the humiliating indignities as the outcasts of Jaffna society at the hands of their Vellala masters. And no one is better qualified to document the agonies of the oppressed Tamils than K. Daniel, a Turumbar.[59]

Nalin de Silva, a mathematician and one of the most prominent Sinhalese nationalist ideologues, has repeatedly analyzed the peopling of Jaffna as composed mainly of agriculturalist castes brought after 1650 from present-day Tamil Nadu by the Dutch to service the tobacco plantations they wanted to develop on a large scale. These people of the Sudra castes in India became Vellalars in Jaffna, were made proprietors of land by the Dutch, and, in the absence of Brahmins, as de Silva explains, became the administrators of the temples as well.[60] The argument that follows is that Tamil nationalism and claims for a homeland are illegitimate and have, from the seventeenth century up to now, been sponsored by foreign powers. The entire history of Jaffna, writes de Silva, was rewritten to sustain the right of the Vellalars to the land. The Dutch were acting on purely economic reasons. They needed a settled population in Jaffna to cultivate tobacco and hence brought agricultural castes from South India for this purpose.[61]

These writings belong to the genre of popular history, obey no academic conventions, and advance unsubstantiated opinions based on partial and select evidence. Yet Mahindapala's outrage is justified. It should be shared by all humanists, even if this means delegitimizing claims of a minority group that has collectively suffered terrible pain over the past three decades.

What does summoning the ghosts achieve? It exposes the cracks and shores up people who are meant to be invisible. The outrage about slavery in Jaffna's past and the reverberations in the present, where even in internally displaced persons camps after the war caste prejudice continues, needs to be reappropriated from the nationalist discourse and upheld by equality and justice minded citizens.[62] The moral illegitimacy of slavery and its afterlives, just as the culpability of those who failed to condemn it in the past and fail to see its ramifications in the present, must be laid bare.

Finally the Coral

According to R. L. Brohier, who wrote from hearsay, the house that was the scene of the murder of the Dutch fiscal Barend van der Swaan and his wife continued to be haunted many years later: "On moonlight nights clad in their period costumes they had been actually seen restlessly wandering alone about the premises sighing loudly, and covering the gaping wounds on their breasts darkly stained by blood with pale trembling hands." But as the house remained unoccupied, it was closed and then converted into a mercantile store during the coffee production years.[63] This apocryphal story invites the reader to listen only to the victims of murder, blissfully ignoring the dark times that presided over these events. Commemorating ghosts in period costumes and commiserating over the death of the fiscal blinds the reader to the world of brutal violence and exploitation that van der Swaan and his like presided over.

Slave in a Palanquin relates what is generally left unsaid. It calls for another way of seeing. It brings to life not only the enslaved men who were condemned for the crime of killing the fiscal and died cruel deaths in the citadel, but other less spectacular acts by men and women who fought their servitude with courage and grit. Registering the harm inflicted and the loss sustained by social violence done in the past is a way of freeing the repressed ghosts and phantoms that blind our vision and destroy the possibility of empathy in the present. Stories of enslavement, invisibility, and hauntings draw me to Mauritian poet Khal Torabully's aspiration for a new form of humanism embodied in multiple crossings: crossings between cultures, heritages, places, generations, gender, historical assertions, and mythical references. Coral epitomizes the form of humanism that can emerge in the Indian Ocean world. Coral, he writes, can be both soft and hard, it can be found in two states, and it is traversed by currents, continuously open to new thoughts and systems. It is a living body with elements that are both vulnerable and solid, a symbol of the fluidity of relationships and influences.[64]

The act of reclaiming for the present, Wayreven, a slave in a palanquin, Valentine, a runaway, as well as Selestina and others who fearlessly crossed the lines drawn by colonial society is a small contribution to uncovering unresolved pasts.

Glossary

ACCOMMODESSANS—land granted in return for duties or services rendered or offices held
ADIGAR—chief officer of state in the Kandyan kingdom
AMILDAR—chief of the South Indian administrators who came to Sri Lanka with the establishment of British rule
ANDOL—palanquin
ARACHCHI—village-level official generally below a korale, or noncommissioned officer in Lascarin force
ATIMAI—"aboriginal" or "stranger" castes in the Jaffna caste system, defined as "slaves" in the Dutch colonial period, which include the Coviyar, Nalavar, Pallar, and the now-extant "Chiandos"
AYAH—a nursemaid or nanny employed by Europeans in the British Raj or similar territories
BATTA—originally allowance made to military personnel or other public servants in the field; small allowance in cash
BHIKKU—an ordained Buddhist monk
BURGHER—originally meaning Europeans working for the VOC and later denoting an ethnic group consisting of the descendants of Europeans in Ceylon
CASTIZ/CASTIZO—term used by Portuguese for people of pure European descent born in Asia but used by the Dutch also to indicate people of mixed descent
CHETTIES /CHETTIAR—a group of South Indian merchants and moneylenders
COLLECTOR—predecessor of the government agent in Ceylon; initially appointed for the management of revenue, this office came to concentrate the major

administrative, financial, and revenue powers of the British administration in the provinces

COOLIE—unskilled laborer (pejorative)

COPRAH—dried meat or kernel of the coconut

COVIYAR/COVIA—caste group defined as slaves by the Dutch; generally domestics of the Vellalars

CRIMINAL ROLLS—records of criminal courts in Dutch Sri Lanka

CUTCHERRY/KACHCHERI—headquarters of a district administration

DHOW—Arab sailing vessel with slanting triangular sails; common in the Red Sea and Indian Ocean

DISAVA—administrative head of a province

DURAVA— Sinhalese caste generally associated with toddy tapping

FISCAAL/FISCAL—an officer who performed numerous functions. In addition to overseeing criminal cases, in Colombo this officer superintended the observance of edicts and orders of the government, inspected the police of the town, and was the justice of the peace. Although appointed by Batavia, the officer was entirely dependent on the governor. Under the British, the term designated the officer charged with the execution of the judgments of the court.

GAMA—Sinhalese term for village

GOYIGAMA/GOVI—cultivators, the dominant caste in the Sinhalese areas

HATANA—war

JA MINISSU—people from Java in Sinhalese

JAVA MANUSAR—people from Java in Tamil

KABERI—also *kapiri*, Sinhalese term for Africans believed to have been forcefully brought to the island as slaves by the Portuguese, derived from the Portuguese word *cafre*, borrowed from the Arabic *kafir*

KAFFIR—from Portuguese *cafre*

KAILAYAMALAI—a chronicle from the Jaffna kingdom

KAMPUNG PANGERAN—prince's quarters located in an area close to the Wolfendhal, Malay quarters

KANGANY—an official in charge of laborers or sometimes soldiers

KARAVA—a Sinhalese caste; seafarers, fisher-folk

KORALE—unit of administration, generally part of a disava

KUTIMAI—"professional" castes conventionally eighteen in number in the Jaffna caste system; served the Vellalars and had to perform various ritual and secular occupations

LANDRAAD—Dutch civil courts of law with cognizance over all land disputes of the local population

LASCAR—sailor or militia member from the Indian subcontinent, Southeast Asia, the Arab world, and other territories located to the east of the Cape of Good Hope

LASCARINS—indigenous soldiers in the service of the king and later colonial governors

LEKAM MITI—traditional registers that recorded the lands liable for *rajakariya* (corvée) and the authority to which the *rajakariya* was due (king, disava, temple, or shrine). Other service lands were also listed. Entries were recorded under the names of villages and fields rather than individual holders.

MADAPALLI—caste group whom Dutch appointed as collectors of revenue and mudaliyars

MADIAGAR—chief headman among the Tamils

MAHABADDA—(literally) Great Revenue, the Cinnamon Department

MARAIKKAYARS—community of Tamil-speaking Muslims of the southeast coast of India; deriving from the Tamil word *marakkalam* (meaning boat)

MATERIAALHUIS—storage house located in the castle where VOC slaves were kept

MESTIZO—descendants of European men and Asian women

MUHANDIRAM—assistant to a Mudaliyar; also an honorary title

MOOR—a term first used by the Portuguese to describe the Muslim community in Sri Lanka

MUDALIYAR—chief headman, an administrator of a korale in British times; also used as an honorary title

MUKKUVAR—a caste group found in the coastal regions of Sri Lanka, Tamil Nadu, and Kerala

NALAVAR/NALLUA—a caste group in the north of Sri Lanka identified as slaves by the Dutch VOC

NITI-NIGHANDUWA—literally the vocabulary of law; compiled after the fall of the Kandyan kingdom; outlines Sinhalese customary law

OLA LEAF—a palm leaf used for writing in South India and Sri Lanka

OOSTERLINGEN—Dutch term meaning Easterners to describe all Southeast Asians brought to Sri Lanka

OPPERHOOFD—Dutch official in control of a subdivision of a disava

PACHAMARS—collective term for depressed castes in Jaffna

PALANQUIN—a covered litter or conveyance, usually for one person, used in India and other Eastern countries, consisting of a large box with wooden shutters like Venetian blinds, carried by four or six (rarely two) men by means of poles projecting before and behind

PALLAR/PALLA—Tamil service caste associated with toddy tapping, identified and legally recognized by the Dutch as slaves

PALMYRA—a type of palm growing in the north of Sri Lanka

PARANGI HATANA—War of the Portuguese; Sinhalese poem composed during the era of Rajasinghe II (1658–1687)

PATAN—a term generally used in South India to refer to Deccani Muslims (Muslims from the Deccan)
PEON—South Indian term for a uniformed orderly
PETTAH/PITA KOTTUVA—outer fort
PLAKAAT—(Dutch) edict or proclamation
RAJARATA—north-central part of the island
RAJAKARIYA—King's Duty; encompassed any service to the king, a lord or a temple in the Kandyan kingdom; in British times denoted compulsory service to the state
SALAGAMA—Sinhalese caste, associated with cinnamon peeling
SEER—a form of weights and measures
SCHIPPER—master of a ship
TAVALAM—resting place in Sinhalese
THESAWALAMAI—code of Tamil laws codified by the Dutch government in 1707
TODDY—alcoholic beverage collected from the sap of various palm trees—palmyra, date, and coconut
TOTTAM—garden lands irrigated by fresh groundwater in Jaffna
TOMBO—list or register of persons or land maintained by the Dutch
TOEPASSES—people of mixed Portuguese-indigenous descent, or people who spoke two languages
ULIYAM—service obligation imposed on Moors and Chetties for being foreigners in the territories under Dutch control
VANNI—dry jungles; name given to the mainland area of the northern province of Sri Lanka
VANNIYARS—semi-independent chieftains; these chieftaincies located between the kingdoms of Jaffna and Kotte emerged in the fourteenth century as a result of the collapse of the Polonnaruwa kingdom
VEDDAS—a community of people in Sri Lanka typologized by Europeans as indigenous and primitive inhabitants of the island
VELLALARS—dominant caste group of landowners in Jaffna
VIDANA—village-level officer, part of the headman system
VIHARA—Buddhist temple
WALAUWAS—local homes and mansions
YALPANA VAIPAVA MALAI—history of the kingdom of Jaffna compiled by Mayivakanan at the request of the Dutch governor in 1736

Notes

Introduction

1. Walter Benjamin, "On the Concept of History," in *Walter Benjamin, Selected Writings*, vol. 4: *1938–1940*, ed. Howard Eiland and Michael W. Jennings (Cambridge Mass: Harvard University Press, 2003), 391.
2. See Walter Johnson, "On Agency," *Journal of Social History*, 37, no. 1 (2003): 113–24, where he warns that scholars need to take some distance from attempts to "give slaves back their agency," which is grounded in the idea of history as a mode of redress.
3. See Lodewijk Wagenaar, *Cinnamon and Elephants; Sri Lanka and the Netherlands from 1600* (Amsterdam: Vantilt, 2016); and Denys Lombard, *Le Carrefour Javanais: Essai Historique d'Histoire Globale* (Paris: Editions de l'EHESS, 1990).
4. Slavery is called an "embarrassing institution" in Orlando Patterson, *Slavery and Social Death: A Comparative Study* (Cambridge, Mass: Harvard University Press, 1982), ix. Some recent publications on abolition are Robert Harms, Bernard K. Fremon, and David W. Blight, eds., *Indian Ocean Slavery in the Age of Abolition* (New Haven, Conn.: Yale University Press, 2013); Andrea Major, *Slavery, Abolitionism and Empire in India 1772–1843* (Liverpool: Liverpool University Press, 2012); Hideaki Suzuki, *Abolitions as a Global Experience* (Singapore: NUS Press, 2016); and Indrani Chatterjee, "British Abolitionism from the Vantage of Pre-Colonial South Asian Regimes," in *The Cambridge World History of Slavery*, vol. 4: *AD 1804–AD 2016*, ed. David Eltis,

Stanley Engerman, Seymour Drescher, and David Richardson (Cambridge: Cambridge University Press, 2017), 441–65.
5. Sri Lanka National Archives (SLNA), *Return of the Population of the Island of Ceylon, 1827* (Colombo: Government Press, 1828). In the British Caribbean colonies, the slave population was 665,000 in 1834. See B. W. Higman, "Population and Labor in the British Caribbean in the Early Nineteenth Century," in *Long Term Factors in American Economic Growth*, ed. Stanley L. Engerman and Robert E. Gallman (Chicago: University of Chicago Press, 1986), 605–39.
6. See, for example, *The Cambridge World History of Slavery*, vol. 3: *AD 1420–AD 1804*, ed. David Eltis and Stanley L. Engerman (Cambridge: Cambridge University Press, 2011). The section on slavery in Asia covers only Southeast Asia and early modern China.
7. On the archive and modes of reading it against the grain and along the grain, see A. L. Stoler, "Colonial Archives and the Arts of Governance," *Archival Science*, no. 2 (2002): 87–109; and A. L Stoler, *Along the Archival Grain: Epistemic Anxieties and Colonial Common Sense* (Princeton, N.J.: Princeton University Press, 2009). For a sharp engagement with the "archival turn" in history, see Benjamin Zachariah, "Travellers in Archives, or the Possibilities of a Post-Post-archival Historiography," *Praticas da Historia*, no. 3 (2016): 11–27.
8. Recent historical projects have collected this data and made it available and searchable online. See Bookkeeper-General Batavia database, http://bgb.huygens.knaw.nl/.
9. Linda Mbeki and Matthias van Rossum, "Private Slave Trade in the Dutch Indian Ocean World: A Study Into the Networks and Backgrounds of the Slavers and the Enslaved in South Asia and South Africa," *Slavery & Abolition: A Journal of Slave and Post-Slave Studies* 38 (2017): 95–116.
10. The governor took residence in Galle in 1659. Remco Raben, "Batavia and Colombo. The Ethnic and Spatial Order of Two Colonial Cities 1600–1800," Ph.D diss., Leiden University, 1996, 45–48.
11. Christopher A. Bayly, *Imperial Meridian: The British Empire and the World 1780–1830* (London: Longmans, 1988).
12. See Major, *Slavery, Abolitionism and Empire in India*, for an exhaustive account of abolitionism in India. On slavery in India, see Indrani Chatterjee, *Gender, Slavery and Law in Colonial India* (New Delhi: Oxford University Press, 1999); Indrani Chatterjee and Richard M. Eaton, eds., *Slavery and South Asian History*, (Bloomington: Indiana University Press, 2006); Howard Temperley, "The Delegalization of Slavery in British India," *Slavery & Abolition* 21, no. 2 (2000): 169–87; and Mark Naidis, "The Abolitionists and Indian Slavery," *Journal of Asian History* 15, no. 2 (1981): 146–58.
13. Nick Draper; "'Possessing Slaves': Ownership, Compensation and Metropolitan Society in Britain at the time of Emancipation, 1834–40," *History*

Workshop Journal 64, no. 1 (2007): 74–102; Harms, Freamon, and Blight, *Indian Ocean Slavery*.
14. Temperley, "The Delegalization of Slavery," 183.
15. W. M. G. Colebrooke, Commission of Eastern Enquiry: Report Upon the Administration of the Government of Ceylon (1831), National Archives, Kew (NA UK), CO/54/122.
16. David Scott, *Refashioning Futures: Criticism After Postcoloniality* (Princeton, N.J.: Princeton University Press, 1999); Niranjan Casinader, Roshan De Silva Wijeyaratne, and Lee Godden, "From Sovereignty to Modernity: Revisiting the Colebrooke-Cameron Reforms—Transforming the Buddhist and Colonial Imaginary in Nineteenth-Century Ceylon," *Comparative Legal History* 6, no. 1 (2018): 34–64.
17. Casinader, Wijeyaratne, and Godden, "From Sovereignty to Modernity," 63; Timothy Mitchell, "The Limits of the State: Beyond Statist Approaches and Their Critics," *American Political Science Review* 85, no. 1 (1991): 77–96.
18. R.A.L.H. Gunawardana, *Robe and Plough: Monasticism and Economic Interest in Early Medieval Sri Lanka* (Tucson: University of Arizona Press, 1979), 121.
19. Lorna Dewaraja, *The Kandyan Kingdom of Sri Lanka, 1707–1782* (Colombo: Lake House, 1988); Ralph Pieris, *Sinhalese Social Organization: The Kandyan Period* (Colombo: Ceylon University Press Board, 1956); Nandadeva Wijesekera, "Slavery in Sri Lanka: Presidential Address Delivered on 20-12-1974," *Journal of the Sri Lanka Branch of the Royal Asiatic Society*, New Series, 18 (1974): 1–22; K. M. de Silva, *Social Policy and Missionary Organizations in Ceylon 1840–1855* (London: Longmans Green, 1965), 206–9.
20. Alicia F. Schrikker and Kate J. Ekama, "Through the Lens of Slavery: Dutch Sri Lanka in the Eighteenth Century," in *Sri Lanka at the Crossroads of History*, ed. Zoltan Biedermann and Alan Strathern (London: UCL Press, 2017), 178–93.
21. Chatterjee and Eaton, *Slavery and South Asian History*, has no mention of Sri Lanka, although since the sixteenth century the area had a large overseas component of enslaved people and multiple forms of servitude.
22. See Rupa Viswanath's argument that colonial officials described Indian slavery in South India as distinct and as "gentle slavery" because it was woven in kinship. Rupa Viswanath, *The Pariah Problem: Caste, Religion and the Social in Modern India* (New York: Columbia University Press, 2014). Although Sanal Mohan's work on Kerala in the nineteenth century starts from the same premise, it shows that missionaries played a role in creating a new idiom of resistance for social groups defined as slave castes. Sanal Mohan, *Modernity of Slavery: Struggles Against Caste Inequality in Colonial Kerala* (Oxford: Oxford University Press, 2015).
23. Matthias van Rossum, *Kleuririjke tragiek: De Geschiedenis van slavernij in Azie onder de VOC* (Hilversum: Uitgeverij Verloren, 2015), shows that slavery in

Asia was not always mild, nor was it always different from labor practices in Atlantic slavery.

24. Gyan Prakash, *Bonded Histories: Genealogies of Labor Servitude in Colonial India* (Cambridge: Cambridge University Press, 1993). See also Nancy Gardner Cassels, *Social Legislation of the East India Company: Public Justice Versus Public Instruction* (New Delhi: Sage, 2010).
25. Patterson, *Slavery and Social Death*, 13.
26. Suzanne Miers and Igor Kopytoff, *Slavery in Africa: Historical and Anthropological Perspectives* (Madison: University of Wisconsin Press, 1977), 4.
27. Robert Edward Luster, "The Amelioration of the Slaves in the British Empire, 1790–1833," Ph.D. diss., New York University, 1988.
28. I borrow this phrase from Veena Das, *Life and Words: Violence and the Descent Into the Ordinary* (Berkeley: University of California Press, 2006).
29. John L. Comaroff and Jean Comaroff, *Of Revelation and Revolution*, vol. 2: *The Dialectics of Modernity on a South African Frontier* (Chicago: University of Chicago Press, 2009), 29.
30. Meghan Vaughan, *Creating the Créole Island* (Durham, N.C.: Duke University Press, 2005); Marina Carter, *Voices from Indenture: Experience of Indian Migrants in the British Empire* (London: Leicester University Press, 1996); Clare Anderson, *Subaltern Lives. Biographies of Colonialism in the Indian Ocean World, 1790–1920* (Cambridge: Cambridge University Press, 2012). See also Anand Yang, "Indian Convict Workers in Southeast Asia in the Late Eighteenth and Early Nineteenth Centuries," *Journal of World History* 24, no. 2 (2003): 179–208.
31. Kerry Ward, *Networks of Empire: Forced Migration in the Dutch East India Company*, (Cambridge: Cambridge University Press, 2009); Ronit Ricci, ed., *Exile in Colonial Asia: Kings, Convicts, Commemoration* (Honolulu: University of Hawaii Press, 2016); Michael Laffan, "From Javanese Court to African Grave: How Noriman Became Tuan Skapie, 1717–1806," *Journal of Indian Ocean World Studies* 1 (2017): 38–59.
32. It is not possible to list here the vast body of scholarship on slavery in South Africa, but seminal works include Robert Ross, *Cape of Torments: Slavery and Resistance in South Africa* (London: Routledge & Kegan Paul, 1983); Nigel Worden, *Slavery in Dutch South Africa* (Cambridge:Cambridge University Press, 1985); Robert C.-H. Shell, *Children of Bondage: A Social History of the Slave Society at the Cape of Good Hope, 1652–1838* (Hanover, N.H.: Wesleyan University Press, 1994); Sirtjo Koolhof and Robert Ross, "Upas, September and the Bugis at the Cape of Good Hope: The Context of a Slave Letter," *Archipel* 70 (2005): 281–308; and Pamela Scully, *Liberating the Family? Gender and British Slave Emancipation in the Rural Western Cape, South Africa, 1823–1853* (Portsmouth, N.H.: Heinemann, 1997).

33. Nigel Worden, "Cape Slaves in the Paper Empire of the VOC," *Kronos* 40, no. 1 (2014): 27.
34. Sue Peabody, *Madeleine's Children: Family, Freedom, Secrets, and Lies in France's Indian Ocean Colonies* (New York: Oxford University Press, 2017).
35. On the early years of labor, see V. K. Jayawardena, *The Rise of the Labor Movement in Ceylon* (Durham, N.C.: Duke University Press, 1972).
36. An example of the elitist feature of feminist historiography is Malathi de Alwis's work on respectability. See, for instance, "'Respectability,' 'Modernity' and the Policing of 'Culture' in Colonial Ceylon," in *Gender Sexuality and Colonial Modernities*, ed. Antoinette Burton (London: Routledge 1999), 179–94.
37. On the plantation era that followed slavery, see Patrick Peebles, *The Plantation Tamils of Ceylon* (London: Leicester University Press, 2001); Rachel Kurian and Kumari Jayawardena, *Class, Patriarchy and Ethnicity on Sri Lankan Plantations: Two Centuries of Power and Protest* (New Delhi: Orient Blackswan, 2015); Donovan Moldrich, *Bitter Berry Bondage: The Nineteenth Century Coffee Workers of Sri Lanka* (Kandy: Co-ordinating Secretariat for Plantation Areas, 1989); and James Duncan, *In the Shadows of the Tropics: Climate, Race and Biopower in Nineteenth Century Ceylon* (London: Routledge, 2007).
38. See Gananath Obeysekere's recent biography of the last king of Kandy, *The Doomed King: A Requiem for Sri Vickrama Rajasinha* (Colombo: Perera-Hussein, 2017).
39. See, for instance, Alain Corbin, *Le Village des Cannibales* (Paris: Aubier 1990); and Ranajit Guha, *Elementary Aspects of Peasant Insurgency in Colonial India* (New Delhi: Oxford University Press, 1983).
40. Das, *Life and Words*.
41. Paul Bijls, "Acts of Equality: Writing Autonomy, Empathy and Community in an Indonesian Slave Narrative," in *Being a Slave in the Indian Ocean World: Histories and Legacies of European Slavery*, ed. Alicia Schrikker and Nira Wickramasinghe (Leiden: Leiden University Press, 2020).
42. Indrani Chatterjee, "A Slave's Quest for Selfhood in Eighteenth-Century Hindustan," *Indian Economic and Social History Review* 37, no. 1 (2000): 53–86.
43. Michael Fisher, "Representation of India, the English East India Company, and Self by an Eighteenth-Century Indian Emigrant to Britain," *Modern Asian Studies* 32, no. 4 (1998): 891–911.
44. Pier M. Larson, "Horrid Journeying: Narratives of Enslavement and the Global African Diaspora," *Journal of World History* 19, no. 4 (2008): 431–64; David Northrup "Becoming African: Identity Formation Among Liberated Slaves in Nineteenth-Century Sierra Leone," *Slavery and Abolition* 27, no. 1 (2006): 1–21.
45. See, for instance, Vincent Carrera, *Equiano the African: Biography of a Self-Made Man* (Athens: University of Georgia Press, 2005).

46. Avery F. Gordon, *Ghostly Matters: Haunting and the Sociological Imagination* (Minneapolis: University of Minnesota Press, 2008), 143–45.
47. The field of study exploring slave narratives is well established. Seminal works include Charles T. Davis and Henry Louis Gates, Jr., eds., *The Slave's Narrative* (New York: Oxford University Press, 1985); and William L. Andrews, *To Tell a Free Story: The First Century of Afro-American Autobiography, 1760–1865* (Urbana: University of Illinois Press, 1988).
48. For an example of legal records creatively used to re-create the lives of enslaved women in India, see Sylvia Vatuk, "Bharattee's Death: Domestic Slave-Women in Nineteenth-Century Madras," in *Slavery and South Asian History*, ed. Indrani Chatterjee and Richard M. Eaton (Bloomington: Indiana University Press, 2006), 210–33.
49. The issue of "slave resistance" has been a central theme in literature in other parts of the world. This has included everyday acts such as theft, foot-dragging, running away, and feigning illness, which were practiced as individuals rather than collectively. The literature is so vast it is only possible to cite a few seminal works: Harold Aptheker, *American Negro Slave Revolts* (New York: Columbia University Press, 1943); Eugene D. Genovese, *From Rebellion to Revolution: Afro-American Slave Revolts in the Making of the Modern World* (Baton Rouge: Louisiana State University Press, 1979); James Scott, *Weapons of the Weak: Everyday Forms of Peasant Resistance* (New Haven, Conn: Yale University Press, 1985).
50. The Digital Humanities Centre at Leiden University provided me with the resources to enter over seven thousand names in spreadsheets, and this volume is only a first step in analyzing them. It juxtaposes this invaluable source with other data to explore specific questions. Registers offer an immense range of possibilities to rethink issues of caste hierarchy, family composition, and labor relations in the northern peninsula, where the numbers of enumerated slaves are overwhelming.
51. The Ancestry database at https://search.ancestry.co.uk/search/db.aspx?dbid=1129 contains the slave registers for the following colonies: Antigua, Barbados, Berbice, Dominica, Grenada, Honduras, Jamaica, Mauritius, Nevis, Sri Lanka (Ceylon), St. Christopher, St. Lucia, St. Vincent, Tobago, Trinidad, Virgin Islands, and Cape of Good Hope.
52. The complete set of slave registers was consulted at the NA UK, CO T71, Slave Registers of Former Colonial Dependencies, 1813–1834. Some of these registers can be accessed on Ancestry.com. These include registers, compiled in the 1820s, that deal with depressed castes, Coviyar, Nalavar, and Palla slaves from Jaffna, Mannar, Tenmoratchie, Patchelapalla, the Islands, Trincomalee, Waddemoratchie, Walligammo, and the Wanny.
53. SLNA, Lot 33/1699, Colombo Kachcheri, 1827.

54. The Moors were, after the Sinhalese and the Tamil, the third largest ethnic group in the country. The term identified Muslims who had lived in the country since as far back as the tenth century. Some claimed Arab descent, but most were descendants of traders from the Coromandel Coast. They spoke Tamil but asserted a distinct identity vis-à-vis Tamil people of the North and East of the island.
55. I borrow this term from Bhavani Raman, *Document Raj: Writing and Scribes in Early Colonial South India* (Chicago: University of Chicago Press, 2012).

1. A Dutch Fiscal's Murder

1. Martin A. Klein, "Looking for Slavery in Colonial Archives," in *African Voices on Slavery and the Slave Trade*, ed. A. Bellagamba, S. Greene, and M. Klein (Cambridge: Cambridge University Press, 2016), 114.
2. The fiscal was an officer with judicial power who functioned as the prosecutor in criminal cases.
3. W. Björkman, "Kāfir," in *Encyclopaedia of Islam*, ed. P. Bearman, T. Bianquis, C. E. Bosworth, E. van Donzel, and W. P. Heinrichs, 2d ed., 2012, http://dx.doi.org/10.1163/1573-3912_islam_SIM_3775.
4. For an account of the presence of Africans in the island, see Shihan de Silva Jayasuriya, "A Forgotten Minority: The Afro-Sri Lankans," *African and Asian Studies* 6 (2007): 227–42; and Shihan de Silva Jayasuriya and Jean Pierre Angenot, eds., *Uncovering the History of Africans in Asia* (Leiden: Brill, 2008). In these detailed works that trace the various forced migratory movements of Africans to Sri Lanka, slaves are always conflated with people of African origin.
5. There is a sizable literature on the Afro–Sri Lankan community or Africana people. For a recent review, see Sureshi M. Jayawardene, "Racialized Casteism: Exposing the Relationship Between Race, Caste, and Colorism Through the Experiences of Africana People in India and Sri Lanka," *Journal of African American Studies* 20 (2016): 323–45.
6. Academic historiography of Dutch rule in Sri Lanka—for example, the valuable works of Kate Ekama, Alicia Schrikker, and Remco Raben—refers to the presence of slaves in Sri Lanka and to their ethnic origin but without connecting slavery to the present.
7. Achille Mbembe, *Critique de la Raison Nègre* (Paris: La Découverte, 2013), 73.
8. In the account of Gadadhar Singh, who was a member of the Seventh Rajput Regiment in China in 1900–1901, Indian sepoys were described as "black" and Chinese as people of "our same colour." See Anand Yang et al., eds., *Thirteen Months in China: A Subaltern Indian and the Colonial World* (New Delhi:

Oxford University Press: 2017). On Afro-Asian solidarity, see Vijay Prasad, *The Darker Nations. A People's History of the Third World* (New York: New Press, 2007).

9. R. L. Brohier, *Changing Face of Colombo (1505–1972): Covering the Portuguese, Dutch and British Periods* (Colombo: Lake House, 1984), 33; Ismeth Raheem, *Views of Colombo (1518–1900)* (Colombo: Lake House, 1984).

10. Brohier, *Changing Face of Colombo*, 33 (emphasis added).

11. For instance, S. Arasaratnam, *Ceylon and the Dutch, 1600–1800: External Influences and Internal Change in Early Modern Sri Lanka* (Aldershot, UK: Variorum, 1996), does not mention a slave rebellion in Colombo.

12. "Dog in dit zelve jaar, stonden de Caneelschillers regen ons op. . . . Ook viel hier un dit jaar (1723) het zeldzaam geval voor, dat de Fiscaal Barent van der Swaan, met zyn Vrouw, door zyne Slaven, jammerlyk, op Colombo vermoord weird. 't Geen zyn Ed. verfataande, is Zyn Ed.drie dagen' er na, de 11 Juni, 1723 (zo men zeg) van schrik overleden." Francois Valentijn, *Oud en Nieuw Oost-Indien, vyfde Deel* (Dordrecht: Van Bram, Oncer de Linden, 1724), 359. My translation from the Dutch.

13. R. G. Anthonisz, *Report on the Dutch Records in the Government Archives at Colombo* (Colombo: H. C. Cottle, 1907), 31.

14. Municipal Council of Colombo, "Slave Island (Colombo 2)," http://colombofort.com/slave.island.htm#, accessed July 31, 2018.

15. Sri Lanka National Archives (SLNA), Lot 1/4603 Criminal Roll, June 1, 1723, 9–15. I thank my Leiden University colleagues Alicia Schrickker and Bente M. de Leede for help with the Dutch-language documents.

16. Bain Attwood, Dipesh Chakrabarty, and Claudio Lomnitz, "The Public Life of History," *Public Culture* 20, no. 1 (February 2008): 2.

17. Markus Vink, "'The World's Oldest Trade': Dutch Slavery and Slave Trade in the Indian Ocean in the Seventeenth Century," *Journal of World History* 14, no. 2 (2003): 139–43; Raben, "Batavia and Colombo," 131.

18. Matthias van Rossum, *Kleurrijke tragiek. De Geschiedenis van Slavernij in Azie onder de VOC* (Verloren: Hilversum, 2015), 23.

19. For an excellent analysis of slave numbers, see Kate Ekama, "Slavery in Dutch Colombo: A Social History," M.A. thesis, University of Leiden, 2012, 10, 15.

20. See Michel Foucault, *Discipline and Punish. The Birth of the Prison*, 2d ed. (New York: Vintage, 1995), for a similar focus in Europe on the corporeal as site of punishment before the penal reforms of the mid-eighteenth century.

21. SLNA, Lot 1/4603 Criminal Roll, June 1, 1723, 9–15.

22. Brohier, *Changing Face of Colombo*, 33.

23. Ashis Nandy calls mythographies narratives that have been delegitimized by disciplinary history. See his *Intimate Enemy: Loss and Recovery of Self Under Colonialism* (New Delhi: Oxford University Press, 1983), 15.

24. Anthonisz, *Report on the Dutch Records*, 6.
25. P. E. Schelinger and R. M. Salkin, eds., *International Dictionary of Historic Places: Asia and Oceania* (London: Routledge, 1996), 201. My emphasis.
26. V. Perniola, *The Catholic Church in Sri Lanka: The Dutch Period*, vol. 1: *1658–1711* (Dehiwela: Tisara Press, 1983), 256, 263.
27. L. Hovy, *Ceylonees Plakkaatboek: Plakkaten en andere wetten uitgevaardigd door het Nederlandse bestuur op Ceylon, 1638–1796* (Hilversum: Verloren, 1991), 2:476–77.
28. James Cordiner, *A Description of Ceylon Containing an Account of the Country, Inhabitants, and Natural Productions: with narratives of a tour round the island in 1800, the campaign in Candy in 1803, and a journey to Ramisseram in 1804* (London: Longman, Hurst, Rees and Orme, 1807), 1:37.
29. James Selkirk, *Recollections of Ceylon, After a Residence of Nearly Thirteen Years: With an Account of the Church Missionary Society's Operations in the Island and Extracts from a Journal*, Church Missionary Society (London: Hatchard, 1844), 5.
30. Hans Hagerdal, *Lords of the Land, Lords of the Sea: Conflict and Adaptation in Early Colonial Timor, 1600–1800* (Leiden: KITLV Press, 2012), 289; Monika Arnez and Jurgen Sarnowlsky, *The Role of Religions in the European Perception of Insular and Mainland Southeast Asia: Travel Accounts of the 16th to the 21st Century* (Cambridge: Cambridge Scholars, 2016), 92.
31. Mahdi Husain, trans. and comm., *The Rehla of Ibn Battuta* (Baroda: Oriental Institute, 1976), https://archive.org/details/TheRehlaOfIbnBattuta/page/n317.
32. Lodewijk Wagenaar, *Cinnamon and Elephants: Sri Lanka and the Netherlands from 1600* (Amsterdam: Vantilt, 2016), 43, 45.
33. Ekama, "Slavery in Dutch Colombo," 20.
34. Jacob Christian Pielat, *Memoir to His Successor Diderik Van Domburg (1734)*, trans. Sophia Pieters (Colombo: Government Printer, 1905), 55.
35. House of Commons Debates, April 15, 1851, vol. 116, cc. 226–86, https://api.parliament.uk/historic-hansard/commons/1851/apr/15/the-kaffir-war; Robert Ross, *The Borders of Race in Colonial South Africa. The Kat River Settlement, 1829–1856* (Cambridge: Cambridge University Press, 2013); Bernth Lindfors, "Hottentot, Bushman, Kaffir: Taxonomic Tendencies in Nineteenth Century Racial Iconography," *Nordic Journal of African Studies* 5, no. 2 (1996): 1–30.
36. N. Worden, E. Van Heyningen, and V. Bickford-Smith, *Cape Town: The Making of a City* (Claremont: Verloren Press. 1998), 61.
37. Ineke van Kessel, "'Courageous but Insolent': African Soldiers in the Dutch East Indies as Seen by Dutch Officials and Indonesian Neighbours," *Transforming Cultures Journal* 4, no. 2 (November 2009): 58.
38. Gabeba Baderoon, *Regarding Muslims: From Slavery to Post-apartheid* (Johannesburg: Wits University Press, 2014), 31–34.

39. J. R. Bruijn, F. S. Gastra, and I. Schoffer, *Dutch Asiatic Shipping in the 17th and 18th Centuries* (The Hague: Martinus Nijhoff, 1987).
40. British Library, Delaware Journal IOR/L/MAR/B/322A, July 29, 1747–July 2, 1750.
41. Zoltan Biederman, "Colombo Versus Cannanore: Contrasting Structures of Two Colonial Port Cities (1500–1700)," *Journal of the Economic and Social History of the Orient* 52, no. 3 (2009): 447.
42. See Jorge Manuel Flores, *Re-exploring the Links: History and Constructed Histories Between Portugal and Sri Lanka* (Wiesbaden: Harrassowitz Verlag, 2007). On the Portuguese tombos, see K. D. Paranavitana, "The Portuguese Tombos as a Source of Sixteenth and Seventeenth Century Sri Lankan History," in Flores, *Re-exploring the Links*, 63–78; Chandra R. de Silva, "The First Portuguese Revenue Register of the Kingdom of Kotte–1599," *Ceylon Journal of Historical and Social Studies*, New Series, 5, no. 1–2 (January–December 1975): 71–153.
43. Raben, "Batavia and Colombo," 131.
44. Gerrit Knaap, "Europeans, Mestizos and Slaves: The Population of Colombo at the End of the Seventeenth Century," *Itinerario* 5, no. 2 (1981): 84–101.
45. Van Rossum, *Kleurrijke tragiek*, 31.
46. Ekama, "Slavery in Dutch Colombo," 9, 17, 26, 51.
47. Van Rossum, *Kleurrijke tragiek*, 31.
48. Knaap, "Europeans, Mestizos and Slaves," 88, 94.
49. Ekama, "Slavery in Dutch Colombo," 10.
50. The Sinhalese are a community speaking the Sinhala language, generally professing Buddhism, and living mainly in the southern districts of the island. They form about 70 percent of the population. The northern and eastern areas of the island are peopled by a majority of Tamils (predominantly Hindu) and Muslims. Among Sinhalese and Tamils, a sizable minority are converts to Christianity.
51. B. L. Panditharatne and S. Selvanayagam, "The Demography of Ceylon: An Introductory Survey," in *History of Ceylon*, vol. 3: *From the Beginning of the Nineteenth Century to 1948*, ed. K. M. de Silva (Peradeniya: University of Peradeniya, 1973), 285.
52. Nadeera Seneviratne-Rupasinghe, "Negotiating Custom: Colonial Law Making in the Galle Landraad," Ph.D diss., Leiden University, 2016, 152.
53. Philippus Baldaeus, *A True and Exact Description of the Most Celebrated East-India Coasts of Malabar and Coromandel; as also of the Isle of Ceylon* (London: Churchill, 1703), 812, https://archive.org/details/trueexactdescripoobald.
54. S. Arasaratnam, *Francois Valentijn's Description of Ceylon* (London: Hakluyt Society 1978), 160–61.
55. E. B. Denham, *Ceylon at the Census of 1911: Being the Review of the Results of the Census of 1911* (Colombo: H. C. Cottle, 1911), 10.

56. Egidius Daalmans, "Notes on Ceylon," *Journal of the Ceylon Branch of the Royal Asiatic Society* 10, no. 35 (1885): 145–74.
57. Michael Roberts et al., *People In Between: Ethnic and Class Prejudices in British Ceylon* (Ratmalana: Sarvodaya, 1989), 8, 41.
58. Lodewijk Wagenaar, *Galle-Vestiging in Ceylon: Beschrijving van een Koloniale Samenleving aan de Vooravond van de Singalese Opstand tegen het Nederlandse Gezag (1760)* (Amsterdam: De Bataafsche Leeuw, 1994), 58.
59. F. R. Bradlow and M. Cairns, *The Early Cape Muslims: A Study of Their Mosques, Genealogy and Origins* (Cape Town: Balkema, 1978), 62–63. The madrasa, which taught precepts from the holy Qur'an and how to read and write the Arabic language, proved extremely popular among the slaves and the free black community. A few years later a masjid was built. Upon Coridon's death the property passed on to his wife, Tryn, a Cape-born former slave whom he had married by Muslim rites, and then to his daughter, Saartje van de Kaap.
60. See, for instance, Nigel Worden, *Slavery in Dutch South Africa* (Cambridge: Cambridge University Press, 1985); and Robert C.-H. Shell, *Children of Bondage: A Social History of Slave Society at the Cape of Good Hope, 1652–1834* (Hanover, N.H.: Wesleyan University Press, 1994).
61. Gert Oostindie, *Dutch Colonialism, Migration and Cultural Heritage: Past and Present*, (Leiden: Brill, 2008), 133.
62. James C. Anderson, "The Slaves 1652–1795," in *The Shaping of South African Society, 1652–1820*, ed. Richard Elphick and Hermann Giliomee (Cape Town: Longman, 1979), 84.
63. SLNA, Lot 7/1, Letter Addressed to the Honorable Court of Directors for the Affairs of the Honorable United Company of Merchants of England Trading to the East Indies at Their House in London Leadenhall Street, London, Colombo, February 26, 1799, 405–7.
64. John D. Rogers makes no mention of slaves or free blacks in his much-cited article on social classification, "Early British Rule and Social Classification in Lanka," *Modern Asian Studies* 38, no. 3 (2004): 625–47.
65. Ann Laura Stoler, "Colonial Aphasia: Race and Disabled Histories in France," *Public Culture* 23, no. 1 (2011): 130.
66. Robert Percival, *An Account of the Island of Ceylon Containing Its History, Geography, Natural History, with the Manners and Customs of Its Various Inhabitants* (London: C. and R. Baldwin, 1803; reprint New Delhi: Asian Educational Services, 1990), 114–15.
67. This point was made eloquently in F. Cooper and A. L. Stoler, eds., *Tensions of Empire: Colonial Cultures in a Bourgeois World* (Berkeley: University of California Press, 1997).
68. M. E. Esteve and Philippe Fabri, eds., *Quelques Notions sur l'Isle de Ceylan. Eudelin de Jonville* (Hambantota: Viator, 2012).

69. Antonio Bertolacci, *A View of the Agricultural, Commercial and Financial Interests of Ceylon* (London: Black, Parbury and Allen, 1817), 39–40.
70. Sujit Sivasundaram, *Islanded: Britain, Sri Lanka and the Bounds of an Indian Ocean Colony* (Chicago: University of Chicago Press, 2013), 105.
71. Ranjit B. Amerasinghe, *The Supreme Court of Sri Lanka: The First 185 Years* (Colombo: Sarvodaya 1986), 511; T. Nadaraja, *The Legal System of Ceylon in Its Historical Setting* (Leiden: Brill 1972), 84.
72. J. S. Buckingham, ed., "Introduction of Trial by Jury and Abolition of Slavery by Sir Alexander Johnston," *Oriental Herald and Colonial Review* 16, no. 49 (January 1828): 125.
73. See Partha Chatterjee's idea of racial binary in *The Nation and Its Fragment: Colonial and Postcolonial Histories* (Princeton, N.J.: Princeton University Press, 1993); and, for instance, Elizabeth Kolsky's critique in "Codification and the Rule of Colonial Difference: Criminal Procedure in British India," *Law and History Review* 23, no. 3 (2005): 631–83.
74. Peter Pels, "The Anthropology of Colonialism: Culture, History and the Emergence of Western Governmentality," *Annual Review of Anthropology* 26, no. 1 (1997), 163–83; Cooper and Stoler, *Tensions of Empire*.
75. Rozina Visram, *Ayahs, Lascars and Princes: Indians in Britain 1700–1947* (London: Pluto Press, 1986), 11–14.
76. Roxann Wheeler, *The Complexion of Race: Categories of Difference in Eighteenth-Century British Culture* (Philadelphia: University of Pennsylvania Press, 2000).
77. Anne McClintock, *Imperial Leather. Race, Gender and Sexuality in the Colonial Contest* (New York: Routledge 1995), 112.
78. Edward Said, *Orientalism* (New York: Pantheon, 1978).
79. Isaac Land, "Bread and Arsenic: Citizenship from the Bottom Up in Georgian London," *Journal of Social History* 39, no. 1 (2005): 93–94.
80. Francisco Bethencourt, *Racisms: From the Crusades to the Twentieth Century* (Princeton, N.J.: Princeton University Press, 2013), 222.
81. Percival, *An Account of the Island of Ceylon*, 133.
82. Nancy Stepan, *The Idea of Race in Science: Great Britain, 1800–1960* (London: St Antony's Macmillan Press, 1982), xviii.
83. Kathrin Levitan, *A Cultural History of the British Census: Envisioning the Multitude in the Nineteenth Century* (Basingstoke, UK: Palgrave Macmillan, 2011), 148. For a differing interpretation in which class, rank, and status rather than race are seen as the defining features of the worldview of administrators, see David Cannadine, *Ornamentalism: How the British Saw Their Empire* (London: Allen Lane, 2001).
84. Christopher Anthony, "Race and the Census in the Commonwealth," *Population, Space and Place* 11 (2005): 103.

85. J. L. Hochschild and B. M. Powell, "Racial Reorganization and the United States Census 1850–1930: Mulattoes, Half-Breeds, Mixed Parentage, Hindoos and the Mexican Race," *Studies in American Political Development* 22, no. 1 (2008): 59–96.
86. For an assessment of the "colonial knowledge" literature and debate, see Leela Gandhi, *Postcolonial Theory. A Critical Introduction* (New York: Columbia University Press, 1998); and, for the Sri Lanka case, Rogers, "Early British Rule."
87. See, for instance, Bruce Curtis, "On the Local Construction of Statistical Knowledge; Making Up the 1861 Census of the Canadas," *Journal of Historical Sociology*, 7, no. 4 (1994): 418.
88. See Nira Wickramasinghe, *Sri Lanka in the Modern Age: A History* (New York: Oxford University Press, 2015), 47–76.
89. Nira Wickramasinghe, *Ethnic Politics in Colonial Ceylon* (New Delhi: Vikas, 1995), 3; Bertolacci, *Agricultural, Commercial and Financial Interests of Ceylon*, 64.
90. N. K. Sarkar, *The Demography of Ceylon* (Colombo: Ceylon Government Press, 1957), 19.
91. Bertolacci, *Agricultural, Commercial and Financial Interests of Ceylon*, 72.
92. SLNA, *Return of the Population of the Maritime Districts of the Island of Ceylon* (Colombo: Government Press, 1816), 24–25, 36, 64, 67.
93. Great Britain House of Commons, March 1, 1838, Slave Trade East India—Slavery in Ceylon—Correspondence on the Slave Trade, Extract from a Report of Lieutenant Colonel Colebrooke 24 Dec 1831, 598.
94. Denham, *Ceylon at the Census of 1911*, 11
95. SLNA, *Return of the Population of the Island of Ceylon 1827*, 57–59, 67–68.
96. H. N. S. Karunatilake, "Social and Economic Statistics of Sri Lanka in the Nineteenth Century," *Royal Asiatic Society of Sri Lanka Branch*, New Series 31 (1986/87): 60. The Blue Books were published from 1821 to 1938 and contain the essential financial data about the colony. The Ceylon Calendar from 1814 to 1862 changed its name during this period to the Ceylon Calendar and Compendium of Useful Information (1840–1850) and then the Ceylon Almanac and Annual Register (1851–1862).
97. In David Scott's explanation of Sri Lanka's colonial modernity, one kind of political rationality—that of mercantilism—was displaced by another after 1832. See David Scott, *Refashioning Futures: Criticism After Postcoloniality* (Princeton, N.J.: Princeton University Press, 1999).
98. See B. S. Cohn, "The Census, Social Structure and Objectification in South Asia," in *An Anthropologist Among Historians* (New Delhi: Oxford University Press, 1987), 224–54.
99. E. A. Benians et al., eds., *Cambridge History of the British Empire (1929–1959)* (Cambridge: Cambridge University Press, 1961), 721.

100. Robert Montgomery Martin, *Statistics of the Colonies of the British Empire, from the Official Records of the Colonial Office* (London: Allen, 1839).
101. For settler colonies such as New Zealand in the Blue Book of Statistics (1840), 89 (http://www.archives.govt.nz/exhibitions/permanentexhibitions/bluebooks/view.php), the population was divided into two categories, Europeans and Aborigines.
102. Benians et al., *Cambridge History of the British Empire*, 105.
103. SLNA, *Blue Book Ceylon*, 1825.
104. Karunatilake, "Social and Economic Statistics of Sri Lanka," 45.
105. See Michel Foucault's preface to *The Order of Things: An Archaeology of the Human Sciences* (New York: Vintage, 1970), 75. Foucault, who has magisterially documented the centrality of statistics as an authoritative form of knowledge, signals also that "the centre of knowledge, in the seventeenth and eighteenth centuries, is the table."
106. G.P.S.H. de Silva, "A Chronological Survey of Sinhalese Lexicographical Works in Ceylon During the Period 1800–1950," *Vidyalaya Journal of Arts, Science and Letters* 1, no. 1 (January 1968): 1–28.
107. Benjamin Clough, *A Sinhalese-English Dictionary*, 1830 (Colombo: Wesleyan Mission, 1892), https://archive.org/details/sinhaleseenglish00clourich.
108. Major, *Slavery, Abolitionism and Empire*, 23.
109. Slave Trade East India Company and Ceylon, Parliamentary Paper 1838, 599.
110. Bruce Curtis, "Surveying the Social: Techniques, Practice, Power," *Histories Social/Social History* 65, no. 39 (May 2002): 83–108.
111. Norbert Peabody, "Cents, Sense, Census: Human Inventories in Late Precolonial and Early Colonial India," *Comparative Studies in Society and History* 43, no. 4 (October 2001): 819–50. More generally, see C. A. Bayly, *Empire and Information: Intelligence Gathering and Social Communication in India 1780–1870* (Cambridge: Cambridge University Press, 1996).
112. For a theorization of colonial rule in India as an ethnographic state, the seminal texts remain B. S. Cohn, *An Anthropologist Among the Historians and Other Essays* (New Delhi: Oxford University Press 1987); Nicholas Dirks, *Castes of Mind: Colonialism and the Making of Modern India* (Princeton, N.J.: Princeton University Press, 1992); Rashmi Pant, "The Cognitive Status of Caste in Colonial Ethnography: A Review of Some Literature on the North West Provinces and Oudh," *Indian Economic and Social History Review* 24, no. 2 (April–June 1987): 145–62; and R. S. Smith, "Rule-by-Records and Rule-by-Reports: Complementary Aspects of the British Imperial Rule of Law," *Contributions to Indian Sociology* 19, 1 (1985): 153–76.
113. Arjun Appadurai, "Numbers in the Colonial Imagination," in *Orientalism and the Postcolonial Predicament: Perspectives on South Asia*, ed. Carol Breckenridge

and Peter van der Veer (Philadelphia: University of Pennsylvania Press, 1993), 317.
114. Slavery in Ceylon, Parliamentary Papers 467, 1838, 1.
115. NA UK, CO T71, Slave Registers Colombo, 1818–1832. The number next to the name in the list below indicates the number of slaves with that name.
116. James C. Scott, *Domination and the Arts of Resistance: Hidden Transcripts* (New Haven, Conn.: Yale University Press, 1990).
117. Orlando Patterson, *Slavery and Social Death: A Comparative Study* (Cambridge, Mass.: Harvard University Press, 1982), 5.
118. Appadurai, "Numbers in the Colonial Imagination," 319.
119. R. Smith, "Rule-by-Records and Rule-by-Reports" cited in Appadurai, "Numbers in the Colonial Imagination," 321.
120. Nira Wickramasinghe, "The Cocos Island Mutiny," paper presented at the conference on Crossfire of Empires: Global Histories of World War II, at Leiden University, May 2015.

2. From Colombo to Galle

1. Carolyn Steedman, "Something She Called a Fever: Michelet, Derrida, and Dust," *American Historical Review* 106, no. 4 (October 2001): 1165.
2. Saidiya Hartman, "Venus in Two Acts," *Small Axe* 12, no. 2 (June 2008): 2.
3. Bookkeeper-General Batavia, http://bgb.huygens.knaw.nl/bgb/voyage/11625, accessed November 11, 2017.
4. There were, however, voyages by VOC ships sent to Madagascar, the Comoros, and Zanzibar to buy slaves for Cape Town in the 1770s. It was not uncommon that more than a hundred slaves were transported in these ships in conditions similar to those of the Middle Passage. I thank Michael Laffan for drawing my attention to this new Middle Passage.
5. Bookkeeper-General Batavia, http://bgb.huygens.knaw.nl/bgb/voyage/11625.
6. I borrow from Veena Das, *Life and Words: Violence and the Descent Into the Ordinary* (Berkeley: University of California Press, 2006), 1, this qualification that gestures toward a contextual and time-dependent understanding of what constitutes "violence."
7. Shahid Amin, "Alternative Histories: A View from India," *Sephis-CSSSC Occasional Paper* (Calcutta: Centre for Studies in Social Sciences, 2002), 28.
8. The emancipation procedures in different regions of the country are dealt with in the following chapters. For a comparison with other Indian Ocean locations, see Indrani Chatterjee and Richard M. Eaton, *Slavery and South*

Asian History (Bloomington: Indiana University Press, 2006); Gyan Prakash, *Bonded Histories: Genealogies of Labor Servitude in Colonial India* (Cambridge: Cambridge University Press, 1993); and Andrea Major, *Slavery, Abolitionism and Empire in India 1772–1843* (Liverpool: Liverpool University Press, 2012).

9. Address to His Royal Highness The Prince Regent for Emancipating Children Born of Slaves after the 12th of August 1816, in G. C. Mendis, *The Colebrooke-Cameron Papers, Documents on British Colonial Policy in Ceylon 1796–1833* (London: Oxford University Press, 1956), 2:361. I was extremely fortunate to find Chris Uhlenbeck, a descendant of C. C. Uhlenbeck, in Leiden and am grateful for his generosity in sharing all the information he possessed about his ancestor.

10. *Journal of Dutch Burgher Union* 9, no. 2 (1916): 66–68; Nigel Penn, "The Voyage Out: Peter Kolb and VOC Voyages to the Cape," in *Many Middle Passages: Forced Migration and the Making of the Modern World*, ed. Emma Christopher et al. (Berkeley: University of California Press, 2007), 72–91.

11. National Archive, The Hague (NA NL), 2.21.165/8, Uhlenbeck Family Papers.

12. National Archives, Kew (NA UK), Slave Registers Colombo, 1818–1832.

13. Sri Lanka National Archives (SLNA), S.A., W. Motthau, Translation of the Minutes of the Consistory of the Dutch Reformed Church of Wolvendaal, Colombo, June 20, 1804, to November 22, 1809, vol. 4, A/5 of the Records at the Wolfendaal Church (Colombo, 1977), 54, Ordinary Meeting of December 30, 1805.

14. NA NL, 2.21.165/8, Uhlenbeck Family Papers, letter from C. C. Uhlenbeck to Secretary of State, Colombo, December 16, 1820.

15. P. H. Molhuysen and P. J. Blok, *Nieuw Nederlandsch Biografish Woordenboek*, A. W. Sijthoffs Uitgevers Maatschappig (Leiden, 1937), 982–83, http://resources.huygens.knaw.nl/retroboeken/nnbw/#page=0&accessor=accessor_index&view=homePane.

16. NA NL, 2.21.165/8, Uhlenbeck Family Papers, letter from 80 Burghers in Colombo to C. C. Uhlenbeck, December 30, 1820, "Hoog geeerde Heer en Vriend." The original Dutch is "De Slaave inboorlingen een der voornaamste personen die met ijver getracht en te weege gebracht heeft dat ze van het juk der Slaafsche Dienstbaarheid bevrijd geworden zijn."

17. *Journal of the Dutch Burgher Union* 23 (July 1933): 52.

18. M. Janse, " 'Holland as a Little England'? British Anti-Slavery Missionaries and Continental Abolitionist Movements in the Mid-Nineteenth Century," *Past and Present* 229, no. 1 (November 2015): 135. The standard text on debates about Dutch abolitionism is Gert Oostindie, ed., *Fifty Years Later: Antislavery, Capitalism and Modernity in the Dutch Orbit* (Leiden: KITLV Press, 1995).

19. M. Janse argues that there were more protests than generally suggested in the mainstream historiography.
20. W. R. van Hoëvell, *Slaven en vrijen onder de Nederlandsche wet* (Zaltbommel: Noman, 1855), cited in Paul Bijl, "Acts of Equality," in *Being a Slave*, ed. A. Schrikker and N. Wickramasinghe (Leiden: Leiden University Press, 2020).
21. Parlement.com, https://www.parlement.com/id/vgo9lljk47yc/g_h_uhlen beck; Janse, in "'Holland as a Little England'?," 148, gives the figure of 13.5 million guilders.
22. Oostindie, *Fifty Years Later*, 200. Slaveholders received between 40 and 350 Dutch guilders per slave; Isabel Tanak-Van Dalen, "Dutch Attitudes Towards Slavery and the Tardy Road to Abolition: The Case of Deshima," in *Abolitions as a Global Experience*, ed. Hideaki Suzuki (Singapore: NUS Press, 2016), 72–112.
23. The term *Burgher* initially related to the Dutch citizens who settled in Sri Lanka. By the eighteenth century it encompassed a growing European community of mixed Portuguese, Dutch, Sinhalese, and Tamil peoples. By the nineteenth century the Burgher community divided into two different communities: Dutch Burghers and Portuguese Burghers. Apart from the Burghers, it is possible, although less probable, that by keeping slaves, local elites were emulating the lifestyle of Kandyan chieftains in the highlands, where slavery was the result of debt, a condition that was not permanent. In the more distant past, before colonial rule, rulers of kingdoms in the island held slaves who were generally concubines or soldiers.
24. P. E. Pieris, ed., *Notes on Some Sinhalese Families*, parts 1–4 (Colombo: Apothecaries, 1902/1911).
25. L. A. Wickremaratne, "Education and Social Change 1832 to c 1900," in *University of Ceylon History of Ceylon*, vol. 3: *From the Beginning of the Nineteenth Century to 1948*, ed. K. M. de Silva (Peradeniya: University of Ceylon, 1973), 169.
26. Kate Ekama, "Slavery in Dutch Colombo," MA thesis, 19–20, citing L. Wagenaar, *Galle: VOC vestiging in Ceylon*, 56.
27. Arnold Wright, *Twentieth Century Impressions of Ceylon: Its History, People, Commerce, Industries and Resources* (London: Lloyd's Greater Britain, 1907), 524.
28. NA UK, Slave registers, Matara district, 1818–1832.
29. Pieris, ed., *Notes on Some Sinhalese Families*, part 3, 20–21.
30. NA NL, 1.11.01.01, 2049, Deeds done by Dutch notaries and the judiciary in Ceylon 1687, 1750–1808, Will of Nicholaas Dias Abesinghe Amereseqere.
31. Alicia Schrikker, *Dutch and British Colonial Intervention in Sri Lanka, 1780–1815: Expansion and Reform* (Leiden: Brill, 2006), 67.
32. Schrikker, *Dutch and British Colonial Intervention*, 68.
33. *Illangakoon Diaries*, in Pieris, *Notes on Some Sinhalese Families*, 70–71.
34. Pieris, *Illangakoon Diaries*, 127.

35. Pieris, *Illangakoon Diaries*, 56; see also the list of slaves shared between the son and daughter of the Maha Mudaliyar Ilangakoon after his death in 1782 (88–89).
36. Pieris, *Illangakoon Diaries*, 116–17; see also twenty slaves listed as part of the estate that Dona Catherina and Dona Assensia, children of Jayatilaka Mudaliyar of Matara left behind (126–27).
37. Robert C.-H. Shell, *Children of Bondage: A Social History of the Slave Society at the Cape 1652–1838* (Hanover, N.H.: Wesleyan University Press, 1994); Robert Ross, *Status and Respectability in the Cape Colony 1750–1870: A Tragedy in Manners* (Cambridge: Cambridge University Press, 2004).
38. Wealthy families in the Kandyan highlands also had slaves in their households who were not alienated folk but local indebted peasants. As they were perceived as traditional and even uncouth, the Kandyan upper classes did not constitute an example to emulate in the manner of the old Low Country bourgeoisie.
39. Patrick Peebles, *Social Change in Nineteenth Century Ceylon* (New Delhi: Navrang, 1995); Kumari Jayawardena, *From Nobodies to Somebodies: The Rise of the Colonial Bourgeoisie in Sri Lanka* (London: Zed, 2000); Michael Roberts, *Caste Conflict and Elite Formation: The Rise of a Karava Elite in Sri Lanka* (Cambridge: Cambridge University Press, 1982); Anoma Peiris, *Architecture and Nationalism in Sri Lanka: The Trouser Under the Cloth* (London: Routledge, 2012).
40. Jayawardena, *From Nobodies to Somebodies*, 7.
41. L. A. Wickremaratne, "The Development of Transportation in Ceylon c 1800–1947," in *University of Ceylon History of Ceylon*, ed. K. M de Silva (Peradeniya: University of Ceylon, 1973), 308–9.
42. Patrick Peebles, "Land Use and Population Growth in Colonial Ceylon," *Contributions to Asian Studies* 6 (1976): 68.
43. Peebles, "Land Use and Population Growth," 70–71.
44. Peebles, "Land Use and Population Growth," 70; Mendis, *Colebrooke Cameron Papers*, 361–65.
45. SLNA, Lot 7/2133, Deed of transfer of slave, June 30, 1809, 361–67.
46. For a precise analysis of the mode of incorporation of Dutch Ceylon into the British Empire, see Schrikker, *Dutch and British Colonial Intervention*, 131–34.
47. U. C. Wickremeratne, *The Conservative Nature of the British Rule of Sri Lanka with Particular Emphasis on the Period 1796–1802* (New Delhi: Navrang, 1996), 151–52.
48. Nira Wickramasinghe, "Many Little Revolts or One Rebellion? The Maritime Provinces of Ceylon/Sri Lanka Between 1796 and 1800," *South Asia: Journal of South Asian Studies*, 32, no. 2 (2009): 170–88.
49. Robert Percival, *An Account of the Island of Ceylon Containing Its History, Geography, Natural History, with the Manners and Customs of Its Various Inhabitants*

(London: C. and R. Baldwin, 1803; reprint New Delhi: Asian Educational Services, 1990: 103.

50. L. Hovy, Ceylonees Plakkaatboek 1:69 (August 7, 1663), 109; 1:111 (April 17, 1674), 169–70; 1:134 (August 13, 1677) 201; 2:415 (May 31, 1757, Colombo/July 4, 1757, Galle), 587–88; 2:608/9 (December 28, 1786), 869.
51. Ekama, "Runaway Slaves from the VOC Cape."
52. British Library, London (BL), IOR/G/11/42 Colombo, February 10, 1800, Dannah for murder; Olke Andringa, WikiTree, https://www.wikitree.com/wiki/Andringa-24, accessed October 1, 2019.
53. For a foray into the shifting nomenclature of Malay and Jawa, see Ronit Ricci, "Jawa, Melayu, Malay or Otherwise? The Shifting Nomenclature of the Sri Lankan Malays," *Indonesia and the Malay World* 44, no. 130 (2016): 1–15; and Michael Laffan, "Finding Java: Muslim Nomenclature of Insular Southeast Asia from Srivijaya to Snouck Hurgronje," in *Southeast Asia and the Middle East: Islam, Movement and the Longue Durée*, ed. Eric Tagliacozzo (Singapore: NUS, 2009), 17–64.
54. Ronit Ricci, "Remembering Java's Islamization: A View from Sri Lanka," *Asia Research Institute Working Paper*, no. 153 (2011); Ronit Ricci, ed., *Exile in Colonial Asia: Kings, Convicts, Commemoration* (Honolulu: University of Hawaii Press, 2016); B. A. Hussainmiya, *Orang Rejimen: The Malays of the Ceylon Rifle Regiment* (Bangi: University Kebangsaan Malaysia, 1990), 48. Hussainmiya acknowledges the presence of Malay slaves in the following manner: "The early Malay population also owes its origin, albeit in a small way, to slaves sent now and then by the Batavian government. Most of them originated from the Moluccas, the lesser Sunda islands."
55. Robert Percival, *An Account of the Island of Ceylon Containing Its History, Geography, Natural History, with the Manners and Customs of Its Various Inhabitants* (London: C. and R. Baldwin, 1803; reprint New Delhi: Asian Educational Services, 1990), 116.
56. Percival, *An Account of the Island of Ceylon*, 120, 148.
57. Tuan Arfin Burah, *Saga of the Exiled Royal Javanese Unearthed* (Dehiwala, Sri Lanka: self-published, 2006), 44.
58. S. Suryadi, "Sepucuk surat dari seorang bangsawan Gowa di tanah pembuangan (Ceylon)," *Wacana* 10, no. 2 (October 2008): 214–45. I thank S. Suryadi for translating this article from Indonesian.
59. In the local languages, Malays today are still known as Ja Minissu (people from Java in Sinhala) and Java Manusar (in Tamil).
60. Hussainmiya, *Orang Rejimen*, 48, citing SLNA Lot 1/4864 Minutes of the Secret War Committee, September 9, 1763; Lot 1/591 Annex to the Minutes of the Dutch Political Council Colombo, October 21, 1781; Lot 1/196 The DPC, April 26, 1786.

61. Percival, *An Account of the Island of Ceylon*, 132.
62. Hussainmiya, *Orang Rejimen*, 61; R. G. Anthonisz, *Report on the Dutch Records in the Ceylon Archives* (Colombo: H. C. Cottle, 1907), 6.
63. Anthonisz, *Report on the Dutch Records*, 6.
64. See J. C. Spores, *Running Amok: An Historical Inquiry* (Athens: Ohio University/Swallow Press, 1988); Nigel Worden, "Public Brawling, Masculinity and Honour," in *Cape Town: Between East and West. Social Identities in a Dutch Colonial Town*, ed. N. Worden (Hilversum: Verloren, 2012), 194–211.
65. The Cape of Good Hope has been the subject of important studies by feminist historians. See P. van der Spuy, "Gender and Slavery: Towards a Feminist Revision," *South African Historical Journal* 25 (1991): 184–95; P. van der Spuy, "'What Then Was the Sexual Outlet for Black Males?' A Feminist Critique of Quantitative Representation of Women Slaves at the Cape of Good Hope in the Eighteenth Century," *Kronos* 23 (1996): 43–56.
66. A. L. Stoler and F. Cooper, "Between Metropole and Colony: Rethinking a Research Agenda," in *Tensions of Empire: Colonial Cultures in a Bourgeois World*, ed. A. L. Stoler and F. Cooper (Berkeley: University of California Press, 1997), 1–56; M. R. Trouillot, *Silencing the Past: Power and the Production of History* (Boston: Beacon Press, 1995); A. L. Stoler, *Carnal Knowledge and Imperial Power: Race and the Intimate in Colonial Rule* (Berkeley: University of California Press, 2002); A. L. Stoler, *Along the Archival Grain: Epistemic Anxieties and Colonial Common Sense* (Princeton, N.J.: Princeton University Press, 2009).
67. Robert Ross, "Oppression, Sexuality and Slavery at the Cape of Good Hope," *Historical Reflections / Réflexions Historiques* 6, no. 2 (1979): 421–33.
68. Pamela Scully, "Narratives of Infanticide in the Aftermath of Slave Emancipation in the Nineteenth-Century Cape Colony, South Africa," *Canadian Journal of African Studies* 30, no. 1 (1996): 88–105. On infanticide in slave societies, see also Kenneth Morgan, "The Struggle for Survival: Slave Infant Mortality in the British Caribbean in the Late Eighteenth and Nineteenth Centuries," in *Children in Slavery Through the Ages*, ed. Gwyn Campbell, Suzanne Miers, and Joseph C. Miller (Athens: Ohio University Press, 2009), 187–203; Deborah Gray White, *Ar'n't I a Woman? Female Slaves in the Plantation South* (New York: Norton, 1985); Raymond A. Bauer and Alice H. Bauer, "Day to Day Resistance to Slavery," in *Rebellions, Resistance, and Runaways Within the Slave South*, ed. Paul Finkelman (New York: Garland, 1989), 84–115.
69. SLNA, Lot 6/494, Sitting Magistrate's Office Colombo to Lusignan Esq Deputy Secretary, January 21, 1822.
70. SLNA, Lot 6/494, statement signed by G. L. Forbes, J. L. Cramer, and G. Ondaatje.
71. SLNA, Lot 6/494, statement signed by G. L. Forbes and M. Mack.
72. SLNA, Lot 6/494, letter of G. L Forbes, January 21, 1822.

73. SLNA, Lot 6/494, statement signed by Forbes, Cramer, Ondaatje, and the mark of Sittee.
74. SLNA, Lot 6/494, statement by Dr. Mack, signed by Cramer and Forbes.
75. SLNA, Lot 6/494, statement by Cramer.
76. SLNA, Lot 6/494, statement by Noor, signed 1803, with a mark.
77. SLNA, Lot 6/494, statement by Selestina, signed with a mark in the presence of Cramer, Ondaatje, and Sitting Magistrate Forbes.
78. SLNA, Lot 6/494, Lot 81, Supreme Court Sitting in Circuit for Colombo, February 1822.
79. NA UK, CO T71, Slave Register Colombo, letter S. This raises the question as to what happened to these two enslaved people, whose names do not appear in the statements relating to Selestina's dead child. Were they emancipated or sold off?
80. For insights into racial and sexual practices and laws under Dutch and British colonialism, see Jean Taylor, *The Social World of Batavia: European and Eurasian in Dutch Asia* (Madison: University of Wisconsin Press, 1983).
81. Percival, *An Account of the Island of Ceylon*, 141.
82. Percival, *An Account of the Island of Ceylon*, 410.
83. Parliamentary Papers 1838, Slave Trade East India and Ceylon, letter to his Royal Highness the Prince of Wales, August 1816, 575.
84. Cited in Kumari Jayawardena, *Erasure of the Euro-Asian: Recovering Early Radicalism and Feminism in South Asia* (Colombo: Social Scientists Association, 2007), 31.
85. See Indrani Chatterjee, "Colouring Subalternity: Slaves, Concubines and Social Orphans in Early Colonial India," *Subaltern Studies* 10 (New Delhi: Oxford University Press, 1999), 49–97; Durba Ghosh, *Sex and the Family in Colonial India* (Cambridge: Cambridge University Press, 2006); and Margot Finn, "Slaves Out of Context: Domestic Slavery and the Anglo-Indian Family, c. 1780–1830," *Transactions of the Royal Historical Society*, sixth series, 19 (2009): 181–203.
86. See Jayawardena, *Erasure of the Euro-Asian*, 37–54.
87. Clare Anderson, "Execution and Its Aftermath in the Nineteenth-Century British Empire," in *A Global History of Execution and the Criminal Corpse*, ed. Richard Ward (Basingstoke, UK: Palgrave Macmillan, 2015), 170–98.
88. Selestina's position resonates with the situation described by Gayathri Chakravorty Spivak in "Can The Subaltern Speak," in *Marxism and the Interpretation of Culture* (Urbana: University of Illinois Press, 1988), ed. C. Nelson and L. Grossberg, 271–315: that of a woman who is structurally muted and whose utterances remain illegible for the state.
89. Yvette Christianse, *Unconfessed* (New York: Other Press, 2006); Toni Morrison, *Beloved* (New York: Knopf, 1987). Pamela Scully, in "Rape, Race and

Colonial Culture: The Sexual Politics of Identity in the Nineteenth Century Cape Colony, South Africa," *American Historical Review* 100, no. 2 (April 1995): 337, points to the curious feature of historiography—applicable to most colonial situations—that authors have focused on the "elusive myths concerning white women as victims of black rapists rather than with the ways in which colonialism created conditions that authorized the pervasive rape of black women by white men."

90. The works of feminist scholars of Sri Lanka have not until now focused on individual working-class women.
91. See Sasha Turner, *Contested Bodies: Pregnancy, Childrearing, and Slavery in Jamaica* (Philadelphia: University of Pennsylvania Press, 2017), 175.
92. BL, G11/46 July–August 1800, 84, 105–20.
93. L. J. Wagenaar, *Galle-Vestiging in Ceylon*. On the early VOC rule, see K. W. Goonewardena, *The Foundation of Dutch Power in Ceylon 1638–1658* (Amsterdam: Djambatan, 1958).
94. Letter from Captain Lachlan Macquarie addressed to Colonel James Stuart, Commanding the Forces of the Island Ceylon, February 23, 1796 (held in Mitchell Library, Sydney, http://www.mq.edu.au).
95. Palghat is 136 kilometers from Cochin and 260 kilometers from Seringapatam.
96. Major Agnew was the commander-in-chief based in Galle after he took over from Captain Macquarie.
97. Testimony of Jan Jacques David D'Estandin in BL, G11/46, July–August 1800.
98. Alicia Schrikker, "Caught Between Empires: VOC Families in Sri Lanka After the British Take-over, 1806–1808," *Annales de démographie historique* 122, no. 2 (2011): 127–47.
99. Mendis, *Colebrooke-Cameron Papers*, 369.
100. NA UK, Slave Registers 1818–1832.
101. E. P. Thompson, "The Moral Economy of the English Crowd in the Eighteenth Century," in *The Essential E. P. Thompson*, ed. Dorothy Thompson (New York: New Press, 2001), 318.
102. Roland Wenzlhuemer, "Indian Labour Immigration and British Labour Policy in Nineteenth Century Ceylon," *Modern Asian Studies* 41, no. 3 (2007): 575–602.
103. Emily Haslam, "Redemption, Colonialism and International Criminal Law," in *Past Law, Present Histories*, ed. Diane Kirkby (Canberra: ANU Press, 2012), 10.
104. Christine Schwobel, *Critical Approaches to International Criminal Law: An Introduction* (London: Routledge, 2014), 184.
105. Jenny Martinez, "Anti-slavery Courts and the Dawn of International Human Rights Law," *Yale Law Journal* 117 (2007): 1–98; Parliamentary Papers 1845

(73) (212) 49, Slave Trade—Slave Vessels: Returns of Cases Adjudged Under Slave Trade Treaties and Number of Slaves Emancipated in Consequence.

106. Sir Alexander Johnston (1775–1849) was the third chief justice of Sri Lanka from 1811 to 1819. His role in the abolition of slavery in Sri Lanka will be dealt with in chapter 3.

107. SLNA, Lot 5/6, Dispatches to the Secretary of State, March 1812–February 1814, The Ceylon Government Gazette (enclosure), Number 611, Wednesday, June 2, 1813; letter by Robert Brownrigg, July 10, 1813.

108. See SLNA, Lot 25.1/27; Tambyah Nadaraja, *The Legal System of Ceylon in Its Historical Setting* (Leiden: Brill, 1972), 83, 85–86.

109. SLNA, Lot 6/476, Advocate fiscal letter to James Sutherland, deputy secretary to the governor, May 15, 1813.

110. Report of the Directors of the African Institution, Appendix G, Proceedings Under the Slave Trade Felony Act in the Island of Ceylon, London, 1815, 96.

111. Pedro Machado, *Oceans of Trade: South Asian Merchants, Africa and the Indian Ocean, c 1750–1850* (Cambridge: Cambridge University Press, 2014), 114. Mocha was once a major port of the Red Sea coast of western Yemen but had significantly declined by 1813.

112. Pedro Machado, "A Forgotten Corner of the Indian Ocean: Gujarati Merchants, Portuguese Indian and the Mozambique Slave Trade, c 1730–1830," in *Structure of Slavery in Indian Ocean Africa and Asia*, ed. Gwyn Campbell (London: Routledge, 2004), 18.

113. Report of the Directors, Appendix G, Africa Institution, 101.

114. Report of the Directors, 107, 108.

115. SLNA, 2nd Additional Supplement to the Ceylon Government Gazette, Tuesday, June 15, 1814.

116. Keynote address by Anthony Reid, Slavery Association Conference, Leiden, June 29, 2017.

117. For a discussion of this approach, see F. Cooper, T. C. Holt, and R. J. Scott, *Beyond Slavery: Explorations of Race, Labor and Citizenship in Postemancipation Societies* (Chapel Hill: University of North Carolina Press, 2000), 5–11.

3. Slave in a Palanquin

1. Nikolai Gogol, *Dead Souls* (New York: Barnes and Noble 2005), 184.
2. Michel de Certeau, *L'Invention du Quotidien*, vol. 1: *"Arts de Faire"* (Paris: Gallimard, 1990), 207.
3. See John Edwin Mason, "Paternalism Under Siege," in *Breaking the Chains: Slavery and Its Legacy in the Nineteenth Century Cape Colony*, ed. Nigel

Worden and Clifton Crais (Johannesburg: Witwaterstrand University Press, 1994), 45–77, for illustrations of the liberal paternalism of colonial officials who were enforcing slavery reform laws in the 1820s and 1830s.
4. Fernand Braudel, cited in Yogesh Sharma, ed., *Coastal Histories* (New Delhi: Primus Books, 2010), xv.
5. See J. C. Heesterman, "Littoral et Interieur de l'Inde," *Itinerario* 4, no. 1 (1980): 89.
6. Radhika Seshan, *Trade and Politics on the Coromandel Coast: Seventeenth and Early Eighteenth Centuries* (New Delhi: Primus, 2012), 7–11.
7. James Cordiner, *A Description of Ceylon*, vol. 1 (London: Longman Hurst, Rees and Orme, 1807), 325–27.
8. James Emerson Tennent, *Ceylon: An Account of the Island*, vol. 1 (London: Longman, Green, Longman and Roberts, 1859), 20.
9. John Penry Lewis, *Manual of the Vanni Districts, Vavuniya and Mullaitivu, of the Northern Province, Ceylon* (London: British Library Historical Prints Editions, 1895), 10.
10. K. M de Silva, *A History of Sri Lanka* (New Delhi: Oxford University Press, 1981), 133–34; K. Indrapala, "The Origin of the Tamil Vanni Chieftancies of Ceylon," *Ceylon Journal of the Humanities* 1, no. 2 (1970): 111–40; Sivasubramaniam Pathmanathan, "Feudal Polity in Medieval Ceylon: An Examination of the Chieftancies of the Vanni," *Ceylon Journal of Historical and Social Studies*, n.s. 2 (1972): 118–30.
11. Alicia Schrikker, *Dutch and British Colonial Intervention in Sri Lanka 1780–1815: Expansion and Reform* (Leiden: Brill, 2007), 88.
12. Talal Asad, *Genealogies of Religion* (Baltimore: Johns Hopkins University Press, 1993), 31.
13. Aya Ikegame, *Princely India Re-imagined: A Historical Anthropology of Mysore from 1799 to the Present* (London: Routledge, 2013), 44.
14. Frank Trentmann, "Materiality in the Future of History: Things, Practices, and Politics," *Journal of British Studies* 48 (April 2009): 300.
15. Michael Banks, "Caste in Jaffna," in *Aspects of Caste in South India, Ceylon and North-West Pakistan*, ed. E. R. Leach (Cambridge: Cambridge University Press, 1960), 61–77; Bryan Pfaffenberger, *Caste in Tamil Culture: The Religious Foundations of Sudra Domination in Tamil Sri Lanka* (Syracuse, N.Y.: Syracuse University Press, 1982).
16. Kenneth David, "The Bound and the Nonbound: Variations in Social and Cultural Structure in Rural Jaffna, Ceylon," Ph.D. diss., University of Chicago, 1972.
17. Prashant Kuganathan "Social Stratification in Jaffna: A Survey of Recent Research on Caste," *Sociology Compass* 8, no. 1 (2014): 86.

18. Rohan Bastin, *The Domain of Constant Excess: Plural Worship at the Munnesvaram Temples in Sri Lanka* (Oxford: Berghahn, 1997), 398.
19. Gananath Obeysekere, "The Coming of the Brahmin Migrants: The Sudra Fate of an Indian Elite in Sri Lanka," *Society and Culture in South Asia* 1, no. 1 (2016): 1–32.
20. Benedicte Hjeile, "Slavery and Agricultural Bondage in South India in the Nineteenth Century," *Scandinavian Economic History Review* 15, no. 1–2 (1967): 71–126; Dharma Kumar, *Land and Caste in South India: Agricultural Labor in the Madras Presidency During the Nineteenth Century* (New York: Cambridge University Press, 1965).
21. Indrani Chatterjee and Richard M. Eaton, eds., *Slavery and South Asian History* (Bloomington: Indiana University Press, 2006).
22. Tikiri Abeyasinghe, *Portuguese Rule in Ceylon 1594–1612* (Colombo: Lake House, 1966), 13–14; Chandra R. de Silva and Sivasubramaniam Pathmanathan, "The Kingdom of Jaffna up to 1620," in *University of Peradeniya: History of Sri Lanka*, vol. 2, ed. K. M. de Silva (Dehiwela: Sridevi, 1995), 106.
23. De Silva and Pathmanathan, "The Kingdom of Jaffna," 2:95. Dutch and later British sources indicate that slaves spoke the Portuguese language in Jaffna.
24. Bryan Pfaffenberger, *Caste in Tamil Culture: The Religious Foundations of Sudra Domination in Tamil Sri Lanka* (Syracuse, N.Y.: Syracuse University Press, 1982), 36, citing Michael Banks, "The Social Organisation of the Jaffna Tamils of North Ceylon, with Special Reference to Kinship, Marriage, and Inheritance," Ph.D. diss., Cambridge University, 1957.
25. Alicia Schrikker and Kate Ekama, "Through the Lens of Slavery: Dutch Sri Lanka in the Eighteenth Century," in *Sri Lanka at the Crossroads of History*, ed. Zoltan Biederman and Alan Strathern (London: UCL Press, 2017), 178–93. For an analysis of the collapse of the Jaffna kingdom, see Zoltan Biedermann, *(Dis)connected Empires: Imperial Portugal, Sri Lankan Diplomacy, and the Making of a Habsburg Conquest in Asia* (New York: Oxford University Press, 2018).
26. Philip Baldeus, *A Description of the Great and Famous Isle of Ceylon* (1672; Delhi: Asian Educational Services, 1996), 817.
27. The name Chandios is not used in Tamil. According to S. Arasaratnam, it is probably a Dutch and Portuguese corruption of the word *Shanar*, a caste that he suggests developed into the Nalavar caste during the Jaffna kingdom. S. Arasaratnam, "Social History of a Dominant Caste Society: The Vellalar of North Ceylon (Sri Lanka) in the 18th Century," *Indian Economic and Social History Review* 18, no. 3–4 (1981): 380–81.
28. Hendrick Zwaardecroon, Commandeur of Jaffnapatam (1697), *Instructions for the Guidance of the Opperkoopman Anthony Pavilioen, Commandeur, and the*

Council of the District of Jaffnapatam with the Adjacent Islands and the Provinces of the Wanni (Colombo: H. C. Cottle 1911), 92.
29. Arasaratnam, "Social History of a Dominant Caste Society," 383.
30. Zwaardecroon, *Instructions*, 11.
31. Pfaffenberger, *Caste in Tamil Culture*, 38–39.
32. Anthropologists have sometimes used the term *atimai* (from the term *ati*, which means base, source, foot) to qualify the praedial castes in Jaffna society, as opposed to the *kutimai* castes, who provided services to the Vellalars. These terms, however, were not used in the eighteenth and nineteenth centuries.
33. Pfaffenberger, *Caste in Tamil Culture*, 36.
34. See Hovy, *Ceylonees Plakkaatboek*, vol. 1, ordinance 205 (April 25/August 14, 1704), "Compendium van plakkaten en ordonanties voor Jaffna." For the question regarding the use of andol by unauthorized persons, see stipulation no. 51.
35. The disava was an official in the precolonial period. The title was retained under Portuguese and Dutch rule.
36. T. Nadaraja, *The Legal System of Ceylon in Its Historical Setting* (Leiden: Brill, 1972).
37. Arasaratnam, "Social History of a Dominant Caste Society," 378.
38. Arasaratnam, "Social History of a Dominant Caste Society," 378–86.
39. C. Brito, *The Yalpana Vaipava Malai or the History of the Kingdom of Jaffna* (1879; New Delhi: Asian Educational Services 2007), 35.
40. Van Vollenhoven, "Ceilonsch volksrecht," 240–80, cited in Schrikker and Ekama, "Through the Lens of Slavery," 189–90.
41. Van Vollenhoven, "Ceilonsch volksrecht."
42. Arasaratnam, "Social History of a Dominant Caste Society."
43. *Memoir of Anthony Mooyaart, Commandeur of Jaffnapatam for the Information and Guidance of His Successor Noel Anthony Lebeck*, 1766, trans. Sophia Pieters (Colombo, H. C. Cottle, 1910), 6.
44. CO (UK), 416/30, December 10, 1829, translation of Tamil version, courtesy of Herman Tieken and R. Cheran.
45. A covered litter or conveyance, usually for one person, used in India and other Asian countries, consisting of a large box with wooden shutters like Venetian blinds, carried by four or six (rarely two) men by means of poles projecting before and behind.
46. CO (UK), 416/17, letter, November 8, 1819.
47. Niels Brimnes, *Constructing the Colonial Encounter: Right and Left Hand Castes in Early Colonial South India* (Richmond: Curzon, 1999); Kanakalatha Mukund, "Caste Conflict in South India in Early Colonial Port Cities, 1650–1800," *Studies in History* 11, no. 1 (1995): 1–27.

48. CO (UK), 416/17, Extract from the Diary of H. W. Hooper, Collector of Jaffna, December 1818.
49. CO (UK), 416/17, Lusignan to Governor Barnes, Matara, July 3, 1820.
50. CO (UK), 416/17, R. Boyd, Commissioner of Revenue, to Governor Barnes, June 19, 1820.
51. CO (UK), 416/17, Chief Justice Harding Giffard and Justice Henry Byrns to Governor Barnes, August 23, 1820.
52. John D. Rogers, *Crime, Justice and Society in Colonial Sri Lanka* (London: Curzon, 1987), 42.
53. Anna Cole and Anna Haebich, "Corporeal Colonialism and Corporal Punishment: A Cross-cultural Perspective on Body Modification," *Social Semiotics* 17, no. 3 (2007): 296.
54. Clare Anderson, *Convicts in the Indian Ocean: Transportation from South Asia to Mauritius 1815–1853* (London: Macmillan, 2000).
55. *A Collection of the Legislative Acts of HM's Government of Ceylon Containing Proclamations and Regulations Issues Since 1st January 1799* (Colombo: Government Office, 1854), 113.
56. Richard Ward, ed., *A Global History of Execution and the Criminal Corpse* (Basingstoke, UK: Palgrave Macmillan, 2015).
57. This example questions a common argument made by historians such as Piet Emmer that people had a different sensibility in the seventeenth and eighteenth centuries, and hence slavery and bondage should not be read through the prism of twenty-first-century humanitarianism.
58. Rogers, *Crime, Justice and Society*, 70. Flogging was gradually restricted, and by the end of the nineteenth century the severity of corporal punishment was reduced, with district courts limited to ordering no more than twenty-five lashes.
59. SLNA, Lot 25.1/19.
60. Cole and Haebich, "Corporeal Colonialism and Corporal Punishment," 305–6.
61. David Arnold, *Colonizing the Body: State Medicine and Epidemic Disease in Nineteenth Century India* (Berkeley: University of California Press, 1993), 8. Arnold has highlighted the coercive nature of colonial rule through his study of the colonization of the body that was enacted by state medical institutions and an array of administrative mechanisms.
62. *A Collection of Legislative Acts of the Ceylon Government from 1796/1833–1833/1852*, Ceylon Regulation 2 of 1821—For defining the meaning of the word Andol, and for giving to Magistrates a discretionary power to inflict corporal punishment on Slaves convicted of Misdemeanors, instead of fine and imprisonment (Colombo: William Skeen, 1854), 264.

63. U. C. Wickremaratne, *The Conservative Nature of the British Rule of Sri Lanka with Particular Emphasis on the Period 1796–1802* (New Delhi: Navrang, 1996), 168.
64. John Holland Rose, ed., *The Cambridge History of the British Empire*, vol. 2 (Cambridge: Cambridge University Press, 1940), 517; Extract of a Dispatch from Lieutenant General Sir R. Brownrigg to Earl Bathurst, September 16, 1816, House of Commons, Parliamentary Papers, 697 (1838) Slave Trade (East India)—Slavery in Ceylon, CO May 16, 1838, 561.
65. SLNA, Lot 20/854, Jaffna Kachcheri—Register of the Supreme Court (1805–1831)— Decree of SC February 24, 1807, signed by Thomas Maitland, given in Colombo on March 31, 1807, by John Rodney.
66. B. W. Higman, *Slave Population and Economy in Jamaica, 1807–1834* (Kingston: University of the West Indies Press, 1995), 45–46; Michael Craton, *Testing the Chains: Resistance to Slavery in the British West Indies* (Ithaca, N.Y.: Cornell University Press 2009).
67. Caroline Quarrier Spence, "Ameliorating Empire: Slavery and Protection in the British Colonies, 1783–1865," Ph.D. diss., Harvard University, 2014.
68. Copy of dispatch from Sir Robert Brownrigg to Earl Bathurst, August 17, 1818, Slave Trade (East India)—Slavery in Ceylon, Parliamentary Papers, 697 (1838), 569.
69. Parliamentary Papers, 697 (1838), letter of Dutch gentlemen of the special Jury to Sir Alexander Johnston, July 14, 1816.
70. Parliamentary Papers, 697 (1838), Article 24 of Regulation 9 of 1818, a Regulation for securing to certain Children emancipated by the Proprietors of the mothers the full benefit of such proprietors intentions, and for establishing an efficient Registry of all slaves and abolishing the joint tenure of Property in the same.
71. Parliamentary Papers, 697 (1838), Article 24 of Regulation 9 of 1818; also see G. C. Mendis, ed., *The Colebrooke-Cameron Papers: Documents on British Colonial Policy in Ceylon 1796–1833* (London: Oxford University Press, 1956). The Jaffna slaveholder signatories were P. Tap, M. Margenout, J. G. Koch, A. de Niese, D. Bast, J. A. Maartenz, P. L. Kroon, J. B. Vanderweff, W. de Rooy, J. Mathheysz, J. Verwyk, Widow Vanderspar, J. A. Stutzer, Widow Van Hek, Widow Saalfelt, Widow Schraader, Widow Tussaint, G. Frankena, and F. B. Rodrigo.
72. NA UK, CO T71 Slave Registers, Domestic Slaves 1818–1832.
73. The rix dollar was equal to twelve Ceylon fanams, according to Benjamin Walter Fernando, *Ceylon Currency, British Period 1796–1936* (New Delhi: Asian Educational Services, 1939).
74. Enclosure 3, in letter from G. Lusignan, Act Secretary to Council, August 13, 1818, to the Collector, the Provincial Judge, the Sitting Magistrate, the

Assistant Collector at Jaffnapatnam, Slave Trade, (East India) Slavery in Ceylon, Parliamentary Papers, 697 (1838), 589.

75. Estimated Stamp Revenue from Registries under the above Regulations, in Parliamentary Papers, 697 (1838), 590.
76. Simon Szreter, "Registration of Identities in Early Modern English Parishes and Among the English Overseas," in *Proceedings of the British Academy* 182 (Oxford: Oxford University Press, 2012), 67–92.
77. Michel Foucault, "The Subject and Power," *Critical Inquiry* 8, no. 4 (Summer 1982): 790.
78. Parliamentary Papers, 697 (1938), 570–74.
79. NA UK, CO T71 Slave Registers, Ceylon 1818–1832.
80. On Craig Robertson's concept of "regime of verification," see Shrimoyee Ghosh, "Of Truth and Taxes: A Material History of Early Stamp't Paper," in *Iterations of Law: Legal Histories from India*, ed. Aparna Balachandran, Rashmi Pant, and Bhavani Raman (Oxford: Oxford University Press, 2017), 211. There is a rich literature on the use of forms and scribal practices. See, e.g., Bhavani Raman, *Document Raj: Writing and Scribes in Early Colonial South India* (Chicago: Chicago University Press, 2012); Velchuru Narayan Rao, David Shulman, and Sanjay Subrahmanyam, *Textures of Time: Writing History in South India 1600–1800* (New York: Other Press, 2003).
81. Emma Tarlo, *Unsettling Memories: Narratives of the Emergency in Delhi* (New Delhi: Permanent Black, 2003).
82. Parliamentary Papers, 697, (1838), 580–86.
83. Cited in Susan Thorne, "Capitalism and Slavery Compensation," *Small Axe* 16, no. 1 (March 2012): 161.
84. Thorne, "Capitalism and Slavery Compensation," 165.
85. See David Scott, *Refashioning Futures: Criticism After Postcoloniality* (Princeton, N.J.: Princeton University Press, 1999); and Nira Wickramasinghe, "Colonial Governmentality and the Political. Thinking Through '1931' in the Crown Colony of Ceylon/Sri Lanka," *Socio* 5 (2015): 99–114.
86. Parliamentary Papers, 697 (1838), Hooper letter, February 20, 1821, 596.
87. Parliamentary Papers, 697 (1838), 591–92.
88. Parliamentary Papers, 697, C. E. Layard, W. H. Hooper, and J. N. Muoyaart, January 4, 1821, 595–96.
89. Parliamentary Papers 697 (1838), Extract from a Report of Piet-Colonel Colebrooke, December 24, 1831, 597–98.
90. Mendis, *Colebrooke-Cameron Papers*, 2:25–26.
91. SLNA, Lot 6/1164, letter from Jaffna Cutchery to Colonial Secretary, October 5, 1833.
92. SLNA, Lot 6/142, From Jaffna Cutchery, December 10, 1822, to Chief Secretary to Government.

93. Megan Vaughan, *Creating the Creole Island: Slavery in Eighteenth-Century Mauritius* (Durham, N.C.: Duke University Press, 2005), 253–55.
94. A. Meredith John, *The Plantation Slaves of Trinidad 1783–1816: A Mathematical and Demographic Enquiry* (Cambridge: Cambridge University Press, 1988), 28.
95. NA UK, CO 416/32, The Humble Petition of the Prisoner Weler Taanduven, a Vellala of Carrewilly to the Commissioner of Enquiry, Jaffna, September 8, 1830.
96. NA UK, CO 416/32, Petition of Cadireser Canagasawe, September 21, 1830.
97. NA UK, CO 416/32, Petition of Renaldus Hendricks de Ortha to Major Colebrooke, Commissioner of Enquiry, ca. 1830.
98. NA UK, CO 416/32 Petition of (illegible) Saeraa, Vellala, September 1830.
99. SLNA, Lot 10/41—letter from Williams, Sitting Magistrate, Point Pedro, to Collector, Jaffna Cutchery, April 14, 1830.
100. Parliamentary Papers, 697 (1838), 573.
101. SLNA, Lot 10/41, extract from criminal diary touching a doubt as to a male child born after the registration from Magistrate, Mallagam to Thomas Eden, Deputy Secretary to Governor, November 23, 1829.
102. SLNA, Lot 6/142–647, letter from the Magistrate to George Lusignan, Mallagam, March 18, 1825.
103. See, for instance, SLNA Lot 6/142–647, Sitting Magistrate Mallagam, October 1, 1825, to Thomas Eden.
104. SLNA, Lot 6/1164, letter from Jaffna Cutchery to Colonial Secretary, October 5, 1833, on charges as civil unfixed contingencies.
105. SLNA, Lot 6/1164, letter from Jaffna Cutchery to Colonial Secretary, November 18, 1833, on civil unfixed contingencies.
106. See chapter 1.
107. NA UK, CO 416/32, Petition of Poroijy Paulo et al., September 2, 1830.
108. Arjun Appadurai, cited in Francis Cody, "Inscribing Subjects to Citizenship: Petitions, Literacy Activism, and the Performativity of Signature in Rural Tamil India," *Cultural Anthropology* 24, no. 3 (2009): 363.
109. For a study of the Joy Tax rebellion of 1800, see Nira Wickramasinghe, "Many Little Revolts or One Rebellion? The Maritime Provinces of Ceylon/Sri Lanka Between 1796 and 1800," *South Asia: Journal of South Asian Studies* 32, no. 2 (2009): 170–88.
110. Michael Herzfeld, *The Social Production of Indifference: Exploring the Symbolic Roots of Western Bureaucracy* (Oxford: Berg, 1992).
111. NA UK, CO 416/32, Petition of Poroijy Paulo et al., September 2, 1830.
112. Joy Mahabir, "Communal Style: Indo-Caribbean Women's Jewelry," *Small Axe* 21, no. 2 (July 2017): 112–22.

113. T. K. Silva et al., *Casteless or Caste blind? Dynamics of Concealed Caste Discrimination, Social Exclusion, and Protest in Sri Lanka* (Copenhagen: International Dalit Solidarity, 2009), 57.
114. Pfaffenberger, *Caste in Tamil Culture*, 90.
115. NA UK, CO 416/32, Petition of Caatty Chasin Cooronader Pulle to the Commission of Eastern Enquiry, May 20, 1828.
116. Pfaffenberger, *Caste in Tamil Culture*, 93.
117. I came across only rare accounts of preaching to "destitute casts." See, e.g., SOAS, Wesleyan Methodist Missionary Society, January 4, 1840, Box 448. For an excellent account of the resistance of Dalits in Kerala, see P. Sanal Mohan, *Modernity of Slavery: Struggles Against Caste Inequality in Colonial Kerala* (New York: Oxford University Press, 2015).
118. SOAS, Wesleyan Methodist Missionary Society, FBN 3—Jaffna, September 3, 1828, Box 446.
119. For insights into domestic slavery in colonial port cities, see Sylvia Vatuk, "Bharattee's Death: Domestic Slave-Women in Nineteenth Century Madras," in *Slavery and South Asian History*, ed. Indrani Chatterjee and Richard M. Eaton (Bloomington: Indiana University Press, 2006), 210–33. For works showing the multiple connections of domestic slaves to indigenous caste and community groupings, see Radhika Singha, "Making the Domestic More Domestic: Criminal Law and the 'Heads of Household' 1772–1843," *Indian Economic and Social History Review* 33, no. 3 (July–September 1996): 309–43; and Indrani Chatterjee, *Gender, Slavery and Law in Colonial India* (New Delhi: Oxford University Press, 1999).
120. SLNA Lot 6/499, Sitting Magistrate Northern province, Malliagam, May 12, 1821, Criminal Diary touching the death of Paripaddy.
121. Banks, "The Social Organization of the Jaffna Tamils," 6, cited in Pfaffenberger, *Caste in Tamil Culture*, 89.
122. There is a vast and varied literature on runaway slaves in the Americas and the Mascarene Islands. See, e.g., John Hope Franklin and Loren Schweninger, *Runaway Slaves: Rebels on the Plantation* (New York: Oxford University Press, 2000). For maroons and marronage, see Sylviane A. Diouf, *Slavery's Exiles: The Story of the American Maroons* (New York: NYU Press, 2016). The best exposé of maroons in Mauritius can be found in Richard B. Allen, *Slaves, Freedmen and Indentured Laborers in Colonial Mauritius* (Cambridge: Cambridge University Press, 1999); and Vaughan, *Creating the Creole Island*. For a broader conceptual analysis of runaway slaves as one category of deserters, see Matthias van Rossum and Jeannette Camp, *Desertion in the Early Modern World: A Comparative History* (London: Bloomsbury, 2016).

123. Nigel Worden, cited in Kate Ekama, "Runaway Slaves from the VOC Cape," in *Desertion in the Early Modern World: A Comparative History*, ed. Matthias van Rossum and Jeannette Kamp (London: Bloomsbury, 2016), 168.
124. Ranajit Guha, "The Prose of Counterinsurgency," in *Selected Subaltern Studies*, ed. R. Guha and G. Chakravorty Spivak (New York: Oxford University Press), 47–48.
125. John Penry Lewis, *Manual of the Vanni Districts, Vavuniya and Mullaitivu, of the Northern Province, Ceylon* (London: British Library Historical Prints Editions, 1895), 20.
126. SLNA, Lot 25.1/18, Christie Section of the Johnston Manuscripts. Report of several cases tried at Criminal Session begun to be holden at Jaffnapatnam on the third of September, 1812—together with some remarks relative to the Administration of Justice in the Second Division of the Supreme Court of Judicature. A letter dated October 23, 1814, from Governor Brownrigg to the chief justice indicates that the report was made by Mr. Coke (Sir William Coke, Puisne judge, 1810).
127. Mohan, *Modernity of Slavery*.
128. NA UK, CO T71 Slave Register, Jaffna, Slaves in the Parish of Nallore.

4. The Chilaw "Experiment"

1. See Trinidad Order in Council in Papers in Explanation of Measures for Amelioration of Condition of Slave Population in W. Indies and S. America, Parliamentary Papers, House of Commons, 1825, 008, vol. 26–27, 124–38.
2. There is copious literature on the rise and decline of free and unfree labor in the world. See, for instance, Jan Lucassen, "Free and Unfree Labour Before the Twentieth Century: A Brief Overview," in *Free and Unfree Labour: The Debate Continues*, ed. Tom Brass and Marcel van der Linden (Bern: Peter Lang, 2000), 45–56; and Marcel van der Linden, "The Origins, Spread and Normalization of Free Wage Labour," in *Free and Unfree Labour: The Debate Continues*, 501–23.
3. Lisa Ford, "Anti-Slavery and the Reconstitution of Empire,"*Australian Historical Studies* 45, no. 1 (2014): 71–86.
4. Conrad Malte-Brun, *Universal Geography: or A Description of All Parts of the World, on a New Plan, According to the Great Natural Divisions of the Globe*, vols. 1–2 (Philadelphia: A. Finley, 1827).
5. Simon Casie Chetty, *The Ceylon Gazetteer: Containing an Accurate Account of the Districts, Provinces, Cities, Towns & of the Island of Ceylon* (Colombo: Cotta Church Mission Press, 1834), 25–26.

6. *A Collection of the Legislative Acts of His Majesty's Government of Ceylon: Containing Proclamations and Regulations, Issued Since 15th January 1799, and Wholly, Or in Part in Force, on 31st May 1821, Arranged Under Their Various Heads*, Government Press, 332.
7. Seymour Drescher, *The Mighty Experiment: Free Labor Versus Slavery in British Emancipation* (New York: Oxford University Press, 2002).
8. Orlando Patterson's body of work has argued that the value of freedom was historically generated out of the experience of slavery. See Patterson, *The Sociology of Slavery*, (Kingston: Sangster's, 1973); and *Slavery and Social Death* (Cambridge, Mass,: Harvard University Press, 1982).
9. David Scott, *Formations of Ritual: Colonial and Anthropological Discourses on the Sinhala Yaktovil* (Minneapolis: University of Minnesota Press, 1994), 139.
10. Willem van Schendel, in "Stretching Labour Historiography: Pointers from South Asia,"*International Review of Social History* 51 (2006): 231, points to the ubiquity of wage labor and the invisibility in South Asian historiography of "numerically far more prominent forms of labour (tenancy, bondedness, sharecropping, domestic labour, family production, etc.)."
11. A *seer* is a traditional weight unit in South Asia. The official size in British India was 0.9 kilogram.
12. SLNA, Lot 20/2015, Collector of Jaffna 1808–1833, CSO to Collector of Jaffna, June 6, 1820.
13. Casie Chetty, *Ceylon Gazetteer*, 25.
14. See David Gilmartin, "Colonialism and Irrigation Technology in the Indus Basin," *Journal of Asian Studies* 53, no. 4 (November 1994): 1127–49.
15. On labour recruitment, see C. Bates and M. Carter, "Sirdars as Intermediaries in Nineteenth-Century Indian Ocean Indentured Labour Migration," *Modern Asian Studies* 51, no. 2 (2017): 462–84; T. Roy, " 'Sardars, Jobbers, Kanganies': The Labour Contractor and Indian Economic History," *Modern Asian Studies* 42, no. 5 (2008): 971–98; and S. Sen, "Commercial Recruiting and Informal Intermediation: Debate Over the Sardari System in Assam Tea Plantations, 1860–1900," *Modern Asian Studies* 44, no. 1 (2010): 3–28.
16. SLNA, Lot 20/1425, Collector of Jaffna to Sitting Magistrate, Point Pedro, May 20, 1820.
17. SLNA, Lot 20/216, Chief Secretary's Office to Sitting Magistrate Jaffnapatam, April 18, 1821.
18. SLNA, Lot 20/2016, CSO to Collector Jaffna, April 18, 1821.
19. Rev. J. D. Palm, "The Educational Establishments of the Dutch in Ceylon," *Journal of the Dutch Burgher Union* 29, no. 2 (October 1939): 44–51.
20. See Anand A. Yang, "A Conversation of Rumours: The Language of Popular 'Mentalites' in Late Nineteenth Century Colonial India," *Journal of Social History* 20, no. 3 (Spring 1987): 485–505; and Pier M. Larson, "The

Vernacular Life of the Street: Ratsitatanina and Indian Ocean Creolité," *Slavery and Abolition* 29, no. 3 (September 2008): 327–59.
21. See E.Valentine Daniel, Henry Bernstein, and Tom Brass, eds., *Plantations, Proletarians and Peasants in Colonial Asia* (London: Frank Cass, 1992), 203.
22. Emerson Tennent, *Ceylon: An Account of the Island*, vol. 2 (London: Longman, Green, Longman and Roberts, 1859), 534.
23. *Report of the Ceylon Tobacco Industry*, Sessional Paper (SP) 6-1912 (Colombo: H. C. Cottle, 1912), 2.
24. *Report of the Ceylon Tobacco Industry*, 2.
25. Casie Chetty, *Gazetteer of Ceylon*, 102.
26. See SLNA, Lot 20/216, CSO Colombo, September 3, 1821, to W. H. Hooper Collector of Jaffna. The privileged position of merchants from Travancore in the tobacco trade continued during British rule, when tobacco became a department of the colonial administration that oversaw the valuing of the produce with copper weight. See also Lot 20/216, letter from CSO May 17, 1821, to W. Eglan, a merchant from Tranquebar, granting permission to enter any port in the island.
27. Sinappah Arasaratnam, "Historical Foundation of the Economy of the Tamils of North Sri Lanka," Chelvanayakam Memorial Lectures, 1982, Lecture 1: The 17th and 18th Centuries (Jaffna, Sri Lanka: Thanthai Chelva Memorial Trust, 1982), 7–8.
28. NA UK, T71, Slave Registers of Jaffna.
29. *Report of the Ceylon Tobacco Industry*, 2.
30. *Report of the Ceylon Tobacco Industry*, 4.
31. SLNA, Lot 6/474 Supreme Court—Letters from the Registrar and Chief Justices to the Colonial Secretary, Jaffnapatam, September 7, 1822, Mody Winsy murder March 21, 1821, at Alivetty on Pody Podien.
32. M. U. de Silva, "Land Tenure, Caste System and the Rajakariya Under Foreign Rule: A Review of Change in Sri Lanka Under Western Powers, 1597–1832," *Journal of the Royal Asiatic Society of Sri Lanka* 37 (1992–1993): 34. De Silva gives a detailed account of the transformation of the land tenure system.
33. Cited in K. M. de Silva, ed., *History of Ceylon*, 3:59; CO 54/20 Maitland to Camden, February 18, 1806, 59.
34. CO 54/20 Maitland to Camden, February 28, 1806, 59.
35. Sujit Sivasundaram, "Tales of the Land: British Geography and Kandyan Resistance in Sri Lanka, c. 1803–1850," *Modern Asian Studies* 41, no. 5 (2007): 925–65.
36. Colvin R. de Silva, *Ceylon Under the British Occupation, 1795–1833: Its Political and Administrative Development*, vol. 2 (Colombo: Navrang with Lake House Book Shop, 1995), 408. For a historical survey of the changes in the rajakariya

system under colonial rule, see M. U. de Silva, "Land Tenure, Caste System and the Rajakariya."

37. Sanayi Marcelline, "Labouring for Salt—Convict Workers in the Levayas of Magampattu in the Early 19th Century," manuscript in progress.

38. G. C. Mendis, *The Colebrooke-Cameron Papers: Documents on British Colonial Policy in Ceylon 1796–1833*, vol. 2 (London: Oxford University Press, 1956), 308.

39. Mendis, *Colebrooke-Cameron Papers*, 2:61.

40. Pim de Zwart, "Population, Labour and Living Standards in Early Modern Ceylon," *Indian Economic and Social History Review* 49, no. 3 (2012): 365–98.

41. de Zwart, "Population, Labour and Living Standards," 386, cites S. B. de Silva, *The Political Economy of Underdevelopment* (London: Taylor and Francis, 1982); see also Chandra R. de Silva, "The First Portuguese Revenue Register of the Kingdom of Kotte—1599," *Ceylon Journal of Historical and Social Studies*, New Series, 5, 1–2 (January–December 1975): 71–153.

42. R. N. Dewasiri, *The Adaptable Peasant: Agrarian Society in Western Sri Lanka Under Dutch Rule, 1740–1800* (Leiden: Brill, 2008), 222. Accommodessans were lands granted as salary for services rendered.

43. Commander Zwaardecroon memoirs cited in de Zwart, "Population, Labour and Living Standards," 387.

44. M. U. de Silva, "Land Tenure, Caste System, and the Rajakariya," 12.

45. Richard B. Allen, *European Slave Trading in the Indian Ocean 1500–1850* (Athens: Ohio University Press, 2014), 199–200; Colvin R. de Silva, *Ceylon Under the British Occupation*, 2:371.

46. Alessandro Stanziani, "Beyond Colonialism: Servants, Wage Earners and Indentured Migrants in Rural France and on Reunion Island (c. 1750–1900)," *Labor History* 54, no. 1 (2013): 65.

47. See a typical indenture contract from 1726 at https://www.albany.edu/history/history316/Indenture-RiceThomas.html.

48. The pie was, under early British rule, the smallest currency after the anna, used in India and Burma as well.

49. SLNA, Lot 20/215, CSO Colombo to Collector of Jaffna, September 5, 1820.

50. SLNA, Lot 20/1425, Collector Jaffna to Magistrate Point Pedro, May 24, 1820.

51. Sidney Chalhoub, "The Politics of Ambiguity: Conditional Manumission, Labor Contracts, and Slave Emancipation in Brazil (1850s–1888)," *International Review of Social History* 60, no. 2 (August 2015): 161–91.

52. See Daina Ramey Berry, *The Price for Their Pound of Flesh: The Value of the Enslaved, from Womb to Grave, in the Building of a Nation* (Boston: Beacon Press, 2017).

53. Parliamentary Papers, 1838, 697, 569.

54. SLNA, Lot 20/1425, Collector Jaffna to CS, June 17, 1820.
55. SLNA, Lot 20/215, CSO Colombo to Collector of Jaffna, September 13, 1820.
56. SLNA, Lot 20/1425, Collector Jaffna Cutcherry to CSO, August 31, 1820.
57. SLNA, Lot 20/ 29, CSO G. Lusignan to C. Scott, Collector of Jaffna, June 5, 1825.
58. SLNA, Lot 20/220, CSO T. Eden to C. Scott, Collector of Jaffna, August 22, 1825.
59. SLNA, Lot 20/1425, Circular—Jaffna Cutcherry to Magistrates of Point Pedro, Mallagam, September 26, 1820.
60. SLNA, Lot 20/1425, Collector Jaffna to Collector Chilaw, August 2, 1820.
61. SLNA, Lot 20/1425, Collector Jaffna to CSO, August 31, 1820.
62. SLNA, Lot 20/1425, Collector Jaffna to Collector Chilaw, October 12, 1820, and October 13, 1820.
63. SLNA, Lot 20/1425, Jaffna Cutcherry to Deputy Acting Governor G. Lusignan, October 5, 1820; Collector Jaffna to CSO, October 25, 1820.
64. SLNA, Lot 20/1425, Collector Jaffna to CSO, November 24, 1820.
65. SLNA, Lot 20/2016, Chief Secretary's Office to Collector Jaffna, January 18, 1821.
66. SLNA, Lot 20/1426, January 15, 1821.
67. *Blue Book Ceylon* 1828, part 1, 289.
68. Chandra R. de Silva, *Ceylon Under the British*, 2:405–6; M. U. de Silva, "Land Tenure, Caste System and the Rajakariya," 38.
69. SLNA, Lot 6/12354, Executive Council (Proceedings) 1822, No. 9 Minute by Governor, October 28, 1822.
70. SLNA, Lot 2/12, Minutes of Council, March 17, 1821–December 23, 1822; SLNA, 6/12354, Executive Council (Proceedings) 1822, No. 9 Minute by Governor, October 28, 1822.
71. SLNA, Lot 6/906, letter from Collector, Jaffna Cutchery, October 16, 1824, to Chief Secretary.
72. SLNA, Lot 6/906, letter from Collector, Jaffna Cutcherry, November 2, 1824, to Chief Secretary; letter from Collector, Jaffna Cutcherry, November 5, 1824.
73. SLNA, Lot 6/906, letter from Collector, Jaffna Cutcherry, November 30, 1824, to Chief Secretary.
74. SLNA, Lot 20/292, 907 B—Collector Jaffna 1825, letter from Collector to Chief Secretary to Government of Colombo.
75. SLNA, Lot 20/295, Jaffna Collector, July 4, 1826, to Chief Secretary.
76. SLNA, Lot 20/295, Jaffna Collector, July 18, 1826.
77. SLNA, Lot 20/295, Jaffna Collector, July 28, 1826.
78. SLNA, Lot 6/971A, Collector Jaffna, July 7, 1829.
79. SLNA, Lot 7/88, CSO to Collector Jaffna, May 13, 1826.

80. SLNA, Lot 6/980B, Collector of Chilaw to CSO, October 17, 1829, map of the canal.
81. SLNA, Lot 6/980B, Collector Chilaw to CSO, October 17, 1829.
82. SLNA, Lot 6/971A, Collector Jaffna May 14 and June 16, 1929, to Chief Secretary.
83. SLNA, Lot 7/332, CSO to Collector Jaffna, November 27, 1828; CSO to Collector Jaffna, April 24, 1829.
84. Patrick Peebles, *Social Change in Nineteenth Century Ceylon* (New Delhi: Navrang 1995), 109.
85. NA UK, CO 416/4 A.15, reply sent March 25, 1830. From the notes of Patrick Peebles, kindly provided to me on December 12, 2018.
86. SLNA, Lot 6/177, statement showing the amount paid to laborers employed in opening the new canal, 1821, Chilaw Cutcherry, September 21, 1821.
87. SLNA, Lot 7/2109, Collector of Chilaw to CSO, December 18, 1828.
88. SLNA, Lot 6/980B, letter Collector Chilaw to Chief Secretary, Colombo, October 27, 1829.
89. Tirthankar Roy, "'Sardars, Jobbers, Kanganies': The Labour Contractor and Indian Economic History," *Modern Asian Studies* 42, no. 5 (2008): 972.
90. SLNA, Lot 6/ 971A, Register of Slaves Sent to Chilaw May 12, 1829.
91. SLNA Lot 6/177, Collector Chilaw, Chilaw cutcherry, September 15, 1821, Subsistence for emancipated slaves August 11 to July 31, 1821.
92. SLNA, Lot 6/178, Collector Chilaw to CSO, January 23, 1822.
93. SLNA, Lot 20/219 Collector Chilaw CSO, July 3, 10, and 29, 1824.
94. SLNA, Lot 20/219, Collector Chilaw to CSO, October 22, 1824; 6/917B, Collector Chilaw to CSO, December 14, 1824.
95. SLNA, Lot 6/918B, Collector Chilaw to CSO, January 6, 9, and 26, 1825.
96. Michael Bennett, "Passage Through India: Global Vaccination and British India, 1800–05," *Journal of Imperial and Commonwealth History* 35, no. 2 (June 2007): 201–20.
97. James Cordiner, *A Description of Ceylon: Containing an Account of the Country, Inhabitants, and Natural Productions*, vol. 1 (London: Longman, Hurst, Rees and Orme, 1807), 255.
98. SLNA, Lot 6/919B, Collector Chilaw to CSO, May 22, 1826.
99. Samuel Ashwell, *Medical and Surgical Monographs* (Philadelphia: Waldie, 1840), 297. Numbers are lacking for the victims of cholera in Ceylon, but in Java it killed 100,000 people. See Alfred Jay Bollet, *Plagues and Poxes: The Impact of Human History on Epidemic Disease* (New York: Demos Medical Publishing, 2004).
100. Colvin R. de Silva, *Ceylon Under the British Occupation*, 1:282.
101. SLNA, Lot 6/177, Collector Chilaw, hospital bills of the emancipated slaves, February 23 to March 23, 1821.

102. Prosper Eve, *Le corps des esclaves de l'île Bourbon. Histoire d'une reconquête* (Paris: Presse de l'Université de Paris-Sorbonne, 2013), 167–86.
103. SLNA, Lot 6/917B, Collector Chilaw to CSO, January 7, 1823.
104. SLNA, Lot 6/919B, Collector Chilaw to CSO, February 15, 1826.
105. SLNA, Lot 6/980B, Collector of Chilaw to CSO, October 23, 1829.
106. SLNA, Lot 6/980B, Collector of Chilaw to CSO, November 26, 1829.
107. SLNA, Lot 20/215, Chilaw Collector, John Wallheoff to G. Lusignan, CSO, Colombo, September 18, 1820?
108. SLNA, Lot 20/215, letter CSO Colombo to the Acting Collector Jaffna, October 1, 1820 (with attachment listing slaves).
109. SLNA, Lot 20/1425, Jaffna Cutcherry to Deputy Acting Governor G. Lusignan, October 5, 1820.
110. SLNA, Lot 20/1426, Collector Jaffna to CSO, April 14, 1821.
111. R. B. Allen, *Slaves, Freedmen and Indentured Laborers in Colonial Mauritius* (Cambridge: Cambridge University Press 1989), 39.
112. SLNA, Lot 20/216, CSO to Collector Jaffna, September 14, 1821.
113. SLNA, Lot 20/216, CSO to Collector of Jaffna, list of emancipated slaves, November 14, 1821.
114. SLNA, Lot 6/918B, Collector Chilaw to CSO, September 15, 1825.
115. SLNA, Lot 7/2109, Collector Chilaw to CSO, July 6, 1829.
116. Richard B. Allen, "Maroonage and Its Legacy in Mauritius and in the Colonial Plantation World," *Outre-Mers. Revue d'Histoire* 89, no. 336–37 (2002): 132–52.
117. William A. Green, *British Slave Emancipation: The Sugar Colonies and the Great Experiment* (Oxford: Clarendon Press, 1991).
118. Patricia Scully, *Liberating the Family? Gender and British Slave Emancipation in the Rural Western Cape, South Africa, 1823–1853* (Portsmouth, N.H.: Heinemann, 1997), 38.
119. See Hansard Parliamentary Debates, new series, vol. 9: "Papers Relating to the Amelioration of the Condition of the Slave Population of the West Indies," March 16, 1824, 1102.
120. "Papers Relating to the Amelioration of the Condition of the Slave Population of the West Indies," 1059.
121. Green, *British Slave Emancipation*, 116.
122. N. Draper, "'Possessing Slaves': Ownership, Compensation and Metropolitan Society in Britain at the Time of Emancipation 1834–40," *History Workshop Journal* 64, no. 1 (2007): 74–102; R. E. P. Wastell, "The History of Slave Compensation, 1838–1845," M.A. thesis, King's College, University of London, 1932.
123. K. M. Butler, *The Economics of Emancipation: Jamaica and Barbados, 1823–1843* (Chapel Hill: University of North Carolina Press 1995); N. Draper, *The Price of Emancipation: Slave-Ownership, Compensation and British Society at the End of Slavery* (Cambridge: Cambridge University Press, 2010); Cécile Ernatus,

"L'indemnité coloniale en Guadeloupe, Guyane et Martinique entre 1848 et 1860: monnaie de pierre, monnaie de sable, monnaie de sang," Ph.D. diss., Université de Paris, 2004.
124. Susan Thorne, "Capitalism and Slavery Compensation," *Small Axe* 16, no. 1 (March 2012): 161.
125. E. A. Alpers, *The Indian Ocean in World History* (Oxford: Oxford University Press, 2014); Richard B. Allen, *European Slave Trading in the Indian Ocean 1550–1850* (Athens: Ohio University Press, 2014); Indrani Chatterjee and Richard M. Eaton, eds., *Slavery and South Asian History* (Bloomington: Indiana University Press, 2006); Andrea Major, *Slavery Abolitionism and Empire in India 1772–1843* (Liverpool: Liverpool University Press, 2012).
126. Frederick Cooper, Thomas C. Holt, and Rebecca J. Scott, *Beyond Slavery: Explorations of Race, Labor, and Citizenship in Postemancipation Societies* (Chapel Hill: University of North Carolina Press, 2000), 20; M. Nwulia, *The History of Slavery in Mauritius and the Seychelles, 1810–1875* (East Brunswick, N.J.: Fairleigh Dickenson University Press, 1981); A. Barker, *Slavery and Anti-Slavery in Mauritius, 1810–33: The Conflict Between Economic Expansion and Humanitarian Reform Under British Rule* (London: Palgrave, Macmillan, 1996); V. Teelock, *Bitter Sugar: Sugar and Slavery in 19th Century Mauritius* (Moka: Mahatma Gandhi Institute, 1998); M. Carter R. d'Unienville, *Unshackling Slaves: Liberation and Adaptation of Ex-Apprentices* (London: Pink Pigeon Press, 2001).
127. Cited in Seymour Dresher, *The Mighty Experiment: Free Labor Versus Slavery in British Emancipation* (New York: Oxford University Press, 2002), 107.
128. Slave Trade Abolition Bill, House of Common Debates, March 17, 1807, vol. 9, 994; David Brion Davis, *The Problem of Slavery in the Age of Revolution 1770–1823* (Ithaca, N.Y.: Cornell University Press, 1975), 412.
129. Adam Smith, *An Inquiry Into the Nature and Causes of the Wealth of Nations* (Edinburgh: Nelson, 1845), 159.
130. Frederick Cooper, "Conditions Analogue to Slavery," in Frederick Cooper, Thomas C. Holt, and Rebecca J.Scott, eds., *Beyond Slavery: Explorations of Race, Labor, and Citizenship in Postemancipation Societies* (Chapel Hill: University of North Carolina Press, 2000), 108.
131. Gyan Prakash, "Colonialism, Capitalism and the Discourse of Freedom," *International Review of Social History* 41 (1996): 9–25.
132. SLNA, Lot 20/1425, Collector of Jaffna to Sitting Magistrate, Point Pedro, May 20, 1820.
133. Bodleian Library, Oxford, Papers of the Anti-Slavery Society, Mss Brit Emp s22/G92A, John Scoble on behalf of the British Foreign Anti-Slavery Society to Lord John Russel, Secretary of State to the Colonies, ca. 1842–1843.
134. Roland Wenzhuelmer, "The Sinhalese Contribution to Estate Labour in Ceylon 1881–1891," *Journal of the Economic and Social History of the Orient* 48,

no. 3 (2005): 442–58. Bertram Bastiampillai points to a little-known flow of workers from Jaffna to the coffee plantations from 1832 onwards in *Northern Ceylon (Sri Lanka) in the 19th Century* (Colombo: Godage, 2006), xx.

5. The Plaint of an Emancipated Slave

1. Amitav Ghosh, *In an Antique Land* (New York: Knopf, 1992), 10.
2. SLNA, Lot 33/1699, letter from G. Deane (collector), September 4, 1825.
3. SLNA, Lot 33/1699, Colombo Kachcheri, 1827.
4. The Moors were, after the Sinhalese and the Tamil, the third largest ethnic group in the country. The term identified Muslims who had lived in the country since as far back as the tenth century. Some claimed Arab descent, but most were descendants of traders from the Coromandel Coast. They spoke Tamil but asserted a distinct identity vis-à-vis Tamil people of the north and east of the island.
5. SLNA, Lot 33/1699, The Humble petition of the undersigned Moor inhabitants of Colombo.
6. Gosh, *In an Antique Land*.
7. When slavery is mentioned in historical works, it is generally in connection with the abolition of slavery acts, or with quantitative figures of slaves in various districts as they appear in slave registers.
8. I borrow this term from Bhavani Raman, *Document Raj: Writing and Scribes in Early Colonial South India* (Chicago: University of Chicago Press, 2012).
9. SLNA, Lot 33/1699, Colombo Kachcheri, 1827.
10. Jacques Rancière, *The Method of Equality: Interviews with Laurent Jeanpierre and Dork Zabunyan* (Hoboken, N.J.: Wiley, 2016), 72.
11. Ameer Ali, "The Genesis of the Muslim Community in Ceylon (Sri Lanka): A Historical Summary," *Asian Studies* 19 (1981): 69. In Sanskrit, the term is Yavana.
12. Edward Alpers, *The Indian Ocean in World History* (Oxford: Oxford University Press, 2013), 40–41.
13. See M. A. M. Shukri, ed., *Muslims of Sri Lanka: Avenues of Antiquity* (Beruwela: Jamiaah Naleemia Institute, 1986); Asif Hussain, *Sarandib: An Ethnological Study of the Muslims of Sri Lanka* (Dehiwela: AJ Prints, 2007); Lorna Dewaraja, *The Muslims of Sri Lanka—One Thousand Years of Ethnic Harmony 900–1915* (Colombo: Lanka Islamic Foundation, 1994); and Dennis McGilvray, "Arabs, Moors, and Muslims: Sri Lanka Muslim Ethnicity in Regional Perspective," *Contributions to Indian Sociology* 32, (1998): 433–83.

14. Dennis McGilvray, "Sri Lankan Muslims: Between Ethnic Nationalism and the Global Ummah," *Nations and Nationalism* 17, no. 1 (2011): 49. See also Sinappah Arasaratnam, *Ceylon* (Englewood, N.J.: Prentice-Hall, 1964); S. F. Dale, *The Mappilas of Malabar, 1498–1922: Islamic Society of the South Asian Frontier* (Oxford: Clarendon Press, 1980); S. Kiribamune, "Muslims and the Trade of the Arabian Sea with Special Reference to Sri Lanka from the Birth of Islam to the Fifteenth Century," in *Muslims of Sri Lanka: Avenues to Antiquity*, ed. M. A. M. Shukri (Beruwela: Jamiah Naleemia Institute, 1986), 89–112; and A. Wink, *Al Hind: The Making of the Indo-Islamic World*, vol 1: *Early Medieval India and the Expansion of Islam, 7th–11th centuries* (Leiden: Brill, 1990).
15. Abdul Sheriff, *Dhow Cultures of the Indian Ocean: Cosmopolitanism, Commerce and Islam* (London: Hurst, 2010), 157.
16. Engseng Ho, *The Graves of Tarim: Genealogy and Mobility Across the Indian Ocean* (Berkeley: University of California Press, 2006), 99–100.
17. Sebastian R. Prange, *Monsoon Islam. Trade and Faith on the Medieval Malabar Coast* (Cambridge: Cambridge University Press, 2018).
18. Markus Vink, *Encounters on the Opposite Coast: The Dutch East Indian Company and the Nayaka State of Madurai in the Seventeenth Century* (Leiden: Brill, 2015), 381.
19. Ronit Ricci, *Islam Translated: Literature, Conversion, and the Arabic Cosmopolis of South and Southeast Asia* (Chicago: University of Chicago Press, 2011).
20. Ameer Ali, "Muslims in Harmony and Conflict in Plural Sri Lanka: A Historical Summary from a Religio-economic and Political Perspective," *Journal of Muslim Minority Affairs* 34, no. 3 (2014): 232. The Arab ancestry of the Moors of Sri Lanka is a contested issue that reached a crescendo with the assertion by P. Ramanathan that Moors were Tamil by race, on the basis of language and various customs. See P. Ramanathan, "The Ethnology of the 'Moors' of Ceylon," *Journal of the Royal Asiatic Society Ceylon Branch* 10, no. 36 (1888): 234–62; and Ilm Abdul Azeez's refutation in *A Criticism of Mr Ramanathan's Ethnology of the Moors of Ceylon* (Colombo: Moors Islamic Cultural Home, 1957; reprint of 1907).
21. Vink, *Encounters on the Opposite Coast*, 123.
22. Tambyah Nadaraja, *The Legal System in Ceylon*, 14.
23. Hussain, *Sarandib*, 14–35.
24. For a lucid account of the ethno-religious identity of the Moors over time, see Sharika Thiranagama, *In My Mother's House: Civil War in Sri Lanka* (Philadelphia: University of Pennsylvania Press, 2011), 112–13.
25. R. L. Brohier, *Changing Face of Colombo (1505–1972)* (Colombo: Lake House, 1984), 13; Nihal Perera, "Indigenising the Colonial City: Late 19th Century Colombo and Its Landscape," *Urban Studies* 39, no. 9 (2002): 1703–21.

26. D. A. Kotelawele, "Muslims Under Dutch Rule in Sri Lanka 1638–1796," in *Muslims of Sri Lanka: Avenues of Antiquity*, ed. M. A. M. Shukri (Beruwela: Jamiaah Naleemia Institute, 1986), 176.
27. K. D. G. Wimalaratne, "Muslims Under British Rule in Ceylon (Sri Lanka) 1796–1948," in *Muslims of Sri Lanka: Avenues of Antiquity*, ed. M. A. M. Shukri (Beruwela: Jamiaah Naleemia Institute, 1986), 416–19.
28. G. C. Mendis, ed., *The Colebrooke-Cameron Papers: Documents on British Colonial Policy in Ceylon 1796–1833*, vol. 2 (Oxford: Oxford University Press, 1956).
29. L. Hovy, *Ceylonees Plakkatboek: Plakkaten en andere Wetten uitgevaardigd door het Nederlandse Bestuur op Ceylon, 1638–1796*, vol. 2 (Hilversum: Verloren, 1991), 548.
30. James Peggs, *Slavery in India: The Present State of East India Slavery: Chiefly Extracted from the Parliamentary Papers on the Subject*, 3rd ed. (London: G. Wightman, 1840), 46.
31. Mendis, *Colebrooke-Cameron Papers*, 2:363–64.
32. Simon Casie Chetty, *The Ceylon Gazetteer: Containing an Accurate Account of the Districts, Provinces, Cities, Towns & of the Island of Ceylon* (Colombo: Cotta Church Mission Press, 1834), 255–56.
33. NA UK, Slave Registers 1818–1832—Colombo District.
34. Hussain, *Sarandib*, cites G. A. Dharmaratna's *Kara-Goi Contest of 1890* and Paul E. Pieris, *Ceylon: The Portuguese Era*, 2:508.
35. See chapter 1.
36. SLNA, Lot 33/1699, To the respectable Headman, Arbitrators and Aliem Saib or High Priest is the complaint made by Packier Pulle Rawothan Naynia an inhabitant of Colombo, May 29, 1826.
37. For accounts of violence against slave women in slaveholding societies, see J. Murray and R. Shell, *Children of Bondage: A Social History of the Slave Society at the Cape of Good Hope 1652–1838* (Johannesburg: Witwatersand University Press, 1994), 285–329; R. Brana-Schute, "Approaching Freeedom: The Manumission of Female Slaves in Suriname, 1760–1828," *Slavery and Abolition* 10 (1989): 40–63.
38. SLNA, Lot 33/1699, signed declaration, January 25, 1827.
39. Orlando Patterson, *Slavery and Social Death: A Comparative Study* (Cambridge, Mass: Harvard University Press, 1982), 211–12.
40. SLNA, Lot 33/169, complaint made by Packier Pulle Rawothan Naynia an inhabitant of Colombo, May 29, 1826.
41. See En Mahiudin Nawawi, *Minhaj et Talibin: A Manual of Muhammadan Law According to the School of Shafii*, trans. E. C. Howard (London: W. Thacker, 1914), 558.
42. Thomas F. McDow, "Deeds of Freed Slaves: Manumission and Economic and Social Mobility in Pre-Abolition Zanzibar," in *Indian Ocean Slavery in*

the Age of Abolition, ed. Robert Harms et al. (New Haven, Conn.: Yale University Press, 2013).

43. Hamid Algar, BARDA and BARDA-DARI. vi. "Regulations Governing Slavery in Islamic Jurisprudence, *Encyclopaedia Iranica*, http://www.iranica online.org/articles/barda-vi.
44. William Gervase Clarence-Smith, *Islam and the Abolition of Slavery* (London: Hurst, 2006).
45. Kyle Harper, *Slavery in the Late Roman World, AD 275–425* (Cambridge: Cambridge University Press, 2011), 468.
46. Patterson, *Slavery and Social Death*, 227.
47. Muhammad Ennaji, *Serving the Master: Slavery and Society in Nineteenth Century Morocco* (London: Macmillan, 1999), 53–54.
48. Patterson, *Slavery and Social Death*, 227.
49. Bernard K. Freamon, "Conceptions of Equality and Slavery in Islamic Law: Tribalism, Piety and Pluralism," Ph.D. diss., Columbia University, 2007, 21.
50. Jonathan E. Brockopp, "Slaves and Slavery," in *Encyclopaedia of the Qur'ān*, gen. ed. Jane Dammen McAuliffe, Georgetown University, Washington DC, http://dx.doi.org/10.1163/1875-3922_q3_EQSIM_00393.
51. Talal Asad, "Equality and Inequality in Islam," *Man* 8, no. 2 (1973): 305–6. See also Louise Marlow, *Hierarchy and Egalitarianism in Islamic Thought* (Cambridge: Cambridge University Press, 1997).
52. SLNA, Lot 33/169, Provincial Court of Colombo, Case 7262, Replication of the plaintiff to the answer of the defendant by G. G. Milleband, his Proctor.
53. SLNA, Lot 33/169, letter from Commissioner of Revenue's to collector, February 9, 1827 (names illegible).
54. Casie Chetty, *Ceylon Gazetteer*. Casie Chetty (1807–1860) was district judge of Chilaw and maniagar of Puttalam, first native to be appointed to the Ceylon Civil Service, appointed a Tamil member of the Legislative Council when this office was rendered vacant owing to the death of Coomaraswamy Mudaliyar. He held this office for seven years and then resigned. He became a member of the Royal Asiatic Society in 1845. He proceeded to Chilaw as district judge, which office he held until his death on November 5, 1860, at the age of fifty-three. Before his death he became a Catholic.
55. Robert Ross, *Status and Respectability in the Cape Colony, 1750–1870: A Tragedy of Manners* (Cambridge: Cambridge University Press, 2011).
56. D. McGilvray and M. Raheem, "Origin of the Sri Lankan Muslims and Varieties of the Muslim Identity," in *The Sri Lanka Reader: History, Culture, Politics*, ed. John Clifford Holt (Durham, N.C: Duke University Press, 2011), 414.
57. Michael Roberts and Ismeth Raheem attempted this to a certain extent in *People in Between: Ethnic and Class Prejudices in British Ceylon* (Ratmalana: Sarvodaya, 1989).

58. SLNA, Lot 5/83, January 31, 1809, List of the Present Inhabitants of Colombo who go in the European Dress mode according to the information given by the constables of the different divisions.
59. Casie Chetty, *Ceylon Gazetteer*, 262.
60. Kotelawele, "Muslims Under Dutch Rule in Sri Lanka," 176.
61. Lennox Mills, *Ceylon Under British Rule* (London: Oxford University Press, 1933), 58.
62. Fazli Sameer, *Muslim Personalities in Sri Lanka Then and Now* (Colombo: Moors Islamic Cultural Home, 1982; rev. ed. 2009), 12.
63. Sameer, *Muslim Personalities*, 13.
64. Replication of the plaintiff Packkier Pulle Rawothan in the Provincial Court of Colombo.
65. The Humble petition of the undersigned Moor inhabitants of Colombo to E. Layard, Collector of Colombo.
66. The Humble petition of the undersigned Moor inhabitants of Colombo to E. Layard.
67. The Humble Report of the undersigned Headmoorman, Arbitrators and Priests of Colombo to L. C. Layard, Collector of Colombo, April 5, 1826.
68. To the respectable Headman, Arbitrators and Aliem Saib or High priest as the complaint made by Packier Pulle Rawothan Naynia as inhabitant of Colombo.
69. Report of the undersigned Arbitrators namely Muhammed Lebbe Secado Mira Lebbe, Headmoorman of the district of Caltura as senior arbitrator et al. to L. C. Layard, Collector, June 8, 1826.
70. Casie Chetty, *Ceylon Gazetteer*, 256.
71. To the respectable Headman, Arbitrators and Aliem Saib or High Priest is the complaint made by Packier Pulle Rawothan Naynia an inhabitant of Colombo.
72. Jessica Murray, in "Gender and Violence in Cape Slave Narratives and Post-Narratives," *South African Historical Journal* 62, no. 3 (2010), 448, cites Jacques Derrida, *Demeure: Ficxtion and Testimony*, trans. E. Rottenberg (Stanford, Calif.: Stanford University Press, 2000), 28. Derrida argues that there is "no testimony that does not structurally imply in itself the possibility of fiction, simulacra, dissimulation, lie and perjury." On the absence of slave narratives in the Dutch Caribbean and the translation of American narrative into Dutch, see Marijke Huisman, "Beyond the Subject: Anglo-American Slave Narratives in the Netherlands, 1789–2013," *European Journal of Life Writing* 4 (2015): VC56–84.
73. See Mathew Hull, *Government of Paper: The Materiality of Bureaucracy in Urban Pakistan* (Berkeley: University of California Press, 2012), for an enticing analysis of petitions as articulating political relationships.

74. C. A. Bayly, *Empire and Information: Intelligence Gathering and Social Communication in India 1780–1870* (Cambridge: Cambridge University Press, 1996).
75. The Humble Petition of Packier Rawothan Naynia. A moorman of Colombo; The Humble Petition of the undersigned Moor inhabitants of Colombo; see Raman, *Document Raj*.
76. Lascarins were indigenous soldiers in the service of the king, and later of colonial governors.
77. Patrick Peebles, *Social Change in Nineteenth Century Ceylon* (New Delhi: Navrang, 1995), 30.
78. India Office Library, G/11/6, Petition by Cornelis de Alwis, February 7, 1801.
79. Raman, *Document Raj*, 163.
80. K. M. de Silva, *History of Sri Lanka* (New Delhi: Oxford University Press, 1981), 327–30.
81. *Asiatic Journal and Monthly Register for British India and Its Dependents* 19, January–June 1825, 850.
82. Ceylon Calendar for 1827 (Colombo: Government Press, 1828), 100.
83. SLNA, Lot 33/1699, letter from Commissioner of Revenue, Robert Boyd, February 9, 1827.
84. SLNA, Lot 33/1699, letter John Deane, Collector, September 4, 1825.
85. SLNA, Lot 33/1699, The Humble Report of the undersigned Headmoorman, Arbitrator and Priests of Colombo; Report of the undersigned arbitrators namely Muhammed Lebbe Secady Mira Lebbe, Headmoorman of the district of Caltura.
86. Veena Das, *Life and Words: Violence and the Descent Into the Ordinary* (Berkeley: University of California Press, 2006), 162.
87. M. U. de Silva, "Land Tenure, Caste System and the Rājakāriya Under Foreign Rule: A Review of Change in Sri Lanka Under Western Powers, 1597–1832," *Journal of the Royal Asiatic Society of Sri Lanka*, New Series 37, (1992): 40–41.
88. Replication of the plaintiff Packier Pulle Rawothan to the answer of the defendants by G. G. Milleband, his proctor.
89. P. D. Kannangara, *The History of the Ceylon Civil Service, 1802–1833* (Dehiwela: Tisara Press, 1966), 71.
90. Patrick Peebles, *History of Sri Lanka* (Westport, Conn.: Greenwood Press, 2006), 48–49.
91. NA UK, CO 54/122, C. H. Cameron, Report upon the judicial establishment and procedure, January 31, 1832.
92. Charles Marshall, Supreme Court Law Reports 1833–1836, Case No. 994, Caltura April 22, 1835, 413.
93. Hannah Arendt, *Eichmann in Jerusalem: A Report on the Banality of Evil* (New York: Viking, 1963); Charles Babour, "The Acts of Faith: On Witnessing in Derrida and Arendt," *Philosophy and Social Criticism* 37, no. 6 (2011): 629–45.

94. Hannah Arendt, *Between Past and Future: Eight Exercises in Political Thought* (New York: Penguin, 1993), 153.
95. Patterson, *Slavery and Social Death*, 240.
96. David Scott, "The Paradox of Freedom: An Interview with Orlando Patterson," *Small Axe* 17, no. 1 (March 2013): 97.
97. Orlando Patterson, *The Sociology of Slavery: An Analysis of the Origins, Development, and Structure of Negro Slave Society in Jamaica* (London: MacGibbon and Kee, 1967), 292, cited in Scott, "The Paradox of Freedom," 96.

6. Eclipse of the Slave

1. Avery F. Gordon, *Ghostly Matters: Haunting and the Sociological Imagination* (Minneapolis: University of Minnesota Press, 2008), xix.
2. Cited in Ulf Hannerz, "The World in Creolisation," *Africa: Journal of the International African Institute* 57, no. 4 (1987): 265.
3. See Walter Benjamin, *Illuminations. Essays and Reflections*, ed. Hannah Arendt (New York: Schocken Books, 1968), for his reading of the past as filled by the now (*Jetzzeit*) and about remembrance (*Eingedenken*) as history's "original vocation."
4. Cited in Encarnación Gutierrez Rodriguez and Shirley Anne Tate, eds., *Creolizing Europe: Legacies and Transformations* (Liverpool: Liverpool University Press, 2015), 27.
5. H. W. Tambiah, *The Laws and the Customs of the Tamils of Jaffna* (Colombo: Women's Education and Research Centre, 2004), 85; K. M. de Silva, *Social Policy and Missionary Organizations in Ceylon 1840–1855* (London: Longmans, Green, 1965), 220.
6. P. L. Simmonds, ed., *Simmond's Colonial Magazine and Foreign Miscellany* 1, (January–April 1844) (London: Foreign and Colonial Office 1844), 363.
7. *Morning Star*, January 14, 1843, 11–12.
8. Paul Ricoeur, *Memory, History, Forgetting* (Chicago: University of Chicago Press, 2004).
9. Edouard Glissant, *Introduction à une Poetique du divers* (Paris: Gallimard, 1996), 18, cited in Gutierrez Rodriguez and Tate, *Creolizing Europe*.
10. Megan Vaughan, *Creating the Creole Island: Slavery in Eighteenth-Century Mauritius* (Durham, N.C.: Duke University Press, 2005).
11. Gananath Obeysekere, "Representations of the Wild Man in Sri Lanka," in *Beyond Primitivism: Indigenous Religious Traditions and Modernity*, ed. J. K. Olupona (New York: Routledge, 2004), 272–95.

12. Eric Meyer makes the important point that scholarship has overemphasized migration waves as compared to continuous population flows between India and Sri Lanka, in "Labour Circulation Between Sri Lanka and South India in Historical Perspective," in *Society and Circulation: Mobile People and Itinerant Cultures in South Asia, 1750–1950*, ed. C. Markovits, Jacques Pouchepadass, and Sanjay Subramanyam (London: Anthem Press, 2006), 55–88. For a recent interpretation of three key Sinhalese ideologues, see Harshana Rambukwella, *The Poetics and Politics of Authenticity: A Cultural Genealogy of Sinhala Nationalism* (London: UCL Press, 2018).
13. Sujit Sivasundaram, "Ethnicity, Indigeneity, and Migration in the Advent of British Rule to Sri Lanka," *American Historical Review* 115, no. 2 (April 2010): 428–52; Gananath Obeysekere, "The Conscience of the Parricide: A Study in Buddhist History," *Man*, New Series, 24, no. 2 (June 1989): 236–54. The Mahavamsa or Great Chronicle is a historical account of Sri Lanka written in the fifth or sixth century, probably by the Buddhist monk Mahanama. It deals mainly with the history of Buddhism in the island and with dynastic succession from about the sixth century BCE to the early fourth century CE.
14. National Archive, The Hague, 1.11.01.0, 1878, Papers concerning slave trade and slave ownership in Ceylon, 18th century.
15. Bookkeeper-General Batavia database, http://bgb.huygens.knaw.nl/, accessed June 13, 2016.
16. Remco Raben, "Batavia and Colombo: The Ethnic and Spatial Order of Two Colonial Cities 1600–1800," Ph.D diss., Leiden University, 1996.
17. R.A.L.H. Gunawardana, *Robe and Plough: Monasticism and Economic Interest in Early Medieval Sri Lanka* (Tucson: University of Arizona Press, 1979).
18. For a detailed account of African soldiers in the regiments of the army from the second decade of the nineteenth century, see Shihan de Silva Jayasuriya and Jean Pierre Angenot, eds., *Uncovering the History of Africans in Asia* (Leiden: Brill, 2008), 17–18.
19. Michael Roberts, "The Collective Consciousness of the Sinhalese During the Kandyan Era: Manichean Images, Associational Logic,"*Asian Ethnicity* 3, no. 1 (March 2002): 40.
20. See Jayasuriya, *Uncovering the History of Africans in Asia*, 157.
21. Kate Ekama, "Slavery in Dutch Colombo: A Social History," M.A. thesis, Leiden University, 2012, 9.
22. Lodewijk Wagenaar, "The Cultural Dimension of the Dutch East India Company Settlements in Dutch Period Ceylon, 1700–1800 with special reference to Galle," in *Mediating Netherlandish Art and Material Culture in Asia*, ed. Thomas Da Costa and Michael North (Amsterdam: Amsterdam University Press, 2015), 151.

23. M. Roberts et al., *People in Between: Ethnic and Class Prejudices in British Ceylon* (Ratmalana: Sarvodaya, 1989), 42.
24. Lodewijk Wagenaar, "The Cultural Dimension of the Dutch East India Company Settlements in Dutch Period Ceylon, 1700–1800—with Special Reference to Galle," in *Mediating Netherlandish Art and Material Culture in Asia*, ed. Thomas DaCosta Kaufmann and Michael North (Amsterdam: Amsterdam University Press, 2015), 151.
25. Roberts, *People in Between*, 161.
26. Ekama, "Slavery in Dutch Colombo," 28–34.
27. P. E. Pieris, ed., *Illangakoon Diaries*, in *Notes on Some Sinhalese Families* (Colombo: Apothecaries, 1902/1911), 116–17, 126–27. Twenty slaves are listed as part of the estate that Dona Catherina and Dona Assensia, children of Jayatilaka Mudaliyar of Matara, left behind.
28. Reprint of a lecture delivered by R. G. Anthonisz, "The Dutch in Ceylon: Glimpses of Their Life and Times," *Journal of the Dutch Burgher Union* 24, no. 4 (April 1935): 129.
29. U. C. Wickremeratne, *The Conservative Nature of the British Rule of Sri Lanka* (New Delhi: Navrang, 1996), 168.
30. Alicia Schrikker, "Caught Between Empires: VOC Families in Sri Lanka After the British Take-over, 1806–1808," *Annales de démographie historique* 122, no. 2 (2011): 127–47.
31. Anna Maria Rugarli and Robert C.-H. Shell, "Historical Relevance? Ten Sketches of Women Illegally Enslaved at the Cape, 1823 to 1830," *New Contree: A Journal of Historical and Human Sciences for Southern Africa*, no. 55 (May 2008): 43–65.
32. Rugarli and Shell, "Historical Relevance?," 53.
33. Great Britain, Parliamentary Papers, vol. 25, 80 (HM Stationery Office, 1829), appendix (L B) Return of Complaints and Applications for Freedom, 127.
34. SLNA, Lot 7/2270, Inward Letters and Documents of the Sitting Magistrate Galle 1802–1805 1), Deposition upon oath taken before me (Babbea emancipated slave).
35. Wickremeratne, *The Conservative Nature*, 160.
36. Mark Whitaker, *Amiable Incoherence: Manipulating Histories and Modernities in a Batticaloa Hindu Temple*, Sri Lankan Studies Series (Amsterdam: VU University Press, 1999).
37. Michael Roberts, *Caste Conflict and Elite Formation: The Rise of a Karava Elite in Sri Lanka 1500–1931* (Cambridge: Cambridge University Press, 1982).
38. Gananath Obeysekere, "The Coming of Brahmin Migrants: The Sudra Fate of an Indian Elite in Sri Lanka," *Society and Culture in South Asia* 1, no. 1 (2015): 1–32.

39. Eric Tagliocozzo, "Trade, Production and Incorporation: The Indian Ocean in Flux, 1600–1900," *Itinerario* 1 (2002): 75–106; Michael Pearson, "Littoral Society: The Case for the Coast," *Great Circle* 7 (1985): 1–8.
40. A. Bertolacci, *A View of the Agricultural, Commercial, and Financial Interests of Ceylon* (London: Black Parbury and Allen, 1817), 60.
41. SLNA, Lot 81/1905, Testament of Peter Mellonius, May 21, 1821.
42. Wagenaar, "The Cultural Dimension of the Dutch East Indian Company," 154.
43. Kabristan Archives, Dutch Reformed Church, Wolvendaal, Colombo Marriages, vols. 1–2, https://www.kabristan.org.uk/.
44. SLNA, Censura Morum held on July 10, 1805. Translation of the Minutes of the Consistory of the Dutch Reformed Church of Wolvendaal, Colombo, 1804 to November 22, 1809, vol. 4A/5 of the Records at the Wolvendaal Church, Colombo, by S. A. W. Mottau, June 6, 1977, 37–38.
45. NA UK, Slave Registers 1818–1832.
46. "Sri Lanka, Colombo District, Dutch Reformed Church Records, 1677–1990," FamilySearch, http://FamilySearch.org, April 28, 2017; Dutch Reformed Church, Wolvendaal.
47. NA UK, Slave Registers 1818–1832, Colombo District.
48. SLNA, 25.1/27, Return Orders and Regulations touching the Supreme Court of Judicature in the Island of Ceylon in Pursuance of His Majesty's Charter dated August 6, 1810 & 1811, C July 15, 1815. The letter is addressed by the Burgher Jurors to the Hon. Sir Alexander Johnston.
49. Roberts, *People in Between*, 123.
50. W. Digby, *Forty Years of Official and Unofficial Life in an Oriental Crown Colony*, vol. 1 (Madras: Higginbotham, 1879), 41.
51. L. A. Wickremaratne, "Education and Social Change 1832 to c 1900," in *University of Ceylon History of Ceylon*, vol. 3: *From the Beginning of the Nineteenth Century to 1948*, ed. K. M. de Silva (Peradeniya: University of Ceylon, 1973), 167.
52. See G. Obeyesekere, "The Ritual Drama of the Sanni Demons: Collective Representations of Disease in Ceylon," *Comparative Studies in Society and History* 2 (1969): 174–216; Obeyesekere, *The Cult of the Goddess Pattini* (Chicago: University of Chicago Press, 1984), 306–12.
53. Ricoeur, *Memory, History, Forgetting*, 414.
54. R. G. Anthonisz, "A Hundred Years Ago," lecture delivered August 29, 1924, *Journal of the Dutch Burgher Union of Ceylon* 14, no. 4 (April 1925): 122.
55. C. Rasanayagam, *Ancient Jaffna: Being a Research Into the History of Jaffna from Very Early Times to the Portuguese Period* (New Delhi: Asian Educational Services, 1984 [1926]), 385.

56. The bottom layer of the Jaffna caste system is collectively referred to as "Panchamar." It consists of Vannar (dhoby), Ampattar (barber), Pallar (agricultural laborer), Nalavar (toddy tapper), and Parayar (funeral drummer) castes. The Panchamar resistance against prohibitions imposed by Vellalar-dominated society began in the 1920s but reached a peak in the 1950–1970s. See Nira Wickramasinghe, *Sri Lanka in the Modern Age: A History* (Oxford: Oxford University Press, 2015): 288–91; Prashant Kuganathan, "Social Stratification in Jaffna: A Survey of Recent Research on Caste," *Sociology Compass* 8, no. 1 (2014): 78–88.
57. K. Daniel, *Mirage, Kanal* (Colombo: Kumaran Book House, 2016).
58. Dilip M. Menon, "A Place Elsewhere: Lower-Caste Malayalam Novels of the Nineteenth Century," in *India's Literary History: Essays on the Nineteenth Century*, ed. S. H. Blackburn and V. Dalmia (New Delhi: Permanent Black, 2004), 483–515; Sanal Mohan, *Modernity of Slavery: Struggles Against Caste Inequality in Colonial Kerala* (New York: Oxford University Press, 2015).
59. H. Mahindapala, "*Mirage*—The Great Tamil Novel of Our Time," *Sunday Times*, March 26, 2017. See also H. L. D. Mahindapala, "Jaffna: The Hell-Hole of Persecuted & Oppressed Tamil Slaves," *Colombo Telegraph*, May 2, 2016.
60. Article by Nalin de Silva, February 26, 2016, http://www1.kalaya.org/2016/02/2016-28.html.
61. Nalin de Silva, *Demala Janathava ge Sangshipath Ithihasaya* (A concise history of the Tamil people) (Boralasgamuwa: Visidunu Press, 2009); de Silva, *Demala Jathivadayata Erehiva* (Against Tamil nationalism) (Maharagama: Chintana parshpadaya, n.d.).
62. P. Thanges and K. T. Silva, "Caste Discrimination in War-Affected Jaffna Society," in *Casteless or Caste Blind? Dynamics of Concealed Caste Discrimination, Social Exclusion, and Protest in Sri Lanka*, ed. K. T. Silva, P. P. Sivapragasam, and Paramsothy Thanges (Copenhagen: International Dalit Solidarity, 2009), 50–76.
63. R. L. Brohier and Ismeth Raheem, *Changing Face of Colombo 1505–1972 Covering the Portuguese, Dutch and British Periods* (Colombo: Lake House, 1984), 34.
64. Khal Torabully, in *Chair Corail, Fragments Coolies* (Guadeloupe: Ibis Rouge Editions, 1999), embraces a Glissantian form of identity-as-relation rather than a single-root identity and thus gestures toward a world of empathy awakened by a new form of humanism.

Bibliography

Archives

Sri Lanka

SRI LANKA NATIONAL ARCHIVES, COLOMBO AND KANDY (SLNA)

Lot 1: Records of the Dutch Administration, 1640–1796.
Lot 2: Records of the Executive Council, 1802–1931.
Lot 5: Dispatches from the Governor to the Secretary of State for the Colonies, 1798–1948.
Lot 6: Letters from Various Departments and Individuals to the Chief Secretary, 1805–1897.
Lot 7: Letters from the Chief Secretary to Various Departments and Individuals Outward, 1795–1889.
Lot 10: Miscellaneous Collection and Cases on Special Subjects, 1767–1872.
Lot 20: (Kandy Branch of SLNA): Jaffna Kachcheri, 1795–1917.
Lot 24: Consistory of the Dutch Reformed Church in Ceylon, 1735–1837.
Lot 25.1: Johnston Papers, Christie Collection, 1834.
Lot 33: Colombo Kachcheri, 1793–1981.
Lot 81: Supreme Court of Ceylon, 1803–1970.

GOVERNMENT PUBLICATIONS, SRI LANKA

Ceylon Blue Books, 1824, 1825, 1828.
Ceylon Calendar, 1827, 1828.
Report of the Ceylon Tobacco Industry, Sessional Paper 6–1912. Colombo: H. C. Cottle, 1912.
Return of the Population of the Maritime Districts of the Island of Ceylon. Colombo: Government Press, 1816.
Return of the Population of the Island of Ceylon, 1827. Colombo: Government Press, 1828.

Netherlands

NATIONAL ARCHIVES, THE HAGUE (NA NL)

1.11.01.0 1878. Papers Concerning Slave Trade and Slave Ownership in Ceylon, eighteenth century, one folder (1960VI).
1.11.01.01 2049. Deeds Done by Dutch Notaries and the Judiciary in Ceylon, 1687, 1750–1808: Will of Nicholaas Dias Abesinghe Amereseqere.
2.21.165/8. Uhlenbeck Family Papers, 1744–1962.

United Kingdom

NATIONAL ARCHIVES, KEW (NA UK)

CO 54: Colonial Office and Predecessors: Ceylon, Original Correspondence, 1798–1949.
CO 55: Colonial Office and Predecessors: Ceylon, Entry Books 1794–1872.
CO 59: War and Colonial Department and Colonial Office: Ceylon, Miscellanea.
CO 416: Commissioners of Eastern Enquiry, Ceylon, 1829–1830.
CO T71 series: Slave Registers of Former Colonial Dependencies, 1813–1834.

PARLIAMENTARY PUBLICATIONS

House of Commons Debates. Slave Trade Abolition Bill. Volume 9. March 17, 1807.
Parliamentary Debates. Papers Relating to the Amelioration of the Condition of the Slave Population of the West Indies, 1056–1198. March 16, 1824.
Parliamentary Papers (House of Commons). Slavery in Ceylon, 467, 1838.

———. Slavery in India, 125, 1828.
———. Slave Trade (East India)—Slavery in Ceylon, 697, 1838.
———. Slave Trade—Slave Vessels: Returns of Cases Adjudged Under Slave Trade Treaties and Number of Slaves Emancipated in Consequence, 73, 212, 1845.
———. Trinidad Order in Council in Papers in Explanation of Measures for Amelioration of Condition of Slave Population in W. Indies and S. America, 008, 1825.

BODLEIAN LIBRARY, UNIVERSITY OF OXFORD

India and Ceylon: Mss Brit. Emp. s 22/G91 (1838–1853, 1880); s22/G92 (1838–1847, 1872–1899).
Papers of the Anti-Slavery Society, 1757–1951.

BRITISH LIBRARY, LONDON (BL)

Delaware Journal IOR/L/MAR/B/322A, 1752–1758.
G/11 Factory Records Ceylon, 1762–1806, 1–2–6.

SCHOOL OF AFRICAN AND ASIAN STUDIES, LONDON

FBN Ceylon Correspondence, 1840, Box 446, 448.
Wesleyan Methodist Missionary Society Papers, 1691–2018.

Secondary Sources

Abeyasinghe, Tikiri. *Portuguese Rule in Ceylon 1594–1612*. Colombo: Lake House Publishers, 1966.
Algar, Hamid. "BARDA and BARDA-DARI vi. Regulations Governing Slavery in Islamic Jurisprudence." *Encyclopaedia Iranica*. http://www.iranicaonline.org/articles/barda-vi.
Ali, Ameer. "The Genesis of the Muslim Community in Ceylon (Sri Lanka): A Historical Summary." *Asian Studies* 19 (1981): 65–82.
———. "Muslims in Harmony and Conflict in Plural Sri Lanka: A Historical Summary from a Religio-economic and Political Perspective." *Journal of Muslim Minority Affairs* 34, no. 3 (2014): 227–42.
Allen, Richard B. *European Slave Trading in the Indian Ocean 1500–1850*. Athens: Ohio University Press, 2014.

———. "Maroonage and Its Legacy in Mauritius and in the Colonial Plantation World." *Outre-Mers. Revue d'Histoire* 89, no. 336–37 (2002): 132–52.

———. *Slaves, Freedmen and Indentured Laborers in Colonial Mauritius.* Cambridge: Cambridge University Press, 1999.

Alpers, E. A. *The Indian Ocean in World History.* Oxford: Oxford University Press, 2014.

Amerasinghe, Ranjit B. *The Supreme Court of Sri Lanka: The First 185 Years.* Colombo: Sarvodaya, 1986.

Amin, Shahid. *Alternative Histories: A View from India.* Sephis-CSSSC Occasional Paper. Calcutta: Centre for Studies in Social Sciences, 2002.

Ancestry. "Former Colonial Dependencies, Slave Registers, 1813–1834." http://search.ancestry.com/search/db.aspx?dbid=1129.

Anderson, Clare. *Convicts in the Indian Ocean: Transportation from South Asia to Mauritius, 1815–1853.* London: Macmillan, 2000.

———. "Execution and Its Aftermath in the Nineteenth-Century British Empire." In *A Global History of Execution and the Criminal Corpse,* ed. Richard Ward, 170–98. Basingstoke, UK: Palgrave Macmillan, 2015.

———. *Subaltern Lives: Biographies of Colonialism in the Indian Ocean World, 1790–1920.* Cambridge: Cambridge University Press, 2012.

Andrews, William L. *To Tell a Free Story: The First Century of Afro-American Autobiography, 1760–1865.* Urbana: University of Illinois Press, 1988.

Anthonisz, R. G. "The Dutch in Ceylon: Glimpses of Their Life and Times." *Journal of the Dutch Burgher Union of Ceylon* 24, no. 4 (1935): 129–32.

———. "A Hundred Years Ago." Lecture delivered August 29, 1924. *Journal of the Dutch Burgher Union of Ceylon* 14, no. 4 (1925): 101–28.

———. *Report on the Dutch Records in the Government Archives at Colombo.* Colombo: H. C. Cottle, 1907.

Appadurai, A. "Numbers in the Colonial Imagination." In *Orientalism and the Postcolonial Predicament: Perspectives on South Asia,* ed. Carol Breckenbridge and Peter van der Veer, 314–40. Philadelphia: University of Pennsylvania Press, 1993.

Aptheker, Harold. *American Negro Slave Revolts.* New York: Columbia University Press, 1943.

Arasaratnam, Sinappah. *Ceylon.* Englewood, N. J.: Prentice-Hall, 1964

———. *Ceylon and the Dutch, 1600–1800: External Influences and Internal Change in Early Modern Sri Lanka.* Aldershot, UK: Variorum, 1996.

———. *Francois Valentijn's Description of Ceylon.* London: Hakluyt Society, 1978.

———. "Historical Foundation of the Economy of the Tamils of North Sri Lanka." Chelvanayakam Memorial Lectures, 1982. Lecture 1: The 17th and 18th Centuries. Jaffna, Sri Lanka: Thanthai Chelva Memorial Trust, 1982.

———. "Social History of a Dominant Caste Society: The Vellalar of North Ceylon (Sri Lanka) in the 18th Century." *Indian Economic and Social History Review* 18, no. 3–4 (1981): 377–91.

Arendt, Hannah. *Between Past and Future: Eight Exercises in Political Thought.* New York: Penguin, 1993.

———. *Eichmann in Jerusalem: A Report on the Banality of Evil.* New York: Viking, 1963.

Armstrong, James C. "The Slaves 1652–1795." In *The Shaping of South African Society, 1652–1820*, ed. Richard Elphick and Hermann Giliomee, 75–115. London: Longman, 1979.

Arnez, Monika, and Jurgen Sarnowsky. *The Role of Religions in the European Perception of Insular and Mainland Southeast Asia: Travel Accounts of the 16th to the 21st Century.* Newcastle upon Tyne, UK: Cambridge Scholars, 2016.

Arnold, David. *Colonizing the Body: State Medicine and Epidemic Disease in Nineteenth Century India.* Berkeley: University of California Press, 1993.

———. "White Colonization and Labour in Nineteenth Century India." *Journal of Imperial and Commonwealth History* 2, no. 2 (1983): 133–58.

Asad, Talal. *Genealogies of Religion.* Baltimore: John Hopkins University Press, 1993.

———. "Equality and Inequality in Islam." *Man* 8, no. 2 (1973): 305–6.

Ashwell, Samuel. *Medical and Surgical Monographs.* Philadelphia: Waldie, 1840.

Attwood, Bain, Dipesh Chakrabarty, and Claudio Lomnitz. "The Public Life of History." *Public Culture* 20, no. 1 (2008): 1–4.

Azeez, Ilm Abdul. *A Criticism of Mr. Ramanathan's Ethnology of the Moors of Ceylon.* Colombo: Moors Islamic Cultural Home, 1957 (1907).

Babour, Charles. "The Acts of Faith: On Witnessing in Derrida and Arendt." *Philosophy and Social Criticism* 37, no. 6 (2011): 629–45.

Baldaeus, Philippus. *A True and Exact Description of the Most Celebrated East-India Coasts of Malabar and Coromandel; as also of the Isle of Ceylon.* London: Churchill, 1703.

———. *A Description of the Great and Famous Isle of Ceylon.* 1672. Delhi: Asian Educational Services, 1996.

Balhatchet, Kenneth. *Race, Sex and Class Under the Raj: Imperial Attitudes and Policies and their Critics 1793–1905.* London: Weidenfeld and Nicholson, 1980.

Banks, Michael. "Caste in Jaffna." In *Aspects of Caste in South India, Ceylon and North-West Pakistan*, ed. E. R. Leach, 61–77. Cambridge: Cambridge University Press, 1960.

Barker, A. *Slavery and Anti-Slavery in Mauritius, 1810–33: The Conflict Between Economic Expansion and Humanitarian Reform Under British Rule.* London: Palgrave Macmillan, 1996.

Bastiampillai, Bertram. *Northern Ceylon (Sri Lanka) in the 19th Century*. Colombo: Godage, 2006.

Bastin, Rohan. *The Domain of Constant Excess: Plural Worship at the Munnesvaram Temples in Sri Lanka*. Oxford: Berghahn Press, 1997.

Bates, Crispin, and Marina Carter. "Sirdars as Intermediaries in Nineteenth-Century Indian Ocean Indentured Labour Migration." *Modern Asian Studies* 51, no. 2 (2017): 462–84.

Bauer, Raymond A., and Alice H. Bauer. "Day to Day Resistance to Slavery" (1942). In *Rebellions, Resistance, and Runaways Within the Slave South*, ed. Paul Finkelman, 84–115. New York: Garland, 1989.

Bayly, C. A. *Imperial Meridian: The British Empire and the World 1780–1830*. London: Longman, 1988.

———. *Empire and Information: Intelligence Gathering and Social Communication in India 1780–1870*. Cambridge: Cambridge University Press, 1996.

Benians, E. A., et al. *Cambridge History of the British Empire (1929–1959)*. 8 vols. Cambridge: Cambridge University Press, 1961.

Benjamin, Walter. *Illuminations*, ed. Hannah Arendt. New York: Schocken Books, 1968.

———. "On the Concept of History." In *Walter Benjamin: Selected Writings*. Vol. 4: *1938–1940*, ed. Howard Eiland and Michael W. Jennings, 389–401. Cambridge, Mass.: Harvard University Press, 2003.

Bertolacci, A. *A View of the Agricultural, Commercial and Financial Interests of Ceylon*. London: Black Parbury and Allen, 1817.

Bethencourt, Francisco. *Racisms: From the Crusades to the Twentieth Century*. Princeton, N.J.: Princeton University Press, 2013.

Biederman, Zoltan. "Colombo Versus Cannanore: Contrasting Structures of Two Colonial Port Cities (1500–1700)." *Journal of the Economic and Social History of the Orient* 52, no. 3 (2009): 413–59.

Bijl, Paul. "Acts of Equality: Writing Autonomy, Empathy and Community in an Indonesian Slave Narrative." In *Being a Slave in the Indian Ocean World: Histories and Legacies of European Slavery*, ed. Alicia Schrikker and Nira Wickramasinghe. Leiden: Leiden University Press, 2020.

Biografish Woordenboek van Nederland (BWN). http://resources.huygens.knaw.nl/.

Björkman, W. "Kāfir." In *Encyclopaedia of Islam*, ed. P. Bearman, T. Bianquis, C. E. Bosworth, E. van Donzel, and W. P. Heinrichs. 2d ed. 2012. http://dx.doi.org/10.1163/1573-3912_islam_SIM_3775.

Bollet, Alfred Jay. *Plagues and Poxes: The Impact of Human History on Epidemic Disease*. New York: Demos Medical, 2004.

Bookkeeper-General Batavia database. http://bgb.huygens.knaw.nl/.

Bradlow, F. R., and M. Cairns. *The Early Cape Muslims: A Study of Their Mosques, Genealogy and Origins*. Cape Town: Balkema, 1978.

Brana-Schute, R. "Approaching Freedom: The Manumission of Female Slaves in Suriname, 1760–1828." *Slavery and Abolition* 10 (1989): 40–63.

Brimnes, Niels. *Constructing the Colonial Encounter: Right and Left Hand Castes in Early Colonial South India*. Richmond: Curzon, 1999.

Brito, Christopher. *The Yalpana Vaipava Malai or the History of the Kingdom of Jaffna*. 1879. New Delhi: Asian Educational Services, 2007.

Brockopp, Jonathan E. "Slaves and Slavery." In *Encyclopaedia of the Qur'ān*, gen. ed. Jane Dammen McAuliffe, Georgetown University, Washington, D.C. Accessed October 1, 2019. http://dx.doi.org/10.1163/1875-3922_q3_EQSIM_00393.

Brohier, R. L. *Changing Face of Colombo (1505–1972)*. Colombo: Lake House, 1984.

———. *Discovering Ceylon*. Lake House: Colombo, 1982.

Bruijn, J. R., F. S. Gastra, and I. Schoffer. *Dutch Asiatic Shipping in the 17th and 18th Centuries*. The Hague: Martinus Nijhoff, 1987.

Buettner, Elizabeth. "Problematic Spaces. Problematic Races: Defining Europeans in Late Colonial India." *Women's History Review* 9, no. 2 (2000): 277–99.

Burah, Tuan Arfin. *Saga of the Exiled Royal Javanese Unearthed*. Dehiwala, Sri Lanka: self-published, 2006.

Butler, K. M. *The Economics of Emancipation: Jamaica and Barbados, 1823–1843*. Chapel Hill: University of North Carolina Press, 1995.

Cannadine, David. *Ornamentalism: How the British Saw Their Empire*. London: Allen Lane, 2001.

Carrera, Vincent. *Equiano the African: Biography of a Self-Made Man*. Athens: University of Georgia Press, 2005.

Carter, Marina. *Voices from Indenture: Experience of Indian Migrants in the British Empire*. London: Leicester University Press, 1996.

Carter, Marina, and R. d'Unienville, *Unshackling Slaves: Liberation and Adaptation of Ex-Apprentices*. London: Pink Pigeon, 2001.

Casie Chetty, Simon. *The Ceylon Gazetteer: Containing an Accurate Account of the Districts, Provinces, Cities, Towns & of the Island of Ceylon*. Colombo: Cotta Church Mission Press, 1834.

Casinader, Niranjan, Roshan De Silva Wijeyaratne, and Lee Godden. "From Sovereignty to Modernity: Revisiting the Colebrooke-Cameron Reforms—Transforming the Buddhist and Colonial Imaginary in Nineteenth-Century Ceylon." *Comparative Legal History* 6, no. 1 (2018): 34–64.

Cassels, Nancy Gardner. *Social Legislation of the East India Company: Public Justice Versus Public Instruction*. New Delhi: Sage, 2010.

Chalhoub, Sidney. "The Politics of Ambiguity: Conditional Manumission, Labor Contracts, and Slave Emancipation in Brazil (1850s–1888)." *International Review of Social History* 60, no. 2 (August 2015): 161–91.

Chatterjee, Indrani. "British Abolitionism from the Vantage of Pre-Colonial South Asian Regimes." In *The Cambridge World History of Slavery*. Vol. 4: *AD 1804–AD 2016*, ed. David Eltis, Stanley Engerman, Seymour Drescher, and David Richardson, 441–65. Cambridge: Cambridge University Press, 2017.

———. *Gender, Slavery and Law in Colonial India*. New Delhi: Oxford University Press, 1999.

———. "A Slave's Quest for Selfhood in Eighteenth-Century Hindustan." *Indian Economic and Social History Review* 37, no. 1 (2000): 53–86.

Chatterjee, Indrani, and Richard M. Eaton, eds. *Slavery and South Asian History*. Bloomington: Indiana University Press, 2006.

Chatterjee, Partha. *The Nation and Its Fragments: Colonial and Postcolonial Histories*. Princeton, N.J.: Princeton University Press, 1993.

Christianse, Yvette. *Unconfessed*. New York: Other Press, 2006.

Christopher, Anthony. "Race and the Census in the Commonwealth." *Population, Space and Place* 11, no. 2 (2005): 103–118.

Christopher, Emma, Cassandra Pybus, Marcus Rediker, and Marcus Buford Rediker. *Many Middle Passages: Forced Migration and the Making of the Modern World*. Berkeley: University of California Press, 2007.

Clarence-Smith, William Gervase. *Islam and the Abolition of Slavery*. London: Hurst, 2006.

Clough, Benjamin. *A Sinhalese-English Dictionary*. 1830. Colombo: Wesleyan Mission Press Kollupitiya, 1892. https://archive.org/details/sinhaleseenglishoo clourich.

Cody, Francis. "Inscribing Subjects to Citizenship: Petitions, Literacy, Activism, and the Performativity of Signature in Rural Tamil India." *Cultural Anthropology* 24, no. 3 (2009): 347–80.

Cohn, B. S. "The Census, Social Structure and Objectification in South Asia." In *An Anthropologist Among Historians*, 224–54. New Delhi: Oxford University Press, 1987.

Cole, Anna, and Anna Haebich. "Corporeal Colonialism and Corporal Punishment: A Cross-cultural Perspective on Body Modification." *Social Semiotics* 17, no. 3 (2007): 293–311.

Comaroff, John L., and Jean Comaroff. *Of Revelation and Revolution*. Vol. 2: *The Dialectics of Modernity on a South African Frontier*. Chicago: Chicago University Press, 2009.

Cooper, Frederick. "Conditions Analogue to Slavery: Imperialism and Free Labour Ideology in Africa." In *Beyond Slavery: Explorations of Race, Labor, and*

Citizenship in Postemancipaton Societies, ed. Frederick Cooper, Thomas C. Holt, and Rebecca J. Scott, 107–50. Chapel Hill: University of North Carolina Press, 2000.

Cooper, Frederick, Thomas C. Holt, and Rebecca J. Scott. *Beyond Slavery: Explorations of Race, Labor and Citizenship in Postemancipation Societies*. Chapel Hill: The University of North Carolina Press, 2000.

Cooper, Fredrick, and Ann Laura Stoler, eds. *Tensions of Empire: Colonial Cultures in a Bourgeois World*. Berkeley: University of California Press, 1997.

Corbin, Alain. *Le Village des Cannibales*. Paris: Aubier, 1990.

Cordiner, James. *A Description of Ceylon: Containing an Account of the Country, Inhabitants, and Natural Productions: with narratives of a tour round the island in 1800, the campaign in Candy in 1803, and a journey to Ramisseram in 1804*. Vol. 1. London: Longman, Hurst, Rees and Orme, 1807.

Craton, Michael. *Testing the Chains: Resistance to Slavery in the British West Indies*. Ithaca, N.Y.: Cornell University Press, 2009.

Curtis, Bruce. "On the Local Construction of Statistical Knowledge: Making Up the 1861 Census of the Canadas." *Journal of Historical Sociology* 7, no. 4 (1994): 416–34.

———. "Surveying the Social: Techniques, Practice, Power." *Histories Social/Social History* 65, no. 39 (2002): 83–108.

Daalmans, Egidius. "Notes on Ceylon." *Journal of the Ceylon Branch of the Royal Asiatic Society* 10, no. 35 (1885): 145–74.

Dale, S. F. *The Mappilas of Malabar, 1498–1922: Islamic Society of the South Asian Frontier*. Oxford: Clarendon Press, 1980.

Daniel, E. Valentine, Henry Bernstein, and Tom Brass, eds. *Plantations, Proletarians and Peasants in Colonial Asia*. London: Frank Cass, 1992.

Daniel, K. *Mirage, Kanal*. Colombo: Kumaran Book House, 2016.

Das, Veena. *Life and Words: Violence and the Descent Into the Ordinary*. Berkeley: University of California Press, 2006.

David, Kenneth. "The Bound and the Nonbound: Variations in Social and Cultural Structure in Rural Jaffna, Ceylon." Ph.D. dissertation, University of Chicago, 1972.

Davis, Charles T., and Henry Louis Gates, Jr., eds. *The Slave's Narrative*. New York: Oxford University Press, 1985.

Davis, David Brion. *The Problem of Slavery in the Age of Revolution 1770–1823*. New York: Oxford University Press, 1999.

de Alwis, Malathi. "'Respectability,' 'Modernity' and the Policing of 'Culture' in Colonial Ceylon." In *Gender Sexuality and Colonial Modernities*, ed. Antoinette Burton, 179–94. London: Routledge, 1999.

de Certeau, Michel. *L'Invention du Quotidien*. Vol. 1: *"Arts de Faire."* Paris: Gallimard, 1990.

Denham, E. B. *Ceylon at the Census of 1911: Being the Review of the Results of the Census of 1911*. Colombo: H. C. Cottle, 1911.

de Silva, Chandra R. "The First Portuguese Revenue Register of the Kingdom of Kotte—1599." *Ceylon Journal of Historical and Social Studies*, New Series, 5, no. 1–2 (January–December 1975): 71–153.

de Silva, Chandra R., and S. Pathmanathan, "The Kingdom of Jaffna up to 1620." In *University of Peradeniya: History of Sri Lanka*, ed. K. M de Silva. Vol. 2, 105–21. Dehiwela: Sridevi, 1995.

de Silva, Colvin R. *Ceylon Under the British Occupation 1795–1833: Its Political and Administrative Development*. Vols. 1–2. Colombo: Navrang with Lake House Book Shop, 1995.

de Silva, G.P.S.H. "A Chronological Survey of Sinhalese Lexicographical Works in Ceylon During the Period 1800–1950." *Vidyalaya Journal of Arts, Science and Letters* 1, no. 1 (1968): 1–28.

de Silva, K. M. *A History of Sri Lanka*. New Delhi: Oxford University Press, 1981.

——. *Social Policy and Missionary Organizations in Ceylon 1840–1855*. London: Longmans, Green, 1965.

de Silva, M. U. "Land Tenure, Caste System and the Rajakariya Under Foreign Rule: A Review of Change in Sri Lanka Under Western Powers, 1597–1832." *Journal of the Royal Asiatic Society of Sri Lanka*, New Series 37 (1992/93): 1–57.

de Silva, Nalin. *Demala Janathava ge Sangshipath Ithihasaya* (A concise history of the Tamil people). Boralasgamuwa: Visidunu Press, 2009.

——. *Demala Jathivadayata Erehiva* (Against Tamil nationalism). Maharagama: Chintana parshpadaya, n.d.).

——. "Pravada naitiva baitakene sinhalayo." http://www1.kalaya.org.

de Silva Jayasuriya, Shihan. "A Forgotten Minority: The Afro-Sri Lankans." *African and Asian Studies* 6 (2007): 227–42.

de Silva Jayasuriya, Shihan, and Jean Pierre Angenot, eds. *Uncovering the History of Africans in Asia*. Leiden: Brill, 2008.

de Zwart, Pim. "Population, Labour and Living Standards in Early Modern Ceylon." *Indian Economic and Social History Review* 49, no. 3 (2012): 365–98.

Derrida, Jacques. *Demeure: Fiction and Testimony*, trans. E. Rottenberg. Stanford, Calif.: Stanford University Press, 2000.

——. *The Kandyan Kingdom of Sri Lanka, 1707–1782*. Colombo: Lake House, 1988.

Dewaraja, L. S. "The Kandyan Kingdom 1638–1739: A Survey of its Political History." In *History of Ceylon c1500 to c1800*, ed. K. M de Silva. Vol. 2, 183–209. Peradenya: University of Peradeniya, 1995.

——. *The Muslims of Sri Lanka: One Thousand Years of Ethnic Harmony 900–1915*. Colombo: Lanka Islamic Foundation, 1994.

Dewasiri, N. R. *The Adaptable Peasant: Agrarian Society in Western Sri Lanka Under Dutch Rule, 1740–1800.* Leiden: Brill, 2008.

Digby, W. *Forty Years of Official and Unofficial Life in an Oriental Crown Colony.* Vol. 1. Madras: Higginbotham, 1879.

Diouf, Sylviane A. *Slavery's Exiles: The Story of the American Maroons.* New York: New York University Press, 2016.

Dirks, Nicholas. *Castes of Mind: Colonialism and the Making of Modern India.* Princeton, N.J.: Princeton University Press, 1992.

———. *The Price of Emancipation: Slave-Ownership, Compensation and British Society at the End of Slavery.* Cambridge: Cambridge University Press, 2010.

Draper, N. "'Possessing Slaves': Ownership, Compensation and Metropolitan Society in Britain at the Time of Emancipation, 1834–40." *History Workshop Journal* 64, no. 1 (2007): 74–102.

Drescher, Seymour. *The Mighty Experiment: Free Labor Versus Slavery in British Emancipation.* New York: Oxford University Press, 2002.

Duncan, James. *In the Shadows of the Tropics: Climate, Race and Biopower in Nineteenth Century Ceylon.* London: Routledge, 2007.

Ekama, Kate. "Runaway Slaves from the VOC Cape." In *Desertion in the Early Modern World: A Comparative History,* ed. Matthias van Rossum and Jeannette Kamp, 161–84. London: Bloomsbury, 2016.

———. "Slavery in Dutch Colombo: A Social History." M.A. thesis, Leiden University, 2012.

Eltis, David, and Stanley L. Engerman, eds. *The Cambridge World History of Slavery.* Vol 3: *AD 1420–AD 1804.* Cambridge: Cambridge University Press, 2011.

Ennaji, Muhammad. *Serving the Master: Slavery and Society in Nineteenth Century Morocco.* London: Macmillan, 1999.

Ernatus Cecile. "L'indemnité Coloniale en Guadeloupe, Guyane et Martiique entre 1848 et 1860: Monnaie de Pierre, Monnaie de Sable, Monnaie de Sang." Ph.D dissertation, Universite de Paris X-Nanterre, 2004.

Esteve, M. E. and Philippe Fabri, eds. *Quelques Notions sur l'Isle de Ceylan. Eudelin de Jonville.* Hambantota: Viator, 2012.

Fernando, Benjamin Walter. *Ceylon Currency, British Period 1796–1936.* New Delhi: Asian Educational Services, 1939.

Fisher, Michael. "Representation of India, the English East India Company, and Self by an Eighteenth-Century Indian Emigrant to Britain." *Modern Asian Studies* 32, no. 4 (1998): 891–911.

Flores, Jorge Manuel, ed. *Re-exploring the Links: History and Constructed Histories Between Portugal and Sri Lanka.* Wiesbaden: Harrassowitz Verlag, 2007.

Ford, Lisa. "Anti-Slavery and the Reconstitution of Empire." *Australian Historical Studies* 45, no. 1 (2014): 71–86.

Foucault, Michel. *Discipline and Punish: The Birth of the Prison.* 2d ed. New York: Vintage, 1995.

——. *The Order of Things: An Archaeology of the Human Sciences.* New York: Vintage, 1970.

——. "The Subject and Power." *Critical Inquiry* 8, no. 4 (1982): 777–95.

Franklin, John Hope, and Loren Schweninger. *Runaway Slaves: Rebels on the Plantation.* New York: Oxford University Press, 2000.

Freamon, Bernard K. "Conceptions of Equality and Slavery in Islamic Law: Tribalism, Piety and Pluralism." Ph.D. dissertation, Columbia University, 2007.

Gandhi, Leela. *Postcolonial Theory: A Critical Introduction.* New York: Columbia University Press, 1998.

Genovese, Eugene D. *From Rebellion to Revolution: Afro-American Slave Revolts in the Making of the Modern World.* Baton Rouge: Louisiana State University Press, 1979.

Ghosh, Amitav. *In an Antique Land.* New York: Knopf, 1992.

Ghosh, Shrimoyee, "Of Truth and Taxes. A Material History of Early Stamp't Paper." In *Iterations of Law: Legal Histories from India*, ed. Aparna Balachandran, Rashmi Pant, and Bhavani Raman, 210–41. Oxford: Oxford University Press, 2017.

Gilmartin, David. "Colonialism and Irrigation Technology in the Indus Basin." *Journal of Asian Studies* 53, no. 4 (1994): 1127–49.

Glissant, Edouard. *Introduction à une Poetique du divers.* Paris: Gallimard, 1996.

Goonewardena, K.W. *The Foundation of Dutch Power in Ceylon 1638–1658.* Amsterdam: Djambatan, 1958.

Gordon, Avery F. *Ghostly Matters: Haunting and the Sociological Imagination.* Minneapolis: University of Minnesota Press, 2008.

Government of Ceylon. *A Collection of the Legislative Acts of His Majesty's Government of Ceylon: Containing Proclamations and Regulations Issued Since 15th January 1799, and Wholly, or in Part in Force, on 31st May 1821, Arranged Under Their Various Heads.* Colombo: Printed at the Government Press by N. Bergman, 1821.

——. *A Collection of the Legislative Acts of HM's Government of Ceylon: Containing Proclamations and Regulations Issued Since 1st January 1799.* Colombo: Government Office, 1854.

Gray White, Deborah. *Ar'n't I a Woman? Female Slaves in the Plantation South.* New York: Norton, 1985.

Green, William A. *British Slave Emancipation: The Sugar Colonies and the Great Experiment.* Oxford: Clarendon Press, 1991.

Guha, Ranajit. *Elementary Aspects of Peasant Insurgency in Colonial India*, New Delhi: Oxford University Press 1983.

———. "The Prose of Counterinsurgency." In *Selected Subaltern Studies*, ed. Ranajit Guha and Gayathri Spivak, 45–86. New York: Oxford University Press, 1988.

Gunawardana, R.A.L.H. *Robe and Plough: Monasticism and Economic Interest in Early Medieval Sri Lanka*. Tucson: University of Arizona Press, 1979.

Gutierrez Rodriguez, Encarnación, and Shirley Anne Tate, eds. *Creolizing Europe: Legacies and Transformations*. Liverpool: University of Liverpool Press, 2015.

Hagerdal, Hans. *Lords of the Land, Lords of the Sea. Conflict and Adaptation in Early Colonial Timor, 1600–1800*. Leiden: KITLV Press, 2012.

Hannerz, Ulf. "The World in Creolisation." *Africa: Journal of the International African Institute* 57, no. 4 (1987): 546–59.

Harms, R., B. K. Freamon and D. W. Blight, eds. *Indian Ocean Slavery in the Age of Abolition*. New Haven, Conn.: Yale University Press, 2013.

Harper, Kyle. *Slavery in the Late Roman World, AD 275–425*. Cambridge: Cambridge University Press, 2011.

Hartman, Saidiya. "Venus in Two Acts." *Small Axe* 12, no. 2 (June 2008).

Haslam, Emily. "Redemption, Colonialism and International Criminal Law." In *Past Law, Present Histories*, ed. Diane Kirkby, 7–22. Canberra: ANU Press, 2012.

Heesterman, J. C. "Littoral et Interieur de l'Inde." *Itinerario* 4, no. 1 (1980): 87–92.

Heidegger, Martin. *Being and Time*. New York: Harper and Row, 1962.

Herzfeld, Michael. *The Social Production of Indifference: Exploring the Symbolic Roots of Western Bureaucracy*. Oxford: Berg, 1992.

Higman, B. W. "Population and Labor in the British Caribbean in the Early Nineteenth Century." In *Long Term Factors in American Economic Growth*, ed. Stanley L. Engerman and Robert E. Gallman, 605–39. Chicago: University of Chicago Press, 1986.

———. *Slave Population and Economy in Jamaica, 1807–1834*. Kingston: University of the West Indies Press, 1995.

Ho, Engseng. *The Graves of Tarim: Genealogy and Mobility Across the Indian Ocean*. Berkeley: University of California Press, 2006.

Hochschild, J. L., and B. M. Powell. "Racial Reorganization and the United States Census 1850–1930: Mulattoes, Half-Breeds, Mixed Parentage, Hindoos and the Mexican Race." *Studies in American Political Development* 22, no.1 (2008): 59–96.

Holland Rose, John, ed. *The Cambridge History of the British Empire*. Vol. 2. Cambridge: Cambridge University Press, 1940.

Holt, John Clifford, ed. *The Sri Lanka Reader: History, Culture, Politics*. Durham, N.C: Duke University Press, 2011.

Hovy, L. *Ceylonees Plakkaatboek: Plakkaten en andere Wetten uitgevaardigd door het Nederlandse Bestuur op Ceylon, 1638–1796*. Vols. 1–2. Hilversum: Verloren, 1991.

Huisman, Marijke. "Beyond the Subject: Anglo-American Slave Narratives in the Netherlands, 1789–2013." *European Journal of Life Writing* 4 (2015): VC56–84.

Hull, Mathew. *Government of Paper: The Materiality of Bureaucracy in Urban Pakistan.* Berkeley: University of California Press, 2012.

Hussaimmiya, B. A. *Orang Rejimen: The Malays of the Ceylon Rifle Regiment.* Bangi: University Kebangsaan Malaysia, 1990.

Hussain, Asif. *Sarandib: An Ethnological Study of the Muslims of Sri Lanka.* Dehiwela: AJ Prints, 2007.

Ikegame, Aya. *Princely India Re-imagined: A Historical Anthropology of Mysore from 1799 to the Present.* London: Routledge, 2013.

Indrapala, K. "The Origin of the Tamil Vanni Chieftancies of Ceylon." *Ceylon Journal of the Humanities* 1, no. 2 (1970): 111–40.

Janse, M. "'Holland as a Little England'? British Anti-Slavery Missionaries and Continental Abolitionist Movements in the Mid Nineteenth Century." *Past and Present* 229, no. 1 (2015): 123–60.

Jayawardena, V. K. *Erasure of the Euro-Asian. Recovering Early Radicalism and Feminism in South Asia*, Colombo: Social Scientists' Association, 2007.

———. *From Nobodies to Somebodies: The Rise of the Colonial Bourgeoisie in Sri Lanka.* London: Zed, 2000.

———. *The Rise of the Labor Movement in Ceylon.* Durham, N.C.: Duke University Press, 1972.

Jayawardene, Sureshi M. "Racialized Casteism: Exposing the Relationship Between Race, Caste, and Colorism Through the Experiences of Africana People in India and Sri Lanka."*Journal of African American Studies* 20 (2016): 323–45.

Johnston, Sir Alexander. "Introduction of Trial by Jury and Abolition of Slavery." In *The Oriental Herald and Journal of General Literature*, ed. J. S. Buckingham, 16, no. 49 (1828): 131–36.

Kabristan Archives. Ireland-Ceylon-India Genealogy. Dutch Reformed Church, Wolvendaal. Colombo Marriages, vols. 1–2. https://www.kabristan.org.uk/.

Kannangara, A. P. *A Survey of Social Change in an Imperial Regime.* Colombo: Vijitha Yapa, 2011.

Kannangara, P. D. *The History of the Ceylon Civil Service, 1802–1833.* Dehiwela: Tisara Press, 1966.

Karunatilake, H. N. S. "Social and Economic Statistics of Sri Lanka in the Nineteenth Century." *Royal Asiatic Society of Sri Lanka Branch New Series* 31 (1986/87): 40–61.

Kenneth, Morgan. "The Struggle for Survival: Slave Infant Mortality in the British Caribbean in the Late Eighteenth and Nineteenth Centuries." In *Children* in *Slavery Through the Ages*, ed. Gwyn Campbell, Suzanne Miers, and Joseph C. Miller, 187–203. Athens: Ohio University Press, 2009.

Kiribamune, S. "Muslims and the Trade of the Arabian Sea with Special Reference to Sri Lanka from the Birth of Islam to the Fifteenth Century." In *Muslims of Sri Lanka: Avenues to Antiquity*, ed. M. A. M. Shukri, 89–112. Beruwela: Jamiah Naleemia Institute, 1986.

Klein, Martin A. "Looking for Slavery in Colonial Archives." In *African Voices on Slavery and the Slave Trade*, ed. A. Bellagamba, S. Greene, and M. Klein, 114–31. Cambridge: Cambridge University Press, 2016.

Knaap, Gerrit. "Europeans, Mestizos and Slaves: The Population of Colombo at the End of the Seventeenth Century." *Itinerario* 5, no. 2 (1981): 84–101.

Kolsky, Elizabeth. "Codification and the Rule of Colonial Difference: Criminal Procedure in British India." *Law and History Review* 23, no. 3 (2005): 631–83.

Koolhof, Sirtjo, and Robert Ross. "Upas, September and the Bugis at the Cape of Good Hope: The Context of a Slave Letter." *Archipel* 70 (2005): 280–308.

Kotelawele, D. A. "Muslims Under Dutch Rule in Sri Lanka 1638–1796." In *Muslims of Sri Lanka: Avenues of Antiquity*, ed. M. A. M. Shukri, 167–88. Beruwela: Jamiaah Naleemia Institute, 1986.

Kuganathan, Prashant. "Social Stratification in Jaffna: A Survey of Recent Research on Caste." *Sociology Compass* 8, no. 1 (2014): 78–88.

Kurian, Rachel, and Kumari Jayawardena. *Class, Patriarchy and Ethnicity on Sri Lankan Plantations: Two Centuries of Power and Protest*. New Delhi: Orient Blackswan, 2015.

Laffan, Michael. "Finding Java: Muslim Nomenclature of Insular Southeast Asia from Srivijaya to Snouck Hurgronje." In *Southeast Asia and the Middle East: Islam, Movement and the Longue Duree*, ed. Eric Tagliacozzo, 17–64. Singapore: NUS, 2009.

——. "From Javanese Court to African Grave: How Noriman Became Tuan Skapie, 1717–1806." *Journal of Indian Ocean World Studies* 1 (2017): 38–59.

Land, Isaac. "Bread and Arsenic: Citizenship from the Bottom up in Georgian London." *Journal of Social History* 39, no. 1 (2005): 93–94.

Larson, Pier M. "Horrid Journeying: Narratives of Enslavement and the Global African Diaspora." *Journal of World History* 19, no. 4 (2008): 431–64.

——. "The Vernacular Life of the Street: Ratsitatanina and Indian Ocean Creolite." *Slavery and Abolition* 29, no. 3 (2008): 327–59.

Levitan, Kathrin. *A Cultural History of the British Census: Envisioning the Multitude in the Nineteenth Century*. Basingstoke, UK: Palgrave Macmillan, 2011.

Lewis, Bernard. *The Political Language of Islam*. Chicago: University of Chicago Press, 1991.

Lewis, John Penry. *Manual of the Vanni Districts, Vavuniya and Mullaitivu, of the Northern Province, Ceylon.* London: British Library Historical Prints Editions, 1895.

Lombard, Denys. *Le Carrefour Javanais: Essai Historique d'Histoire Globale.* Paris: Editions de l'EHESS, 1990.

Lucassen, Jan. "Free and Unfree Labour Before the Twentieth Century: A Brief Overview." In *Free and Unfree Labour: The Debate Continues*, ed. Tom Brass and Marcel van der Linden, 45–56. Bern: Peter Lang, 2000.

Luster, Robert Edward. "The Amelioration of the Slaves in the British Empire, 1790–1833." Ph.D. dissertation, New York University, 1988.

Machado, Pedro. "A Forgotten Corner of the Indian Ocean: Gujarati Merchants, Portuguese Indian and the Mozambique Slave Trade, c 1730–1830." In *Structure of Slavery in Indian Ocean Africa and Asia*, ed. Gwyn Campbell, 16–34. London: Routledge, 2004.

———. *Oceans of Trade: South Asian Merchants, Africa and the Indian Ocean, c 1750–1850.* Cambridge: Cambridge University Press, 2014.

Mahindapala, H. L. D. "Jaffna: The Hell-Hole of Persecuted & Oppressed Tamil Slaves." *Colombo Telegraph*, May 2, 2016.

———. "*Mirage*: The Great Tamil Novel of Our Time." *Sunday Times*, March 26, 2017.

Major, Andrea. *Slavery, Abolitionism and Empire in India 1772–1843.* Liverpool: Liverpool University Press, 2012.

Malte-Brun, Conrad. *Universal Geography: or A Description of all Parts of the World, on a New Plan, According to the Great Natural Divisions of the Globe.* Vols. 1–2. Philadelphia: A. Finley, 1827.

Marcelline, Sanayi. "Labouring for Salt: Convict Workers in the Levayas of Magampattu, in the Early 19th Century." Unpublished manuscript.

Marlow, Louise. *Hierarchy and Egalitarianism in Islamic Thought.* Cambridge: Cambridge University Press, 1997.

Marshall, Peter. "The Whites of British India 1780–1830: A Failed Colonial Society?" *International History Review* 12, no. 1 (1995): 26–44.

Martin, Robert Montgomery. *Statistics of the Colonies of the British Empire, from the Official Records of the Colonial Office.* London: Allen, 1839.

Martinez, Jenny. "Anti-slavery Courts and the Dawn of International Human Rights Law." *Yale Law Journal* 117 (2007): 1–98.

Mbeki, Linda, and Matthias van Rossum. "Private Slave Trade in the Dutch Indian Ocean World: A Study Into the Networks and Backgrounds of the Slavers and the Enslaved in South Asia and South Africa." *Slavery & Abolition: A Journal of Slave and Post-Slave Studies* 38 (2017): 95–116.

Mbembe, Achille. *Critique de la Raison Nègre.* Paris: La Decouverte, 2013.

McClintock, Anne. *Imperial Leather: Race, Gender and Sexuality in the Colonial Contest.* New York: Routledge, 1995.

McDow, Thomas F. "Deeds of Freed Slaves: Manumission and Economic and Social Mobility in Pre-Abolition Zanzibar." In *Indian Ocean Slavery in the Age of Abolition*, ed. Robert Harms et al., 160–83. New Haven, Conn.: Yale University Press, 2013.

McGilvray, Dennis. "Arabs, Moors, and Muslims: Sri Lanka Muslim Ethnicity in Regional Perspective." *Contributions to Indian Sociology* 32, no. 2 (1998): 433–83.

———. "Sri Lankan Muslims: Between Ethnic Nationalism and the Global Ummah." *Nations and Nationalism* 17, no. 1 (2011): 45–64.

McGilvray, Dennis, and Mirak Raheem. "Origin of the Sri Lankan Muslims and Varieties of the Muslim Identity." In *The Sri Lanka Reader: History, Culture, Politics*, ed. John Clifford Holt, 410–19. Durham, N.C.: Duke University Press, 2011.

Mendis, G. C. *The Colebrooke-Cameron Papers: Documents on British Colonial Policy in Ceylon 1796–1833.* 2 vols. London: Oxford University Press, 1956.

Menon, Dilip M. *A Place Elsewhere. Lower-Caste Malayalam Novels of the Nineteenth Century.* In *India's Literary History: Essays on the Nineteenth Century*, ed. S. H. Blackburn and V. Dalmia, 483–515. Delhi: Permanent Black, 2004.

Meyer, Eric. "Labour Circulation Between Sri Lanka and South India in Historical Perspective." In *Society and Circulation: Mobile People and Itinerant Cultures in South Asia*, ed. C. Markovits, Jacques Pouchepadasss, and Sanjay Subramanyam, 55–88. London: Anthem Press, 2006.

Miers, Suzanne, and Igor Kopytoff. *Slavery in Africa: Historical and Anthropological Perspectives.* Madison: University of Wisconsin Press, 1977.

Mills, Lennox. *Ceylon Under British Rule.* London: Oxford University Press, 1933.

Mitchell, Timothy. "The Limits of the State: Beyond Statist Approaches and Their Critics." *American Political Science Review* 85, no. 1 (1991): 77–96.

Mizutani, Satoshi. "Historicising Whiteness: From the Case of Late Colonial India." *ACRAWSA* 2, no. 1 (2006): 1–15.

Mohan, P. Sanal. *Modernity of Slavery: Struggles Against Caste Inequality in Colonial Kerala.* Oxford: Oxford University Press, 2015.

Moldrich, Donovan. *Bitter Berry Bondage: The Nineteenth Century Coffee Workers of Sri Lanka.* Kandy: Co-ordinating Secretariat for Plantation Areas, 1989.

Mooyaart, Anthony, *Memoir of Anthony Mooyaart, Commandeur of Jaffnapatam for the Information and Guidance of His Successor Noel Anthony Lebeck*, trans. Sophia Pieters. 1766. Colombo: H. C. Cottle, 1910.

Morrison, Toni. *Beloved.* New York: Knopf, 1987.

Mukund, Kanakalatha. "Caste Conflict in South India in Early Colonial Port Cities—1650–1800." *Studies in History* 11, no. 1 (1995): 1–27.

Murray, Jessica. "Gender and Violence in Cape Slave Narratives and Post-Narratives." *South African Historical Journal* 62, no. 3 (2010): 444–62.

Murray, J., and R. Shell. *Children of Bondage: A Social History of the Slave Society at the Cape of Good Hope 1652–1838.* Johannesburg: Witwatersrand University Press, 1994.

Nadaraja, T. *The Legal System of Ceylon in its Historical Setting.* Leiden: Brill, 1972.

Naidis, Mark. "The Abolitionists and Indian Slavery." *Journal of Asian History* 15, no. 2 (1981): 146–58.

Nandy, Ashis. *Intimate Enemy: Loss and Recovery of Self Under Colonialism.* Delhi: Oxford University Press, 1983.

Nawawi, en. Mahiudin. *Minhaj et Talibin: A Manual of Muhammadan Law According to the School of Shafii*, trans. E. C. Howard. London: Thacker, 1914.

New Zealand. Blue Book of Statistics. 1840. http://www.archives.govt.nz.

Northrup, David. "Becoming African: Identity Formation Among Liberated Slaves in Nineteenth-Century Sierra Leone." *Slavery and Abolition* 27, no. 1 (2006): 1–21.

Nwulia, N. *The History of Slavery in Mauritius and the Seychelles, 1810–1875.* East Brunswick, N.J.: Fairleigh Dickenson University Press, 1981.

Obeysekere, Gananath. "The Coming of the Brahmin Migrants: The Sudra Fate of an Indian Elite in Sri Lanka." *Society and Culture in South Asia* 1, no. 1 (2016): 1–32.

———. "The Conscience of the Parricide: A Study in Buddhist History." *Man*, New Series 24, no. 2 (1989): 236–54.

———. *The Cult of the Goddess Pattini.* Chicago: University of Chicago Press, 1984.

———. *The Doomed King: A Requiem for Sri Vickrama Rajasinha.* Colombo: Perera-Hussein, 2017.

———. "Representations of the Wild Man in Sri Lanka." In *Beyond Primitivism: Indigenous Religious Traditions and Modernity*, ed. J. K. Olupona, 272–95. New York: Routledge, 2004.

———. "The Ritual Drama of the Sanni Demons: Collective Representations of Disease in Ceylon." *Comparative Studies in Society and History* 2 (1969): 174–216.

Oostindie, Gert, ed. *Dutch Colonialism, Migration and Cultural Heritage: Past and Present.* Leiden: Brill, 2008.

———. *Fifty Years Later: Antislavery, Capitalism and Modernity in the Dutch Orbit.* Leiden: KITLV Press, 1995.

Palm, Rev. J. D. "The Educational Establishments of the Dutch in Ceylon." *Journal of the Dutch Burgher Union* 29, no. 2 (1939): 44–51.

Panditharatne, B. L., and S. Selvanayagam, "The Demography of Ceylon. An Introductory Survey." In *History of Ceylon*. Vol. 3: *From the Beginning of the Nineteenth Century to 1948*, ed. K. M. de Silva, 285–302. Peradeniya: University of Peradeniya, 1973.

Pant, Rashmi. "The Cognitive Status of Caste in Colonial Ethnography: A Review of Some Literature on the North West Provinces and Oudh." *Indian Economic and Social History Review* 24, no. 2 (1987): 145–62.

Paranavitana, K. D. "The Portuguese Tombos as a Source of Sixteenth and Seventeenth Century Sri Lankan History." In *Re-exploring the Links: History and Constructed Histories Between Portugal and Sri Lanka*, ed. Jorge Manuel Flores, 63–78. Wiesbaden: Harrassowitz, 2007.

Pathmanathan, S. "Feudal Polity in Medieval Ceylon: An Examination of the Chieftancies of the Vanni." *Ceylon Journal of Historical and Social Studies* 2 (1972): 118–30.

Patterson, Orlando. *The Sociology of Slavery: An Analysis of the Origins, Development, and Structure of Negro Slave Society in Jamaica*. London: MacGibbon and Kee, 1967.

——. *Slavery and Social Death: A Comparative Study*. Cambridge, Mass.: Harvard University Press, 1982.

Peabody, Norbert. "Cents, Sense, Census: Human Inventories in Late Precolonial and Early Colonial India." *Comparative Studies in Society and History* 43, no. 4 (2001): 819–50.

Peabody, Sue. *Madeleine's Children: Family, Freedom, Secrets, and Lies in France's Indian Ocean Colonies*. New York: Oxford University Press, 2017.

Pearson, Michael. "Littoral Society: the Case for the Coast." *Great Circle* 7 (1985): 1–8.

Peebles, Patrick. *History of Sri Lanka*. Westport: Greenwood, 2006.

——. "Land Use and Population Growth in Colonial Ceylon." *Contributions to Asian Studies* 6 (1976): 64–79.

——. *The Plantation Tamils of Ceylon*. London: Leicester University Press, 2001.

——. *Social Change in Nineteenth Century Ceylon*. New Delhi: Navrang, 1995.

Peggs, James. *Slavery in India: The Present State of East India Slavery: Chiefly Extracted from the Parliamentary Papers on the Subject*. 3rd ed. London: Wightman, 1840.

Peiris, Anoma. *Architecture and Nationalism in Sri Lanka: The Trouser Under the Cloth*. New York: Routledge, 2012.

Pels, Peter. "The Anthropology of Colonialism: Culture, History and the Emergence of Western Governmentality." *Annual Review of Anthropology* 26, no. 1 (1997): 163–83.

Penn, Nigel. "The Voyage Out: Peter Kolb and VOC Voyages to the Cape." In *Many Middle Passages: Forced Migration and the Making of the Modern World*, ed. Emma Christopher et al., 72–91. Berkeley: University of California Press, 2007.

Percival, Robert. *An Account of the Island of Ceylon Containing Its History, Geography, Natural History, with the Manners and Customs of Its Various Inhabitants*. London: C. and R. Baldwin, 1803; reprint New Delhi: Asian Educational Services, 1990.

Perera, Nihal. "Indigenising the Colonial City: Late 19th Century Colombo and Its Landscape." *Urban Studies* 39, no. 9 (2002): 1703–21.

Perniola, V. *The Catholic Church in Sri Lanka: The Dutch Period.* Vol. 1: *1658–1711.* (Original documents translated into English.) Dehiwela: Tisara Press, 1983.

Pfaffenberger, Bryan. *Caste in Tamil Culture: The Religious Foundations of Sudra Domination in Tamil Sri Lanka.* Syracuse, N.Y.: Syracuse University Press, 1982.

Pielat, Jacob Christian. *Memoir to his Successor Diderik Van Domburg (1734),* trans. Sophia Pieters. Colombo: Government Printer, 1905.

Pieris, P. E., ed. *Ceylon. The Portuguese Era: Being a History of the Island for the Period 1505–1658.* Colombo: Colombo Apothecaries, 1913/1914.

——. *Notes on Some Sinhalese Families.* Parts 1–4. Colombo: Apothecaries, 1902/1911.

Pieris, Ralph. *Sinhalese Social Organization: The Kandyan Period.* Colombo: Ceylon University Press Board, 1956.

Prakash, Gyan. *Bonded Histories: Genealogies of Labor Servitude in Colonial India.* Cambridge: Cambridge University Press, 1993.

——. "Colonialism, Capitalism and the Discourse of Freedom." *International Review of Social History* 41 (1996): 9–25.

Prange, Sebastian R. *Monsoon Islam: Trade and Faith on the Medieval Malabar Coast.* Cambridge: Cambridge University Press, 2018.

Prasad, Vijay. *The Darker Nations: A People's History of the Third World.* New York: New Press, 2007.

Raben, Remco. "Batavia and Colombo: The Ethnic and Spatial Order of Two Colonial Cities 1600–1800." Ph.D dissertation, Leiden University, 1996.

Raheem, Ismeth. *Views of Colombo (1518–1900).* Colombo: Lake House, 1984.

Raman, Bhavani. *Document Raj. Writing and Scribes in Early Colonial South India.* Chicago: University of Chicago Press, 2012.

Ramanathan, P. "The Ethnology of the 'Moors' of Ceylon." *Journal of the Royal Asiatic Society, Ceylon Branch* 10, no. 36 (1888): 234–62.

Rambukwella, Harshana. *The Poetics and Politics of Authenticity: A Cultural Genealogy of Sinhala Nationalism.* London: UCL Press, 2018.

Ramey Berry, Daina. *The Price for Their Pound of Flesh: The Value of the Enslaved, from Womb to Grave, in the Building of a Nation.* Boston: Beacon Press, 2017.

Ranciere, Jacques. *The Method of Equality: Interviews with Laurent Jeanpierre and Dork Zabunyan.* Hoboken, N.J.: Wiley, 2016.

Rao, Velchuru Narayana, David Shulman, and Sanjay Subrahmanyam. *Textures of Time: Writing History in South India 1600–1800.* New York: Other Press, 2003.

Rasanayagam C. *Ancient Jaffna: Being a Research Into the History of Jaffna from Very Early Times to the Portuguese Period.* 1926. New Delhi: Asian Educational Services, 1984.

Reid, Anthony. "Slavery and Forced Labour in Asia: Status Quaestionis." Keynote address, Slavery Association Conference. Leiden, June 2017.
Report of the Directors of the African Institution. Appendix G, Proceedings Under the Slave Trade Felony Act in the Island of Ceylon. London, 1812/13.
Ricci, Ronit, ed. *Exile in Colonial Asia: Kings, Convicts, Commemoration*. Honolulu: University of Hawaii Press, 2016.
——. *Islam Translated: Literature, Conversion, and the Arabic Cosmopolis of South and Southeast Asia*. Chicago: University of Chicago Press, 2011.
——. "Jawa, Melayu, Malay or Otherwise: The Shifting Nomenclature of the Sri Lankan Malays." *Indonesia and the Malay World* 44, no. 130 (2016): 1–15.
——. "Remembering Java's Islamization: A View from Sri Lanka."*Asia Research Institute Working Paper* no. 153 (2011).
Ricoeur, Paul. *Memory, History, Forgetting*, trans. Kathleen Blamey and David Pellauer. Chicago: University of Chicago Press, 2004.
Roberts, Michael. *Caste Conflict and Elite Formation: The Rise of a Karava Elite in Sri Lanka*. Cambridge: Cambridge University Press, 1982.
——. "The Collective Consciousness of the Sinhalese During the Kandyan Era: Manichean Images, Associational Logic." *Asian Ethnicity* 3, no. 1 (2002): 29–46.
Roberts, Michael, et al. *People In Between: Ethnic and Class Prejudices in British Ceylon*. Ratmalana: Sarvodaya, 1989.
Rogers, John D. *Crime, Justice and Society in Colonial Sri Lanka*. London: Curzon Press, 1987.
——. "Early British Rule and Social Classification in Lanka."*Modern Asian Studies* 38, no. 3 (2004): 625–47.
Ross, Robert. *Cape of Torments: Slavery and Resistance in South Africa*. London: Routledge and Kegan Paul, 1983.
——. *Status and Respectability in the Cape Colony 1750–1870. A Tragedy in Manners*. Cambridge: Cambridge University Press, 2004.
Roy, T. "'Sardars, Jobbers, Kanganies': The Labour Contractor and Indian Economic History." *Modern Asian Studies* 42, no. 5 (2008): 971–98.
Rugarli, Anna Maria, and Robert C.-H. Shell. "Historical Relevance?: Ten Sketches of Women Illegally Enslaved at the Cape, 1823 to 1830." *New Contree*, no. 55 (2008), 43–65.
Said, Edward. *Orientalism*. New York: Pantheon, 1978.
Sameer, Fazli, *Muslim Personalities in Sri Lanka Then and Now*. Colombo: Moors Islamic Cultural Home, 1982.
Sanal Mohan, P. *Modernity of Slavery: Struggles Against Caste Inequality in Colonial Kerala*. Oxford: Oxford University Press, 2015.

Sarkar, N. K. *The Demography of Ceylon*. Colombo: Ceylon Government Press, 1957.

Schelinger, P. E., and R. M. Salkin, eds. *International Dictionary of Historic Places: Asia and Oceania*. London: Routledge, 1996.

Schrikker A. F., and K. J. Ekama. *Dutch and British Colonial Intervention in Sri Lanka, 1780–1815: Expansion and Reform*. Leiden: Brill, 2006.

———. "Through the Lens of Slavery: Dutch Sri Lanka in the Eighteenth Century." In *Sri Lanka at the Crossroads of History*, ed. Z. Biedermann and A. Strathern, 178–93. London: UCL Press, 2017.

Schrikker, Alicia. "Caught Between Empires: VOC Families in Sri Lanka After the British Take-over, 1806–1808." *Annales de démographie historique* 122, no. 2 (2011): 127–47.

Schwobel, Christine. *Critical Approaches to International Criminal Law: An Introduction*. London: Routledge, 2014.

Scott, David. *Formations of Ritual: Colonial and Anthropological Discourses on the Sinhala Yaktovil*. Minneapolis: University of Minnesota Press, 1994.

———. "The Paradox of Freedom: An Interview with Orlando Patterson." *Small Axe* 17, no. 1 (2013): 96–242.

———. *Refashioning Futures: Criticism after Postcoloniality*. Princeton, N.J.: Princeton University Press, 1999.

Scott, James. *Domination and the Arts of Resistance: Hidden Transcripts*. New Haven, Conn.: Yale University Press, 1990.

———. *Weapons of the Weak: Everyday Forms of Peasant Resistance*. New Haven, Conn: Yale University Press, 1985.

Scully, Pamela. *Liberating the Family? Gender and British Slave Emancipation in the Rural Western Cape, South Africa, 1823–1853*. Portsmouth, N.H.: Heinemann, 1997.

———. "Narratives of Infanticide in the Aftermath of Slave Emancipation in the Nineteenth-Century Cape Colony, South Africa." *Canadian Journal of African Studies* 30, no. 1 (1996): 88–105.

———. "Rape, Race and Colonial Culture: The Sexual Politics of Identity in the Nineteenth Century Cape Colony, South Africa." *American Historical Review* 100, no. 2 (1995): 335–59.

Selkirk, Rev. James. *Recollections of Ceylon, After a Residence of Nearly Thirteen Years: with an Account of the Church Missionary Society's Operations in the Island and Extracts from a Journal*. Church Missionary Society. London: Hatchard, 1844.

Sen, S. "Commercial Recruiting and Informal Intermediation: Debate Over the Sardari System in Assam Tea Plantations, 1860–1900." *Modern Asian Studies* 44, no. 1 (2010): 3–28.

Seneviratne-Rupasinghe, Nadeera. "Negotiating Custom: Colonial Lawmaking in the Galle Landraad." Ph.D dissertation, Leiden University, 2016.

Seshan, Radhika. *Trade and Politics on the Coromandel Coast: Seventeenth and Early Eighteenth Centuries*. New Delhi: Primus, 2012.

Sharma, Yogesh, ed. *Coastal Histories*. New Delhi: Primus Books, 2010.

Shell, Robert C.-H. *Children of Bondage: A Social History of the Slave Society at the Cape 1652–1838*. Hanover, N.H.: Wesleyan University Press, 1994.

Sheriff, Abdul. *Dhow Cultures of the Indian Ocean: Cosmopolitanism, Commerce and Islam*. London: Hurst, 2010.

Shukri, M. A. M., ed. *Muslims of Sri Lanka: Avenues of Antiquity*. Beruwela: Jamiaah Naleemia Institute, 1986.

Silva, T. K., et al. *Casteless or Caste Blind? Dynamics of Concealed Caste Discrimination, Social Exclusion, and Protest in Sri Lanka*. Copenhagen: International Dalit Solidarity, 2009.

Simmonds, P. L., ed. *Simmond's Colonial Magazine and Foreign Miscellany*. Vol. 1. London: Foreign and Colonial Office, 1844.

Sinha, Mrinali. *Colonial Masculinity: The Manly Englishman and the Effeminate Bengali in the Late Nineteenth Century*. Manchester: Manchester University Press, 1995.

Sivasundaram, Sujit. "Ethnicity, Indigeneity, and Migration in the Advent of British Rule to Sri Lanka." *American Historical Review* 115, no. 2 (April 2010): 428–52.

———. *Islanded: Britain, Sri Lanka and the Bounds of an Indian Ocean Colony*. Chicago: University of Chicago Press, 2013.

———. "Tales of the Land: British Geography and Kandyan Resistance in Sri Lanka, c. 1803–1850." *Modern Asian Studies* 41, no. 5 (2007): 925–65.

Smith, R. S. "Rule-by-Records and Rule-by-Reports: Complementary Aspects of the British Imperial Rule of Law." *Contributions to Indian Sociology* 19, no. 1 (1985): 153–76

Spence, Caroline Quarrier. "Ameliorating Empire: Slavery and Protection in the British Colonies, 1783–1865." Ph.D. dissertation, Harvard University, 2014.

Spivak, Gayathri C. "Can the Subaltern Speak?" In *Marxism and the Interpretation of Culture*, ed. C. Nelson and L. Grossberg, 271–315.Urbana: University of Illinois Press, 1988.

Spores, J. C. *Running Amok: An Historical Inquiry*. Athens: Ohio University/Swallow Press, 1988.

Stanziani, Alessandro. "Beyond Colonialism: Servants, Wage Earners and Indentured Migrants in Rural France and on Reunion Island (c. 1750 –1900)." *Labor History* 54, no. 1 (2013): 64–87.

Steedman, Carolyn. "Something She Called a Fever: Michelet, Derrida, and Dust." *American Historical Review* 106, no. 4 (October 2001).

Stepan, Nancy. *The Idea of Race in Science: Great Britain, 1800–1960*. London: St. Antony's Macmillan Press, 1982.

Stephen, Martin. *Scapegoat: The Death of HMS Prince of Wales and Repulse*. Barnsley: Pen and Sword Books, 2014.

Stoler, Ann Laura. *Along the Archival Grain: Epistemic Anxieties and Colonial Common Sense*. Princeton, N.J.: Princeton University Press, 2009.

———. *Carnal Knowledge and Imperial Power: Race and the Intimate in Colonial Rule*. Berkeley: University of California Press, 2002.

———. "Colonial Aphasia: Race and Disabled Histories in France." *Public Culture* 23, no. 1 (2011): 121–56.

———. "Colonial Archives and the Arts of Governance." *Archival Science* 2 (2002): 87–109.

———. "Rethinking Colonial Categories: European Communities and the Boundaries of Rule." *Comparative Studies in Society and History* 31, no.1 (1989): 134–61.

Stoler, Ann Laura, and F. Cooper. "Between Metropole and Colony: Rethinking a Research Agenda." In *Tensions of Empire: Colonial Cultures in a Bourgeois World*, ed. A. L. Stoler and F. Cooper, 1–56. Berkeley: University of California Press, 1997.

Suryadi, S. "Sepucuk Surat dari seorang bangsawan Gowa di tanah pembuangan (Ceylon)." *Wacana: Journal of the Humanities of Indonesia* 10, no. 2 (2008): 214–45.

Suzuki, Hideaki. *Abolitions as a Global Experience*. Singapore: NUS Press, 2016.

Szreter, Simon. "Registration of Identities in Early Modern English Parishes and Among the English Overseas." In *Registration and Recognition: Documenting the Person in World History*, ed. Keith Breckenbridge and Simon Szreter, 67–92. Oxford: Oxford University Press, 2012.

Tagliocozzo, Eric. "Trade, Production and Incorporation: The Indian Ocean in Flux, 1600–1900." *Itinerario* 1 (2002): 75–106.

Tambiah, H. W. *The Laws and the Customs of the Tamils of Jaffna*. Colombo: Women's Education and Research Centre, 2004.

Tanak-Van Dalen, Isabel. "Dutch Attitudes Towards Slavery and the Tardy Road to Abolition: The Case of Deshima." In *Abolitions as a Global Experience*, ed. Hideaki Suzuki, 72–112. Singapore: NUS Press, 2016.

Tarlo, Emma. *Unsettling Memories: Narratives of the Emergency in Delhi*. New Delhi: Permanent Black, 2003.

Taylor, Jean. *The Social World of Batavia: European and Eurasian in Dutch Asia*. Madison University of Wisconsin Press, 1983.

Teelock, V. *Bitter Sugar: Sugar and Slavery in 19th Century Mauritius*. Moka: Mahatma Gandhi Institute, 1998.

Temperley, Howard. "The Delegalization of Slavery in British India." *Slavery and Abolition* 21, no. 2 (2000): 169–87.

Tennent, James Emerson. *Ceylon: An Account of the Island*. 2 vols. London: Longman, Green, Longman and Roberts, 1859.

Thanges P., and K. T. Silva." Caste Discrimination in War-Affected Jaffna Society." In *Casteless or Caste Blind? Dynamics of Concealed Caste Discrimination, Social Exclusion, and Protest in Sri Lanka*, ed. K. T. Silva, P. P. Sivapragasam, and Paramsothy Thanges, 50–76. Copenhagen: International Dalit Solidarity, 2009.

Thiranagama, Sharika. *In My Mother's House: Civil War in Sri Lanka*. Philadelphia: University of Pennsylvania Press, 2011.

Thompson, E. P. "The Moral Economy of the English Crowd in the Eighteenth Century." In *The Essential E.P. Thompson,* ed. Dorothy Thompson, 316–77. New York: New Press, 2001.

Thorne, Susan. "Capitalism and Slavery Compensation." *Small Axe* 16, no. 1 (37) (2012): 154–67.

Torabully, Khal.*Chair Corail, Fragments Coolies.* Guadeloupe: Ibis Rouge Editions, 1999

Trentmann, Frank. "Materiality in the Future of History: Things, Practices, and Politics." *Journal of British Studies* 48 (2009): 283–307.

Trouillot, M. R. *Silencing the Past: Power and the Production of History.* Boston: Beacon Press, 1995.

Turner, Sasha. *Contested Bodies: Pregnancy, Childrearing, and Slavery in Jamaica.* Philadelphia: University of Pennsylvania Press, 2017.

Valentijn, Francois. *Oud en Nieuw Oost-Indien, vyfde Deel.* Dordrecht: Van Bram, Oncer de Linden, 1724.

van der Linden, Marcel. "The Origins, Spread and Normalization of Free Wage Labour." In *Free and Unfree Labour: The Debate Continues*, ed. Tom Brass and Marcel van der Linden, 501–23. Bern: Peter Lang, 2000.

van der Spuy, P. "Gender and Slavery: Towards a Feminist Revision." *South African Historical Journal* 25 (1991): 184–95.

———. "'What Then Was the Sexual Outlet for Black Males?': A Feminist Critique of Quantitative Representation of Women Slaves at the Cape of Good Hope in the Eighteenth Century." *Kronos* 23 (1996): 43–56.

van Rossum, Matthias. *Kleurrijke Tragiek: De Geschiedenis van Slavernij in Azië onder de VOC.* Hilversum: Uitgeverij Verloren, 2015.

van Rossum, Matthias, and Jeannette Camp. *Desertion in the Early Modern World: A Comparative History.* London: Bloomsbury, 2016.

van Schendel, Willem. "Stretching Labour Historiography: Pointers from South Asia." *International Review of Social History* 51 (2006): 229–61.

Vatuk, Sylvia. "Bharattee's Death: Domestic Slave-Women in Nineteenth-Century Madras." In *Slavery and South Asian History*, ed. Indrani Chatterjee and Richard M. Eaton, 210–33. Bloomington: Indiana University Press, 2006.

Vaughan, Megan. *Creating the Creole Island: Slavery in Eighteenth-Century Mauritius.* Durham, N.C.: Duke University Press, 2005.

Verges, F. "Creolization and Resistance." In *Creolizing Europe: Legacies and Transformations*, ed. Encarnacion Gutierez Rodriguez and Shirley Anne Tate, 38–56. Liverpool: Liverpool University Press, 2015.

Vink, Markus. *Encounters on the Opposite Coast: The Dutch East Indian Company and the Nayaka State of Madurai in the Seventeenth Century.* Leiden: Brill, 2015.

———. "'The World's Oldest Trade': Dutch Slavery and Slave Trade in the Indian Ocean in the Seventeenth Century." *Journal of World History* 14, no. 2 (2003): 131–77.

Visram, Rozina. *Ayahs, Lascars and Princes: Indians in Britain 1700–1947.* London: Pluto Press, 1986.

Viswanath, Rupa. *The Pariah Problem: Caste, Religion and the Social in Modern India.* New York: Columbia University Press, 2014.

Wagenaar, L. J. *Cinnamon and Elephants: Sri Lanka and the Netherlands from 1600.* Amsterdam: Vantilt, 2016.

———. "The Cultural Dimension of the Dutch East India Company Settlements in Dutch Period Ceylon, 1700–1800—with Special Reference to Galle." In *Mediating Netherlandish Art and Material Culture in Asia*, ed. Thomas DaCosta Kaufmann and Michael North, 141–76. Amsterdam: Amsterdam University Press, 2015.

———. *Galle-Vestiging in Ceylon: Beschrijving van een Koloniale Samenleving aan de Vooravond van de Singalese Opstand tegen het Nederlandse Gezag.* 1760. Amsterdam: De Bataafsche Leeuw, 1994.

Ward, Kerry. *Networks of Empire: Forced Migration in the Dutch East India Company.* Cambridge: Cambridge University Press, 2009.

Ward, Richard, ed. *A Global History of Execution and the Criminal Corpse.* Basingstoke, UK: Palgrave Macmillan, 2015.

Wastell, R. E. P. "The History of Slave Compensation, 1838–1845." M.A. thesis, King's College, University of London, 1932.

Wenzlhuemer, Roland. "Indian Labour Immigration and British Labour Policy in Nineteenth Century Ceylon."*Modern Asian Studies* 41, no. 3 (2007): 575–602.

Wheeler, Roxann. *The Complexion of Race: Categories of Difference in Eighteenth-Century British Culture.* Philadelphia: University of Pennsylvania Press, 2000.

Whitaker, Mark. *Amiable Incoherence: Manipulating Histories and Modernities in a Batticaloa Hindu Temple.* Amsterdam: VU University Press, 1999.

Wickramasinghe, Nira. "Colonial Governmentality and the Political: Thinking Through '1931' in the Crown Colony of Ceylon/Sri Lanka." *Socio* 5 (2015): 99–114.

———. *Ethnic Politics in Colonial Ceylon.* Delhi: Vikas, 1995.

———. "Many Little Revolts or One Rebellion? The Maritime Provinces of Ceylon/Sri Lanka Between 1796 and 1800." *South Asia: Journal of South Asian Studies* 32, no. 2 (2009): 170–88.

———. *Sri Lanka in the Modern Age: A History*. Oxford: Oxford University Press, 2015.

Wickremaratne, L. A. "The Development of Transportation in Ceylon c 1800–1947." In *University of Ceylon History of Ceylon*. Vol. 3: *From the Beginning of the Nineteenth Century to 1948*, ed. K. M de Silva, 303–16. Peradeniya: University of Ceylon, 1973.

———. "Education and Social Change 1832 to c 1900." In *University of Ceylon History of Ceylon*. Vol. 3: *From the Beginning of the Nineteenth Century to 1948*, ed. K. M de Silva, 165–86. Peradeniya: University of Ceylon, 1973.

Wickremeratne, U. C. *The Conservative Nature of the British Rule of Sri Lanka with Particular Emphasis on the Period 1796–1802*. New Delhi: Navrang, 1996.

Wijesekera, Nandadeva, "Slavery in Sri Lanka: Presidential Address Delivered on 20-12-74." *Journal of the Sri Lanka Branch of the Royal Asiatic Society*, New Series 18 (1974): 1–22.

Wimalaratne, K. D. G. "Muslims Under British Rule in Ceylon (Sri Lanka) 1796–1948." In *Muslims of Sri Lanka: Avenues to Antiquity*, ed. M. A. M. Shukri, 89–112. Beruwela: Jamiah Naleemia Institute, 1986.

Wink, A. *Al Hind: The Making of the Indo-Islamic World*. Vol. 1: *Early Medieval India and the Expansion of Islam, 7th–11th Centuries*. Leiden: Brill, 1990.

Wolvendaal Church Records. "Sri Lanka, Colombo District, Dutch Reformed Church Records, 1677–1990." FamilySearch. Database with images. http://FamilySearch.org.

Worden, Nigel. "Cape Slaves in the Paper Empire of the VOC." *Kronos* 40, no. 1 (2014): 23–44.

———. "Public Brawling, Masculinity and Honour." In *Cape Town: Between East and West. Social Identities in a Dutch Colonial Town*, ed. N. Worden, 194–211. Hilversum: Verloren, 2012.

———. *Slavery in Dutch South Africa*. Cambridge: Cambridge University Press, 1985.

Wright, Arnold. *Twentieth Century Impressions of Ceylon: Its History, People, Commerce, Industries and Resources*. London: Lloyd's Greater Britain, 1907.

Yang, Anand A. "A Conversation of Rumours: The Language of Popular 'Mentalites' in Late Nineteenth Century Colonial India." *Journal of Social History* 20, no. 3 (1987): 485–505.

———. "Indian Convict Workers in Southeast Asia in the Late Eighteenth and Early Nineteenth Centuries." *Journal of World History* 24, no. 2 (2003): 179–208.

Yang, Anand A., et al, eds. *Thirteen Months in China: A Subaltern Indian and the Colonial World*. New Delhi: Oxford University Press, 2017.

Zachariah, Benjamin. "Travellers in Archives, or the Possibilities of a Post-Post-archival Historiography." *Praticas da Historia*, no. 3 (2016): 11–27.

Zwaardecroon, Hendrick, Commandeur of Jaffnapatam. *Instructions for the Guidance of the Opperkoopman Anthony Pavilioen, Commandeur, and the Council of the District of Jaffnapatan with the Adjacent Islands and the Provinces of the Wanni*. 1697. Memoir. Colombo: H. C Cottle, 1911.

Index

abolition of slavery: in British Empire, 49, 154; in Cape Colony, 155, 156; in East Indies, 57; gradual, 41, 47, 53, 105, 130, 156, 169; movement for, 11, 12, 51; in Sri Lanka; 40, 46–47, 51, 56, 105, 107; Slavery Abolition Act of 1833, 5, 155; in West Indies, 155. *See* Regulation 9–10 of 1818; Regulation 8 of 1821

abolitionists: in British Parliament, 41, 106, 156; C. C. Uhlenbeck, 53–57; James Steven, 156; in the Netherlands, 57. *See also* anti-slavery

abortion: as an act of resistance, 75–76; as crime, 75

Abyssinians, 27

accommodessans, 138, 177, 247n42

Address to His Royal Highness the Prince Regent for Emancipating Children Born of Slaves after the 12th of August 1816: signatories of, 112, 167–68

Africans: in Britain, 37; as slaves, 27, 50, 51, 169. *See also* soldiers

Afro-Sri Lankans, 16–17, 169, 193–94, 203

Amangkurat III, 66

amelioration policies: in Cape Colony, 154, 155, 156; in the Caribbean, 154

andol. *See* palanquin

Andringa, Olke, 66, 68, 176

Annales historians, 9–10

anti-slavery, 5, 57, 158

Anuradhapura period: and slavery, 6

apprenticeship: in Great Britain, 155 in Mauritius, 156; in Slavery Abolition Act of August 28, 1833, 155

Arabia, 85, 163, 164, 165

Arabian slave market, 13, 52

Arabic, 10–11, 16, 22, 163, 164, 180

archives: of the VOC, 7, 9, 21, 22. *See also* colonial archives

atimai: in Jaffna society, 204; in South Indian society, 95

autobiography: of emancipated slaves, 10

Baldaeus, Philippus, 31, 96

baptism: of slave children, 200–201, 201f

[291]

Barbados, 106
barber: and circumcision, 173, 174, 179, 180, 184
Batavia: Statutes of 1749, 167; New Statutes of (1766), 165
Beloved, 75–76
Bertolacci, Antonio, 35, 36, 40, 84
blackness: idea of, in Britain, 34, 37–39; as racialized identity, 18; in Sri Lanka, 17–18, 34
blacks: in Cape Colony, 33; as category of classification, 17–18, 32–33, 38, 43, 49. *See also* free blacks
Blue Books: categories of classification in, 13; history of, 42–43
Bombay, 17, 35, 37, 84, 85
Boursse, Esaias, 27
Brandes, Jan, 30
Brohier, R.L., 18–19, 22, 166, 207; on Slave Island, 23, 25
Brownrigg, Sir Robert, 84, 138, 178, 185
Burghers: as signatories of Address of 1816 on emancipation, 79, 107; as slaveholders, 53, 108, 109, 167; status and respectability of, 175–77; and trial by jury, 201–2. *See also under* Dutch Burghers; Portuguese Burghers

Caffre, 16; Caffre Corps, 17. *See also* Kaffir
canal: labor on, 14, 126
Cape Colony, 4, 9, 32, 120, 196; amelioration policies in, 154–56, 197
Cape of Good Hope, 9, 23, 28, 32–33, 51, 106
Casie Chitty, Simon, 128, 134, 158, 168, 180; on circumcision, 174
caste: in census, 45–46; cinnamon peelers, 55, 64; Dalits,118, 125; Dutch rule and slave castes, 95–97, 99; in Jaffna, 94–97, 101, 116, 120; in Kerala, 118–19, 125, 205 ; and missionaries, 119; oppressed castes in Thesawalamai code, 99–100. *See also* Coviyar, Durawa, Goyigama, Karayar, Madapalli, Nalavar, Panchamar, Pallar, Vellalar
Castiz, 30
Catholicism. *See* Roman Catholicism
census: of 1684, 30, 194–95; of 1694, 30; of 1789, 30; of 1801 and understanding of social difference, 34; of 1814, 40, 166; of 1824, 39, 41,43, 112, 166; in Britain, 38, 39; as bureaucratic instrument, 49; categories of classification in, 37, 46; of India, 45; Kaffir as category of, 27; skin color in, 42, 43; slave as category of, 34, 40, 42, 46; and verifiable evidence, 41
Ceylon Calendar: of 1821, 5; of 1824, 178
Chandernago, 9
Chandios, 96
Chilaw: canal, 131–32, 143, 145–47, 150; hospital, 149–50
cholera, 149, 150
Christians, 30, 32, 95–96, 138, 167, 195–96
Cinnamon Department, 137
cinnamon peelers, and unrest, 21
circumcision: Muslim rite, 173–74; of slaves, 179. *See also* Casie Chitty
Clough, Rev. Benjamin, 44–45
Cochin, 7, 13, 52, 76, 78, 79,
Colebrooke-Cameron: Commission, 5, 41, 62, 128, 146; reforms, 5, 14, 41, 46, 110, 130, 138, 166; Report, 5, 42
collector, office of, 184
Colombo: capitulation (1796), 77; Fort, 65, 166, 179

[292]   INDEX

colonial archives, 8, 11, 51, 70, 94, 160
compensation: in British Slave Compensation Act of 1837, 110; for mothers in Regulation 8 of 1821, 111; for slaveholders, 57, 90, 111, 115
conversion: to Christianity, 119, 125; to Islam, 198; to Roman Catholicism, 96, 204
convict, 57, 129, 136, 137
coolie: and kangany, 147; in pioneers corps, 83, 143, 146
Corea, Johannes, 146
Coridon of Ceylon, 32–33
Coromandel, Coast, 4, 31, 91, 133, 143, 164
court case, 14, 21, 65–66, 160, 170, 187
Coviyar: as palanquin bearer 96–97, 101; purchase of freedom of, 141; in slave registers, 47, 109; value of, 111, 141
Creole: Portuguese, 203
Creolization, 189

Daalmans, Egidius, 32
Daniel, K., 206
death: of emancipated slaves, 148–49; of Governor Rumpf, 21; of slaves in materiaalhuis lists, 23
De Jonville, Eudelin: *Some Notions About the Island of Ceylon*, 35–36
Delaware ship: logbook of, 29
De Saram, Cornelis, 44
De Silva, Nalin, 206
Dias Bandaranaike, Don Jacobus, 44
domestic slaves: Coviyars as, 111; in Jaffna, 107–8; in slave registers, 47, 108, 109, 110
Douglass, Frederick, 11
D'Oyly, John, 36
Durawa, 185
Dutch: and Africans, 22, 26, 27, 169, 194; Burghers, 58, 84, 176, 229n23; census of population, 194–95; in Jaffna, 93, 96–100; members of jury, 85, 176; missions, 133; and mixed marriage, 75, 194; Reformed Church, 183, 199, 200; rule, 61, 103, 106, 177, 195, 199; rule and status of Moors, 165; slaveholders, 53, 81, 167; tombos, 31, 100; treatment of slaves, 74; use of term 'black', 32, 33–34

East India Company, British: in India, 5, 37, 77, 119, 155, 158; rule over Sri Lanka, 6, 8, 53, 136
East India Company, Dutch. *See* Vereenigde Oostindishe Compagnie (VOC)
East Indies, slaves from, 6, 17, 22, 26–27, 51, 67, 190, 198–200
emancipated slaves: death of, 129, 148–50
emancipation: by purchase by the government, 141–45; ritual of, 171–72 (*see* manumission); terms of, 60, 139–42; in wills of slaveholders, 58, 60–61
enumeration: colonial population, 45–46, 49; in U.S., 38–39. *See also* census
Equiano, Olaudah, 11
Eurasians, 75, 194
exiles: from the East Indies (Southeast Asia, Indonesia), 9, 66, 67

Falck, I.W., 165, 182
family, of emancipated slaves, 148, 153
fines, for omitting to register slaves, 107, 109
fiscal: of Galle, 79; murder of Barent van der Swaan, 16, 19, 21, 207

flogging: in British colonies, 104; in Europe, 103; as punishment for traveling in a palanquin, 102, 104
forgetting, 191, 203
fragments, of lives of slaves, 52, 88, 120, 128
free black: in Blue Books, 13, 43; in Cape Colony, 32–33, 223n59; in Sri Lanka, 32, 43
Free Coloured, 43
freedom: certificates of, 111; in exchange for labor, 14, 145; purchase of, 141. *See also* manumission

Galle: Fort, 76–77; graveyard, 32; under Portuguese, 76; under VOC, 76–77, 78
gardens, spice, 62–63
gender, of slaves, 41, 58–59, 70, 71f, 195
Glissant, Edouard, 189
Goa: Portuguese in, 19
Gosh, Amitav, 161
Gowa, sultan of, 66, 67
Goyigama, 95, 198; as proprietors of slaves, 167; and rajakariya, 137
guardian of slaves, 154–55, 196–97

Hadramis, 164
Hall, Stuart, 189
He, Zheng, 164
headman, of the Muslim community, 160, 177
hierarchies: of caste, 46, 89, 96, 116; in Jaffna society, 96, 102, 116, 118, 119, 123
Hooper, W.H.: in Galle case, 85; and palanquin case in Jaffna, 102, 110–11

Ibn Battuta, 27
Indian Ocean: Arabic language in, 163; British territories in the, 4; as interconnected space, 17, 198; Islam in the, 160–61, 163–65, 172; Portuguese in the, 165; slave trade in the, 4, 51, 53, 85, 169–70; slavery, 2, 10, 17, 28, 95; slavery studies, 3
infanticide, 13, 52, 76
insurrection: of Kaffir slaves, 19, 21, 24–26
invisibility, 15, 189, 192–93, 203–4, 207
Isaaksz, Claas, 98
Islam: egalitarian ethos in, 172–73; Encyclopaedia of, 16; in the Indian Ocean, 160–61, 164; manumission in, 171–72; slavery and, 171
Islamic law, 163, 174

Jaffna: caste relations in, 94, 97, 101, 116, 120; caste servitude in, 204; collector of, 89, 104, 110, 131–32, 142–45, 152–53; cultivation in, 98, 133–34, 135; customary law in, 98; domestic slavery in, 119, 112; Dutch rule in, 93, 95–101; inhabitants of, 31, 102; kachcheri, 112, 139, 142; kingdom of, 98–99, 117; magistrate of, 113, 133; missionaries in, 119, 125, 133; money economy in, 138; novels about, 204; peninsula, 6, 90–91, 95, 116, 121–22, 134–35; population of, 95, 134; Portuguese rule in, 90–91, 96, 116; provincial court of, 112, 141; recruitment of labor from, 132–33; slaveholders in, 99, 104, 108, 113–14, 133, 141, 191; social stratification in, 94; Thesawalamai code in, 99–100; tobacco, 97–98, 99, 112, 133–36, 204, 206
Jayewardene, Adrian, 145
jewelry, tax on. *See* Joy tax
Johnston, Alexander: in Admiralty Commission, 84; emancipation of slaves, 107, 157; and jury system, 36, 201–2

[294] INDEX

Joy tax, 116
jurors, 85, 202
jury system, introduction of, 36

kachcheri: Batticaloa, 197; Chilaw, 128; Colombo, 14, 161; Jaffna, 112, 139, 142
Kaffir: as census category, 27–28, 32; insurrection of, 13, 16, 19, 21, 24–26; nonracial meaning, 28; in South Africa, 28
Kailayamalai, 98–99
Kalpitiya, 128, 129, 131, 186
Kandasamy temple, 93
Kandyan kingdom: British wars against, 143, 145; law in, 6; as refuge for Moors, 165; slavery in, 6
kangany, 147
Karatota Kirti Sri Dhammarama, 36
Karayar, 97
Kerala, 118, 164, 204, 205
Khoikhoi, 28
kutimai, 95

labor: agreement, 139–42; Chinese, 138–39; and Colebrooke-Cameron Commission, 41, 138; convict, 57, 136, 137; contract, 131, 136, 139–43; corvée, 61, 62; European needs for, 7, 191; freedom as ideology, 129, 157; indentured, 139, 140; Indian, 83, 138, 143, 156; migration, 28, 83, 130, 193; in public works, 83, 112, 126, 131, 136–37, 143, 150; as punishment, 103; slave, 30, 49, 63, 129, 132, 156; VOC dependence on slave, 30; wage based, 126, 129, 130, 137–38, 155, 157
landowners: of coconut plantations, 145; in the early nineteenth century, 62; in Jaffna, 94; testamentary cases of, 58; in tombos, 29
lascar, 85, 86

law: customary, 6, 98, 165; international, 84; Kandyan, 6; Muslim, 165; and performance of freedom, 162–63; and punishment, 65, 89; Roman Dutch, 182, 186
Legislative Act 2 of 1821, 104
Legislative Council, 41–42, 46, 166
lekam miti, 31
liberalism, 90, 93, 131
liberated Africans, 11
Libertines, 195–96
logbook, 29

Madapalli, 97, 99
Madapalli, mudaliyars, 99
Madras, 29, 38, 69
magistrate's court, 73–74, 78, 79, 172, 176; in Jaffna, 102, 117, 132, 133, 140. *See also* sitting magistrate
Maitland, Governor: and Chinese migrant worker scheme, 138–39; and power of native chiefs, 177; registers, 47, 105; and service tenure, 137
Malabars, 31, 36, 40, 41, 128; as slaveholders, 168
Malay: emancipated slaves, 68–69, 198; language, 66, 67, 68; regiment, 26, 69; slaves, 8, 23, 74; soldiers, 66–67, 68, 122; stereotype of, 69; sultan, 64; world, 8
Malaya, 38
Mannar: Christians in, 95–96; disturbances in, 116; Pandara Wannian, 121–22; slaveholders in, 107
manumission: 156, 173, 187, 190, 195; in Cape Colony, 59, 156; conditional, 140; Islam on, 171–72; as pious act, 172; Orlando Patterson on, 171, 187
marriage, mixed, 75, 166, 194
Matara, slaveholders in, 79, 81–83

Mauritius, 113, 126, 139, 191; enslaved in, 8, 23, 27, 126, 152; gradual abolition in, 156, indentured labor in, 151; registration in, 106; runaways in, 153

memory, of slavery, 14, 23, 50, 128, 189, 190

Mestizo, 30

Miskin, Tahmas, 10

missionaries, 118, 119, 133, 137, 175

modernity: and Colebrooke-Cameron Report, 42, 130; genealogy of, 5

Moors: class among, 175, 177, 179; during Dutch rule, 165; headman of, 14, 160; origin of, 163–65; during Portuguese rule, 165; racial identity of, 175; as slaveholders, 81–82, 167–69

Mozambique, 19, 38

Mudaliyars: in Jaffna, 99; and land grants by British, 62, 145; petition against, 183; power over manumitted slaves, 100

Mysore, kingdom of, 77, 94

Nalavar: compensation given to 141; in K. Daniel's novel *Mirage*, 204; people after abolition of slavery, 204; petition by, 115–18; and right to be taxed, 116; in the Thesawalamai, 99–100; in tobacco farms, 133–34, 136, 204; value of, 111, 140–41

Nallur, temple in, 90, 115, 116, 118

North, Sir Frederick: and abolition of service tenure, 62; formation of Ceylon Rifle Regiment, 66–67; establishment of hospitals, 149; joy tax, 116; and Malay troops, 69; and pioneer corps, 83; proclamation of 1801, 47; reforms of 1799–1800, 105

Office for the Registry of Colonial Slaves, 12

Office of the Guardian of Slaves. *See* guardian of slaves

Ordinance 7 of 1843, 190

Ordinance 20 of 1844, 190

palanquin: bearers, 96, 101; in Jaffna, 93–94, 93f, 101–5; in Mysore, 94

Pallar: after abolition of slavery, 204; and compensation to slaveholders, 132, 141; defined as slaves, 96, 125; as outdoor servants, 97; purchase of freedom of, 14, 126, 141, 143; rebellious nature of, 120; in registers, 47, 109–10, 134; status according to Dutch, 95, 96, 100; in Thesawalamai, 99–100; value of, 111, 140–41

palmyrah, 91

Panchamar, 204

Pandara Wannian/ Pandaram Wanni, 90, 121–23

Paraiya, 100

Parangi Hatana, 27, 194

Pasqual Mudaliyar, 198

Patterson, Orlando: on the act of manumission, 187; and acts of refusal, 188; definition of slavery, 49; renaming slaves, 49; rituals of redemption, 171

pay, of laborers, 137

Percival, Robert, 35, 38, 65, 67, 69, 74

performance: of freedom, 162; of personhood, 139, 163

petition: by emancipated slave, 150–51; and justice claims, 161, 183–84; language in, 182, 187; by Lascarins, 183; and the making of political subjects, 116, 182; by Nalavars, 115–18; regulation of by colonial government, 183; by slaveholders,

100, 113, 114, 167; as source for historians, 11, 12, 181–82; writer, 9, 116, 117, 151, 182
Pettah: inhabitants, 38; Moors and Tamils in, 178–79; Portuguese and Dutch descendants in, 166
Pielat, Jacob Christiaan, 27
Pioneer Corps, 83, 143, 146–47
Polonnaruwa period: and slavery, 6
population: in Blue Books, 42, 43; categories used to classify, 40–41; in Colombo under Portuguese rule, 29; Dutch accounts of, 29, 31; Dutch census of, 30, 194–95; of enslaved in Suriname, 57; free and enslaved, 30; and gender ratio of slaves, 70; of Jaffna, 95; literacy of, 133; of Moors in Colombo, 166–67; and number of slaves, 45, 46; and slaves in Jaffna, 112, 134; survey by Bertolacci, 40
Portuguese: and Africans, 19, 27, 169, 194; Burgher, 15, 202, 229n23; and conversion to Roman Catholicism, 96; descendants of, 32, 166, 194, 202; in Goa, 19, 95–96; language, 203–4; marriages with local women, 202; and Moors, 165; rule over Jaffna, 90–91, 96, 116; rule over maritime provinces, 6
Prediger, Rudolph, 79, 196
prisoners: and Kaffirs, 27; punishment of, 24, 103–4
proprietors of slaves: per ethnicity, 55f, 81–83; in Galle, 79–83; payment to, 147, 155–56; proportion of Muslim, 167–69; and slave registration, 12, 47, 107–10, 112–13, 190; status of, 132
provincial court, 14, 60, 161; and emancipation, 141, 161, 162, 184; registration at, 107, 108, 115, 112
punishment, 24, 65, 89, 102–4, 109

Qur'an, 16, 98, 173

race: in Britain in the 18th century, 37–38; as category of classification, 17–18, 37–39; and colonial difference, 33, 34, 37; ideas of, 37–39; mixed, 75
rajakariya, 62, 136–38, 150
Rajasiha Hatana, 27
Rajasinghe I, 194
recruitment, 132–33
reenslavement, 196
Regulation of 1706, 103
Regulation 13 of 1806, 105
Regulation No 9 and 10 of 1818, 47, 106, 107–10, 111–12, 115, 139–41
Regulation No 8 of 1821, 110–15
respectability: for Burghers, 175–77; and clothing, 177; for Muslims, 163, 173, 175–77, 178
Ricoeur Paul, 203
Rumpf, Isaac Augustin, 21
runaway: from Chilaw, 152–53; and punishment under Dutch, 65

Shafi'i legal school, 164
Sierra Leone, 11, 84
Simons, Cornelis Joan, 98, 102
Sinhalese-English Dictionary of 1830, 44–45
sitting magistrate, 70–71, 113, 114–15
slave children: age and sex of, 108, 109, 112; christening of, 198; education of, 133; emancipation of, 41, 107, 110, 112, 115, 154, 157; labor extracted from, 140; number of, 133; registration of birth, 107, 114; in Thesawalamai, 99–100; in wills, 58–59, 66
Slave Island: murder in 1723, 16, 69; naming of, 21, 24–26

slaveholders: in Colombo, 53–56, 167; ethnic distribution of, 57–58, 79–83; and fraud, 113, 114–15; as landowners, 58–64; violence committed by, 52, 69–70, 74

slavery: Abolition Act of 1833, 5, 155; abolition in East Indies and West Indian islands, 57; Abolition of Slavery Ordinance of 1844, 50, 156, 193; and abolitionists, 12, 41, 53–57, 106, 156; amelioration of, 8, 40, 154–59; as 'bundle of rights', 136; and caste-based service labor, 96–98, 99; and Colebrooke-Cameron commission, 128; in K. Daniel's *Mirage*, 204, 206; delegalization in India, 5; dominant model of (Atlantic), 17; in the Galle district, 79–82; gradual abolition of, 41, 47, 53, 105, 130, 154, 169; in India, 40, 205; in the Indian Ocean world, 2, 10, 17, 51, 88, 150, 181; Islam on, 171–72; in the Kandyan kingdom, 6; and liberalism, 90, 93, 131; local practice of, 6, 95; in Malayalam novels, 205; memory of, 14, 23, 50, 128, 189, 190; as 'social death', 49; in South Africa, 61; South Asian, 7, 95; studies on, 2, 3; in the Thesawalamai, 99–100

slaves: Abolition Act (1807), 84, 156; African, 27, 50, 51; blackening of, 13, 17, 22–23; bonds, 47, 79, 139; as census category, 34, 40, 42, 46; child of, 13, 52, 70, 72–76, 107, 111, 112; contract of, 136, 139–42; deed of transfer of, 63f; domestic, 16, 26–27, 41, 108, 112, 196, 200; emancipated, 68, 113f, 130–32, 142, 176, 195–98, 202–3; gender distribution of, 71f; interdiction to purchase, 167; manumitted, 33, 46, 99, 100, 154, 195; monetary value of, 142; naming of, 23, 46, 48; number of, 30, 41, 45, 46, 134–35, 135f, 190; owned by VOC, 23, 99, 105; origin of, 17, 22, 23, 47–48, 195, 199; registers of, 12, 46, 47, 48, 105, 168–69; registers of in Barbados, 106; registers of in Jaffna, 110, 134; registers of in Trinidad, 106, 113, 155; registration and fines, 107, 109; revolt of, 26; sickness of, 133, 148–50; trade in, 4, 57, 84, 85, 99, 169–70; Trade Felony Act (1811), 84; violence against women, 13, 52, 69–70, 119–20, 204

Smith, Adam, 129, 157

soldiers: African 17, 194; Javanese, 66; Malay, 66–67, 68–69, 122

South Africa, 28, 32–33, 61, 151

South Asia: bondage as a norm in, 88; historiography of slavery in, 7

Stephen, James, 156

Supreme Court, 64, 73, 73f, 76, 84, 114, 117, 120, 186; decision on palanquin case, 89, 102–4, 185; decree of February 24, 1807, 106

Surapati, Untung, 10

Thesawalamai: slavery in, 99–100

Tipu Sultan, 77

tobacco: cultivation in Jaffna, 98–99, 133–35; cultivation in Virginia, 134; export to Travancore, 98; and slave labor, 133–34

Toepasses/Toepas: in census of Colombo, 195; as descendants of manumitted slaves, 194–95, 202; in Portuguese Empire, 194; and wearing of hat, 194, 195. *See also under* Portuguese Burghers

Tolfrey, William, 36

tombos: Dutch, 31, 100; Portuguese, 29, 31
Torabully, Khal, 207–8
Trincomalee, 41, 64, 94, 109, 121, 138, 149
Trinidad, 106, 113, 118, 126, 154–55
Tuan Guru, 33

Uhlenbeck, C.C., 53–57
uliyam, 177
Unconfessed, 75

vaccination, 149
Valentijn, Francois, 21, 31
Van Balie, Wange, memoir of, 10
Van de Graaf, Governor, 30, 69
Van der Swaan, Barent, murder of, 16, 19, 21, 27, 207
Van Dort, W.G., 202
Van Rhee, Thomas, 30
Vanni, 90, 91–92, 92f, 120, 121, 122, 134
Vanniyars, 92
Vavuniya, 92, 122
Vellalars: castes in the service of, 94–97; description of Baldaeus of, 96; and difficult past, 15, 189, 190; domestics of, 97; as dominant landowners, 94; and Madapalli, 99; use of palanquins by, 102
Vereenigde Oostindishe Compagnie (VOC): appropriation of service labor in Jaffna by, 96, 99; Europeans working under, 166; mobility of slaves in territories of, 65; shipping network of, 4; slaves kept by, 23, 30, 99, 105, 196; working wages in Sri Lanka under rule of, 137–38
Verges, Françoise, 189
Vice Admiralty court, 84
violence: bodily, 13; domestic, 119–20; inter-caste, 89, 117; against women, 13, 52, 69–70, 204

Wanni. *See* Vanni
whip, 90
white, in bureaucratic language, 34, 38, 42, 43
Wilberforce, William, 106, 156
Wolfendaal Church (Wolvendaal), 199, 200

Xhosa wars, 28

Zanzibar, 85

GPSR Authorized Representative: Easy Access System Europe, Mustamäe tee 50, 10621 Tallinn, Estonia, gpsr.requests@easproject.com